STRONGHOLD
BRITAIN

FOUR THOUSAND YEARS
OF BRITISH FORTIFICATIONS

GEOFFREY WILLIAMS

SUTTON PUBLISHING

First published in the United Kingdom 1999 by
Sutton Publishing Limited · Phoenix Mill
Thrupp · Stroud · Gloucestershire · GL5 2BU

This paperback edition first published in 2003

British Library Cataloguing in Publication Data
A catalogue record for this book is available from the British Library

ISBN 0 7509 3519 7

Typeset in 10/14pt Sabon.
Typesetting and origination by
Sutton Publishing Limited.
Printed and bound in Great Britain by
J.H. Haynes & Co. Ltd, Sparkford.

CONTENTS

ACKNOWLEDGEMENTS

I am not keen on long acknowledgements and, let's face it who reads them in any case? Even so, many organizations, libraries, authors, historians, site custodians and others aided this book, somewhere along the line. There were others who worked behind the scenes, from those at Sutton Publishing who had faith in the project, especially Jane Crompton and Sarah Fowle, who guided and managed the project, to those who tailored, produced and finally sold it. My special thanks to you all.

Christine Sieniawska produced all the plans and drawings, to liven up the book. Tim Chambre, the branch librarian at Portswood, Southampton, always enthusiastically came up trumps when other, supposedly more prestigious, institutions promised the earth and delivered a handful of dust. Ewen Isaacs, Noel Clark and all the staff at City Photographic, Southampton, gave much advice and assistance with photographic equipment, ideas and tips; this is one shop where service excels. Finally, thanks to my fellow players at Old Edwardians' Hockey Club. They ensured that, instead of conscientiously typing away at the computer, I was out there at 10.30 p.m., on freezing and wet January nights, losing my knees and knuckles on the astroturf and loving every minute of it, I think . . .

INTRODUCTION

'You're always the last one out at night. Can't you practise your guitar in the day?'

'No, I'm reading History, not Music, so I have a bash in the evening,' I replied as the porter hastily ushered me from the music rooms.

'Ah well' he said wearily, 'at least History's one subject that never changes.'

'You must be joking, my old flower!'

For a start, today's news is tomorrow's history. Not the tedious trivia that pads out the puerile offerings of our self-important press, nor the sordid allegations of impropriety by our politicians or public servants, but events or actions of genuine significance. Then there is the on-going reinterpretation of historical evidence or, more often, the revision of older theories in the light of new evidence. Of course, basic facts seldom change; for example, the Romans invaded England in AD 43 and Nelson won the Battle of Trafalgar in 1805. Like it or not, historians can re-analyse, re-examine and reinterpret until the cows come home, but such facts are beyond dispute. The minor details may be open to question, the causes and consequences might offer the opportunity for hours of academic debate – but the facts cannot be altered.

On the other hand, supposing events had turned out rather differently, what then? Let us go back in time to the evening news on 14 October 1066 and see how things might have been.

'Good evening. After a day of almost unremitting fighting at Senlac Hill, a few miles north of Hastings, the invading Normans are now in full retreat, hunted by our brave warriors. For the very latest news of the day's astounding events, we can now go over live to our reporter at the scene, Katia AD.'

'I am standing beside King Harold and his men, jubilant after their second great victory in little over a fortnight. It has been a tense, fierce encounter with the Normans often holding the upper hand. The battle was won in mid-afternoon, as King Harold withheld his troops after the Normans tried to draw them into a trap. Norman arrows and cavalry fell not, as intended, among our own brave soldiers, but amid the invaders' ranks. Caught in disarray, the Normans were then slaughtered and driven from the field in a valiant counter-attack, our soldiers cutting them to pieces with heavy axes. I am now joined by two of the king's victorious housecarls.

Some two thousand years before the pillbox was built, Old Berwick Hill was a very comprehensively defended hillfort. Nearby are some cup and ring marked stones, dating back a further two thousand years before the hillfort.

'Edwin, you have just returned from the fighting – what is the position at the moment?'

'Well, Katia, the Normans scattered and fled, and we pursued them towards the coast. As it is dark, we have just recalled our men, but will divide into parties that can continue searching into the night and prevent the surviving Normans regrouping.'

'Cealwin, you led the decisive attack into the stalled Norman advance. How did you achieve such spectacular results?'

'I led one of the three prongs of attack, Katia. Etherlred of Banbury was responsible for the frontal assault, Morcar of London wheeled round from the left flank to cut off their retreat, and my men worked round the back from the right to head off any counter-attack from the main Norman position.'

'Edwin, what is the intention now?'

'The Normans have lost over half their forces and we must prevent the remainder from regrouping. As you know, Katia, they destroyed all their ships, so there is no chance of an escape.'

'Desperate men make dangerous foes, Katia, so reinforcements have been requested from London to help seek out and destroy the remaining Normans.'

'I quite agree, Cealwin, they were prepared to destroy and conquer England; we must show no mercy. Duke William fell in action, about two hours ago. His knights must share the same fate.'

'Thank you for sharing those thoughts with me. This is Katia AD at the victorious royal camp on Senlac Hill, for the Saxon Broadcasting Corporation six o'clock news, handing you back to the studio.'

Now, only a tyrant could get away with such a comprehensive revision of history, but consider the impact of such meddling, not just for Saxon England, but Britain, Europe and even world history. For a start, Chapter 4 would be irrelevant. Castles, cathedrals, towns and even feudalism might not have developed and, of course, society would have taken an entirely different course. Who knows, England, Scotland and Wales might have united centuries earlier than they did, bloodlessly. Then again . . .

History, or at least our perception of it, changes remorselessly, mostly bolstered by new evidence. Not so long ago, when I was at school in fact, children were taught that, as Britain's shores were constantly battered by waves, wind and rain from the west, so her people were being beaten and plundered by a steady stream of invaders from the east. The Beakers were followed by the Celts, and then the Belgae. The Romans arrived to establish 350 years' stability, before giving us up as a bad job. Then came a further 650 years of Angles, Saxons, Jutes, Irish, Norse, Danes and, finally, Norman invaders, each wishing to control and subdue our green and pleasant land.

That was the 'invasion thesis'; a widely accepted theory. Quote it today and you will be laughed at. Indeed, many recent theories have been challenged – and there is no stopping historians now. Was Britain really the first industrial nation in the world? What about the Netherlands 150 years earlier, or China during the Ming dynasty? The future is not simply formed by the past, it changes the past!

Moreover, history itself has diversified. Long gone are the days when history was about kings, battles and castles. Now we have Economic History, Social History and, who knows, one day students might even be able to study for a joint-honours degree reading the History of the Development of Business Studies! History has changed and evolved – there is no going back.

None of that should bother us too much, and all the squabbling over historical minutiae can be left to the experts. We can simply go out to see, appreciate, understand and enjoy Britain's numerous strongholds. Perhaps you have visited many already – but even so, there are still thousands more. Maybe this is your first visit to Britain; if so, then prepare yourself for an invigorating journey to strongholds built over a period exceeding five thousand years.

Many strongholds are, of course, ruins – some of which are quite magnificent – but to really appreciate the history before your eyes, one must look beyond the obvious; try to envisage them in their contemporary world. Who built them, how and why? Few were built in one go, so why were they developed? Perhaps most important, what were they like as living strongholds? Was offence or defence the prime consideration, or an afterthought? How did a stronghold relate to the world about it? Why did a stronghold prosper and then decline? Quite often, answers to all, or any, of these questions are elusive, but when visiting the tumbled remains of an Iron Age dun in the wilds of Scotland, such thoughts can only be enhancing. They might even transform it from a visual pleasure to an all-round historical experience, without the need for jolly re-enactments.

History can be all things to all people. Some think that by analysing the past we can predict the future. Others assume we can learn about the present by understanding the past. They might be right, but one can gain great pleasure simply by visiting our vast heritage, something we British tend to overlook – after all it's all around us. Some years ago, while writing a book about Iron Age hillforts, I met an eminent archaeologist who had excavated at several hillforts but, despite a lifetime's work in this field, had visited far fewer than I had. How odd! Fancy spending countless hours poring over dreary archaeological reports and other academic tomes, and not visiting hillforts galore. To me, it was like writing a book about hockey and not playing the game.

This should not concern us too much, though. Whether you bought this book, borrowed it from the library, or received it as a present, bite the bullet and put it to use. Get yourself organized and visit your local strongholds. Better still, read a relevant chapter or two and then find some strongholds I have omitted, or missed!

This book is merely one key to a door that leads to the exciting, invigorating, even uplifting world that is Stronghold Britain. Even if you do not agree with everything I've written, the important thing is to get out and visit strongholds, and enjoy them in your own way. An archaeologist once strongly criticized me for encouraging people to visit hillforts. He felt they were a valuable resource that could only be damaged by visitors, but archaeologists and historians have no more right to our historic sites than you or me, especially those on public land. So, get up, get ready and get out to see Stronghold Britain. You will be amazed, astounded and even, on occasions, antagonized, but never will you be ambivalent towards the sheer diversity of Britain's living history.

USE OF IMPERIAL MEASUREMENTS

As this is a book about British strongholds, I have used the appropriate imperial measurements and weights. Body measurements, such as the foot, are more relevant to prehistoric strongholds, and the imperial system developed from the long and protracted use of units that were easily identified by all.

It is three decades since archaeology sold its soul to the great metric god. Nowadays, you might hear archaeologists say that the ditch of a Martello Tower – built against Napoleonic France, no less – was 3 metres deep, and not bat an eyelid! They who know so much, understand so little . . . Despite the treachery of successive, small-minded governments, imperial measurements *are* relevant to our immediate, historic and prehistoric past and, if we British have any sense, to our present and future.

C H A P T E R   1

PREHISTORIC BRITAIN

Not so very long ago, the prospect of travelling two thousand years back in time was about as enticing as, say, the annual pilgrimage to the in-laws; the option of visiting the Stone Age was considered worse than going on holiday with them. Much of this rather off-putting image was due to the Romans. They regarded the peoples of our insignificant island off the north-west coast of Europe as barbarians at best – or as wild, woad-painted and quite uncivilized savages at worst.

The Romans recognized these peoples as Celts – the very savages who had sacked their beloved Rome in 390 BC. Furthermore, some of the Belgic-Celts who were driven from Gaul by the onslaughts of Julius Caesar in the first century BC had taken refuge on that not-so-distant island. Finally, just to confirm Roman prejudice against our less than green and pleasant land, it was also the spiritual centre of the dreaded Druids. The Romans feared these crazed, wild-haired men and shrieking women who practised the ultimate heresy – human sacrifice – and perhaps even cannibalism. Little wonder our present-day authorities keep the modern druidic adherents at arms' length.

These sweeping impressions have filtered down to us, because several Roman accounts have survived the turmoil of the passing centuries. Our traditional classical education spread such ideas far and wide, these being further reinforced by archaeology's own prehistoric invasion thesis of 'wave after wave' of foreigners invading our less-than-peaceful shores. There is no doubt about it – on the basis of such evidence, our prospective time-traveller had much to fear had his time-machine landed in Britain in about 1 BC.

And yet . . . if only it were so simple. The last fifty years have seen many archaeological theories do more apparent double-turns, backflips and somersaults than an Olympic acrobat, in an attempt to accommodate the latest evidence. Scottish brochs, traditionally said to herald from the first century BC, may now date back to c. 600 BC. Iron Age hillforts, most of which were dated to c. 200 BC (perhaps 300 BC at a pinch), are now known to have been built centuries earlier, even well before the Iron Age itself. Neolithic causeway camps – assumed to be ceremonial centres – now show

Viewed from the neolithic West Kennet long barrow, Silbury Hill looks for all the world like a great Norman motte. Europe's largest prehistoric monument, it remains an enigma. Nobody knows why it was built.

signs of being occasionally occupied, and some were even defended. The once-hallowed 'invasion thesis' is now considered as a distinctly shabby old hat. Oh yes, just like the proverbial slow train arriving half an hour late at Crewe, it's 'all change' for archaeology. The express train to the understanding of our prehistoric past is about to depart – and it waits for nobody.

Today, Britain is often perceived as a fairly homogeneous society, but is this accurate? Take a crofter on the Shetland Islands. His daily life has little in common with a townie from Lerwick, still less with a cosmopolitan Glaswegian. One would be sticking one's neck out to call a Shetland islander a Scotsman, and heaven help anyone who suggests to a Glaswegian that Scotland is under the English thumb. Similar parallels could easily be drawn between a Londoner, a Northumbrian and a hill farmer from Snowdonia. Far from being a single united nation, modern Britain is still a diverse and eclectic mix, even without taking into account the mass immigration of the last fifty years. Two thousand and more years ago the differences were even more marked.

In front of me I have a book by an eminent archaeologist, written barely forty years ago, that suggests Britain's few inhabitants at the tail-end of the Old Stone Age were little more than wandering foragers. Thirty years before, some archaeologists still believed that prehistoric Britons lived in pit-dwellings – these are now recognized as storage, ceremonial or rubbish pits. More recently, though, we have found that not only was Paleolithic man living on our island fully 500,000 years ago but, far from being a poor wandering soul, a whole seemingly settled landscape has emerged, as discovered at Boxgrove in Sussex – the Bedrock of the British Flintstones perhaps?

To date, the remarkable Boxgrove site is unique, but who knows what might turn up in the future? Between the time early man lived in and near Boxgrove and the end of the Paleolithic era (the Old Stone Age) around 9000 BC, the climate blew successively hot and cold. It is usually assumed that very few people inhabited Britain at the end of the last Ice Age, *c*. 11000 BC, but as the ice retreated, so man soon returned in its wake.

Nomadic at first, ancient man began to settle, if not permanently, for at least a season or two. Wessex, a part of England with a long, well-defined history, has fewer than a dozen known Paleolithic sites – little chance of Fred Flintstone and Barney Rubble getting up to their tricks there, then. On the other hand caves in the Mendip Hills and Derbyshire, to say nothing of Kent's Cavern, have been far more forthcoming. Ultimately, a fire in a cave's entrance was the first stronghold. By that definition, though, modern deadlocks, padlocks and all-action security systems of flashing lights and ringing bells would transform even the most modest house into a stronghold: I think not.

THE FIRST STRONGHOLDS

The Mesolithic period (or Middle Stone Age) lasted from *c.* 9000 to *c.* 4500 BC. It was during this period, in about 6000 BC, that the North Sea finally broke through to create Europe's largest island. Whatever had happened before, there is now increasing evidence of man settling all over Britain; not quite from Land's End to John O' Groats, but at least as far north as the west coast of Scotland. Evidence of palisade fences enclosing a Mesolithic settlement might be as rare as moon-dust, but with various wild animals roaming about, you can bet someone, somewhere hit upon the bright idea. Suddenly, there you have it, the first true, man-made stronghold.

West Kennet long barrow is a rarity in southern England: a Neolithic burial chamber that can be entered. The mound is about 330 ft long and 10 ft high. It is pictured here from the top of Silbury Hill.

Of course, one would not expect to see the remains of such a stronghold today, but evidence of banks and palisade fences of Mesolithic antiquity have been uncovered. By the time the Neolithic period (New Stone Age) began, *c.* 4500 BC, things changed rapidly; forest clearance was well underway for a start. Undoubtedly, the population was increasing and, far from wandering about in a vast, empty landscape in search of food, people were living in settlements. Naturally, evidence of such lightly built settlements, dating back some six thousand years, is hard to find on the ground today; however, there are some splendid jewels in our landscape's crown.

Take long-barrow earthen burial mounds (or stone cairns) for instance. There are hundreds scattered throughout Britain. Yet, following the drought of 1995, aerial photography was able to locate still more, surviving only as soil marks. Many long-barrows remained in use for several centuries, some for well over five hundred years, suggesting that the people either returned to a particular mound to bury their dead or, more likely, lived nearby. Far from a few isolated pockets of Britain being occupied during the Neolithic Age, it is looking increasingly likely that most of the land was inhabited, albeit with a low population density.

Indeed, we must look to the Neolithic Age for our first true strongholds. The Iron Age was formerly seen as the era of the prehistoric stronghold, with Neolithic and Bronze Age man being considered nomadic. The Iron Age is still the great age of fortified settlements, no question there, but more evidence is constantly being found of defences at Neolithic sites.

Britain's oldest man-made dwelling, the Knap of Howar, on Orkney's Papa Westray, is a splendid example of a Neolithic house and adjoining workshop.

North-west Europe's oldest known stone dwelling, the Knap of Howar on the Orcadian island of Papa Westray, comprises a large living room and an adjoining work room, dating to about 3500 BC. This small but fascinating site appears rather less defended than an open prison – in other words, not at all. Your eyes, though, may deceive you. Five-and-a-half thousand years ago, the sound that separates Papay from Westray was probably a bay; Papa Westray was not an island. Not only did the Knap of Howar sit further inland than it does today, but it lay behind

Bronze Age stone row on
Dartmoor.

a protective screen of sand dunes along with other settlements. Was the Knap of Howar, not unlike the later Skara Brae on Orkney's Mainland, one of several dwellings defended by a palisade fence in the sand dunes? While there is no direct evidence to back such a theory, absence of evidence is not evidence of absence. Who knows what might turn up at any future excavation.

NEOLITHIC MONUMENTS

Cursus and Henge:
for Settlement or Ceremony?

Apart from burial mounds there are several other types of Neolithic monuments visible in our landscape. The typical cursus, so-called because early antiquarians thought they were prehistoric race-courses, has about as much in common with defence as do bows and arrows today. The roughly parallel banks and ditches *could* have been used to keep out unwanted visitors, especially if topped by a palisade fence, but given their sometimes extreme length – the Dorset Cursus, for example, is about 6 miles long – perhaps they were used to delineate sacred ground. Describing a cursus as a stronghold is, very likely, a bit far-fetched.

Henges on the other hand are widely recognized as being ceremonial centres, perhaps the best known being those at Stonehenge and Avebury, but are they? Henges usually comprise an earth bank with an inner ditch in a slightly flattened ellipse, often with two opposing entrances. As the bank lies *outside* the ditch at a henge (an arrangement not unlike that of the old Berlin Wall – more appropriate to keeping people in), perhaps they were intended to create an aura of mystique by keeping out prying eyes? Gradually, evidence is coming to light to show that some henges were, at least temporarily, occupied. Or were henges prehistoric concentration camps or prisoner-of-war centres? There is still clearly much work to be done with henges, though it is doubtful if they were strongholds.

Neolithic Causeway Camps

It is no easier with causeway camps either. Once again, these were traditionally thought to be either ceremonial sites, trading centres, theatres or something along those lines, but most definitely not defended settlements. As they usually comprise concentric banks and ditches, both being crossed by several causeways (not necessarily aligned), so they have defensive limitations: too many entrances rather spoils the impregnable effect.

Modern archaeology is constantly challenging these older ideas and, if not quite casting them totally aside, is certainly beginning to modify them. For a

WHITE SHEET CASTLE (Promontory Hillfort and Causeway Camp)
Wiltshire O/S map 183 ref. 804346 (hillfort) 802352 (causeway camp)
Directions: From Mere, head north towards Wood Farm, crossing the by-pass. Continue to the end of the track, before the farm, and follow the path up the ridge of hills to the drove road. Turn left and the hillfort is on the left. The causeway camp is about ¼ mile beyond the hillfort, before the track descends the hill.

A single bank and ditch runs round the west escarpment of the hillfort, and opens out to three wide-spaced ramparts and ditches across the neck of the promontory in the east. There are several gaps, not all of which were entrances. About 15 acres are enclosed at this prominently located hillfort.

Cross-banks cut off the plateau to the east and north-west, and they continue down the escarpment. They may have formed a stock enclosure, while the animals might have been herded between the hillfort's ramparts in times of danger. Beyond the cross-bank in the north-west lies the causeway camp, an oval earthwork with twenty-one causeways across its ditch and bank, enclosing about 4 acres. Of several Bronze Age round barrows nearby, one lies over the ditch in the south-east, but excavation confirmed the Neolithic date of the causeway camp.

This whole area, with its Neolithic, Bronze Age and Iron Age sites, plus a drove road derived from an ancient trackway, simply oozes history. There is much to see, but it takes time to appreciate it all. Whatever the use of the causeway camp, the hillfort was certainly a stronghold, one that is quite unusual in Wessex.

start, several Iron Age hillforts were built over, or in the immediate vicinity of, causeway camps. Crickley Hill, Hembury and Rybury Camp, along with Maiden Castle, Hambledon Hill and White Sheet Hill, all fall into this category. It was once thought that causeway camps were not only deserted, but largely unknown to the hillfort builders, some two thousand years later. Really? As many can still be seen today, they must surely have been pretty obvious in the Iron Age. There is also increasing evidence of settlement in and near causeway camps between the Neolithic and Iron Ages, so perhaps many had not been deserted for two thousand years either. Who knows what evidence might be revealed in the future.

So far, evidence of causeway camps being used as strongholds is severely limited. There is a strong temptation in archaeology to assume that, for example, as one causeway camp was a defended stronghold, so the rest must have been. Such sweeping generalizations have more uncertainties than flying abroad when

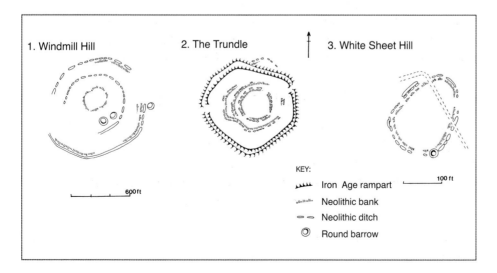

1. Windmill Hill 2. The Trundle 3. White Sheet Hill

KEY:
⌃⌃⌃ Iron Age rampart
⸗⸗⸗ Neolithic bank
⌐ ⌐ Neolithic ditch
◎ Round barrow

600 ft

100 ft

Causeway enclosures.

the French or Spanish air-traffic controllers are having their annual work-to-rule. No, each site must be taken strictly on its merits. None the less, such all-encompassing hypotheses are far from extinct. It may be, though, that the causeway camps at Maiden Castle, The Trundle and Knap Hill developed into defended enclosures, while banks at Crickley Hill, Hambledon Hill and Windmill Hill were certainly timber-revetted. In addition, a number of flint arrow-heads were found near burnt palisade timbers at Crickley Hill suggesting, at least, a highly coincidental – not to say unfortunate – accident. At Carn Brea, meanwhile, a wide spread of arrow-heads, with no sign of the usual manufacturing detritus, may point to something more than a group of visitors getting a bit upset.

Best of all is the Neolithic landscape that was partially excavated at Hambledon Hill. The big causeway camp there might have been a large open cemetery with, incidentally, about 60 per cent of the human remains belonging to children – not too unusual for a subsistence economy. There is no certainty that this site was ever fortified, nor the smaller adjacent one on the Stepleton Spur, but there is plenty of evidence for other contemporary defences. Hambledon Hill, then, most certainly was a Neolithic stronghold of sorts.

Maumbury Rings, a Neolithic henge, was later used as an amphitheatre by the Romans. The Civil War gun ramps are also shown in this photograph.

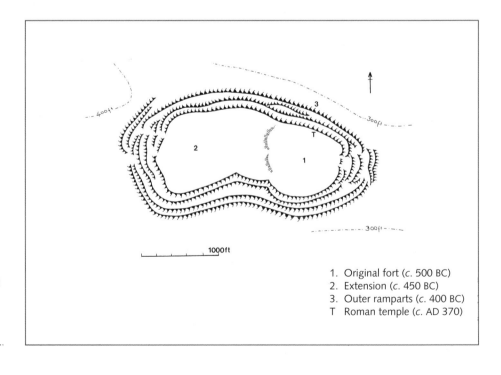

Maiden Castle was originally a Neolithic causeway camp, dating to the fourth millennium BC. Successive developments in the Iron Age turned this into one of the greatest, and most famous, of all hillforts.

1000ft

1. Original fort (c. 500 BC)
2. Extension (c. 450 BC)
3. Outer ramparts (c. 400 BC)
T Roman temple (c. AD 370)

There is no finer Neolithic causeway camp than Knap Hill. The numerous causeways that cross the ditch still clearly stand out, and the site overlooks the Vale of Pewsey. Within ½ mile are Bronze Age round barrows, an Iron Age enclosure and the Dark Age linear earthwork, the east Wansdyke.

It is clear that Hambledon Hill was not a transitory camp either, for pottery has been found there that was manufactured in the Bath area and on The Lizard peninsula, together with axes from South Wales, Cornwall and Langdale in Westmorland, among others. Not only does this suggest that Hambledon was a place of some importance in the fourth millennium BC, but shows that trade was widespread, with all that this entails, including transport and exchange rituals.

So, why was there a need for defence and strongholds in the Neolithic Age? Not unnaturally, protection for man and his cattle – an important factor of the Hambledon economy – from wild animals and hostile raiders was vital. Archaeology has made huge strides in discovering how developed was the landscape in Neolithic Britain and, in the vicinity of Avebury, evidence of lynchet field boundaries has been found 12 feet below the present ground level. Avebury was most certainly an important area, and one with a considerable density of occupation. Once a patch of land had been cleared, it would have been tempting for someone to try to drive the incumbent off, rather than undertake all the hard graft to clear their own. So, it had to be defended. Multiply this notion from individuals into groups of people, and you have a settlement which, in turn, brings about the stronghold, or defended settlement.

That is but one scenario. Immigration is another. As today, this was certainly a problem faced by our Neolithic forebears. It might be that the people of Neolithic Scotland spoke a language not unrelated to Gaelic. In other words,

KNAP HILL
Wiltshire O/S map 173 ref. 121636
Directions: From Pewsey, take the minor road north-west to Alton Priors. Turn right at the cross-roads, continue for about a mile northwards and the car park is on the right. The causeway camp is clearly seen on top of the hill.

To date, there is little direct evidence that Neolithic causeway camps were anything other than ceremonial sites. However, some seem to have been attacked, so it may be that a few – if by no means all – had some means of defence.

Knap Hill is superbly located above the Vale of Pewsey and gives the impression that it might have had defensive capabilities. A single ditch, crossed by five causeways, encloses the north and west arc of the summit, about 4 acres. The bank is now very low, but might have been continued, or been intended to be, round the other sides. It is unclear but perhaps the causeway camp was never finished. Certainly, silting of the ditch began soon after it was completed and debris has been C-14 dated to *c.* 3500 BC.

Knap Hill might never have been a stronghold, but it is one of the most obviously defensible causeway camps. Its magnificent location would make it ideal as a ceremonial centre or a stronghold. Either way, with its two Bronze Age round barrows and an Iron Age enclosure to the north, this is a site occupied by prehistoric man on and off for over three thousand years. Given its location, that is no surprise.

they may not have been too far removed from the Celts of the Iron Age. If those peoples migrated to Scotland early in the Neolithic Age, then so it could have been for England and Wales. Of course, this is impossible to confirm.

An alternative theory is that as the native Neolithic population grew, so the demand for land increased. Though the population was minuscule in comparison with that of modern Britain, farming methods and husbandry, in particular crop yields, were as vital as they still are. Today, yields have increased enormously. Two hundred years ago, a good yield would have been about 5:1. This figure was a little above that of the Norman era and, one might assume, still more over that of prehistoric times. So, more land was needed to feed the same size population in the Neolithic Age than, say, in the Middle Ages. There is no doubt, though, that defended settlements existed in the Neolithic Age. Whether it was through the demands of an increasing population, the desire to protect private or communal land, or the need to stave off an influx of foreigners, the age of stronghold building began at least as early as the third millennium BC.

BRONZE AGE

Clearly, Britain's first strongholds emerged before the techniques for making metal objects had reached our shores. Copper is found in various parts of Britain, and it is assumed that there was a brief Copper Age between the Neolithic Age and the Bronze Age proper, probably somewhere between 2500 and 2000 BC. Bronze is an alloy of copper and tin, and the latter is only found in Cornwall. So, while bronze implements had been made in some parts of Britain a few centuries before 2000 BC, it was hardly universal. For instance, the Neolithic Age on the Shetland Islands seems to have lasted until about 1500 BC. So, for our purposes, let us say the Bronze Age began *c.* 2000 BC and it is easy to be more than three hundred years out either way.

The most obvious use of metal is for tools and weapons: in particular daggers, swords and shield bosses. Not for the last time, Britain lagged behind the world's

YEAVERING BELL (Hillfort)
Northumberland O/S maps 74 or 75 ref. 928293
Directions: Head north from Wooler on the A697 and turn left on the B6351. After 2 miles, turn left on a track to Old Yeavering. Follow the track through the farmyard and turn left through the gateway just before the stream. Cross the field diagonally to the steps over the stone wall. Walk straight to the top of the steep hill.

The twin peaks of Yeavering Bell stand bleakly against the sky. On a dark winter's day, one can easily imagine all sorts of evil deeds being enacted within the hillfort. Unlike the many hundreds of small prehistoric defended settlements that abound in the Votadini tribal area, Yeavering Bell is comparatively large: 13½ acres enclosed by the tumbled stone wall. Shaped like a running-track, the wall was about 12 ft thick and probably 10 ft high. It might have been destroyed by the Romans – although there is no evidence of this – and a short, low section still stands in the west. This was no stone-faced rampart, but a true solid wall. There are entrances in the north, south and east, with crescent-shaped enclosures – probably for cattle – at the east and west.

This was not the first fortified settlement on the site. When it was excavated in the 1950s, a small palisade enclosure was discovered round the eastern summit. This overlay some of the 130 circular hut platforms that can be clearly seen within the larger hillfort, so people might have lived on this seemingly uninhabitable hill in the Bronze Age. Quite unexpectedly, it was also found that the huts were not built of stone but of wood. The density of about 10 huts per acre is almost double that of many hillforts in the south. Of course, not all were contemporary, but there could have been a population of about 500 people. It would have been quite something on a stormy winter's night, trapped within your wooden thatched hut; it was certainly not a place for the faint-hearted.

Yeavering Bell is one of the largest stone-walled hillforts in England, though there are many in Scotland. The Anglo-Saxon royal township of Ad Gefryn lies across the main road at ref. 926305. Although this dates to the seventh century AD, there was a Neolithic cemetery, Celtic fields and an Iron Age enclosure there before. The relationship between this site and Yeavering Bell would be quite interesting to discover.

leaders in such technological matters. The Egyptians had long been building pyramids, the Sumerian/Mesopotamian/Babylonian city states were building hanging gardens and ziggurats, and bronze had been used in the Middle East for almost 1,500 years. And some people think Britain is technologically backward today! (At least we had our stone circles coming on stream, and so another new industry was born.)

One might assume that the advent of metal weapons set the scene for a minor prehistoric arms-race; once a settlement's residents had so armed themselves, their neighbours could hardly sit back and do nothing. Primitive defensive systems would need to be revised and beefed-up. The idea that palisade enclosures first emerged in the last centuries of the Bronze Age was widespread until fairly recently. As we have seen though, defensive banks, fences and ditches had existed since Neolithic times so, given the advance in weaponry, one might expect something a little more sophisticated than a paltry wooden fence, but probably not too early in the Bronze Age. Why? Swords did not appear until the second millennium BC and, let's face it, there are numerous open settlements that date to the Bronze and Iron Ages. Maybe, just maybe, life was more peaceful than we imagine; if not all sweetness and honey, it was far from being a case of constantly looking over one's shoulder, just in case.

Let there be no doubt about it, though, whatever the cause, from about 1000 BC (if not a few hundred years before) there was a veritable explosion of defended settlements all over Britain. In fact, this growth in strongholds was more akin to a nuclear explosion, with its expanding ripple effect. British stronghold building began as a trickle, but soon grew into a great rush that lasted for 1,500 years. Oh yes, in the meantime, the Romans came, saw and – mostly – conquered, but they never entirely quashed the use of native strongholds, at least in Scotland.

Crannogs

These strongholds, whether for an extended family or a village settlement, took their form in the later Bronze Age and not, as was often supposed, in the Iron Age. So, we have Flag Fen in the old, wonderfully named, Soke of Peterborough, in which an artificial island was built in a lake or marsh about 1000 BC. This crannog-type affair was fully 3 acres in area, being built on over one million (yes, a million) wooden piles; it was truly massive and a fantastic feat of engineering and organization. This is an outstanding place to visit, but it was certainly not a stronghold – more likely a ritual site.

There were probably other crannogs in the East Anglian fens, not nearly so large as Flag Fen, that were strongholds; the remains of many were undoubtedly destroyed in subsequent drainage schemes. Others have been found in Wales, but Scotland and Ireland are the usual homes of these artificial islands. Modern archaeology has, once again, been able to turn the accepted norm on its head; crannogs were initially thought to have originated in Ireland and been copied in Scotland. Recent research from several sites suggests that not only is the reverse most likely but also, though this is a very, very tentative theory, that Scottish crannogs date back to at least 800 BC. This date, although on the Bronze Age/Iron Age border for much of Britain, sits fully two hundred years back into the Scottish Bronze Age. It might not be the earliest either, for a crannog has recently been discovered in Loch Olabhat, in North Uist, which may be of Neolithic origin. This site has produced much pottery, waterlogged timbers and evidence of possibly twelve buildings.

A crannog was a relatively simple form of stronghold. Stones were placed offshore, usually in a lake, and secured by wooden piles to create an island. Many were connected to the shore by a causeway (a few of which were either

Din Lligwy is one of the finest late Iron Age open settlements in Britain. The small village is enclosed by a low wall as shown. Occupied into the Dark Ages, Din Lligwy is a mixture of rectangular and circular huts.

sunken or included a trap to catch out unwanted guests), but others were true islands. Of course, nothing of their usually wooden superstructure remains, but some probably had fences and a few even a stone wall. Water was the main defence, though very few crannogs were big enough for anything other than an extended family. One can argue as to whether or not that disqualifies such crannogs from being classed as strongholds, but as far as we are concerned, they will do nicely, thank you.

Farms and Homesteads

Bronze Age fortified farmsteads are rarely seen today, and only a few are known to have survived, although there are several on military land on Salisbury Plain. Their small scale has meant that many have been obliterated by ploughing and modern farming methods, especially those on the gentle rolling hills of southern England. Nevertheless, more sites are being discovered that can be dated back to the middle Bronze Age.

On higher ground such defended homesteads or settlements have survived rather better, especially in Scotland. As the Bronze Age progressed to about 1500 BC, there was a move to farm the less productive, lighter soils of the hills and the tree-cover was accordingly cut back. Perhaps this is a tangible sign of an ever-growing population? Again, the pattern of clearing land and then defending both it and the homestead, as had happened in the valleys of Neolithic Britain, was repeated, often at heights of up to 1,500 feet above sea level.

Bronze Age Stronghold Settlements – everything but the hillfort

Some of the best surviving examples, not only of defended settlements, but also of long rectangular field boundaries (reaves), can be seen on Dartmoor. Large areas of what is now peaty moorland were once used both for arable and cattle farming, and evidence of posts and hedgerows of still earlier boundaries has been found beneath reaves. While there are pockets of huts and open settlements from the middle Bronze Age, it is the defended pounds that are of relevance here. Grimspound is the premier surviving example. This is a later pound, *c.* 1000 BC, which might explain why it is the biggest, but its tumbled stone wall shows that this was every inch a stronghold settlement. Indeed, except for its location on the slopes between two tors, it is little different from many Scottish Iron Age hillforts.

Grimspound is far from being an isolated example. There are also Rough Tor and Mam Tor and, at lower altitudes, Rams Hill, Ffridd Faldwyn and The Breiddin; Traprain Law and many other hillforts originated as late Bronze Age defended settlements. It is also conceivable that the Atlantic roundhouses, which eventually developed into brochs and duns, can be

There is no better example of a late Bronze Age settlement in Britain. Grimspound's tumbled stone walls might have stood about 10 ft high.

GRIMSPOUND
Devon O/S map 191 ref. 701809
Directions: From Moretonhampstead, take the B3212 across Dartmoor. After about 3 miles, cross a cattle-grid followed by sharp right and left bends and a car park. Turn left ¼ mile after these and follow the minor road to Widecombe, for 1½ miles. Park just before a right-hand bend, and follow the stream uphill to the pound, on the left.

Standing nearly 1,500 ft above sea level, nobody would relish living on and farming these Dartmoor hills today. This is not surprising, given the inclement and rapidly changing weather, but Grimspound is proof that Dartmoor was indeed farmed in warmer prehistoric times.

Grimspound was the defended settlement of a cattle- and sheep-rearing people, rather than of the arable farmers associated with the reeves elsewhere on the moors. It dates from the late Bronze Age, *c.* 1000 BC, and was inhabited until the climate deteriorated, *c.* 800 BC; man departed the moors as the peat took over.

A single stone wall about 10 ft thick defended a circular enclosure of 4 acres on the slopes between Hookney and Hameldown Tors. As one would expect, the wall is a tumbled mass of stones, but short lengths were partially restored in the nineteenth century. There was a single paved entrance in the south-east, facing Hameldown Tor; all the other gaps are post-settlement. The wall is visible for the entire circuit, and is a rare survivor in such fine condition.

Inside, in the centre and the south, are sixteen hut circles. Many of these had a hearth, door-jambs and a central post-hole, probably a roof support; two huts also had porches. Perhaps indicating that the weather was beginning to take a turn for the worse, the hut walls were lined inside and out with vertical slabs, the gap was filled with smaller stones and turf. The roofs would have been either turf or thatch.

To the north, as many as eight much simpler circular foundations can be seen, none of which had a hearth. These may have been storage rooms or barns, for the quality of build was inferior to that of the huts. Some cattle pens are located beside the perimeter wall in the west. With its single entrance, a stream running through the settlement under the walls, and internal cattle pens, the inhabitants clearly appreciated the defensive capabilities of the site. Yet even if the wall was 10 ft high, the enclosure is overlooked on three sides. Surely, then, this was not the best of locations to build a stronghold if defence was a critical priority?

Reconstruction of Grimspound.

traced back to at least the last centuries of the Scottish Bronze Age, well before 600 BC.

However, we are leaping ahead of ourselves. From about 2000 to 1500 BC there was certainly increased clearance and occupation of high ground. One might suggest that the reasons for this were similar to those given for the defended settlements in the Neolithic Age: namely, personal property, population growth and immigration. Connected with the latter are the so-called Beaker people, whose distinctive pottery emerged in our landscape, along with round barrow burial mounds, during the last centuries of the third millennium BC.

Older theories that the Beaker people had a different shaped head to the native population, or even a big nose – hence an alternative source for their name, are now considered as fanciful as day-trips to the Moon – for the present, at least.

It was assumed that the Beaker people were one of the many waves who indulged themselves by invading our shores with impunity, and this cannot be entirely ruled out. A more recent suggestion is that they arrived as peaceful immigrants with their specialist pottery, burial rites and, who knows, perhaps they even introduced bronze-making. The more favoured option is the possibility that there was no mass-migration at all, but that change came through trade. None of these theses can be either proved or disproved with any degree of certainty and, as surely as night follows day, tomorrow's archaeologists will concoct an entirely new set of ideas.

Bronze Age Climatic Change

Not only that, but change was, quite literally, in the air. Just as there was increased farming of the high ground early in the second millennium BC, probably due to a rising population, so the last centuries saw a retreat from the uplands and also from many non-coastal areas of Scotland. Beneath the current blankets of peat, signs of Iron Age landscapes on the Isle of Lewis and Neolithic (but 2nd millennium BC) settlements on the Shetland Isles are gradually being uncovered. Given the vast tracts of Britain that are still engulfed by peat bog, the possibilities for future excavations could be almost limitless.

What caused this apparent climatic change, the opposite to our global warming? Rather like today's destruction of the tropical rainforests, the drive to cultivate and farm higher ground led to the clearance of great tracts of woodland and forest. Dartmoor was just about cleared of trees, but the Pennines, Lake District, Peak District, North Yorkshire Moors, large areas of Wales, and southern and western Scotland had also been effectively deforested by about 1500 BC. The consequences of such actions must have been, at the very least, detrimental to soil regeneration.

The light infertile soils of the uplands, rocky islands and coastal areas, especially in Scotland, could never sustain an intensive agricultural economy. In any case, if yields were low on the rich soils of the valleys, one might assume they would be distinctly marginal on the higher ground, even in good years. Poor farming methods and low yields required more land to produce enough food, and thus contributed to soil degeneration. At any time from c. 1500 BC in north Scotland, and certainly by 1200 BC, the peat blanket was beginning to form. Why?

One favoured theory is the gradual deterioration in the climate: it became both cooler and wetter – just the right conditions for peat. This was no mini Ice Age: all it takes is a small drop in the average temperature, and a few more inches of rain a year – each and every year – and crops will not grow or ripen at above, say, 1,000 feet. After a couple of such years, the barren land would be, not unnaturally, abandoned, which is when the peat takes over. Just like a bulldog, once peat took a hold it was very difficult to shake off. Even today, peat is a relentless opponent. On the Shetland island of Yell crofters claim the odd victory, but they are quickly

BUTSER ANCIENT FARM
Hampshire O/S map 197 ref. 710168
Directions: Take the A3 south from Petersfield and turn left at the sign for Chalton. Turn immediately right and the farm is ¼ mile down the road, on the right.

The Butser Ancient Farm Project is a living, open-air research station, not a recreated museum. Not only are there various reconstructed Iron Age huts, each built using traditional methods and materials, but there are storage pits, crops, animals, metal manufacturing and an enclosing ditch, bank and palisade fence. Visitors may wander around and view it all from close range; sometimes they are asked to give a helping hand – a real journey back in time. To all intents and purposes, this is just what an Iron Age farm could have been like.

Few of the strongholds featured in this book are seen in their working environment or condition. The further back in time one goes, naturally the less this is so. Iron Age hillforts were most emphatically not the quiet, pleasantly green spaces enclosed by a rolling bank and ditch they often appear today. The Butser Ancient Farm gives an outstanding impression of how a farmstead might have looked and includes much of what would have been familiar to the inhabitants of the later Iron Age hillforts and farms.

The Butser Ancient Farm Project is not the only place where one can see recreated Iron Age round huts, but it is by far the best and most comprehensive in Britain. It really ought to be visited before one goes to see any prehistoric stronghold. Cut out the romantic, barbaric or other fanciful notions; it was a relatively dirty, smelly and rustic world, but one that was well ordered and not without its less mundane aspects. Nowhere else can one come so near to the world of our prehistoric forebears.

Top: A general view of the Butser Iron Age Farm. Middle: Pimperne House, at Butser. Bottom: A ring of posts supporting the unfinished thatch roof of a hut at Butser.

pushed back on the defensive, fighting yet another rearguard action, despite tractors and fertilizer. Three thousand years ago it was a hopeless task.

So, was the deteriorating climate connected with the mass clearance of the upland woods? It certainly cannot have helped, but there is a bit more to it. In 1159 BC the Icelandic volcano Hekla erupted and caused something akin to a nuclear winter. There was some fall-out over Scotland and Ireland, and a dust-cloud that partially blocked the sun. This, though, does not explain what happened in England and Wales, unless the effects of such a natural cataclysm have been vastly underestimated. On the other hand, neither does it account for the deteriorating weather before Hekla blew its top. Perhaps it was a combination of a small climatic change, exacerbated by the mass clearance of trees, the poor farming methods and finally the eruption of Hekla that pushed farmers over the edge, or off the hills.

HILLFORTS AND THE IRON AGE

In case you thought I had forgotten the plot, this book is about strongholds. However, the above might go some way to explaining the greatest change to take place in Britain's landscape over the following two thousand years: the appearance of hillforts. There are about three thousand in Britain, ranging in size from barely half an acre to one of over 800 acres. Though most (but by no means all) are situated on hills, the vast majority lie below the 1,000 feet contour, which might have been the limit of permanent occupation in the first millennium BC.

Britain's climate probably reached its nadir in about 800 BC, the beginning of the Iron Age in England and Wales. Thereafter, it seems to have improved steadily so that by about 400 BC, peat growth in Scotland was minimal, and by the time of the Roman invasion in AD 43, the climate was similar to that of today (as I write, it is typically cold and wet).

Hillforts, especially the smaller ones, certainly date from as early as 1000 BC, well before the Iron Age. Many were also built in Scotland before the onset of their Iron Age, *c.* 600 BC. On the whole, though, hillfort building took off from 800 BC onwards. So why was this? Did the exodus from the higher ground result in previously undefended lowland settlements cooperating to protect their lands, while those moving down from the high ground built strongholds to secure their new base? Or should we look elsewhere for an explanation, say the introduction of iron weapons? As usual, the reality is likely to be a combination of factors,

Archaeology has uncovered evidence that South Cadbury Castle was occupied in the Neolithic, Bronze Age, Iron Age and Roman times. Still later, it was the fortress of a Dark Age warrior of some considerable significance (was it Camelot?), became a Wessex *burh*, and was still occupied in medieval times. Aside from its Arthurian associations, South Cadbury Castle is famous for having some of the most extensive defences of any Iron Age hillfort.

Regrettably, the thatch roof of this hut at Chysauster has now been removed.

although the migration to the lower lands would have added considerably to the population density.

Let us make one thing absolutely clear, though. Whatever tensions or circumstances caused the rapid building of strongholds throughout the first millennium BC and beyond, be they hillforts, duns, brochs or crannogs, there are also many, many examples of contemporary open settlements. Some of these can still be seen today, such as Chysauster, Ty Mawr and Kilphedir. In other words, life was most certainly not all mayhem and turmoil. Indeed, archaeological evidence increasingly points to something completely different.

Hillforts can be found just about anywhere, and it will come as no surprise to discover that people who enjoy putting things into neat packages have had something of a field day with hillfort categories. Not only that, but it is a wild mistake to assume that all hillforts were in simultaneous use. A good number grew in both size and scale, and lasted many centuries. Some floundered while others flourished. Many were founded well into, if not late in, the Iron Age; some grew into large tribal capitals, while others expanded and then contracted, ending life smaller than when they were originally built. Like doing the football pools, the permutations are endless.

Contour and Plateau Hillforts

The earliest hillforts utilized defences little changed from Neolithic times: a bank, ditch and palisade fence. Contour hillforts, with their defences following the shape of the hill at a particular height, are, by inference, the most simple to plan and the earliest built. This, no doubt, is often correct, but visit Hod Hill or Hambledon Hill and you will find nothing simple about either. As it was the

MOEL TRIGARN (Hillfort)
Pembrokeshire O/S map 145 ref. 158336
Directions: Head south from Cardigan on the A478. Turn right at Crymych and turn left after 1¼ miles. Turn almost immediately right again and follow the minor road round. You will need to cross fields before reaching the hill.

There are 145 known hillforts in Pembrokeshire and Moel Trigarn stands on the north-east of the Preseli Mountains, from where stones might have been taken to Stonehenge. The three Bronze Age cairns on the summit which give the hillfort its name – the reputed burial-places of the kings Mon, Maelen and Madog – are the most easily identifiable feature from afar.

A 3 acre inner enclosure is defended by a single part-drystone wall/part stone-faced rampart, except at the south-west where the ridge requires no artificial defence. An additional 2 acres are enclosed by a slighter wall to the north and east, a little lower down the hill. A simple entrance leads from the higher to the lower enclosure in the east, while a second entrance faces west. The lower enclosure also has two north-facing postern gates.

Both enclosures have numerous hut platforms and circles, in total about 140; there are more on a terrace to the south, but none is especially visible. Several huts have been investigated, but artefacts were few and far between, though some seem to pre-date the hillfort. The hillfort was probably occupied from the sixth century BC until Roman times, and would have been a quite wild location for about 500 or so people to live in.

Towards the end of its use, a further 2 acre enclosure was built on the east side, through which the main track to the entrance passed. The relatively slight scale of the wall suggests that this was more of a stock enclosure although, again, there are a number of huts and hut platforms.

Whether Moel Trigarn was ever a Demetae tribal centre is unknown, but it is certainly a large hillfort for the area. It commands the locality and, perhaps more importantly, can be seen to do so by all and sundry.

summits of such hills that were fortified, so contour hillforts often had the advantage of height and, should it be necessary, enhancing the defences was rarely difficult, although enlarging the hillfort might be.

Plateau hillforts are also fairly straightforward, the layout usually being determined by the lie of the land. Defences at this type of hillfort probably needed to be quite substantial, as the approach was often over level ground. Arbury Banks is one such example, although Edinshall, which is built on a plateau on the side of a hill, is easily overlooked.

Promontory Hillforts

The promontory fort is probably the most common type of hillfort. There are numerous cliff-castles in Cornwall and south-west Wales, and they can be found as far north as the Shetland Islands; some promontory forts are the most spectacularly sited strongholds to be seen. However, not all are on the coast. Crickley Hill and Bredon Hill are just two of many inland examples. Of the hundreds of coastal promontory forts, Sudbrook Camp is barely above the high water mark, Hamble Common Camp is much larger and is practically at sea level, the Brough of Stoal, on Yell, is minuscule yet still has three ramparts, and the inappropriately named Dane's Dyke encloses a truly massive area.

The great attraction of the promontory fort was, of course, that man harnessed nature to provide sections of defences. So, both St John's Point and The Rumps have just one line of defence cutting across the neck of the promontory. Elsewhere, such as Bredon Hill, man-made defences enclose about half of the site, forming two of the sides, while at Sudbrook man-made defences

A courtyard house at Chysauster.

The open village at Ty Mawr included round and rectangular huts, built over many centuries.

Ladle Hill is Britain's best example of an unfinished hillfort. It is separated from Beacon Hill by the A34.

account for two out of three sides. Even there, though, the building work was considerably reduced.

Ridge-top and Valley Hillforts

There are also ridge-top hillforts that do not enclose the whole of a summit, perhaps like the first phase at Burnswark or Eggardon Hill. These often combine natural and artificial defences and have the added advantage of having space to expand, or to create further enclosures – say for cattle – immediately outside.

Valley hillforts, though, are a distinctly rare subspecies. One major defensive advantage of a hillfort is, as might be expected, its height over the immediate surroundings. Risbury Camp is positively dominated by its neighbouring hills, while Cherbury Camp lies in the wide upper Thames valley. Both of these have substantial defences though, the latter possibly including a moat.

Hill-slope, Rounds and Multiple Enclosure Hillforts

Hill-slope forts, or hillforts with widely spaced defences known as rounds, are even more of a curiosity, though they are quite a feature of the West Country. Goosehill is a rare exception outside that region. Beware, though, as not all rounds are on the slopes of hills – Castle-an-Dinas for example is at the summit. Neither are all hill-slope forts rounds: for example, Stockland Great Camp and Harding's Down are quite different. The main feature of the rounds is the assumed division of enclosures between the inhabitants and their cattle. Clovelly Dykes gives a clear idea of this arrangement; though not on the side of a hill, defence was clearly not the sole factor in its location. On the other hand, many hillforts with concentric, widely spaced defences can be found in Scotland, usually on top of hills, such as Barmekin of Echt, Arbory Hill and the Brown Caterthun.

So, like most things, hillforts are not a cut-and-dried type of stronghold. In fact, the above is a simplified view – perhaps over-simplified, as some archaeologists like to be even more specific and refer to, for example, semi-contour or cliff-edge hillforts. It is, however, the defences that are the most visible aspect of hillforts today and, presumably, were most vital to the inhabitants. The simplest form of defence is to dig a wide, deep ditch and pile the rock and spoil inside to form a glacis rampart. One would expect that this most basic method was the earliest type of hillfort defence. Perhaps, with a palisade fence on top, it was, but there is much evidence to the contrary.

THE RUMPS (Promontory Hillfort)
Cornwall O/S map 200 ref. 933811
Directions: Head north from Wadebridge on the A39 and turn left on the B3314. After 4¼ miles turn left towards Polzeath and first left towards New Polzeath. Turn right at a cross-roads and then left along a track to park at Pentire Farm. Leave by the notice-board and turn right along the path and cliff-top walk to The Rumps.

This is probably the best of Cornwall's many spectacular promontory forts or cliff-castles. It is simplicity itself and shows that economy of effort was certainly not lost on Iron Age man. The inner and third ramparts across the neck of the promontory were the earliest defences, with the large second and outer ramparts, the latter now with a wall on it, being later additions. Thus, three stone-faced ramparts and ditches, complete with a wooden bridge over the entrance passage, formed the final phase of almost 500 years' occupation, probably ending in the first century AD. The Rumps might have been quite a breezy spot, but the defences could not be simpler and yet they would have been virtually impregnable.

Huts were found in the sheltered dip between the two headlands, and in the lee of the ramparts, when the site was excavated in the 1960s. Pottery from Gaul and the Mediterranean region – including wine amphorae – was also found thereabouts. Thus The Rumps might have been a stronghold with overseas trading links, not uncommon in the West Country.

An alternative scenario is that The Rumps was occupied and refurbished by refugees from Gaul in the first century BC. This cannot be proved either way, but is the less likely option. The Rumps is a splendid hillfort to visit with magnificent coastal views, especially northwards to Tintagel Castle.

Intra-mural stairs at Edinshall broch.

HILLFORT DEFENCES

Hillfort defences usually utilized materials that were available in the immediate vicinity. Thus, as a rough guide, wooden-faced, revetted or box ramparts were the norm in the south and east, and stone-faced ramparts, or stone walls in the north and west. Scotland had its own speciality: a drystone wall laced with horizontal supporting timbers. Naturally, the timber-lacing has long-since gone, and the collapse of these often massive ramparts may be due to the decay of the timber. This building technique, known as *murus gallicus*, was used in Germany early in the first millennium BC, suggesting trade, or other connections, between the two regions. Alternatively, of course, such building techniques may have developed independently of each other.

Vitrified Hillforts

Timber's inherent weakness is that it decays and needs replacing. However, when used for defences, there is a rather more obvious deficiency: it burns. Stone, however, will liquify if subjected to a fierce heat, perhaps caused by burning timber-lacing, and then fuse as it cools: hence Scotland's vitrified hillforts. There are about a hundred such hillforts, but by no means all were burnt by raiders. It seems likely that those hillforts with vitrified material near the entrance succumbed to attack, but most only have vitrified material elsewhere on the rampart.

Many hillforts had lean-to houses built against the ramparts. Probably made of wood, and with a thatch or turf roof, there was plenty of combustible material. If an inhabitant was a bit careless, well, the ensuing scenario is not difficult to imagine. The timber-laced rampart could easily catch fire and suddenly there is a major catastrophe and a collapsing wall. On the other hand, lighted javelins or arrows fired into the thatched roofs of lean-to huts would have the same effect. So why attack at the most obvious place, the heavily defended entrance? All of this is, of course, pure speculation but, whether by accident or attack, many Scottish hillforts were so blighted. Sites showing vitrified material include Finavon and Knockfarrel, while Dun Skeig has both a vitrified hillfort and a later vitrified dun. Almondbury was also burned in the same way, and some Welsh hillforts succumbed likewise. Mind you, considering the numbers of vitrified hillforts in Scotland, it took the people long enough to realize something was amiss in the basic design.

Ramparts

Stone walls without timber-lacing and lacking a ditch can be seen at many hillforts. Tre'r Ceiri is undoubtedly the finest example, but there are many others in Wales and Scotland with partially collapsed ramparts; Chun Castle is one of several in

Plan of Tre'r Ceiri hillfort.

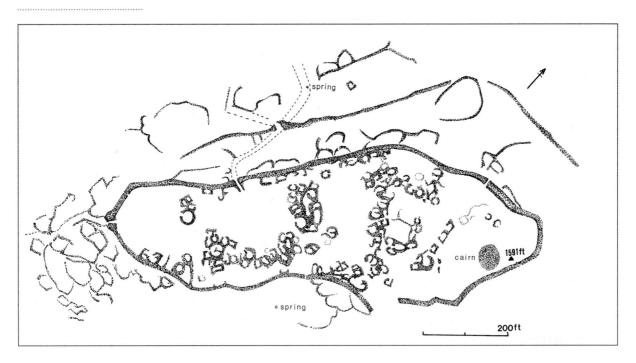

CLOVELLY DYKES (Hillfort)
Devon O/S map 190 ref. 312235

Directions: Leave Barnstaple on the A39 heading west. Turn right at Clovelly Cross roundabout on the B3237. Permission to visit the site is required from the East Dyke Farm, the second farm on the left.

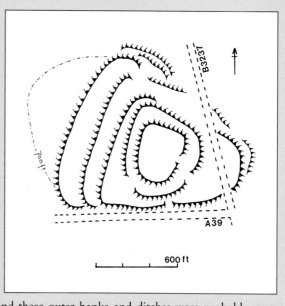

Clovelly Dykes is the finest example of the West Country 'rounds' type multiple-enclosure hillfort. Indeed, it is almost unique insofar as its outer enclosures are still used for herding cattle, just as they were two thousand years ago.

Standing 700 ft above the sea, and at a junction of three ancient trackways, the hillfort was probably a major centre for the, supposed, export of cattle in the last centuries of the first millennium BC. A rampart and ditch enclosed about 2¼ acres, with a second – much stronger – rampart and ditch enclosing a further 2 acres outside this. The original entrances in the east were slightly off-set and, as such, the whole is not untypical of many 'rounds' hillforts.

What makes Clovelly Dykes so special are the crescent-shaped, east enclosure and the three parallel west enclosures. Ultimately, the site covers fully 23 acres and these outer banks and ditches were probably more defensible cattle enclosures than part of the stronghold itself. All the ramparts are now covered in hedgerows, making them easy to see.

Of course, it is pure speculation that Clovelly Dykes was a cattle-distribution point, but this seems to be a best-guess. It is assumed that 'rounds' hillforts combined a stronghold with cattle enclosures, which suggests that then, as now, cattle and sheep farming formed a major part of the local economy. It is a rare example of such continuity of use.

England. There are some examples where the stone is overgrown and barely visible, as at Rainsborough Camp; only excavation can confirm their construction.

The timber box, or timber wall, ramparts are some of the earliest hillfort defences. Naturally, a few years' exposure to our inclement weather would soon make the spoil filling unstable, causing the revetment to bow and eventually to break. Horizontal ties, not unlike timber-lacing, were thus needed to hold the rampart together. Even these would need regular replacing though; the stoutest timbers might have lasted about twenty-five years (a little less than an average Iron Age lifetime).

Stone walls, timber-laced stone ramparts, timber box, wall and stone-faced ramparts were all, first and foremost, defences. To be effective, a minimum height of at least 10 feet was desirable, often with a wall-walk and parapet above that. They would probably have been about the same thickness, but both measurements vary greatly. Height over an attacking force was vital, while a good width would hinder undermining, a favoured Roman tactic.

The glacis rampart was not only widely used, but can be clearly seen as a later addition at many hillforts. It was simple to construct and, with a stone parapet on top, as at Hod Hill, highly effective. A glacis rampart is virtually a mirror image of its outer ditch, assuming that is where the material came from. Some were also quarried from the hillfort interior, the spoil being thrown down the hill

Finavon hillfort was occupied from c. 800 BC but met a fiery end some three hundred years later. This photograph shows some of the vitrified stone on the ramparts.

to build, or enhance the rampart. Height and width were again vital, and you do not need to be mathematical genius to work out that if a rampart was 15 feet high then, from the bottom of its ditch, an attacker had to climb fully 30 feet up a steep slope while missiles rained down. To see just how effective these seemingly simple defences can be, visit Maiden Castle or Badbury Rings. Remember, though, not only have they weathered over the last two thousand years, but the defenders would not have been cheering on one's progress either.

Glacis ramparts usually run at a constant angle from the bottom of the ditch upwards. Sometimes this angle changed, as at Caer Caradoc, Clun, but for most wall, box or stone ramparts there was a berm, or strip of level ground, between the rampart and the ditch. This helped to prevent the rampart from sliding into the ditch. Similarly, a few glacis ramparts were revetted at the back, as at Sudbrook Camp, presumably to prevent their collapse on to the internal buildings.

Occasionally, glacis ramparts were built on top of earlier ramparts, but they are usually found as outer defences at multivallate hillforts (those with more than two lines of defences). These are surprisingly common and most date from the middle Iron Age. The big question is, *why* were they built? Were they designed to impress, a sort of prehistoric keeping up with the Joneses? A more popular reason is that weapon development, in particular the advent of the sling, necessitated the extension of hillfort defences.

Have you ever seen a sling in action? Its most renowned use was, of course, when David felled poor Goliath, who never got anywhere near him, but an expert slinger could fire with, literally, deadly accuracy over more than 50 yards. A range of 100 yards was certainly possible, if less accurate, but a section of a hillfort's rampart could certainly have been cleared in advance of a storming party by concentrated volleys of sling-stones.

Clumps of trees were planted at several hillforts from the seventeenth century onwards, to enhance the vista for landowners. A close inspection will show that, even though the site was abandoned for two thousand years, the ramparts and ditches of Badbury Rings would still make formidable defences.

Few hillforts have defences over 75 yards wide but, remember, the attacker would be at a disadvantage, usually having to sling uphill, while the defending slingers held all the aces by firing downhill. Of course, the idea that the sling caused hillforts to gain multiple lines of defence is somwehat speculative. However, large magazines of pebbles have been found at several hillforts – especially the 250,000 at Maiden Castle: coincidence?

Ditches

Very few hillforts were defended by a rampart alone. The vast majority had a ditch outside every rampart. Today, these often appear as little more than an apparent nuisance to an attacker, although some are still massive: once again, see Maiden Castle. Most are now silted up and heavily weathered, but they could be a formidable obstacle to an attacking force. Anything up to 20 feet deep, they could also be fully 40 feet wide, and were not simply trifling impediments, at least not

The defences at Maiden Castle hillfort were even more formidable. Not to the Romans though.

when avoiding sling-stones and spears. Yet there was far more to a ditch than that.

As has been mentioned, the outer ditch at Cherbury Camp was probably a moat for most of the year. This was a rarity, but was not unique. Other ditches may have contained sharpened wooden stakes, known as *chevaux de frise*. These could be particularly deadly but, again, the extent of their use is unknown, although a few hillforts, such as Dreva Craig, Pen-y-Gaer or Cademuir II, have stone *chevaux de frise* defending the easier approaches to their walls.

The northern defences at
Hod Hill.

Ditches usually had either a V-shaped or a flat-bottomed profile. Stanwick
hillfort has a short length of reconstructed ditch, whose effectiveness is quite
obvious. Ditches with a U-shaped profile are also known, but it is seldom easy to
distinguish between these varieties owing to silting. Doubtless silting also
occurred when the hillforts were occupied. Indeed, the clearing and repairing of
ditches must have been an unwelcome annual task. This could yield an
additional benefit, though, as the silt would be piled on the outer lip of the ditch
and eventually, over the years, would form a counterscarp bank. These could
become quite large and early antiquarians were occasionally fooled into thinking
they were an additional rampart, as at Beacon Hill.

It is quite clear, then, that hillfort defences continually evolved. Improved
weapons, particularly the sling and the metal-tipped javelin, led to the use of
ever-wider, multiple lines of defence. Instead of the simple contour hillfort, with
its rampart and ditch of the late Bronze Age/early Iron Age, later sites were
carefully chosen for their potential for expansion and also for extending the
defences. So at, say, Danebury – the most comprehensively excavated large
hillfort, incidentally – the defences were progressively improved over several
centuries. At Traprain Law though, the initial hillfort was extended from about
10 acres to 40 acres over a period of a thousand years. There are many other
examples throughout Britain.

Entrances

At any stronghold the entrance is the potential weakspot. Throughout history, it
is clear that defences evolved as building techniques, weapon development, the
degree of unrest in society and, yes, even fashion changed. While entrances have
developed more than any other feature of strongholds over five thousand years,

On a wet day, the hill alone makes a visit to South Cadbury Castle something of an adventure. With gates, bridges and the keen attention of Iron Age guards, the inhabitants surely held all the aces.

two factors have remained constant: the need to enhance the defences at an entrance, and the need to have as few entrances as possible. Whether one considers an ancient hillfort or an army post in Northern Ireland, each adheres to these basic tenets. It is the sheer number of gaps in the defences at hillforts such as the Brown Caterthun, and at causeway camps, such as Knap Hill, that leads archaeologists to query whether they were ever, first and foremost, fortified settlements.

The simplest form of entrance is, of course, a gap through a rampart, probably closed by a wooden gate, with a causeway over the ditch. This might deter the odd unwelcome visitor, but would be vulnerable to a determined raid. By turning in the rampart ends to form a passage leading to the gates, the attackers' movement is restricted; should they enter the passageway, they would be vulnerable to missiles thrown down from the side walls. Nevertheless, if the attackers linked shields over their heads for protection (as in the Roman *testudo* or tortoise), they could perhaps burn the gates and force an entry.

Other elaborations, or variations, on this basic defensive theme were therefore needed, and included the building of a bridge over the passageway, allowing yet more defenders to rain missiles down on the attackers, or using more than one set of gates: Old Oswestry had at least three sets at its exposed western entrance. Neither gates nor bridges can, of course, be seen at hillforts today, but their use has been determined by excavation.

As with the popular inturned entrances, so there are many other defensive improvements still to be seen. In particular, two or more ramparts allowed the approach to the entrance to be staggered, forcing attackers to turn and expose an undefended flank. These developed into entrances with a right-angled approach, as at Hod Hill and Hambledon Hill.

STANWICK (Hillfort)
Yorkshire O/S map 92 ref. 178123
Directions: Turn right off the A66 on to the B6274 2 miles west of Scotch Corner. The road cuts through the outer rampart. Turn right opposite Forcett Church, and right again after 100 yd. At the end of the houses is the signpost to 'Stanwick Camp' on the left.

Stanwick is a massive stronghold, only very loosely described as a hillfort, which exceeds over 700 acres, yes 700, in size. It is the largest known prehistoric stronghold in Britain. It was built in the first century AD, possibly in one go – although Sir Mortimer Wheeler felt it had been developed over three phases. Its defences are, in the main, a single rampart and ditch; these are nothing special – except for their length. But wait . . .

Fortunately, Wheeler left open a section of the flat-bottomed ditch, over 15 ft deep and 40 ft wide, and reconstructed a short length of the drystone-faced earth rampart. These demonstrate just how formidable hillfort defences could be. Of course, hillforts in the south and Midlands would usually have wood-revetted ramparts, while V-shaped ditches were common, but just try to envisage the work involved in the construction of such a hillfort. Even relatively simple defences like a bank and ditch, when seen in their true scale and not as ancient ruins, were an enormous obstacle in the Iron Age – to all, that is, except the Romans.

Stanwick may have been built as a result of internecine warfare in the Brigantian tribe, between the rival factions of King Venutius and his pro-Roman Queen Cartimandua. That is Wheeler's hypothesis, but this is being challenged. Whatever the conclusions, Stanwick, like no other hillfort, allows us a brief glimpse as to what Iron Age defences really looked like.

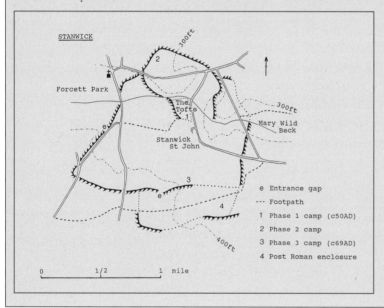

STANWICK

Forcett Park

The Tofts

Mary Wild Beck

Stanwick St John

e Entrance gap
--- Footpath
1 Phase 1 camp (c50AD)
2 Phase 2 camp
3 Phase 3 camp (c69AD)
4 Post Roman enclosure

0   1/2   1 mile

Finally, outworkings were built, ranging from a bank outside the entrance passage to prevent a head-on approach, through to the great elaborate maze-like schemes at Maiden Castle, combining almost every conceivable option available to Iron Age man. Not only did these prevent a direct approach, but attackers were forced to undergo all sorts of tests before even reaching the main gates. It seems, though, that the Romans passed everything with impunity.

Perhaps the most unusual type of hillfort entrance is to be found at a surprising number of the stone-walled hillforts in Scotland. The White Caterthun is one of many examples where there is no apparent gateway to the citadel; this is in stark contrast to its neighbour, the Brown Caterthun, which has entrances facing all points of the compass. It is probable that a removable wooden

Though the stone wall at Caer-y-Twr hillfort can be traced all round the circuit, this is the only stretch that still stands. One section is thought to have been dismantled by the Romans, possibly during siege training.

structure, or even just ladders, gave entry over the wall: not convenient for the inhabitants perhaps, but it certainly eliminated the stronghold's weak link. Many such hillforts, incidentally, had an outer enclosure more akin to the usual hillfort. This, presumably, was for the cattle, sheep, carts and other possessions that were all, ultimately, disposable if the worst came to the worst.

Scottish Duns and Brochs

Scotland is, in fact, home to the last two types of widely used prehistoric stronghold: duns and brochs. Both are developments of the Atlantic roundhouse, and their lineage seems to be interwoven. Indeed, there are duns that are considered to be brochs, and brochs that are thought to be duns, all rather depending on a particular archaeologist's view. While we can deftly sidestep such traps, one needs to be wary for more detailed reference. As an aside, Dun Telve and Dun Troddan are – without the slightest doubt – brochs. They are not the only examples of confusing nomenclature either: many undefended hills are also called dun something or

The single outer and paired inner gate posts at Chun Castle hillfort.

another. Duns are also found in Ireland, but brochs are unique to Scotland and its islands; they represent the very pinnacle of British drystone building.

If the number of different types of hillfort is something of a surprise, duns can be equally bewildering. Kildonan is an undoubted dun, while the main outer wall at Nybster Broch has been considered to be that of a promontory dun. Duns are mainly located in Argyll, the Western Isles and Perthshire, with a few promontory duns in the north. As with the promontory hillfort, this latter type comprises a simple

wall cutting off a headland, though it is the build of the wall itself that differentiates the dun from the hillfort. Sometimes, as at Sgarbach, the main defence is a stone wall across the neck of the promontory, but at others, such as Dun Grugaig, all sides of the promontory are enclosed.

Dun Grugaig is more akin to the usual dun: a sort of halfway house between a small hillfort or defended homestead and a broch. Kildonan is a fairly typical dun, though they can be much smaller. Naturally, considering most duns are built on restricted sites, such as knolls, their shape is seldom any more regular than that of hillforts, but many of them are round or oval.

The first duns/brochs probably developed late in the Scottish Bronze Age, before *c*. 600 BC, from circular stone dwellings. The walls were thickened to allow for greater height, and duns often took on a more irregular shape, probably increasing the enclosed area; that is one scenario, anyway. Two types of wall seem to have developed: that with a rubble core and stone facing, or its near relation the (sometimes timber-laced) solid stone wall, as at Dun Skeig, and the galleried wall. The latter has been considered to be the more recent development, and was possibly the catalyst for the brochs. Some duns combined galleried and solid wall sections, as at Kildonan.

Strathgarry is a solid walled dun, while Dun Torcuill on North Uist is not only a galleried dun but, like many in the Hebrides, also occupies an island in a loch. This dun, incidentally, has also been called a broch. Herein lies a major difference between a dun and a broch, often still visible today. At Dun Torcuill, the wall varies in thickness from about 7 to 13 feet. A broch was an almost circular drystone tower that rose from 20 feet to perhaps 50 feet in height. Not only are thick walls essential to a broch, as height was its principal defence, but variations in thickness round the circumference had to be avoided as the stability of the tower would be seriously undermined.

Not unlike a hillfort, a dun's wall would be between 10 and 20 feet high, many having a wall-head walk, occasionally with intra-mural stairs. This is one of several

A dun, a broch or a semi-broch? Dun Ardtrok, on Skye, has been regarded as an example of the latter and, as a result, has featured in fierce academic debates about the nature of semi-brochs. Would the inhabitants have cared? I doubt it.

DUN KILDONAN (Dun)
Argyll O/S map 68 ref. 780277

Directions: Take the B842 north from Campbeltown, for 6½ miles, to the Forestry Commission car park at Ballochgair. The dun is across the road, 100 yd to the south-east.

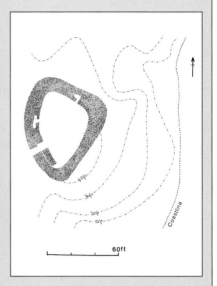

Lying just 40 ft above the sea, a javelin throw to the east, Dun Kildonan is not only one of Scotland's better preserved duns, but it occupies a panoramic location. It sits on a rocky knoll with a level approach from the west, and a steep descent to the beach. Not only could the inhabitants have fished in Kildonan Bay, but they would have enjoyed the spectacular view across Kilbrannan Sound to the ever-cloudy Isle of Arran.

Dun Kildonan is often clad in bracken in the summer, but the main features are visible. A D-shaped wall encloses a courtyard measuring about 70 ft × 40 ft. This wall is stone-faced with a rubble core and varies in thickness from 5 to 13 ft, with an additional facing most of the way round. It was probably built in one stage – the inner section not being a later addition, with the median facing stabilizing the whole structure. Perhaps that is one reason why it has survived so well, when many other duns are nothing but piles of rubble?

Another reason is that part of the wall was restored during excavations in the late 1930s; stones had been robbed to construct roadside walls and dykes. The wall is up to 6 ft high internally, and nearly 8 ft externally, the outer face starting at a lower level. Despite having some broch-like features, there is no doubt that Kildonan was a dun, but it was probably only about 15 ft high.

The west-facing entrance includes a door-jamb and bar-hole, while there is a short length of galleried wall immediately to its south. This is not very thick and could have been part guard-chamber/part wall strengthening at the entrance. A double stair-case leads to the wall-head, from which unwanted guests could have been encouraged to go away. These stairs are in good condition, with tiny steps, while the median wall-face is best viewed from this point. There is a small mural cell in the north-east, and a possible bottom step of a ladder to the wall-head in the east.

Dun Kildonan was briefly excavated in 1984 and from this, and earlier excavations, it has been deduced that there were three main periods of occupation. It was built in the first century BC, and occupied for about three hundred years. These dates have not been confirmed by C-14 dating so, given recent results from other sites, they may need placing a little further back in time. The double-stairs were filled in soon after, to be cleared out in the 1930s. At least three hearths and up to six small huts were in use at that time, suggesting it was probably occupied by an extended family rather than a small tribe.

Then followed a long period of abandonment until the site was reoccupied in the seventh to ninth centuries. This was a time of Norse raids and when the Scotti came over from Ireland.

The tiny steps of the intra-mural stairs at Dun Kildonan.

Some huts have been uncovered that might date from this period, along with a brooch and enamelled disc. Finally, after another period of disuse, Dun Kildonan was reoccupied in the thirteenth and fourteenth centuries.

Though many artefacts have been found, it was their poor quality that the excavators noted. This is all the more surprising in view of the high quality of the dun itself. For the visitor, that is of more importance, and Kildonan is one of Scotland's best duns. With its fine views, a fresh-water stream and proximity to the sea, this was a good site for a stronghold and it remains a worthy and easy place to visit.

Stronghold, look-out or
lighthouse? Like many
brochs, Dun Carloway on
the Isle of Lewis is sited
near the coast. Significant?
If only more of these
magnificent towers had
survived.

features shared with brochs. Dun entrances were often
low and cramped, and many had the door halfway along
the passage. This was secured by jambs and a wooden
beam protruding into the walls via bar-holes, and
perhaps one or two intra-mural guard chambers. There
are even duns where gaps between the lintels above the
entrance passage allowed defenders to jab spears into
attackers caught within the dark and narrow confines. A
combination of all or any of these can also be found at
many brochs. A final similarity is that each usually has a
single entrance, with no other external openings.

Within duns, people lived either in huts or lean-to
buildings, just as in hillforts. It is unlikely that people lived
within the wall gallery, but intra-mural cells may have
served as living quarters, at least in some form. Despite
the fire risks posed by huts with thatched roofs and
wooden lean-to buildings, duns enjoyed a long period of
use. For example, Kildonan was in use, on and off, for
well over one thousand years, right into the Medieval period. Indeed, Hebridean
duns were undoubtedly built in the Dark Ages and even in medieval times so, when
visiting these most fascinating of strongholds, be aware: it might not be prehistoric.

Clearly, brochs and duns have much in common. While some had outer
defences, Burrian Broch having four ramparts, the broch's height and blank
exterior wall were its outstanding defensive features. Some brochs had a galleried
wall down to the ground, as at Dun Mor (Tiree), while others had a solid wall to
first floor-level, as at Dun Telve; all had a galleried wall – tied together with

Though Dun Carloway
Broch is badly damaged, an
idea of its size can be
gained from the figure in
the intra-mural gallery.

The tumbled remains and surrounding rampart at Kilphedir Broch.

cross-slabs – from the first floor upwards. This simple, ingenious expedient allowed the walls to reach an unbelievable height. Today, 40 feet plus might not seem much, but visit Mousa and you will soon realize the enormity of the task and the magnificence of its execution. Remember as well that brochs were of drystone build – held together simply by their own weight.

As with a few duns, some brochs had two doors in the entrance, such as Kintradwell, while a small number had two entrances, possibly the Keiss Road Broch. An odd one might even have had a covered tunnel leading to the entrance, as at, possibly, Carn Liath. As for the door itself, most were made of wood but, especially in north Caithness and the northern islands, a stone slab might have been used instead, these being more readily available. Heavy it might have been, but it would surely pass all fire regulations.

The finest prehistoric stronghold of all? Mousa Broch is perhaps the greatest drystone building in Britain.

As with hillforts, duns and crannogs, brochs vary immensely in size: Edinshall is dun-like in its proportions, being nearly twice the diameter of some brochs. Not all were anywhere near as tall as the tapered majesty of Mousa either, and no others remain so complete today, which is one reason for disputes as to whether a particular stronghold might be a dun or broch.

Inside, brochs did not have a great deal of space. Stairs wound up through the galleries to the wall-head, so they could not be used for living in, and though many have intra-mural cells, some do not. At Dun Troddan a circle of post-holes was found in the courtyard floor, and it is thought that this supported

MOUSA (Broch)

Shetland (Mousa) O/S map 4 ref. 457237

Directions: From Lerwick, take the A970 south for about 12 miles and turn left along the minor road to the pier at Leebotten. It is important to telephone Mr T. Jamieson on Sandwick 01950 431367 at least a day in advance to book the boat trip to Mousa island.

The approach to Mousa, especially the journey across the sound on the small boat, is one of the most invigorating of any stronghold in this book. Not only is this the best and only complete broch, it is the finest example of a drystone prehistoric building in Britain. If not one of the Seven Wonders of the Ancient World, it is one of the most significant historic sites in Europe. Mousa is truly majestic.

In bald figures its height of 44 ft – up to 6 ft lower than it was originally – is modest to our eyes; its overall diameter of 50 ft is much smaller than many brochs; even its 15 ft thick wall is nothing special. The ratio of wall thickness:overall diameter – about 2:3 – is the highest of any known broch though, and suggests that Mousa might have been the tallest broch. Has it survived because it was special?

The courtyard is only 20 ft across, though the original floor level was below that seen today. The interior was converted into a wheelhouse in the third or fourth centuries AD; the piers were removed when it was first excavated in 1861. There is a scarcement ledge at first floor level, probably to support a wooden mezzanine floor; a second scarcement, only 12 ft above the floor, is particularly low and may have supported a roof or an upper floor.

As usual, the galleried wall begins at first floor level. Narrow stairs rise through six storeys and two landings to the wall-head. The gallery is relatively wide, even near the top, and the wall has rows of vertical openings, probably to reduce the weight while ventilating the galleries.

Entrance

Ground plan and elevation of the southern half of Mousa Broch.

Once you have climbed to the wall-head, Mousa really comes into its own. Sumburgh Head can be seen in the south as can the ruined Broch of Burraland across the sound on Mainland. Mousa commands its immediate vicinity on the island. There are traces of a ring-wall below, but height was Mousa's main defence and one can see just how invincible it would be in a raid or even a siege. Arrows, javelins, ladders – none of these would have any real effect on the wall-head defenders. However, an enclosed roof would be an extremely vulnerable Achilles heel, if lighted arrows or javelins were propelled in that direction. This is one reason to doubt that brochs, the ultimate in prehistoric defensive homesteads, ever had a fully enclosed roof.

The stonework positively demands inspection. Here is the supreme example of how Iron Age man was capable of planning and building such a stronghold. Yes, Mousa may be the foremost broch, but many others were probably about 40 ft high. Mousa is certainly the jewel in Britain's majestic prehistoric crown. You can go and see the pyramids, the Inca temples or the Greek cities to appreciate some of the finest stonework in history, but Mousa is a gem in its own magnificent way.

either a full or mezzanine floor. Balcony-like galleries might also have been used. Such post-holes have been found at other brochs, but it is impossible to tell if they were anything like universal.

Likewise, the thatched roof. I am inclined to think that brochs did not have a fully enclosed roof – and any roof would certainly place additional stresses on the wall. A full roof would make the interior very dark and dismal. More important, this finest engineered of prehistoric strongholds could be rendered not

Despite its fallen stones, Culswick Broch is an unforgettable stronghold to visit. Its glorious location, beautiful red granite and wild exposure must have been a constant inspiration to the inhabitants.

only useless, but a positive death-trap, by one lighted-spear thrown over the wall-head. A shortened roof covering a balcony, either part-way up the wall or at the wall-head, was probably most common.

As to their location and use, most brochs are found in northern Scotland, the Orkney and Shetland Islands, and the Hebrides, with odd ones in the Western Highlands, the central Lowlands, Tayside, the Borders and Galloway. There are over five hundred assumed brochs, begging the question who owned them? Surely not all were the stronghold of a chief? Three are close together at Keiss while Dun Telve and Dun Troddan are almost within throwing distance: rather too many chiefs? Some brochs could have belonged to an extended family, but the Keiss brochs and especially Gurness – plus others in the north and the northern islands, although not the Hebrides – stand amid, what may be contemporary out-buildings. Could those brochs have been a central refuge for the settlement?

Other brochs stand on an island in a loch, as at Bragor, while some occupy coastal promontories, seemingly like great prehistoric lighthouses. The Broch of Burland is an outstanding example. They were not beacons, though some may have served as look-outs. It is possible that those brochs with few external buildings were the stronghold of an extended family; those amid a larger settlement might have served as a temporary refuge for a chief and his retainers, or simply for a village.

Some of the secondary internal features at Mid-Howe Broch, on Rousay, Orkney.

Double door-jambs, Carn Liath Broch.

Above right: Carn Liath Broch and settlement, and Dunrobin Castle.

Despite all that, brochs are specialist buildings, surely not built by general labour to a rough plan. Were there, perhaps, specialist broch-builders, rather like there were many specialists involved in building medieval castles and cathedrals? If so, how were they paid and employed? We can never know the answer to such questions, but brochs, more than any other prehistoric stronghold, are suggestive of a society organized at levels far beyond the barbaric descriptions portrayed in Roman literature.

Blockhouses

There are other types of stronghold found solely in a particular region that do not fit into any of the aforementioned categories. On the Shetland Islands, there are five known blockhouses, a combination of an inner gatehouse and possibly a chief's citadel. These have not been recognized anywhere else so far. The best example is at Clickimin. This was probably three storeys high and had lean-to buildings on its inner face. There is a central entrance, similar to those at brochs

Gurness Broch, the path between the huts.

Below right: The blockhouse and causeway, Clickimin.

DUN TELVE and DUN TRODDAN (Brochs)
Inverness-shire O/S map 33 (Telve) ref. 829173 (Troddan) ref. 834173
Directions: Take the A87 south from Kyle of Lochalsh. At Shiel Bridge, turn left over the 'Old Military Road' through Glenmore to Glenelg. Turn left through Glenelg and left again up Glen Beag for about 1½ miles. Dun Telve is beside the road on the right, Dun Troddan a ¼ mile further along.

In one afternoon, one can visit two brochs, a dun, Georgian barracks and a small hillfort without too much effort. This area might seem a fairly infertile and inhospitable place today, but clearly it was not always so. Duns Telve and Troddan are the finest brochs still to be seen on mainland Scotland. Each has the classic, tapered profile, a solid wall up to the first floor and a galleried wall thereafter; each clearly shows the broch's unique method of construction. Dun Telve is 33 ft high and its wall has four levels of galleries, and begins a fifth, while it is one of the few brochs with a second scarcement; in 1722 it stood at least 6 ft higher. Dun Troddan is 25 ft high, but stood 33 ft high in 1720.

Dun Telve's wall is 14 ft thick, enclosing a 32 ft diameter courtyard; a wall:courtyard ratio of less than the 1:1 used to suggest that a broch may have reached up to 40 ft in height. Given its known height in 1722, this shows that the ratio is, at best, arbitrary. Dun Troddan's courtyard is 28 ft across, and its wall 14 ft thick. This gives the classic 1:1 ratio and, if it means anything, the implication is that Dun Troddan was higher than Dun Telve. Dun Troddan stands on the edge of a ridge above the valley. Dun Telve is lower down and has evidence of, possibly secondary, external buildings and the remains of an outer entrance, perhaps a barbican-type structure. Dun Troddan lacks both.

Brochs so close together are rare but not unique. The similarities in design and build suggest that the two owners – be they local chiefs or members of an extended family – were not at loggerheads. These brochs are of advanced design and may date to the first centuries BC or AD. Indeed, when excavated in 1920 Dun Troddan revealed a ring of post-holes to support a raised floor, another supposed feature of many brochs. Very little is known about the peoples who built and lived in these brochs, but at least their buildings have survived. The massive blank wall at Dun Troddan conveys some idea of just how impregnable a broch would have been. Whatever else, these people certainly knew how to protect themselves.

Dun Telve entrance and highest scarcement.

Intra-mural stairs at Dun Telve.

BROCH OF GURNESS
Orkney Islands (Mainland) O/S map 6 ref. 383268 (Historic Scotland)
Directions: From Stromness, take the A967 north and turn right on the B9057 to the north-east coast. Turn right on the A966 and left up the minor road leading to the coast. There is a car park beside the site, which includes a small museum.

Although it lacks the majesty of Mousa Broch, and the massive build of the White Caterthun hillfort, Gurness Broch is nevertheless one of Britain's great prehistoric strongholds. Facing the island of Rousay across Eynhallow Sound, this is one of eight known brochs along that stretch of water, which shows just how important it must have been in the Iron Age. One can easily imagine a thriving community centred round the broch tower.

Seventy-odd years ago, and for many centuries before, Gurness was simply a great earthen mound. During the late 1920s and 1930s this was gradually cleared to reveal the broch and the most extensive set of surrounding buildings then discovered; that still applies. Unfortunately, nature had already taken a hand and the northern section has suffered quite a bit of erosion. This, then, is an exposed location, yet one that was inhabited for possibly a thousand years, right into the Dark Ages.

The broch is the earliest visible building at the site. A galleried wall about 15 ft thick encloses a courtyard 34 ft in diameter. The wall stands 12 ft above the present floor level, the original floor being several feet below. Thus the broch could have been over 30 ft high, despite the model in the museum showing it as barely 20 ft.

There is rather more to Gurness than that, though. Some brochs stand in splendid isolation but Gurness is further protected by a unique rampart with projecting bastions, a drystone-faced ditch about 6 ft deep, and two more ramparts. It is not known whether these encircled the site, thanks to the coastal erosion.

The broch entrance has some later out-workings and is flanked by guard cells leading to the wall galleries. Inside, the courtyard contains the finest set of secondary features to be seen: great vertical stone slabs dividing the interior into several chambers; a hearth and two sets of stairs; and a hearth, well and a water tank at the original floor level. This is one of the very few brochs where the internal layout, whether of primary or secondary use, can still be seen.

Yet still there is more. The broch is surrounded by fourteen courtyard houses, which were initially thought to have been post-broch although this is now disputed. Some archaeologists now think that the courtyard houses, each with its various chambers and shelters, formed a village round the broch, this being either a communal refuge, or the home of a chief. This theory is given further credence by the fact that the path from the broch to the rampart entrance is clear of buildings. As such, Gurness may be a precursor of the Norman motte and bailey castles.

The similarities in design with Mid-Howe Broch – just across the water on Rousay – are most apparent. At the latter though, some external buildings are built over the outer defences. The scale of Gurness, its remains from at least three periods of occupation – including the relocated Pict shamrock-shaped house, the museum and its magnificent, if exposed, location make this one of the most important and impressive of Britain's prehistoric sites.

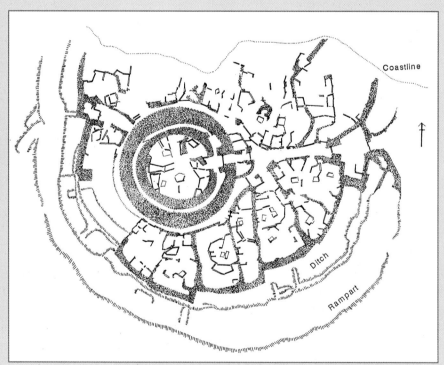

Plan showing the layout of Gurness Broch.

and duns, but the blockhouse stands within an older outer wall. Indeed, each blockhouse is quite different. That at the Loch of Huxter (Whalsay) forms an entrance to the small fort, but this appears to be the odd-man out. Blockhouses date from perhaps the fourth century BC onwards; they are clearly unique and yet utilize various building designs and techniques featured in duns and brochs.

Belgic *Oppida*

Leaving Scotland, the lake villages of Glastonbury and Meare used water as their chief defence. Elsewhere in southern England can be seen the remains of a great cultural and social change that swept the area from about 100 BC until the Roman invasion. Coins had begun to appear before that time, while a heavier plough and wheel-thrown pottery also came to be used. Far from being the start of a prehistoric pre-industrial revolution, there is much evidence to suggest the arrival of a new people on the scene: the Belgic-Celts.

These Belgic-Celts were evidently war-like and, while they never mounted a D-Day type invasion, they seem to have been far from welcomed or welcoming; perhaps they were the first political refugees to hit our shores? Danebury hillfort was burned and abandoned at this time, and others might have suffered a similar fate. There emerged in the central south of England, eventually spreading as far as East Anglia and Gloucestershire, a new type of stronghold: the *oppidum*. Chichester Dykes is one example. These were large strongholds, and there are not too many about. Quite often, their defences of long banks and ditches were no better than those of the earliest hillforts, but they were more akin to medieval walled towns than to citadel strongholds. They were usually built on low-lying land, and a number eventually spawned Roman towns, such as Winchester (Venta Belgarum), Colchester (Camulodunum) and St Albans (Verulamium). Others, such as Dyke Hills were replaced by a nearby Roman town, in this case Dorchester on Thames.

DEMISE

Why were the prehistoric strongholds abandoned? Well, Neolithic causeway camps – if they were ever fortified – might have been succeeded as ceremonial centres by henges. These in turn were ousted or, in rare cases, enhanced by stone circles. The arrival of the Romans ensured that fortified hillforts, *oppida* and crannogs were abandoned in England and Wales. They certainly knew how to deal with such strongholds, but in Scotland it was not quite so simple.

While the Romans enjoyed their pound of Scottish flesh, and strongholds were abandoned at various times, the Scottish Iron Age continued until *c.* AD 500. However, brochs had probably begun to be deserted some two hundred years before so, we must ask, just why were these very specialist strongholds built? The Picts first appeared in Roman literature in AD 297, as the painted peoples north of Hadrian's Wall. Many brochs are located close to the coast; were they strongholds against raiders, possibly Celtic Picts, or were the nineteenth-century

HAMBLEDON HILL
Dorset O/S map 194 (Hillfort) ref. 845125 (Causeway camp) ref. 849122
Directions: Head north from Blandford Forum on the A350 and turn left at Iwerne Courtney or Shroton. Park near the church, turn left at the next road and take the footpath to the left of the cricket ground. Follow the path through the gate and fence, then head west up the Shroton spur to Hambledon Hill.

Archaeology is undecided whether Neolithic causeway camps were fortified. They were surely not defended settlements, like hillforts, but some seem to have been partially fortified. As one ascends the spur from Shroton, there are three low banks near the bottom. These are the scant remains of the inner, middle and outer outworks of a Neolithic settlement dating to *c.* 3000 BC.

Excavation has shown that the inner outwork was a massively fortified barrier with a complex entrance. This was contemporary with the large causeway camp on the summit plateau. Further outworks and a small causeway camp on the Stepleton spur, coupled with yet more enclosures on the Hanford spur, show the Hambledon Neolithic settlement to be of massive proportions. The fortified nature of the cross-banks on the Shroton spur were the first confirmation of defended Neolithic settlements. And to think, our Stone Age ancestors are still often thought of as primitive, uncivilized nomads! Think again.

Should you walk from nearby Hod Hill, you pass the cross-banks on the Hanford spur, just before reaching the large summit causeway camp. These are fully five thousand years old, have seen Iron Age and Dark Age settlements come and go, and the summit is still farmed today. Yet sections are still visible.

The Iron Age hillfort encloses the northern spur of Hambledon Hill. There is a Neolithic long barrow clearly visible on the summit, and this spur was possibly occupied to a similar extent as the others in Neolithic times. Yet, as you will have seen, the two ramparts and ditches, with counterscarp bank, enclose 24 acres and cling to the hillside to create a most beautiful hillfort. Indeed, some so-called fringe archaeo-scientists used to regard hillforts not as fortified settlements, but as either landscape architecture or something akin to earth-energy power stations.

Hambledon Hill goes a long way to disproving such mumbo-jumbo by dint of its physical remains. Hod Hill has visible hut circles, but at Hambledon the hillfort is covered in hut platforms, cut into the sides of the hill, on which huts were built. Indeed, Hambledon Hill is not one, but three hillforts. The northern tip of 7 acres was the original hillfort, and the slight remains of the cross-rampart and ditch can just be seen north of the central mound. This mound was later enclosed by a rampart to the south, doubling the size of the hillfort. Finally, the hillfort as we see it today was completed. It is this sequence of development that gave rise to the notion that nearby Hod Hill was an overspill hillfort, as Hamble-don Hill's population outgrew the hillfort. Why could not the other spurs of the hill have been used, as in Neolithic times, though?

The ruins of the north entrance are poor, while that at the south-east is a pretty basic one. The south-west entrance is altogether more complex and impressive, and is a mirror image of the north-east entrance at Hod Hill – further evidence of close ties between the two sets of inhabitants? Perhaps, but Hambledon Hill is one of the most spectacular and attractive of British hillforts.

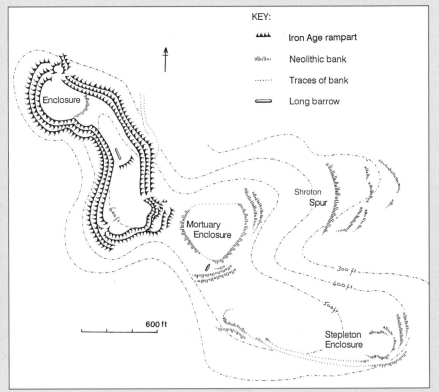

KEY:

⌃⌃⌃ Iron Age rampart

ᴜᴜᴜ Neolithic bank

······· Traces of bank

▭ Long barrow

Enclosure

Shroton Spur

Mortuary Enclosure

300 ft
400 ft
500 ft

Stepleton Enclosure

600 ft

CHICHESTER DYKES (Oppidum)

Sussex O/S map 181 refs 826081–859081; 890085–918086; 818066; 841067–853067 (not complete)

It seems that The Trundle hillfort was abandoned in the first century BC, possibly after the arrival of Belgic-Celts from Gaul, driven out by Julius Caesar's invasion. Before long, Caesar had turned his attention to Britain, but this part of Sussex did not succumb to his raids.

Since those times the Sussex coastline has been tortured and twisted by the sea. Much of the Selsey peninsula has been eroded, while the inland water between Bosham and Boxgrove has apparently greatly diminished since the late Iron Age, at least if one is to make any sense of the dykes as a defensive system, which they undoubtedly were.

Several hundred acres were enclosed by the dykes and somewhere within lay the tribal capital of the Regni. This was the seat of Verica, c. AD 10–43, who had gold and silver coins minted. He was pro-Roman, but was expelled before the Claudian invasion in AD 43, and was succeeded by Cogidubnos. Whether the latter fought the Romans is not clear, but he was one of eleven native leaders who submitted to the Emperor Claudius at Camulodunum (Colchester). Thereafter, Cogidubnos became a faithful client-king of the Romans.

The Chichester Dykes were built before the Romans invaded and they would certainly have defined and defended a large area. Several good lengths exist, but they are mostly covered in trees. Such dykes may be regarded as an alternative to the hillfort and, though not so dramatic, physically mark a major change in society in southern England during the century or so before the Roman invasion.

antiquarians right to describe them as Pictish Towers – i.e., those of the invaders? It might *just* be possible that the Picts arrived in Scotland in the first millennium BC and took many centuries to assert themselves. The only problem is that north-east Scotland appears to have been the Pictish heartland, and there are no brochs or duns in that area.

Not surprisingly, our knowledge of prehistoric society is, at best, minimal. We cannot hope to learn who built the strongholds and why, and who lived in them. Archaeology has achieved minor miracles in understanding prehistoric society, but there are inevitably limits. The strongholds, their development and finally their demise have played an enormous role in relaying the many theories about our prehistoric forebears. They remain the finest visual elements of those times. Of course, Stonehenge, Silbury Hill, Avebury, Maes Howe and Callanish are equally magnificent examples of prehistoric workmanship and planning, and there are many others as well. Nevertheless, many strongholds are equally astounding, and their numbers are quite staggering.

If the population of late Iron Age Britain was about 2–4 million, then these people left behind an extraordinarily diverse range of strongholds. Their often superb locations undoubtedly add to their attraction, but I wonder if our own ruins will be described as examples of 'landscape architecture' in two thousand years? Somehow, I think there might be just a modicum of dissent.

Britain's prehistoric past is, not surprisingly, the least understood period of our history. Over four thousand years of stronghold building cannot be adequately covered in a single chapter; we can, though, appreciate and, most importantly, visit them. Without a shadow of doubt, they represent some of the finest building achievements in our islands. Yet they were all built by hand with stone tools, antler picks, pelvic shovels, ropes and sheer hard graft. Above all though, there was ingenuity. Barbarians? Uncivilized? Could the Romans really have been describing our prehistoric forebears – or their own society with their ritual mass-slaughter at the Coliseum to keep their citizens happy.

ROMAN BRITAIN

Britain, by the immeasurable sea stranded,
Remote, barbaric, beset by unapproachable shores.

So began a poem to commemorate the successful invasion of Britannia by the forces of Emperor Claudius in AD 43. Remote and barbaric? This image of our prehistoric past has been handed down through the centuries, and remains a widely held view to this day. For many, the arrival of the Romans in Britain was the ancient equivalent of Mao Tse Tung's Great Leap Forward and yet, as Chapter 1 suggested, there is ever more evidence to the contrary.

As with most things, so archaeological fashions and fads come and go, depending on the results, interpretation and artefacts from the most recent excavations. Such work has mounted a challenge to the orthodox view that, far from dragging our barbaric ancestors from the dark into the light, Britain's Roman interlude was a distinctly backward step. The natural progression of society was stymied for a thousand years, certainly as far as southern England was concerned. In another twenty years, this view might be dismissed as fanciful poppycock, but current and future research might also enhance its credibility.

The tribes of southern and eastern England were certainly well organized, technologically advanced and economically developed. Once the dust had settled, by about AD 47, the Romans divided their new province into *civitates* – based on the native tribal areas, often with the former chiefs ruling on the Romans' behalf. This was the principle of divide and rule, as copied by the British when administering their empire. Naturally, the new, ever-expanding province of Britannia had a Roman governor, but once tribal allegiance had been sworn to the emperor, the legions were moved from the conquered territories to expand the empire's borders. For a whole generation thereafter, life carried on almost as before, except that taxes were channelled back to Rome, and native settlements were rendered defenceless.

In one important respect, though, the native Britons' horizons were broadened; it was thanks to the Romans that the concept of Britain as an entity came about. Prior to their arrival, people belonged to a tribe: usually a large, autonomous tribe in the southern half of England, and smaller and diverse tribes in the north and west. Each tribe had its territory, the borders of which might change after a season's raiding or a confederacy agreement, but each person would have considered himself a member of his tribe, and not a Briton. This transition did not occur overnight, and was relevant only to the occupied territories in any case but, in its way, it was a revolutionary proposition.

It is more a matter of personal interpretation than clear historical fact as to whether the long Roman interlude was beneficial to Britain. We can argue about the niceties of the matter forever and a day, but the Romans were the undoubted rulers and masters of the greater part of our islands. As regards England and Wales, they came, they saw and they conquered. Stronghold Britain it might have been, but the strongholds were built and located to control the natives. Like it or not, our forebears were subjugated within their own land and, however decently the Romans might have acted, it was not widely regarded as the most pleasant of experiences. Remember, during the Second World War the Nazi Germans lorded it over the French for a mere four years; the Romans occupied our lands for almost four hundred years. This rather puts the impact of the Latin invaders into its true perspective.

Walltown Crags, an isolated stretch of Hadrian's Wall.

Well before their departure, and to no great surprise, many natives adopted and adapted the Roman way of life. By the time the Angles, Saxons, Jutes and others began raiding our shores, it was not just the Celts who were put firmly on to the back foot, but the Romano-British. That, then, was the way of the Roman Empire: to invade a territory, impose their system of government, win over the native leaders by making them active participants in that system, and then reap the benefits of low administration costs. An additional bonus was the reduced need for a large-scale military presence. It was a system that worked time and time again.

THE ROMAN ARMY

Not surprisingly, the most important element in this seemingly simple system of control was the renowned Roman army. As with the British Raj in India, where there was a small British army and the Indian Army (comprising native troops mostly commanded by Britons), the Romans also divided their forces. In the first century AD, there were about thirty legions to guard and expand the entire empire, supported by a similar number of auxiliaries recruited from conquered territories. Quite naturally, the legions – the soldiers of which were all Roman citizens – were the prestigious backbone of the army. Each legion had a number and usually a title denoting its origin or founder, such as the II Augusta legion. It was not dissimilar to our own regimental system.

The hierarchy was based on social background (some things never change) and each legion was commanded by a legate, who might be a senator. His second-in-command was the senior tribune, a young man of similar social standing, and below that were (usually) five military tribunes, all of lesser nobility. Each officer served for about three years (a sort of short service

Turret 51B, Hadrian's Wall.

commission) but continuity was provided by the prefect, an officer of equal standing to the tribunes. He was the senior long-serving officer and was usually appointed from the centurions.

Ah ha, the centurion: part myth, part legend with a pinch of reality, but certainly not part-time. A sort of sergeant-major figure, yet with duties more akin to those of a company commander – say, a captain – the centurions effectively ran the legion on a daily basis. Each centurion would usually have risen from the ranks, having been a junior officer, and would be in charge of eighty men. Nine of the ten cohorts that made up a legion were formed of six centuries, with ten centuries in the first cohort. So, with about 150 cavalry and trumpeters and others, a full-strength legion mustered about 5,500 men.

Let us make no mistake about it, the legendary deeds and reputations of the legions were exploited to the full when on campaign; they were admired by friends, respected and feared by foes. Nobody likes to go into battle against crack troops. In the Second World War British morale always suffered if a regiment of the line faced an élite Panzer unit. It was no different two thousand years ago. At that time, the world had not seen a more effective, well-drilled and efficient fighting, even killing, machine. Once a Roman legion had you in its vice-like grip, there was no easy way out. Highly trained, rigidly disciplined, well armed, durable and thoroughly professional, Rome's legions regularly wiped out forces of far greater size, and yet fighting was only one of their many duties.

In many respects the legionary soldiers were the most highly skilled construction force of all time. Of course, each legion had its specialists, such as surveyors and engineers, but it was the soldiers who built the roads on which they marched relentlessly; they who built the fortresses, forts, fortlets, walls, bridges and signal stations that feature in this chapter; they who built and policed the empire. It is quite remarkable to think that, for all the military highways in Britain, the hundreds of forts and the two great walls, not forgetting the invasion and subsequent campaigns, there were never more than four legions stationed here.

Yet, for all that, there was another absolutely essential side to the Roman army: the auxiliaries. These were the support troops, recruited from conquered peoples. Initially, they rarely served in their own land; thus auxiliaries serving in Britain came from all over Europe, while auxiliary regiments from Britain served in Europe and even North Africa. Such units were commanded by a prefect or tribune, often a former centurion from a legion, and varied in size according to the type of regiment: a crack cavalry regiment, or *ala*, had 512 men; an infantry cohort, 480 men; and a mixed cavalry/infantry unit, the *cohort equitata*, 608 men.

Other units or divisions were made up of specialists, such as archers, javelin throwers or cavalry, all of which could support a legion on campaign. Auxiliary cohorts would also undertake routine work, such as patrols, guard duties and escorts: essentially the mopping-up after the action had died down. It was auxiliaries who usually guarded Hadrian's Wall, for example.

Caerleon boasts Britain's best preserved amphitheatre, just outside the town's west wall. Amphitheatres were used not only for entertainment but also for training troops.

A legion on campaign was a formidable opponent. Not unnaturally, the Romans preferred to fight on their own terms, whatever the odds. They would line up on a ridge with the infantry in the middle and the cavalry on the flanks. The legionaries were well protected with armour and each soldier carried two javelins. They would wait in ordered ranks for the enemy to attack and then let fly, at a range of barely 50 yards, with both javelins in quick succession. The sky would momentarily blacken with these terrifying missiles, whose shafts were designed to bend on impact so they could not be returned, and the opposition would be swamped in utter confusion. Even if a javelin failed to find a target, it remained an awkward obstacle amid advancing, bunched-up men.

The javelin attack was the signal for the legionaries to close ranks, link their shields together, and advance into the enemy in tight wedge-shaped formations. Their short swords were ideal for close combat, and they systematically stabbed the naked torsos of the Celtic foe, then ruthlessly stamped the wounded bodies into the earth beneath their heavy boots. Should the opposition break ranks and flee, the cavalry, armed with long swords and lances, would charge after them to complete the slaughter. There was an almost horrific beauty and symmetry to their tactics, and they worked again and again and again. (Indeed, substituting batons for swords, on the 1,900th anniversary of the Battle of Mons Graupius in AD 84, almost identical tactics were used by Britain's police forces against pickets during the miners' strike, usually with an equally devastating effect.)

THE FIRST ROMAN INVASIONS OF BRITAIN

That, of course, was the theory; it was also, more often than not, the practical outcome. The Roman army was, most emphatically, an offensive force during the first and much of the second century AD. By the third century the army's role was more one of occupation, and a century later it was certainly on the defensive. The change-over from offence to defence came with the establishment of permanent, fixed frontiers (it usually does), but that was not how Julius Caesar viewed Britannia.

In August 55 BC Caesar landed near Deal with the VII and X legions to test the water. He hardly got off the beaches before a good old Channel storm blew up and wrecked half his ships; it was the first of many such occasions when the weather has come to our aid. Unaware of the plight the Romans were in, the native forces agreed to a peace settlement, allowing Caesar to withdraw, dishevelled but otherwise unharmed. Surely, this was one of the greatest missed opportunities in history?

The Britons were to rue this error the following year. Caesar returned, landing on 6 July, again near Deal, with 5 legions and 2,000 cavalry, in about 800 specially built, shallow-draught boats. He rapidly moved inland and swamped Bigbury hillfort, before returning to base as the Channel had again done its worst. This time, though, there was to be no respite for the natives.

Caesar drove inland again, crossed the Thames in the vicinity of modern London and vanquished the Catuvellaunian chief Cassivellaunus at his tribal

RICHBOROUGH (Saxon Shore Fort)
Kent O/S map 179 ref. 325602
Directions: Leave Sandwich on the old A257 towards the bypass. Just before crossing the railway, turn right. The fort is signposted.

The West Gate, Richborough. Britannia beckons.

Rutupiae is, Hadrian's Wall notwithstanding, the foremost symbolic Roman site in Britain. How lucky we are that, despite its location, it has survived over 1,900 years of continuous change. It was here, then lapped by the waters of the English Channel, that the Romans first landed in AD 43. A pair of V-shaped ditches ran for almost ½ mile to cut off a narrow peninsula, which became the invasion beach-head. Once Kent was overrun, these were filled in, but a short section has been uncovered and can be seen within the later fort walls.

Richborough then grew into a port town, with a massive, four-way triumphal arch, built towards the end of the first century, as the gateway to the province Britannia. This was no mere symbol either, for here the great Watling Street began and passed through the west gate.

Early in the third century the arch became the basis of a signal station, its rampart protected by the three ditches still visible today. Before the century was out, Richborough was comprehensively rebuilt as a Saxon Shore Fort, defended by the great stone walls that still stand up to 25 ft high. Fully 6 acres were enclosed by this wall, with its bastions and two ditches. The main gates were at the east and west, with postern gates through the north and south walls. Buildings and barracks were of timber.

As with Burgh Castle, Richborough has lost one of its walls, and it too served an ecclesiastical use somewhat later. Here, though, is evidence of at least three strongholds. How close we came to losing it can be seen by the proximity of the railway. No doubt the last Romans departed through here, just as they had arrived here almost four hundred years earlier.

stronghold of Wheathampstead, despite being harried by some four thousand charioteers. This was to be no conquest though, for Caesar took hostages and tribute – and then departed. The native Britons were to enjoy a further ninety-odd years of freedom before the iron fist of Rome came again, this time to stay.

THE ROMAN CONQUEST OF BRITAIN

It must be quite clear by now that the Romans did not dither and mess about amending their plans of action. Events elsewhere in the empire had taken the heat off Britain, not least an apparently innocuous execution in Palestine. Before much longer though, the riches from our green island were too much to ignore: plentiful raw materials and, in particular, slaves. Certainly Claudius was tempted and so, in AD 43 three waves of ships carrying Claudius' army set out from France. They reputedly landed at Richborough, and this time nature did not intervene. The invasion was on.

Aulus Plautius had four legions under his command – II Augusta, IX Hispana, XIV Gemina and XX Valeria – plus a similar number of auxiliaries, a total of

The mightily impressive north wall and postern gate at the Richborough Saxon Shore fort.

The Roman temple at Maiden Castle was built some 250 years after the hillfort fell to the II Augusta legion.

about 40,000 men. Opposition was far from united and was masterminded by two brothers, Caradoc and Togodumnus, sons of the late Catuvellaunian king Cunobeline. Under these two, Catuvellaunian rule and influence had spread rapidly across southern England, but was often less than welcome; at least two deposed tribal chiefs had pleaded with Rome for help. And intervene the Romans most certainly did.

After winning a two-day battle at the River Medway, the Roman army halted at the River Thames, possibly near London Bridge. Emperor Claudius arrived post-haste from Rome and, if not in the vanguard was certainly in attendance as the legions drove on and captured the tribal capital at Colchester. Although Caradoc himself had long since fled, eleven native kings reputedly submitted to Claudius during his ten days' stay at Colchester, and the conquered territories were quickly disarmed.

Meanwhile, the II Augusta legion, under the command of Vespasian, was dispatched to subdue the south-western tribes, and what a joyous and successful time they had. According to Roman accounts, Vespasian fought thirty battles and overcame twenty *oppida* in an orgy of victorious conquest; our hillforts were no

BRECON GAER (Roman Fort)
Brecknockshire O/S map 160 ref. 002297
Directions: Leave Brecon heading west on the A40. Turn right on the first minor road, after about 3 miles, and then right again towards Cradoc. Park beside the bridge over the stream, and follow the path up the hill to the farm. The north gate is just beyond the end of the farmyard.

Brecon Gaer was built *c.* AD 80 as a cavalry fort and encloses about 5 acres. It has a dominating location on a high plateau and is in surprisingly good condition. Having the usual rectangular shape, its turf walls can be seen for their whole circuit, while the south, west and east gateways each have their stone foundations and sections of wall cleared. The gateway at the south is double, and the guard room foundations are all laid bare.

Later, the wall was faced in stone. Little or nothing of this is visible at the three sides where the gateways remain, but there is a good long section of wall, up to 10 ft high, at the north-east. The ditch also remains at this point, making this the finest auxiliary fort in Wales.

Brecon Gaer west gate.

match for a well-organized siege. Of those twenty hillforts, Maiden Castle and Hod Hill have provided evidence of probable skirmishes, while Spetisbury Rings produced a mass grave containing more than a hundred British and Roman bodies. As for the other seventeen, well, either archaeologists have much work to do, or the Roman accounts are wildly exaggerated.

However by AD 47 the Romans ruled all of England east of a frontier roughly along a line from the River Exe, the Severn estuary, the River Avon and the River Trent to the River Humber. In addition, the Brigantian tribal confederacy, which occupied Yorkshire and the Pennines, was generally friendly and the legions moved up to fortresses along the frontier. The rapid assimilation of the conquered tribes into the new order ensured that many Roman military strongholds usually had but a brief life. Take the Roman fort at Hod Hill: destroyed by accidental fire in AD 51, it was not rebuilt as the area was, by then, considered secure.

A number of factors, both in Britain and elsewhere, combined to slow down the advance. Then, in AD 59, Suetonius Paulinus was appointed governor and set off to sort out the Deceangli and Ordovices tribes in North Wales. More especially, he annihilated the Druids on their sacred island of Anglesey: these religious leaders had been a thorn in Roman sides since Julius Caesar's campaigns in Gaul. Though the Romans were generally tolerant towards the

CAERLEON (Legionary Fortress)
Monmouthshire O/S map 171 ref. 339906
Directions: From Newport or the M4, take the B4236 into Caerleon. Signs direct you to the amphitheatre just outside the west gate.

Of the several legionary fortresses in Britain, disappointingly little remains to be seen. Caerleon, or Isca Silurum, tops the list, although the modern town overlays most of the stronghold.

It was built *c.* AD 75 as the headquarters of the II Augusta legion and remained so, even though the legion was often away on campaign, for about two hundred years. Initially, Caerleon was the centre for the Roman campaign to overcome the Silures and Demetae tribes of South Wales, and could easily be provisioned from boats on the River Usk. Built of timber and turf, its ramparts were faced and rebuilt in stone in the second century. Little remains of the defences, save for a length of wall in the south-west. There is, though, more to Caerleon than that.

Just outside the west gate stands Britain's most complete amphitheatre. It was built at the same time as the fortress and probably held about six thousand people

The barracks of the II Augusta legion, at Caerleon.

(about the strength of the II Legion). This may have been used as a training ground as much as for staging entertainment.

Further to the north, within the fortress, can be seen the only uncovered foundations of legionary barracks in Europe, complete with latrines, cookhouse and ovens. Of the three visible barrack blocks, only that nearest the wall is original; the others are recent reconstructions. Twelve pairs of rooms, each housing eight men, can be seen, with the larger set of rooms to the north for the centurion and officers. Spare rooms were used for offices, recruits and such-like.

While Caerleon's defences are some way short of being earth-shattering, they combine with the amphitheatre, barracks and baths – in the town centre – to provide the most comprehensive legionary fortress currently visible in Britain.

religions of occupied territories, the Druids, with their human sacrifices and suspected cannibalism, were shown no mercy and were invariably massacred.

Paulinus' campaign did not reach fruition as the Iceni tribe rebelled the following year against the harsh and corrupt Roman regime in East Anglia. In no time at all, they had comprehensively sacked Colchester, London and St Albans, and advanced north to smash the remaining Roman army. Boudicca had proved to be a mightily inspirational leader but, possibly near Mancetter (Warks.), she met her match. Her rag-bag army of (reputedly) 100,000 was comprehensively slaughtered. Once the revolt was put down, the Romans exacted a brief but merciless and bloody revenge; lessons were harshly taught in those days. A decade of consolidation followed, which included greater direct control from the governor to prevent the local corruption that first ignited the revolt.

In northern England though, by about AD 70, all was not going too well with the Brigantian confederacy. The Romans went to the aid of their supporter, Queen Cartimandua – ironically ranged against her husband Venutius – and the IX Hispana legion put down the rebellion and extended the area of direct Roman rule as far north as Teesdale. By that time only three legions were stationed in

Britain, the XIV Gemina legion having been withdrawn. These were based at Gloucester (II Augusta); Wroxeter (XX Valeria Vitrix); and York (IX Hispana).

The Arrival of Agricola

During the 70s, the Romans campaigned against the Silurian tribe of south-east Wales – setting up a new legionary fortress at Caerleon – at the behest of the new emperor, the old warrior Vespasian. Then, in about AD 77, one Gnaeus Julius Agricola was appointed governor of Britain. Suddenly, the game was up. Within a single campaign season, the tribes of north and central Wales, who had previously inflicted the occasional setback on Roman forces, were comprehensively defeated by this truly great general, leading the XX Valeria Vitrix legion. The troublesome Ordovices were all but annihilated. A legionary base was founded at Chester, and a string of auxiliary forts was established as Wales yielded beneath the mighty Roman hammer. That was just the start for Agricola, who was determined to subjugate all Britain's tribes to Roman rule.

In AD 80 Agricola led the IX and XX legions into Scotland, quickly subduing the Borders' tribes, such as the Selgovae and Novantae, but leaving the friendly Votadini pretty much alone. The two legions strode northwards in a double-pincer movement, meeting up on the banks of the Firth of Forth at Inveresk; hillforts and other native strongholds were simply swept aside or rendered useless. It is possible that cohorts from each legion pushed farther on to the Tay, establishing the odd fort on the way. Not unnaturally, after such a rapid advance, the following year was spent in consolidation. Agricola probably led a land and seaborne invasion of Galloway in AD 82, and even contemplated invading Ulster, which he could see across the Irish Sea. Given subsequent history, it is probably just as well for his reputation that he did not try.

Then, in AD 83, Agricola returned to the Forth/Clyde isthmus to complete the invasion of Britain. He divided his forces, with the fleet in support, and marched north-east. The fleet spread terror among the natives and supplied the army – but by dividing his troops Agricola almost came a cropper. The IX legion was attacked one night, and was only rescued by the governor's direct intervention. It was not a particularly successful campaign season either for, although the Romans pushed north, the Caledonians – a confederacy of small tribes – refused to be drawn into battle and engaged in bothersome, harrying guerrilla actions. This rather deviated from Agricola's plan to bring the enemy to battle and comprehensively beat them.

The Battle of Mons Graupius

While the campaign was hardly a stalemate, it was not an entirely satisfactory position for either side; it was costly for the Romans, while the Caledonians were slowly but surely pushed back into the Highland glens. Eventually, the massed ranks of both armies were drawn up for the Battle of Mons Graupius. The site of this momentous conflict remains elusive, but it might have taken place on the slopes beneath the distinctive hillfort of Mither Tap o' Bennachie. As events turned out, it was hardly a copybook example of Roman battle tactics and it was the home team, the Caledonians, who held the high ground.

Reputedly, about 30,000 Caledonians lined up to face Agricola's army. The Roman forces comprised about 8,000 auxiliaries in the centre, flanked by some 5,000 cavalry, with the two legions drawn up behind. Assuming these were at full strength, Roman forces would have comfortably exceeded 20,000, although the Roman historian Tacitus claims there were only 11,000. Initially, the Caledonian charioteers paraded in front of their lines and taunted the Romans, who replied by delivering their javelin volleys; the natives hardly batted an eyelid, which impressed the Romans. Then they got down to serious business and Agricola led the auxiliaries into the mass of the natives in close combat, while his cavalry routed the chariots.

The rear ranks of Caledonians then surged down the hill, but Agricola sent forth the four cavalry squadrons held back for such an eventuality. They swept through the Caledonian ranks, attacked from behind and, in the ensuing chaos, some 10,000 natives were left dead on the battlefield. Reputedly only 360 Roman soldiers bit the dust. This was a comprehensive victory and so, surely, the rest of Scotland was at Agricola's mercy? As it happened, he was recalled to Rome, having served a double-term of six years as governor. The Scottish campaigns had proved enormously expensive and, despite a period of consolidation, Scotland was all but given up as the second century dawned.

Interestingly, neither legion took an active role in the fighting, they just let the auxiliaries get on with it, and as many as 20,000 Caledonians escaped. This was certainly not part of the Roman master-plan, and an effective force survived to fight another day. A series of forts was built to keep the natives hemmed into their glens, and a great new legionary fortress was begun, but never finished, at Inchtuthil. It took some time, but, although the Romans won the battle, the Caledonians, while not exactly winning the war, saw them off in the end.

Hadrian's Wall

The rain, the wind, the sleet, the snow,
  Over the parapet, they ceaselessly blow.
The cold, the damp, the Barbarians' call,
  I joined up for action, not to guard a wall.

The Roman forts built along the Stanegate frontier, from the River Tyne to the Solway Firth, came under increasing attack from the Scottish tribes and suffered heavy losses following a revolt in AD 117. This was the signal for Emperor Hadrian to visit Britain and to authorize the building of his great wall; the transition from offensive to holding or even defensive strongholds was underway. The new wall was built of stone from Wallsend, on the River Tyne, to the River Irthing and, initially – owing to a shortage of good quality stone, of turf to Bowness, on the Solway Firth; a distance of 80 Roman miles. A number of fortlets and turrets were also built along the western coast, possibly as far south as St Bee's Head.

The general defensive format of the new frontier comprised a V-shaped ditch north of the wall; the wall itself, this being about 20 feet high to the parapet; the

Hadrian's Wall at Cawfields Crags, looking east.

Military Way road to the south, built in the 160s; and, finally, the vallum, a wide, flat-bottomed ditch with 10 feet high banks on either side. The vallum probably defined the military zone and was crossed by gated causeways. The wall itself varied in thickness from 8 Roman feet at the extreme east, to 10 feet between Newcastle and milecastle 27, and back to 8 feet thick on the broad foundations to the River Irthing. The original turf wall was about 20 feet thick and 12 feet high, with a wooden parapet on top. Its replacement by a 9 feet thick stone wall began soon after the turf wall was completed and was finished during the major refurbishment of the wall in the 160s, occasionally taking a different alignment.

The vallum, at Cawfields. Did this define the military zone?

There was a fortlet or milecastle every mile, with two turrets in between; the turf wall milecastles were originally built in turf, but all the turrets were of stone. In addition, and most important since the wall was more a frontier post than a defensive barrier, there were sixteen adjoining forts. Together these housed about ten thousand troops, whose duties were both to man the wall and to go out and meet an enemy in open combat. The original plan had been to use the earlier Stanegate forts as bases for the troops. Possibly at the personal direction of Hadrian, however, new forts were built against, or even astride, the wall. Those forts in the

HADRIAN'S WALL (Frontier Wall and Forts)
Cumberland and Northumberland

Perhaps the most surprising thing about this great frontier is not how much remains, but how little. It was, of course, a valuable source of good quality stone over the centuries, yet much of its destruction took place in the eighteenth and nineteenth centuries. Even so, there are still many fine sections to be seen, though none in original condition. In particular, the B6318 follows the line of the stone wall for much of its length. Doubtless this road's construction was to the detriment of the wall, but it makes for easy access to the many stretches still worth visiting.

Milecastle 37.

Not surprisingly, the turf wall has fared even worse, while the sprawl of Newcastle upon Tyne and its environs has all but obliterated the wall at its eastern extremity. Starting out from Brampton on the A69 and working eastwards, some of the best sections of wall, forts, milecastles, turrets or signal towers are listed below.

Hare Hill
O/S map 86 ref. 562646. A short length of wall up to 9 ft high.
Banks East Turret (52A) and Pike Hill Signal Tower
O/S map 86 refs 575647 and 577647.
Turrets 51A and 51B
O/S map 86 refs 588653 and 583651. Beside road leading east to Birdoswald Fort.
Birdoswald Fort, Turret 49B, Milecastle 49 and Wall
O/S map 86 ref. 615663. Long section of wall from fort to milecastle.
Willowford Bridge abutment, Milecastle 48 and Wall
O/S map 86 refs 623664 and 634662. Access from Willowford Farm, Gilsland.
Walltown Crags Turret 45A and Wall
O/S map 87 ref. 674664.
Cawfields Milecastle 42, Wall and Vallum
O/S map 87 ref. 716667
Vindolanda (Chesterholm) Fort, Civilian Settlement and Museum
O/S map 87 ref. 771664. Former Stanegate fort with impressive attached civilian settlement. Recent discovery of what might have been a prisoner-of-war camp. Outstanding reconstructed stone wall turret and turf wall milecastle entrance.
Housesteads Fort and Museum, Milecastles 37, 38 and 39 and Wall
O/S map 87 ref. 790687. The finest Roman fort in Britain, Housesteads covers 5 acres and has the remains of a civilian settlement. It also has the best stretches of wall, with 3 miles west to Steel Rigg, including a very fine milecastle, Castle Nick 39, and further stretches east to Sewingshields with more milecastles and turrets.
Black Carts Turret 29A and Wall
O/S map 87 ref. 884712. 500 yd of wall.
Chesters Fort and Bridge abutments
O/S map 87 ref. 913701. Cavalry fort built astride Hadrian's Wall.
Bruton Turret 26B and Wall
O/S map 87 ref. 922698. Off A6079 towards Hexham. One of the best turrets.
Planetrees
O/S map 87 ref. 928696. A short but interesting stretch of narrow wall on wide foundations.
Corbridge Fort, Military Supply Depot, Town and Museum
O/S map 87 ref. 982648. In Corbridge off the A68 about 4 miles south of Hadrian's Wall. The fort was replaced by a town at the important junction of the Stanegate, east to west, and Dere Street, north to south.
Heddon on the Wall
O/S map 88 ref. 136669. Remains of almost 300 yd of wall.

Reconstruction of a milecastle, with a turret beyond.

east tended to reach beyond the wall and were mostly for cavalry; forts in the west, with the odd exception, abutted the wall and were for infantry cohorts. There were also several outlying, fully manned forts to the north.

Hadrian's Wall was a means of controlling the empire's frontier. Though not really intended to be an impregnable obstacle, it indicated a change in outlook for the Roman army, from an offensive towards a defensive force. The whole entity, wall and forts, was built by the legions, but manned by auxiliaries. It was a magnificent physical achievement and its still visible diversity of building style and proportions indicates that each cohort had their own ideas about details. Not only did it take six years to complete, but alterations were continually undertaken, such as rebuilding the turf wall in stone, or building and expanding forts. Indeed, Hadrian's Wall was less than twenty years old when it was abandoned in favour of the Antonine Wall, although it was reoccupied a few decades later.

What is not known is the impact the barrier had on the natives. It was built entirely for Roman convenience, taking no account of tribal boundaries or native tracks, probably on the principal of a modern motorway – like it or lump it. No doubt many natives were aggrieved and, as the verse on p. 50 suggests, it was hardly the most prized posting in the empire for the soldiers, either. The auxiliaries at first came from central Europe – and could hardly have appreciated our northern winter, but later most wall guards would have been native Britons.

As with the Romans themselves, Hadrian's Wall did not go out with a bang. True, there were occasions when it was overrun, such as in the 180s and again in 367, but it was probably abandoned when the Romans left in 407, and the soldiers' pay failed to arrive. Thereafter, the wall was a huge, irresistible quarry and many local buildings contain material from the frontier or its forts. Indeed, there are not many good lengths of wall left, and none in original condition, but it can be traced for most of its length: an enigmatic, yet endearing scar snaking its way across northern England.

The finest surviving Roman fort in Britain: Housesteads Fort, adjoining Hadrian's Wall.

Hadrian's Wall country. The undulating view east towards Housesteads Fort.

Hadrian's Wall milecastle 42.

The isolated fortlet at Durisdeer guards the pass from Nithsdale to Clydesdale.

HARDKNOTT CASTLE (Auxiliary Fort)
Cumberland O/S map 89 ref. 218014
Directions: Leave Ambleside on the A593 heading west, and turn right along the minor road a mile after passing the B5343. Follow this over the Wrynose Pass, and turn right on the narrow, winding and very steep (1 in 3) road over the Hardknott Pass. The fort is ½ mile beyond the summit to the right of the road.

Though not the highest Roman fort in England, Hardknott boasts the most spectacular location and dramatic approach. It can also be reached direct from Ravenglass, or Glannaventa, where the Romans had another fort, by following the road up Eskdale or, best of all, by taking the narrow-gauge Ravenglass and Eskdale Railway, and walking from the terminus.

Built during Hadrian's reign and garrisoned by the 4th cohort of Dalmatians, this 2¾ acre auxiliary fort commands Eskdale and the road from Ravenglass to Ambleside. Mediobogdum sits on a promontory between Eskdale and the pass, and its stone wall is still mostly about 6 ft high. Much of this has been rebuilt using the original fallen stones.

There are entrances along each side, all except the north having double portals, and the foundations of the *Principia*, the commandant's house, and granaries can be seen. Also of historical interest is the parade ground, the best still to be seen in Britain. Due to the space restrictions, this is 200 yd beyond the east gate on a plateau above the fort. The raised mounds of what may have been the tribune's rostrum are also visible.

This remote yet wonderfully attractive site is one of the finest Roman forts in Britain. It is wholly orthodox in design and probably never saw any action in what might have been a relatively short service life. One wonders what those poor Balkan troops thought of the harsh, wet Lakeland winter.

SOUTH SHIELDS (Roman Fort)
Co. Durham O/S map 88 ref. 365679
Directions: Follow the A194(M) and A194 from the A1 into South Shields. The fort is well signposted in the town.

Built by Hadrian *c.* 130 as a 4 acre fort to control the mouth of the River Tyne, a few miles east of his wall, South Shields, or Arbeia, underwent many changes during the following 370 years.

Initially timber buildings housed a cavalry regiment, but the former were soon replaced by stone buildings, and the latter also moved on. By the time Severus invaded Scotland, the fort was extended by about an acre to the south. It became a supply base for the campaign and over twenty granaries have been found, both in the extension and also replacing barracks.

Still later there was a reversal and barracks replaced the granaries. By the end of the third century, the fort might have been abandoned, although surely some presence was maintained at this strategic site. Soon it was occupied again and appears to have remained active until the early fifth century, probably when Hadrian's Wall was finally abandoned.

Despite being surrounded by housing, most of the fort is visible, but not the River Tyne. There is a good museum, along with foundations of many buildings and a little over half of the perimeter wall. Undoubtedly of most interest is the outstanding replica west gateway, built in 1986. Here, one can see just what a twin portal gateway really looked like; short stretches of the outer ditches have been restored as well. This gateway alone makes the journey to South Shields well worthwhile. Reproductions are not always to be derided.

The replica gateway, South Shields.

The Antonine Wall

Fate has not been kind to the most northerly frontier of the Roman Empire, probably due to its being built entirely of turf on a stone base. A timber palisade fence sat atop the wall, which might have been revetted to prevent it from sliding into the ditch. It ran for 37 miles from Bo'ness, on the Forth, to Old Kilpatrick, on the Clyde, and effectively cut Scotland in half. So ideal and accessible is its course that, for the most part, the wall and its sixteen known (and nineteen supposed), forts have been destroyed or built over.

As with the southern barrier, a network of forts – often built on or near those of the Agricolan campaigns – supported the wall; these also penetrated far to the north. Unlike Hadrian's Wall, the Antonine Wall was an offensive, aggressive declaration of intent; it was not simply a means of securing the frontier, but a springboard for advance – just what the Roman army was used to.

Antoninus Pius succeeded Hadrian as emperor in AD 138. He soon instigated incursions into Scotland and by 142 the wall was underway; certainly, Antoninus accepted the salutation of *Imperator* for the invasion, the only military accolade to his name. The three legions stationed in Britain built the wall: II Augusta, VI Vitrix and the XX Valeria Vitrix, so the campaign had the full weight of Roman military power behind it.

The Antonine Wall was, understandably, heavily garrisoned. This did not last long, for by the mid-150s trouble was brewing in the former Brigantian territory,

---

ANTONINE WALL (Roman Wall)
Stirlingshire O/S map 65 Seabegs Wood ref. 814793; Tentfield Plantation ref. 855798; Watling Lodge ref. 865798
Directions: *Watling Lodge.* Leave Falkirk on the A803 and turn left on to the B816 towards High Bonnybridge at Camelon, along Tamfourhill Road. A signpost indicates the site.
Tentfield Plantation. Continue further west along the B816. Turn right at the cross-roads and a sign indicates the site on the left.
Seabegs Wood. Continue west on the B816, under two railway bridges (the road leading to Rough Castle is on the right) and turn left to Castlecary. A sign indicates the site, about a mile along the road on the left.

The Antonine Wall was one of Rome's greatest structures. Built of turf on a stone base, it runs for 37 miles from Bo'ness to Old Kilpatrick and effectively cuts Scotland in half. It is easy to reach and, as a result, most of the wall, ditch and the sixteen known, and nineteen supposed, forts have been destroyed or subsequently built over. The ruins do not compare with Hadrian's Wall, but there are several sections worth visiting. The three sites mentioned here all show various aspects of the Antonine Wall and, together with Rough Castle, can be visited in one go.

Watling Lodge was the site of the main north gateway, though it now lies under the house of that name. There is a well-preserved length of V-shaped ditch, 40 ft wide and 15 ft deep. Unfortunately, there is little sign of the wall. Also not visible, but revealed by excavation between 1972 and 1974, was a fortlet, measuring 50 ft × 60 ft now lying beneath some houses.

One can walk through Tentfield Plantation to Rough Castle, but it is often overgrown in the summer. The wall here is still about 4 ft high and can be traced through the woods. Two of the six known beacon platforms are also visible, one about 170 yd beyond Lime Road and the second 45 yd east of the railway crossing.

Nothing can be seen of the fort at Seabegs Wood, but there is a good length of ditch, with the wall up to 3 ft 6 in high behind it. There is also the best preserved section of the Military Way that ran parallel to the wall. This appears as a mound about 1 ft high and 24 ft wide and can be seen to the south of the wall.

The stretch of the Antonine Wall west of Rough Castle is the best preserved and is easy to reach.

and the new wall was evacuated to deploy the troops further south. This was too good an opportunity for the natives to miss and, it seems, the Romans were at least helped on their way. There is evidence of slaughter at Newstead Fort, but it is not known if any wall forts faced a similar fate; some were burnt, most probably by the departing Romans. The uprising put down, the Antonine Wall was reoccupied, in about 160, but was abandoned again after the death of Antoninus. That might have been the end of it, although some historians consider it was occupied again, late in the second century. As yet, the evidence, either way, is far from conclusive.

The north entrance at Rough Castle was protected by lilia: holes with a wooden stake at the bottom.

Quite why Antoninus authorized the invasion of Scotland is a matter for conjecture. None of the Scottish campaigns, from Agricola onwards, ever gave

the Romans a substantial economic or political return, so why did Antoninus think he could do any better? One theory contends that, as he had no military reputation, he took the opportunity to gain one at little or no risk. After all, a military reverse by the disunited tribes of Scotland would hardly threaten the empire, while their very disunity increased the likelihood of an easy victory. If this was the case, then Antoninus seems to have been both successful and justified in his judgement.

Thereafter, apart from the Scottish campaigns of Septimus Severus between 208 and 211, the Roman army was no longer an offensive force. Severus built at least fifteen temporary forts, from the Forth through Strathmore right up into the north-east. There was no battle on the scale of Mons Graupius, yet for almost a century England was virtually free from northern raids. Why was this? One theory contends that, before returning to the south, Severus' army destroyed all crops and devastated the land: in other words, genocide. From then on, what had once been temporary offensive strongholds, especially those built of turf and wood, metamorphosed into stone defensive strongholds, symbols of power – many of which grew fat to encompass a civilian settlement. Never again did the Romans go on the attack to the extent that they had done under Vespasian, Agricola and Severus.

The turf Antonine Wall was built on a stone base. Two lengths are exposed in New Kilpatrick cemetery.

ROMAN STRONGHOLDS

Generally speaking, whether one considers a 50 acre legionary fortress, an auxiliary fortress one-tenth of the size, temporary marching camps, a fortlet or a milecastle on Hadrian's Wall, Roman strongholds conformed to a universal standard layout. With good reason, for the Roman stronghold had proved itself in the field time and time again. Most forts were rectangular, although no two were identical. A V-shaped outer ditch (although Ardoch fort had six) would protect a rampart, with an entrance at the centre of each side. Small fortlets naturally had only one or two entrances but, as they are a stronghold's weakspot, why did bigger forts have so many? The answer is probably that the Roman army was an offensive, not a defensive, force. If attacked, whether in an overnight camp, a fort or even a legionary fortress, the troops would quickly muster to meet the enemy in the open, attack being the best form of defence. (This scenario is not dissimilar to the skirmishes of the Britons outside their hillforts.) The temporary fortifications might seem defensively limited, in comparison with, say, the great hillfort at Maiden Castle, but, and this is the important thing, they worked astoundingly well.

The internal layout also followed a typical standard pattern, unlike the native strongholds which varied widely. In the centre was the *Principia*, or headquarters, with the officers' quarters nearby. The troops were housed in rows with their centurion at their head. This layout applied to both a legionary fortress and an overnight camp with everyone in tents, and even the fortlets and milecastles followed these broad principles. In the permanent strongholds, there would be roads, storehouses, a hospital and other specialist buildings, while a bathhouse and workshops might well be contained in an annexe.

In any attack the gateways were the obvious target and were in consequence elaborately defended. A wonderful wooden entrance has been reconstructed at The Lunt, and an imposing stone entrance at South Shields. Regrettably, no original Roman fort entrances have survived. However good the basic defensive format though, Roman forts were occasionally overrun, as was Newstead in about AD 100, and again in the mid-second century. The evidence is far from conclusive, but several other Borders forts and supply bases might also have bitten the dust at the same times. Oh yes, even the Romans had their off-days.

The Legionary Fortress

Camulodunum was the first such stronghold in Britain, and it developed into the capital after the legions moved on to extend the province. Thereafter, legionary strongholds sprang up and either flourished or died, depending on the rate of advance (or, in one exception, retreat). Thus the II Legion soon moved from Exeter to Gloucester, to Usk and finally to Caerleon. Similarly, the XX Legion followed the XIV Legion to Wroxeter and then moved north to Chester; the IX Legion made York their base in the 70s. In addition to these, the legions built many temporary bases, especially after the Claudian invasion; the locations of some remain unknown. Others, such as Exeter, Gloucester and Wroxeter developed into important towns after their main military function had ceased, while Caerleon, Chester and York all became large, walled towns as well as legionary headquarters. These transitions most certainly did not happen overnight.

As one might expect, legionary strongholds conformed to the usual rectangular shape and their initial defences were built of wood and turf. Caerleon is the best example to be seen today. It was built in *c.* 75 with the usual V-shaped ditch, a turf rampart with a wooden parapet on top and about thirty timber towers. The whole fortress, including the internal buildings, was rebuilt in stone early in the second century. Thereafter, although detachments of the II Legion were usually away on campaign – for example, they helped to build Hadrian's Wall – Caerleon was their regimental base until the dawn of the fourth century. It was quite different for York, Chester, Colchester and Wroxeter. The first three remained important settlements and the medieval walls even encompassed the legionary strongholds. As for Wroxeter, this expanded massively to become the fourth largest town in Britain. Wroxeter – where?

There is, however, one legionary fortress of which little can be seen today, although the site is easy to visit, yet it is probably the most important example for archaeologists. Inchtuthil was typically orthodox in all respects: it was of rectangular shape, built of wood and turf, and covered about 50 acres. As with all legionary strongholds, it was the focal point of a campaign of conquest – in this case Agricola's attempt to subdue the Caledonians. As we know, Agricola swept northwards with nary a backward glance; the thought of retreat never entered his mind. By 83 he was having trouble in bringing the Caledonians to battle, but that did not stop work on the new legionary stronghold. Despite Agricola's recall to Rome at the end of 84, work continued until Inchtuthil was nearly finished, including the bathhouse beside the River Tay. Then came the

THE LUNT (Roman Fort)
Warwickshire O/S map 140 ref. 344753
Directions: Take the A46 south from Coventry city centre. At the A45 (by-pass) roundabout, turn right towards Baginton, turning immediately left and first left again, along Mill Hill. Continue through the village for ½ mile. The Lunt is on the left.

The Lunt was hastily built in AD 60 to house troops recalled from the North Wales campaign to tackle the destructive might unleashed by Boudicca and her Iceni tribesmen. The final showdown, at nearby Mancetter, saw a resounding victory for the highly organized but vastly outnumbered Roman forces.

In its short fifteen years' existence, The Lunt was remodelled three times yet it was never, apparently, a textbook example of a Roman fort. Even so, it would hardly warrant a visit except for two matters, both products of the last twenty-odd years: the great towering wooden double gateway, and the adjoining turf rampart topped by a wooden palisade fence. Of course, both are reconstructions, but after all the ruins one usually sees, most of which severely tax the imagination, one cannot beat the real thing. Here, at The Lunt, it takes little effort to imagine a cavalry troop about to ride out for their next patrol.

Cavalry? Well, inside is a reconstructed *gyrus*, a circular arena with a raised walk-way, where horses were trained: a military riding school, no less. This is the only one known in Britain, yet there may have been others in the immediate vicinity. A reconstructed granary further adds to the realism, this housing a museum.

order to withdraw to the Forth/Clyde isthmus and the Romans, quite deliberately and systematically, destroyed their intended Scottish headquarters, a Chester or York in the making.

This was fortunate for archaeologists as, thanks to years of careful, painstaking excavation, the whole layout has now been mapped. The *Principia*, legate's quarters, officers' quarters, barracks, granaries, stores, workshops and a hospital were all found laid out in the typical grid pattern. It is quite amazing what a seemingly ordinary plot of land, much of which is now a golf course, can hide. Talk about buried treasure!

So, even the legionary fortress was a partly offensive/partly defensive stronghold. In time, once an area became fully assimilated into the Roman order, forts took on the guise of the modern army camp: capable of being defended if necessary, but more important as recruiting and training bases. Eventually, like Wroxeter and Colchester, Chester and York sprouted civilian settlements and the legionary function was diluted. So it is with many military strongholds: they either wither and die, or the military role plays second fiddle to the burgeoning civilian development. Those Roman legionary strongholds must have been quite daunting in their day, though.

The Auxiliary Fort

As with prehistoric strongholds there are hundreds of Roman forts and, one would presume, many more still to be found. As a matter of fact, the term auxiliary fort is not an accurate description for many permanent forts of 2–10 acres or more, as they often housed legionary cohorts, sometimes alongside auxiliaries. Once again, as they were usually in the vanguard, many forts were built by the legions and the size of the subsequent detachment was, naturally, dictated by that of the fort.

ARDOCH (Roman fort)
Perthshire O/S map 57 ref. 839099
Directions: Take the A9 north from Stirling, through Dunblane. Turn left on the A822 and on leaving Braco at a sharp left-hand bend, there is a small parking area. The Roman fort is through a gate on the right of the road.

The Roman earthwork defences at Ardoch are not only among the finest in Britain, but some of the best anywhere. They were very effective when built and remain very impressive, and are rightly renowned, both in general and for their complexity.

As seen today, Ardoch dates from the Antonine era and is one of up to six forts or marching camps hereabouts. Traces of these can still be seen, especially at map refs 840107 and 839109. Two date from *c.* AD 80, the others from the campaigns of Septimus Severus in AD 208/9.

The main legionary fort encloses about 5 acres. The western defences have been decimated by the road and the southern ones eroded, but the inner rampart – built of turf on a stone base, just like the Antonine Wall itself – and ditch are complete for the whole circuit. It is the east side, with five additional ditches enclosed by an outer rampart, that is the most impressive. There is a causeway across the ditches with an off-set outer gateway; another gateway can be seen in the north. The inner rampart would have been surmounted by a wooden palisade fence.

Certainly, the eastern defences were not uniform round the whole fort, for the northern ditches are more widely spaced and have an additional rampart; these, after all, faced hostile territory. The outer rampart is continued round and, with marshy ground to the east and south, the fort would have been a risky place to attack. The interior had the usual array of buildings associated with Roman forts, but little is visible today.

In the 150s Ardoch was the major Roman fort north of the Antonine Wall. Today, it offers a magnificent example of Roman defences which would probably have been well-nigh impregnable.

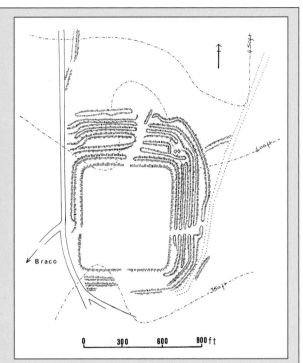

East entrance and causeway, Ardoch.

Some forts developed from campaign camps, especially those that commanded a strategic location, such as a river crossing (Littleborough, Notts.), or high ground (Hod Hill), while others sat centrally in an area of expected tribal unrest (Caernarvon). Newstead fort, on the other hand, was the initial fulcrum for Agricola's Scottish campaign, and later acted as a forward post deep within enemy territory. Agricola gave his Borders forts enough provisions to survive a winter cut off from the main forces, though not all forts endured such a precarious existence.

Not surprisingly, the best surviving examples are to be found in the more remote areas of Roman Britain. The fort within Hod Hill hillfort, Lydsbury Rings, is a rare survivor in southern England. Excavation uncovered most of the

The Romans cleared Burnswark hillfort and used it for siege practice. They also built two forts and three artillery mounds, known as the Three Brethren. These and the south fort, with the small Agricolan fort in the north-east corner, all bask in the evening sunlight.

internal layout, with the usual bits in the usual places, and barrack accommodation for about 600 infantry and 250 cavalry. It was, of course, built of timber and turf and, although accidentally burnt down in AD 51, was probably being run-down by that time anyway; certainly it was never rebuilt. Hod Hill was not alone. The Romans also built forts within the hillforts of Ham Hill, Hembury and may have used Maiden Castle as well. Utilizing native strongholds made economic sense, though it was mostly Vespasian's II Legion that undertook this useful expedient.

Hardknott fort interior, looking south-west.

North entrance and wall, Hardknott fort.

Elsewhere, forts have often survived only because their defences were rebuilt in stone. Thus, High Rochester has some scant remains, while other Borders forts, such as Newstead, Dalswinton and Glenlochar, have little or nothing. On the other hand, where the turf and timber defences were singularly impressive, such as the six ditches at Ardoch, a fort can be worth a visit, but these are few and far between.

INCHTUTHIL (Roman Legionary Fort)
Perthshire O/S map 53 refs (hillfort) 115393 (Roman fort) 125397
Directions: Leave Dunkeld heading east on the A984. Just after Spitalfield, at a sharp left-hand bend, follow the track on the right through the woods for ¾ mile, and a footpath leads to the Roman fort.

This fort is now mostly covered by a golf course, but for the natives of these parts 1,900 years ago there would have been far more to watch out for than a wayward white ball. Here, on this plateau formed by the shifting course of the River Tay, was a Roman legionary fortress from which it was intended to subdue Scotland. Yet, within five years, this massive stronghold had been and gone.

Inchtuthil, or Pinnata Castra, covered fully 50 acres in the classic Roman style. It was to have been the base of the XX Valeria Vitrix legion. Begun in c. AD 83, a stone and wood-faced rampart and ditch provided the defences. Inside was the full complement of wooden buildings for every conceivable need, all to the usual Roman layout. This was, though, no temporary stronghold; the Romans came, and they intended to conquer and stay, but Agricola was recalled to Rome and soon after the Romans departed.

Before they left, they destroyed all that could not be carried. Thus, pottery and glass were ground into the earth. The timber buildings were dismantled and carted off, and about a million iron nails – fully 12 tons in weight – were buried beneath a workshop. Whether they were coming or going, the Romans never did things by halves.

A series of excavations between 1952 and 1965 uncovered the layout of the fort and added much to our knowledge of the Scottish campaigns and how the Roman army worked. A redoubt was discovered beside the River Tay, to the south-east, which enclosed almost 5 acres – twice the size of many forts. A bath-house was also found, while a long ditch further to the west cut off the approach to the fort from that direction; there may have been others.

Despite the size of Inchtuthil, there is little to see today. The ditch is visible at the east and the south rampart is impressive. Other than that, it is a case of using one's imagination. Nevertheless, this is an important site, one which, had it not been for events in Rome itself, might have changed Scotland's history. Had the Romans gone on to conquer the rest of Scotland, the name Inchtuthil might have been impressed on every Scot today, rather in the manner of Stirling Castle.

Almost ½ mile to the south-west lies a small post-Roman hillfort. Five ramparts and ditches enclose an area of 250 ft × 150 ft. This may not have been able to withstand the Romans had they returned, but it has one of the most comprehensive sets of Iron Age defences. These covered a greater area than the hillfort itself, despite only defending the east side; the river afforded protection elsewhere. The inner rampart was faced with stone from the Roman fort, so the natives did gain something after all.

Strange bedfellows, these: the truly great stronghold has all but disappeared, yet the historically insignificant one remains – a bit of an archaeological David and Goliath. Some barrows overlay the Roman earthworks as a rare example of Iron Age burials if, indeed, that is what they are.

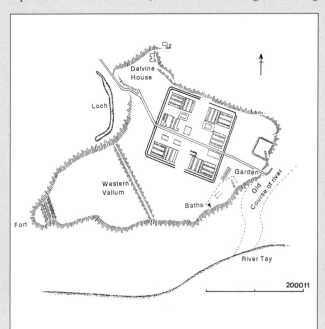

It is another matter with forts built (or rebuilt) in stone, such as Hardknott with its fine wall and detached parade ground; several also have building foundations. Few are better than those near Hadrian's Wall, with Housesteads, Chesters and Chesterholm being well to the fore. South Shields is yet another and, should one wish to see what a timber fort looked like, The Lunt cannot be beaten. At all these, and others, one can gain an impression of the auxiliary fort in its heyday, with troops on patrol and troops relaxing. At Chesterholm a civilian settlement formed an annexe where off-duty soldiers could spend their earnings and enjoy some of the trappings for which they toiled manfully. There was far more to Roman military life than campaigns and patrols.

Replica turret at Chesterholm (Vindolanda) fort.

Thus it was the auxiliary forts, rather than the legionary strongholds, that were the bastions of Roman conquest and rule. From these, they campaigned and exerted their authority, and the forts themselves were an ever-present symbol of Roman power. Later they often became the focal point for a new settlement or town, from Carlisle to Caernarvon and Carmarthen to Chichester; they were no longer offensive but rather, if anything, defensive strongholds. Soldiers were allowed to marry after about AD 200, and then the forts occasionally even merged into the adjoining town, the military presence being little more than that of a modern police force.

As for the soldiers, they might be detachments from a legion or an auxiliary unit, and often served at a fort for several years at a time. In such a case the fort may as well have been a legionary stronghold: it was, to all intents and purposes, their home base. Small wonder then, that civilian settlements grew alongside, as a regular supply of customers is essential to any business. After a while, a fort could meld with its neighbouring settlement, the two becoming largely indivisible, perhaps with the fort even losing its status as a stronghold. For a fort that was built on or near a native settlement, the wheel had come full circle.

Fortlets and Signal Towers

Just as the legionary strongholds and the auxiliary forts were built to a similar layout, it will come as no surprise to find that fortlets and signal towers bore a more-than-passing resemblance to their big-brother strongholds. A fortlet might guard a strategic point, such as a road junction or a pass, or could be used for surveillance. As such, they were self-contained strongholds, perhaps housing a semi-permanent detachment from a fort. Fortlets varied in size. On the one hand, Barburgh Mill housed a full century of troops, but others, such as Durisdeer, were smaller. Usually rectangular or square-shaped, a fortlet's defences comprised a ditch protecting a rampart, and a single entrance. Hadrian's Wall milecastles were similar to fortlets but dispensed with the ditch and had two entrances. There was neither the room, nor the need for a full array of buildings, and the

The interior of the replica timber gateway and rampart at Chesterholm (Vindolanda) fort.

barracks and storerooms ran along the sides of the fortlet. Each was a self-contained fort in miniature.

The signal tower was often still smaller. Not all were fortified, but Agricola built a whole series running north-east from the Ochil Hills to keep an eye on the Caledonians. Built of turf and timber, they were defended by a rampart and ditch. A central watch-tower was the important part, and one assumes that the soldiers' quarters were lower down. Some signal stations were built of stone, as were the turrets on Hadrian's Wall. It is likely that the troops who manned these were stationed at the nearest milecastle, so they are not a direct relation to independent signal stations such as Parkneuk.

Later, in the third and fourth centuries, some larger signal stations were built along the north-east coast of England, perhaps to warn against Anglo-Saxon raiders. They were much bigger than the earlier ones, some having towers up to 100 feet high on a base 30 feet across. They were almost a forerunner of the Norman rectangular keeps, with the soldiers being housed at the lower levels of the tower. Like the fortlets, the towers were defended by a rampart and ditch and, though not specifically strongholds, they fall within our sphere because they were Roman defended works that may have influenced later strongholds. For example, Scarborough Castle contains the stone footings of one of these towers.

Marching or Temporary Camps

Although hundreds of these are known throughout Britain, there are probably many more to be discovered. While on the move a Roman force, ranging from something less than a cohort to legions plus auxiliaries, would set up camp each night. As well as carrying weapons, three days' food and other items of kit, each soldier marched with two stakes. Once the scouts had found and marked out a suitable place for the evening's camp, the main force would arrive and divide, with one group digging, the other guarding.

The marching camp was a simplified version of the fort, and was equally well planned. A ditch was dug and the spoil used to build an inner rampart. The ditch had to be at least 5 feet deep, the rampart 6 feet high. The latter was topped with rows of stakes and there were entrances at each side. Remember, the Roman army was an offensive force; if attacked, they would want to get at the enemy in double-quick time. Tents were lined up in rows, with a large one for the centurion at the head of his men. The officers' tents were in the middle. This followed the same basic layout as the fort, including wide tracks to assist rapid deployment. They took no chances. Each century provided sixteen guards throughout the night. How do we know? Simple, each century of eighty men, had eight tents that housed eight men; the rest were the sentries, presumably on a rota basis.

Such organization, such orderliness, even for an overnight stop. Is it any wonder that the Roman army was such a mighty fighting force? Perhaps we should wonder how the IX Legion was caught napping in its camp by the Caledonians, and had to be rescued by Agricola. To no great surprise then, it is in Scotland where the best marching camps can still be seen. In addition, many forts, such as Ardoch or The Birrens, were built on or near the site of Agricola's temporary forts, and often several overlaid one another.

As with the forts, a marching camp would vary in size depending on the number of soldiers. Quite obviously, if a cohort of about 500 men was on the march, the camp would be a couple of acres or so. At the other extreme, the largest of the four camps at Pennymuir covers fully 42 acres: large enough for two full legions under canvas. There are also four camps not far away at Chew Green (both of these are referred to under Woden Law), and these developed to become something of a semi-permanent staging post in the mid-second century. Wagon parks were provided fronting on to Dere Street, an ancient forerunner of the motorway service station and motel, perhaps?

Siege Practice Camps

How does one tell the difference between a practice siege and the real thing? Quite remarkably, archaeologists have been able to do this for several decades, by the simple expedient of finding ballista-bolts embedded in the rampart, after confirming the hillfort had been cleared. Only two such sites are known with any certainty, Burnswark and Woden Law, but presumably there were others. Practice and training was something the Romans took very seriously – mess

WODEN LAW (Hillfort and Roman Practice Camp)
Roxburghshire O/S map 80 ref. 768125
Directions: Take the minor road from Jedburgh through Oxnam and turn left along the road that follows Oxnam Water, past Swinside Hall. At the junction, turn left for a mile, and then turn right to cross Kale Water at the ford. The track ahead follows Dere Street and once at the top, Woden Law is on the right.

On initial acquaintance, Woden Law gives the impression of being a multi-vallate hillfort; it is, in fact, a product of three distinct phases. The most obvious aspect of the hillfort is its dominating location, yet despite being fully 1,390 ft above sea level, the land to the east would be easy to farm.

A single, grass-covered stone wall enclosed 450 ft × 180 ft to form the first hillfort – the second bank out from the interior. This had entrances in the north and the south-west and was probably built about the mid-first millennium BC. As such, it is similar to hundreds of other Borders hillforts.

Later, possibly in response to an external threat – such as the arrival of Agricola and the Romans *c*. AD 80, a pair of ramparts, with a median ditch, were built outside the original wall on all bar the inaccessible west side. The inner rampart used spoil from the original rampart and was faced by its stone. The outer rampart was of glacis construction revetted with timber. These defences offered greater protection in depth, though the interior was still within range of a javelin or sling-stone. An enclosure was added at the south, possibly for cattle and sheep.

These defences were demolished and the hillfort cleared by the Romans. No matter what pact the Latin invaders had with the Votadini tribe – and Woden Law was probably within the Selgovae tribal area anyway – they would not allow the natives to occupy a such a well-located hillfort. One can easily see how it commands both the Pennymuir camps and Dere Street for miles into the distance.

Surrounding all this are the two banks and three ditches that were the first Roman siege works, built for practice, and not the real thing. These are within easy throwing distance of the hillfort: far too close for comfort. Roman soldiers had a reputation of being brave and fearless fighters, but building such works under a hail of missiles would surely have been beyond even them.

Still further out are two sets of incomplete ditches with a median rampart. These are joined by an east–west traverse, considered to be a later work, possibly following the re-occupation of the Borders in the mid-second century. Near the traverse is a ballista mound, just for good measure. These are an impressive set of siege-works, clearly a bit over the top for what would have been a relatively easy hillfort to capture. A limited excavation in 1950 showed that these siege-works were, indeed, merely for practice.

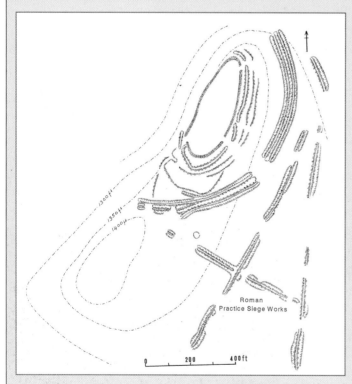

Roman
Practice Siege Works

0   200   400 ft

Returning to the hillfort, at some stage after the Romans left – and possibly as late as the Dark Ages – Woden Law was again refortified. The inner-most wall, another grass-covered mound about 9 ft wide, enclosed about 400 ft × 160 ft within the line of the original wall. There are traces of four round huts in the grassy interior, although they might belong to any of the three phases of native occupation.

Woden Law is a most impressive site, both as a hillfort and for the outstanding Roman siege-works. It is also compact and easy to visit, while still being secluded; it is just the sort of place where one's imagination can run wild. At any minute, one might expect a cohort of Roman soldiers to come marching out of the mist along Dere Street.

about with them at your peril. Artillery platforms are visible at both of these sites. Two forts and a fortlet isolate Burnswark, but Woden Law is merely cut off by banks and ditches; had it been a true siege, the Romans evidently did not rate the natives' defences very highly.

More surprising is the lack of evidence to suggest that hillforts, or other prehistoric strongholds, were defended against the Romans. There were over two thousand of them – not all fortified at the time of the Romans, of course – but only a tiny proportion showed signs of resistance. Did the inhabitants simply capitulate when they saw the mighty Roman forces? Vespasian is supposed to have overcome twenty hillforts; where are they all? Of course, many hillforts could have been used for siege practice once cleared; without finding ballista-bolts, we cannot tell. Yeavering Bell might have had its walls pulled down by the Romans: practice or the real thing? We can be sure of one thing, though, the Roman army was meticulous in its preparations. There must be more siege practice camps out there, somewhere . . .

Forts of the Saxon Shore

On the whole the Roman strongholds referred to in this book, with the exception of those connected with Hadrian's Wall, were built with offence in mind. Even the Antonine Wall and its associated forts acted as a springboard for attacks as much as a defensive barrier. Yes, legionary fortresses were usually built behind a frontier, but they were often the main bases for an offensive campaign. Roman strongholds only became more defensive in purpose when they were rebuilt in stone, and then mostly when associated with an immobile protective barrier.

After the Severan campaigns in Scotland early in the third century, the Romans never again embarked on an expansive attack, except when regaining lost territory or exacting revenge. By the last decades of that century, their soldiers mostly manned static defensive strongholds at the empire's borders, and were beginning to come under increasing attack. In particular, the East Anglian and south-east coasts were susceptible to raids from unconquered territory across the North Sea: the Romans even created an officer to deal with the problem – the Count of the Saxon Shore.

The solution was to build a series of broadly rectangular stone forts – at least nine, and maybe eleven – from Brancaster in north-west Norfolk to Portchester in Hampshire, and possibly Carisbrooke on the Isle of Wight. There is no doubt that these forts were defensive strongholds. Garrisoned and possibly supported by a fleet to deter raids up the many creeks and estuaries of the long coastline, for about a century they had a fair degree of success. The Saxon Shore forts dispensed with the usual layout of the earlier forts, despite generally retaining a regular plan. The stone

A bastion added to the Saxon Shore fort at Burgh Castle after construction of the wall had begun.

The still impressive western entrance to the Roman fort at Pevensey Castle.

The south wall, bastions and ditch at Portchester Castle.

A replica it might be, but the north gate at Cardiff Castle shows just how formidable were permanent Roman defences. With its Norman motte, medieval castle and extravagant nineteenth-century restoration, Cardiff Castle is the crowning glory at the heart of the Welsh capital city.

wall still had an external ditch but, as if to emphasize the change from offence to defence, there were far fewer entrances. If circular bastions were not originally built, they were soon added, both at corners and along the sides; some were clearly strengthened to carry artillery. This was hardly the work of a confident army looking to attack at every opportunity, rather the strategy of an army expecting to be attacked.

Despite being built of stone, not all the Saxon Shore forts have survived. Brancaster is barely visible on the surface, Walton Castle is now under the sea, much of Bradwell and Reculver forts have been eroded away, Dover is under the town and Lympne has mostly been lost. Four survive to a decent extent, though, and three of these were comprehensively refortified, well over five hundred years after they were first abandoned – which says quite a bit about their viability. The Saxon Shore forts were not entirely unique in Roman Britain either: Cardiff also had a similar contemporary fort that was probably a naval supply depot, but they signal a change from an expanding empire to one on the wane.

But were the Saxon Shore forts really built to fend off marauding bands of brigands? One theory contends they were the work of a Belgic mariner, an almost 'official' Roman pirate called Carausius. Taking advantage of Imperial weakness, he ruled Britain for seven years from about 290, even going so far as to title himself emperor. He rather expected that the 'real' emperor, Maximian, would hardly let

SILCHESTER (Roman Town)
Hampshire O/S map 175 ref. 640625
Directions: Leave Basingstoke on the A340 and turn right at Pamber End. Take the road to Bramley Corner and turn left to the site, by St Mary's Church.

For about six hundred years, until the mid-sixth century, Silchester, or Calleva Atrebatum, was an important town. It was probably begun in the first century BC as the capital of the Atrebates tribe. The defences enclosed about 230 acres, and coins were minted there. Little of the pre-Roman town remains.

Not only did the Romans establish Silchester as the civitas capital of the Atrebates, but it also became an important junction for several roads. These ran from London to Exeter, Dorchester and Winchester/Bitterne, and others went to St Albans, Cirencester and Dorchester-on-Thames.

Towards the end of the second century, Silchester was reduced to its current 107 acres, and a rampart and ditch were built along the line of the present wall. This wall, which is virtually complete for its whole circuit, was built in the mid-third century, quite possibly a time when many towns did likewise – for defence not show.

There are the usual four main gateways, plus three postern gates. The masonry reinforced the earth rampart; there is no finer Roman town wall in Britain. Silchester was extensively excavated in the late nineteenth century, and its grid street plan was mapped, though it is not visible today.

Nobody knows why Silchester was abandoned or, perhaps more pertinently, why it was never extensively reused in later times, as many important Roman towns were. Certainly, it is our good fortune that it has survived. An amphitheatre, able to seat about 2,700 people, can be seen outside the east gate. This might give a fairly accurate indication of the town's population. Silchester's impressive wall still rises almost to its original 20 ft in places. The many artefacts are mostly in Reading Museum.

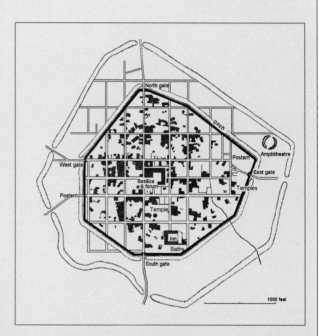

Entrance to the Roman town of Calleva Atrebatum, Silchester.

sleeping dogs lie and would try to regain his lost province at the earliest opportunity. Hence the building of the Saxon Shore forts, *against* the main Roman forces. Fact, or a glib historical theory? There is no proof either way, of course, but history favours the assumption that the forts were built by the Romans against Anglo-Saxon raiders. However appealing the story of Carausius, this was certainly the use to which the forts were put in the fourth century.

Walled Towns

Many, though not all, civilian settlements that grew alongside, or even supplanted, Roman forts were eventually defended by a wall. Some, such as Lincoln, which was a colony for retired soldiers, were understandably so protected, but more interesting are those towns that were purpose-built as the capital of a *civitas*, or former tribal area. Thus, we have Winchester – Venta Belgarum, capital of the Belgae; Dorchester – Durnovaria, capital of the Durotriges; and Canterbury – Durovernum Cantiacorum, capital of the Cantiaci. There are few remains of the Roman occupation at any of these towns, not surprisingly, but there were also others.

Silchester – Calleva Atrebatum, capital of the Atrebates, and Caerwent – Venta Silurum, capital of the Silures, are fine surviving examples of these new towns, intended to seduce the natives with the Roman way of life. Silchester was built on the site of a native *oppidum*, but Caerwent, like Dorchester and others, probably occupied a fresh site several decades after the Claudian invasion; stone

---

BLACKSTONE EDGE (Roman Road)
Lancashire O/S map 109 ref. 973171
Directions: Leave Littleborough heading east on the A58. After about 2 miles, a minor road joins on the right. The Roman road can be seen going straight up the hill as the A58 bends to the left.

Doubt has been raised about the authenticity of the stone setts but, assuming the surface is Roman, then this is the finest stretch of Roman road in Britain. The stone setts are in remarkably good condition (too good?) and the surface is about 15 ft wide. There is a wide groove down the middle in which a cart's brake pole ran to steady its descent. Although partially overgrown in the summer, this road is easy to reach and, like no other, shows just how Roman roads looked.

The Roman road at Blackstone Edge.

WADE'S CAUSEWAY (Roman Road)
Yorkshire (North Riding) O/S map 94 refs 793938 to 812988
Directions: From Grosmont, take the minor road south-west and then south to cross Wheeldale Moor. Once over Wheeldale Gill, a signpost on the left, after a mile or so, locates the road.

Although its route can be followed across the North Yorkshire moors, it is the mile or more of exposed stone foundations on Wheeldale Moor that are the most interesting. This is not quite so visually appealing as Blackstone Edge, but is considerably longer. Wade's Causeway is also usually peaceful, so one can easily imagine the moors echoing to the tramp of marching feet. That is somewhat ironic, as the point of departure and destination of the road remain unknown.

CAERWENT (Walled Town)
Monmouthshire O/S map 171 ref. 469905
Directions: From Caerleon, take the B4236 to the A48, heading east. This by-passes the village. The road runs through the east and west gates.

Soon after defeating the Silures tribe, the Romans built the civitas capital of Caerwent, or Venta Silurum. This was a relatively modest town of 44 acres, but still had the usual full array of civic buildings, baths and temple associated with Roman towns. Some of their foundations can still be seen.

Along with other towns, Caerwent gained a turf wall and ditch *c.* 200, probably when Clodius Albinus took most of Britain's Roman army with him in his failed attempt to become emperor. These earthwork defences were replaced by the current stone walls in the third century, and the polygonal bastions were added a century later; these were built to hold artillery.

South wall and bastions, Caerwent.

Caerwent has one of the best circuits of Roman town walls to be seen in Britain, and easily the best in Wales. It is complete from the east to west gates, via the south gate – the only one that remains to any extent. While the facing stones are often missing, long sections are intact to remind us that, at many Roman walls, it is mostly the central core we see today, and not the finished article. Clearly, this wall would not have been out of place a thousand years later.

walls were added a generation or so later. These were not military strongholds but defended settlements, rather like many hillforts. It is likely that the gates were closed at night, and if one was late getting back, well, it was just like college days – only I dare say the punishment for getting caught climbing in was a good deal more severe than a dressing-down from the Master.

These towns were not necessarily rectangular in shape, but had a grid-pattern street layout with the main civic buildings in the centre. There was the usual gateway facing each of the four winds, and possibly the odd postern gate, much like many medieval town walls which often, initially at least, followed the line of the Roman walls. The wall-walk would have been an ideal place from which to keep an eye on the townsfolk, even if there was little chance of an external threat. As with many medieval town walls, few Roman walls have survived owing to the restrictions they imposed as the town expanded, but Caerwent still has long sections of wall, including the fourth-century bastions. Silchester is even more fortunate, retaining almost the full circuit, and its interior has not been built over. This has provided the best example of a Roman street plan, although there is little to be seen on the ground today.

Newport Arch, Lincoln, is Britain's only surviving Roman gateway over a road.

COLCHESTER (Roman Walled Town and Norman Castle)
Essex O/S map 168
Directions: The Roman walls are best at the west and north. The castle is within the castle park. The Lexden earthworks (Iron Age) are along Straight Road, ref. 965246, and Bluebottle Grove, ref. 965245.

The proud local boast is that Colchester is the oldest town in England. Debatable perhaps, but there is little doubt that it is one of the longest permanently inhabited sites in the country.

A couple of miles from the town centre are the Lexden earthworks, the inner-most of a series of banks and ditches that defended the Trinovantian and later Catuvellaunian oppidum in the late Iron Age. Other earthworks can be seen at several locations to the west and south of the town, and the O/S map will help locate them.

The oppidum was mostly to the west of the later Roman town, and was much bigger to boot. On the other hand, the buildings were probably the usual wooden thatched huts, so this tribal capital would not have been so substantial or impressive as the Roman town.

In AD 43 the Emperor Claudius visited Colchester during his brief stay in Britain, and a legionary base was established, to be followed by a colonia, or settlement for retired soldiers. For a few years the new town of Camulodunum was the capital of the expanding Roman Britannia, but in AD 60 it was sacked by Boudicca and her rampaging, revengeful Iceni tribe. London and St Albans soon suffered the same fate. Though rebuilt, Camulodunum never regained its former status: that mantle passed to Londinium.

Still, that did not stop Colchester getting a stone wall early in the second century. Fully 108 acres are enclosed by this wall, of which considerable proportions, somewhat surprisingly, still survive. Standing, in places, beside the roar of a dual carriageway, elsewhere poking between houses, even having buildings built against and on to it, the wall's circuit is far from complete, yet it makes for a fascinating journey. Most impressive is the Balkerne Gate, at the west. The remains of the north portal are now beneath a pub but, though a mere shadow of its once great self, the southern arch still stands. It might be quite modest – certainly in comparison to its former glory – but, except for Lincoln's magnificent Newport Arch, it is all we have.

In the centre of the Roman colonia lay a great temple dedicated to the Emperor Claudius. It was here that a final stand was made against the marauding Iceni, but to no avail, as all were slaughtered. On that site now stands the largest Norman castle keep, not only in England, but in Europe. Measuring 152 ft × 111 ft and now with its upper storeys missing, it resembles an Italian basilica. This appearance is assisted by the use of Roman materials, and also the manner of its restoration for use as a worthy museum.

Of particular interest is the outline of battlements in the stonework at first-floor level. This is no fancy decoration, but might have been a hasty improvisation to defend the unfinished keep, begun before 1080. England was then far from being a settled Garden of Eden so far as the Normans were concerned. The recently ousted Danes were keen to regain lost ground, while even the local Saxons might just have sensed an opportunity for revenge.

What a mighty stronghold this royal castle must have been. Like the similar Tower of London, it was used as a prison in the later Middle Ages. Though it escaped slighting after the Civil War, it was sold for demolition in 1683 but, as luck would have it, the contractor went bankrupt before the job was complete. Today, its baileys resound to the massed bands of the Army at the annual tattoo: a quite fitting retirement for a once-mighty stronghold, in a still-busy garrison town.

The surviving half of the Balkerne Gate, Colchester.

The Roman west wall looking towards the Balkerne Gate.

CONCLUSION

Having worked our way through Britain's main categories of Roman strongholds, we can observe a distinct change from the offensive, designed to expand the empire, through the containing, intended to secure the empire and to act as a base to go forward should the desire arise, to the purely defensive, indicating the empire in decline and retreat. Naturally, the more negative the planned use of a stronghold, the greater its capacity for defence, and some of these are today the most visually impressive sites from almost four hundred years of Roman rule.

One does not usually expect a static fortress to be a means of offence. Yet this was clearly the case for the Romans, especially in the first century AD. A campaign camp and even a fort could be defended, but its purpose was to support an attacking campaign. This was quite different from the use to which our native strongholds were put – they really were defensive. That some Roman offensive strongholds evolved into defensive citadels is beyond doubt, while others became symbols of the power and might of the invaders, serving to deter any opposition.

Today, the remains of Roman strongholds often appear less defensively capable than the best of the native hillforts. Yet hillforts were no match for the Romans. This was entirely due to the discipline of the Roman army. Time and again, history has shown how a well-organized army can overcome a ramshackle force of far greater size. Discipline, method and structure in everything, and especially in stronghold-building, was the order of the Roman day. For innovation, economy of effort and suitability for its intended task, the Roman stronghold has few equals. It might not always look the most impressive, but none was more effective.

CHAPTER 3
THE DARK AGES

As the fourth century progressed, the iron grip in which the Romans once held Britannia slackened with each passing year. The incandescent Roman candle that had illuminated the ever-widening path from prehistory first flickered, then died until, by the end of the century, it shone no more and Britain was plunged into a new age; one darker and bleaker than anything known for over a thousand years. Or was it?

Thanks to the archaeological excavation and analytical expertise of the last few decades, the former impenetrability of the ensuing Dark Ages has been lightened a touch. It now, more or less, equates to a deepening squall on the filthiest of winter mornings: gloomy perhaps, but with the prospect of a slight improvement. Indeed, by the time the seventh century turned the corner, distinct shafts of light begin to penetrate the murk, these becoming ever-brighter towards the end of the first millennium and beyond.

Britannia, by AD 400, was no longer a single Roman province, but four or five of these forming a diocese. Even so, the Roman troops gradually withdrew from our shores, as the empire was squeezed on all fronts. By 407 the last soldiers had gone, and a request to Rome for assistance against the increasingly frequent raids from across the North Sea met with a blank response: tough! What happened next is far from certain, but it seems that life carried on with England, at least, being divided roughly along the lines of the former *civitates*. Certainly there was the Kingdom of Dumnonia, possibly based on the Dumnonii *civitas*; there were probably others. These *civitates*-based kingdoms probably embraced many aspects of Roman life for two centuries after the Roman withdrawal, such as

Reconstruction of a Saxon farm.

The east Wansdyke winds
its way westwards along
the Wiltshire downs.

Roman law, the use of Latin, Roman measurements and so forth. Britannia most certainly did not simply descend spinelessly into violent chaos. Even in the south-east and East Anglia, the two regions most affected by raiding, several decades passed before the interlopers were able to impose their will.

Of the possible five Roman provinces that covered England and Wales, only two were initially seriously threatened by the raids by Angles, Saxons and Jutes. Left to fend for themselves, the wealthy Romano-Britons, and those Celts who had not wholeheartedly embraced the empire, hired mercenaries to do their fighting for them. For a short while this unheroic tactic worked, but these foreigners rather liked what they saw and decided to stay.

In Scotland, the Roman impact was rather less assured. The Picts ruled the roost north of the Forth/Clyde isthmus and had some, albeit modest, influence as far south as Galloway. Even so, though hardly plagued by raiders from mainland Europe, members of Ulster's Scotti tribe, had already landed in remotest Argyll: the nascent Dalriada was born. Pictland was to be increasingly threatened.

Wales was not without its problems either, and matters were soon to degenerate much further. As the infamous Angles, Saxons and Jutes migrated to England in ever-greater numbers, pushing the Romano-Britons and Celts steadily westwards, so the inhabitants of Wales faced immense pressures. It is not known how many retreating Britons descended on Wales, the West Country, Cumberland, Galloway and Strathclyde, but that there was a less than enthusiastic migration is beyond doubt. On top of that, Britons from Galloway found their way into North Wales, while there was considerable movement from Ireland to both North and South Wales. In other words, Wales was something of a cosmopolitan melting-pot of Celts and others from all parts of Britain and Ireland, and nothing like the homogeneous land some would have us believe it to be.

SOUTH CADBURY CASTLE (Reused Hillfort and Saxon *Burh*)
Somerset O/S map 183 ref. 629253
Directions: Leave the A303 west of Wincanton, at the turning for South and North Cadbury, and continue into the village. Castle Lane leads up to the hillfort.

This outstanding hill, rising to 500 ft, has been home to man for almost 4,500 years. The Iron Age settlement was the longest established, but it was the Dark Ages refortification that gives this hill its foremost claim to fame. This is the favoured location for none other than King Arthur's Camelot.

Cadbury's distinguished past came to light following excavations undertaken by Professor Leslie Alcock, from 1966 to 1970. This was one of the more extensive hillfort excavations ever undertaken but, even so, only about 6 per cent of the enclosed 18 acres was excavated; that, more than anything, puts the limitations of excavation results into perspective. The hill was first occupied *c.* 3300 BC, as an undefended settlement on the summit plateau. Once abandoned, it was apparently not occupied again until *c.* 1000 BC, but may then have been continuously inhabited from then until Roman times. The first defences were a box rampart and ditch along the line of the current inner rampart, built *c.* 500 BC, by which time the community was well established.

Thereafter, the defences were refurbished on five or six occasions, at times showing considerable signs of neglect. By *c.* 200 BC the defences comprised a massive stone-faced inner rampart and three outer glacis ramparts, each having a ditch, with entrances in the south-west and the north-east. These defences are up to 400 ft wide and without a doubt were some of the most formidable at any hillfort. Just the thing for a bustling trading centre.

At the turn of the millennium the defences were refurbished again. The south-west entrance was rebuilt, having become turf-covered and seemingly abandoned. Apparently only a temple and its processional way stood at the summit. The hillfort might have become a religious centre, rather than a settlement.

Even so, by the time Vespasian and the Roman II Legion arrived, *c.* AD 43, the population was fairly high once again and the defences had been refurbished. A little later, probably after Boudicca's revolt, some thirty people, including women and children, were massacred at the south-west gate. Their bodies were left where they fell, to became a gruesome larder for wild animals. Ten years later their remains were covered and the Romans erected a camp within the hillfort while they dismantled the latter's defences. Thereafter, Cadbury Castle was undefended, but many coins of the third and fourth centuries attest to its later use.

For many hillforts, that would have been the end, but Cadbury Castle was refortified on two further occasions. After *c.* 450, the inner rampart was rebuilt with a timber-frame and stone reveting. The south-west gateway was restored and its track metalled. A hall, measuring 60 ft × 35 ft, and much pottery – including some of Mediterranean origin – dating to that period were found. By the scale of contemporary settlements, this was clearly of some importance and it lasted for several generations.

Was this the fabled Camelot? One may or may not believe the various legends, but the scale of the refortification, though modest by Iron Age standards, suggests that Cadbury Castle could have been the headquarters of an Arthurian type of warrior-leader. One, perhaps, of regional omnipotence?

Cadbury Castle enjoyed yet another comeback during the reign of Ethelred the Unready, 978–1016, when it became a Saxon *burh*. It had a 20 ft wide stone-revetted earth rampart, and there was also a mint that produced silver coins from 1009 to 1020. This might overstate the importance of Cadbury Castle as many *burhs* had a mint. Cadbury was destroyed in about 1020, possibly on the orders of King Canute.

It is apt that, for a hillfort with such a distinguished past, it should enjoy a prominent present, and its defences remain formidable to this day. This could be one of the most fabled sites in history. It is the only contender for the title of Camelot that can provide definite proof of a substantial occupation from the time of the brave King Arthur.

KING ARTHUR TO THE RESCUE

Perhaps it is just as well that we know so little about how bleak the fifth century was for the Britons. As the Angles and Saxons continued to arrive in greater numbers, eventually with their families in tow, so the natives gradually ceded land to the usurpers. Then, at about the turn of the sixth century, the Saxon advance was firmly halted, perhaps even driven back for a generation or two.

This reversal of fortune has long been popularly attributed to the legendary exploits of the mythical Arthur, King of all the Britons. Well, that was myth for a start, while the sword in the stone, the quest for the Holy Grail and much else is closer to cartoon than reality. On the other hand . . . There is no doubt, according to the few written accounts from the early Dark Ages, that the Saxon advance ran out of steam at about that time. Was the east Wansdyke a frontier built to prevent the Saxons from advancing up the Thames valley? A possible site for the battle of Mount Badon, which the Britons won, is Liddington Castle hillfort, just south of the Ridgeway. Nearby, at Barbury Castle, an inconclusive battle was fought in 556 but thereafter the Saxons pushed west in earnest again. This time there was no King Arthur – real, legend, myth or otherwise – to stop them.

Genuine hard evidence to support Arthur's existence is as tenuous as that for the Yeti. South Cadbury Castle hillfort was heavily refortified in the period 475–550, this being so unusual that, when it was excavated, the archaeologist thought it was probably the base for a chief of more than local stature. More recently, however, it has been claimed that Arthur's Camelot was in Shropshire. Nevertheless, it seems that the West Country Britons were more than able to put the wind up the Saxons for a while. Their leader's exploits were undoubtedly heroic in comparison with other apparently feeble attempts at resistance. Small wonder, then, that all over Britain beleaguered natives also dreamed of having such a courageous and daring leader. Perhaps that is why there are monuments and Arthurian legends all the way from Scotland to Cornwall, via Wales.

Resistance could not last and as the sixth century drew to its close so a dark veil was drawn over the last remnants of Celtic England; the land was soon divided into the seven embryonic Anglo-Saxon kingdoms of the Heptarchy. Indeed, by the seventh century the invaders flourished in Northumbria, Mercia, East Anglia, East, South and West Saxons, and Kent. In Wales the eclectic racial cauldron

---

TINTAGEL
Cornwall O/S map 200 ref. 051892
Directions: From the village centre, a steep walk leads out to the headland.

As the supposed birthplace of the legendary King Arthur, thanks to the works of Geoffrey of Monmouth, no Dark Age stronghold has a more popular appeal. People travel from all over the world to visit the sites of the Arthurian legends, and nowhere is more important than Tintagel.

There it stands, a mighty towering headland, pounded by the Atlantic waves and the whirling winds. The gaunt ruins almost mystically beckon one onwards and upwards towards them. Once there, the defences must surely be those familiar to the young Arthur. One can imagine the boy running about in gay abandon on the summit, surveying all that one day would be his.

Unfortunately not. The outer castle defences are thirteenth century, the inner ones a hundred or so years older. The remains from the Dark Ages consist of low walls, once thought to be cells and other parts of a fifth-century monastery, but more recently considered to be a palace of sorts. The remnants of the inner curtain wall crown the Dark Age bank and ditch. Surely those of a stronghold, one might think; quite possibly, but do not be too hasty to draw conclusions.

The notion of Tintagel being a Dark Age stronghold is far from certain – yet what an exciting prospect! The quantity of imported pottery from the fifth/sixth centuries suggests a rather grand existence for monks, and a royal household is the current fancied theory. As for a Norman/medieval castle? There are certainly better examples, even in Cornwall. However, add the dramatic location into the equation, especially the romantic ruins, and Tintagel comes into its own. Despite all the indeterminate evidence, Tintagel might well have been a Dark Age stronghold and, if so, then perhaps the legend is right and Arthur really was born and grew up there.

occasionally boiled over, while in Scotland there was ever more friction between the Picts and the Dalriadans in the north, and between the Picts and Britons of Strathclyde further south. In a land divided to a greater extent than at any time since the Iron Age, there was, though, one increasingly unifying force: Christianity.

By the mid-sixth century, St Columba had reached Iona, St Ninian had been and gone in Galloway, and Christianity had spread into northern England. At the end of the century St Augustine landed in Kent, and the extent to which Christianity had flourished during the latter years of Roman rule was soon to be completely eclipsed. Groups of monks formed monasteries to spread the word and, one by one, the various kingdoms embraced Christianity. Of course, religion has never prevented war, and while the mantle of importance passed from Northumbria to Mercia as the eighth century dawned, so the Catholic Church of Rome firmly extinguished the light of the Celtic Church. Wessex grew ever stronger, and King Offa of Mercia initiated the building of a barrier between his kingdom and that of the unruly peoples of Wales, but on the whole a relative peace descended over the land we now call England.

In Scotland the Angles banished the Britons from Galloway, while the Picts ruled to the north of the Forth/Clyde isthmus. Yet it was not all downhill for the Picts from that point on; by about 850 Kenneth MacAlpin of Dalriada had united the Picts and the Scotti, and a new nation had begun to take shape.

THE COMING OF THE VIKINGS

Britain was becoming a steadily more settled land until, in 789 a relatively minor but bloody raid on the Isle of Portland brought the Saxons into conflict for the first time with Nordic raiders – the Vikings had arrived. This was the precursor of another 250 years of increasing violence. In 793 they returned to sack, burn and loot the monastery at Lindisfarne, and to put the rather pathetic, undefended and weak monks to the most horrific and gruesome of deaths. Whatever the influence of the Anglo-Saxon, Danish and Norwegian languages on English, the words prisoner and mercy did not emanate from the Viking vocabulary.

While there was an apparent paucity of stronghold building against the Angles and Saxons, apart from some refortifying of hillforts, the fighting at that time was mild compared to the venomous violence of the Vikings. Killing and looting were almost a sport to them, and they embraced both with almost demonic vigour. Their longships would quietly slip up an estuary, and between thirty and fifty heavily armed men would disembark from each ship and attack their target in the most frenzied of assaults: a Dark Ages' blitzkrieg. Gathering their loot, the Vikings would then depart and sail back to Scandinavia. It may seem a risky operation to us, but Britain provided much easier pickings than long-haul trading expeditions to the Mediterranean.

These were generally small-scale raids, involving hundreds rather than thousands of men. Then, in the mid-ninth century, long-established Viking trade routes to the Middle and Far East were severely disrupted. Suddenly, the relatively prosperous island of Britain looked an even more attractive proposition. Judging

General view of the Iron
Age Castle Haven Dun,
expanded in the Dark Ages.

by the experiences of the previous fifty years or so, it was, in any case, ripe for the taking.

Raids resumed in earnest in about 840, though more as large-scale, full-blooded assaults. The island groups of Orkney, Shetland and the Hebrides soon succumbed, probably resulting in the reoccupation, or indeed building, of duns. It was all to no avail, as these peripheral islands not only provided the Vikings with land, but were ideally placed havens en route to settlements in Iceland and Ireland. The Hebrides were ceded to the Scottish crown by the Treaty of Perth in 1280, following the Battle of Largs, but despite the Orkney Islands coming under Scottish lordship from the thirteenth century, these and the Shetland Islands did not finally return to the Scottish crown until 1468/9. They were under Norse rule longer than they have been under Scottish or British. Little wonder that Shetland islanders get upset if you call them Scots!

While the arrival of the Vikings was little more than a nuisance to the peoples of mainland Scotland, their impact in England was little short of devastating. The earlier wounds inflicted on the inhabitants of the east coast were as nothing compared with the increased frequency and scale of the raids during the mid-ninth century. This culminated in the Vikings over-wintering on the Isle of Thanet, in 850. Within twenty-five years, or about an average lifetime, the Vikings had overrun East Anglia, Northumbria and Mercia, and had forced the ruler of Wessex, King Alfred, to take refuge at Athelney, deep in the Somerset marshes – burnt cakes and all.

KING ALFRED THE GREAT

If ever a country needed an heroic warrior, this was it. Unlike Arthur, though, Alfred the Great was a true hero, at least in Wessex. There was nothing mythical about him either, although legend has over-embellished some of his deeds and exploits. From the humiliation of being a fugitive within his own lands, hiding from the Danes in the marshes of Athelney, Alfred fought back and won a great victory at Edington in 878. This was the first time the Vikings had been comprehensively defeated, and an uneasy truce, or at least a wary and cautious stand-off, ensued. Eventually, the land to the north and east of the old Watling Street was ceded to the Vikings, becoming known as the Danelaw, while that to the south and west was Saxon Wessex, with Alfred as its undisputed ruler.

True to his reputation of being a wise king, Alfred used this hiatus to instigate a series of measures to curtail Viking terror, if not forever, at least for a century or so. Despite the almost constant state of war at that time, Alfred's army was not a professional force. It was not unusual, even until recent times, for a leader to be sitting smugly at the head of a great army one day, only to find his forces hopelessly depleted the next – harvest time had arrived. Fully aware of this tendency, even when engaged in a fight for the very existence of his kingdom, Alfred took only half the available men to fight, the rest stayed behind to work the land.

Secondly, though with perhaps less effect than is often assumed, Alfred built a fleet of ships to deter sporadic Viking raids. This was not a true navy and it seems as though his ships might have regularly come off second-best in a skirmish, but they acted as a deterrent. Finally, and most importantly, Alfred created a web of fortified *burhs*, or stronghold towns, throughout Wessex, similar to those of Offa's Mercia.

Eventually, there was a fortified *burh* every 20 miles or so – or, in other words, a stronghold within a day's walk of every village. Here, probably for the first time since Roman days, was a series of new and reused strongholds. Not all had brand new defences, though. For example, South Cadbury was a *burh* within a former hillfort and Dark Age fortress, and Portchester Castle was also reused. When the Vikings next decided that Wessex was ripe for the taking, in the 890s, the combination of the standing army, Alfred's ships and the *burhs* helped to ensure that Wessex survived.

The next century saw large tracts of the Danelaw recaptured by Alfred's successors; even the Welsh pitched in. The Vikings were reduced to undertaking small raids again until, from 991, a marked increase in the scale of the raids forced the unfortunate Ethelred the Unready to try to buy them off with his infamous Danegeld. To no great surprise, the Danish king realized that if he could get away with the ruse once, and England was able and willing to pay for peace, he could do so again, and again, and again. In the end, though he was neither crowned nor fully acknowledged, England briefly had a king by the name of Sweyn Forkbeard. Thereafter, until 1042, England was part of the Danish empire, but then enjoyed a brief twenty-four years of Saxon rule in a united land. The Dark Ages' story had become increasingly bright and merry until, quite suddenly, its parchment was to be set ablaze once again, when the Normans, or French Vikings, invaded in 1066.

STRONGHOLDS OF THE DARK AGES

Reused Hillforts

Recalling the extensive unrest that swept through England in the fifth and sixth centuries, one might assume that former hillforts would have been widely reused as defended refuges. Increasingly evidence seems to back this proposition, at least in southern England and the West Country. No doubt a modest renovation of the ramparts, perhaps merely adding a palisade fence and clearing the ditch, would have afforded some degree of protection in those turbulent times. Major battles were also fought at, or in the immediate vicinity of, several former hillforts which, one might assume, formed a useful stronghold for one side or another.

Rebuilding took place on an altogether grander scale at South Cadbury Castle. A major refortification took place in the late fifth century, with a new inner rampart using stone revetting quarried from the ruined buildings. A long hall has been found dating to this period, along with Mediterranean pottery. All the indications point to this being the stronghold of someone of considerable importance. A King Arthur figure? Well, just maybe.

As much as anything, it is surface evidence of rectangular huts within a fortified site that denotes its use, or reuse, in the Dark Ages. Chun Castle hillfort is one where these can be clearly seen, even overlaying the circular Iron Age huts. More often than not, though, the reuse of hillforts – or even duns and, just possibly, brochs – was usually as an open settlement. Even when refortified, as at South Cadbury Castle, the new defences were usually inferior to those of the Iron Age. Hillforts and duns may have served as temporary refuges, but for true strongholds from the early Dark Ages, we must look elsewhere.

CASTLE DORE (Reused Hillfort)
Cornwall O/S map 200 ref. 103548. Tristan Stone ref. 112522
Directions: Leave Fowey on the B3269 towards Lostwithiel. Castle Dore lies immediately east of the road just after the staggered junction with the Tywardreath–Golant road. Go through a gate into the field.

A circular rampart and ditch, the former rising to 8 ft high, enclose some 1¼ acres; an outer rampart and ditch, which have since succumbed to the ravages of the plough, offered further protection. The outer defences are close to the inner ones, but open out to form a barbican at the entrance. At one time, two banks defined a passage between the outer and inner gateways and a wooden bridge spanned the rebuilt, in-turned entrance.

The hillfort dates to the middle Iron Age, probably the fourth century BC, and was further strengthened in the first century BC. At that time the inner rampart was heightened and revetted in stone. Circular huts were clustered near the entrance, some having been rebuilt.

Castle Dore was abandoned early in the Roman era, but was reoccupied for several generations in the Dark Ages, probably during the fifth and sixth centuries. Apart from a modest refurbishment of the defences, two long halls, one of them 90 ft long, and a rectangular kitchen were built. The 7 ft Tristan Stone was found within the hillfort: Tristan was the son of Mark, King of Dumnonia, of which Cornwall was part. This adds credence to the suggestion that Castle Dore was his stronghold home. Myth, legend or fact?

Clearly, Castle Dore was a Dark Age stronghold of not inconsiderable importance. It is a dominating site, which explains its reuse. Its good location came to the fore again in 1644 when it was used as a temporary refuge during the skirmish for nearby Lostwithiel during the Civil War.

LIDDINGTON CASTLE (Reused Hillfort)
Wiltshire O/S map 174 ref. 208797
Directions: From Swindon, head south on the A345. Turn left just after the B4005 at Chisledon. This is the original Ridgeway track. After ¾ mile, a path on the right leads up to the hillfort.

Like Barbury Castle, Liddington Castle commands the Ridgeway track, as well as long stretches of downland and, most impressively, the Thames valley below. It is also oval-shaped, though its 7½ acres are defended by a single rampart and ditch, with a south-east entrance. The similarities of the two former Iron Age hillforts go even further, for Liddington Castle was refortified in the Dark Ages, when its ramparts were heightened, and it too might have witnessed a great battle.

The battle of Mons Badonicus, at which King Arthur scored a decisive victory over the Anglo-Saxons in the late fifth century, might have been fought hereabouts. Until a few centuries ago, Liddington Castle was known as Badbury Castle, after the nearest village. It is unlikely that Badbury – 'the hill country of Badon' – just referred to the hillfort and its immediate surroundings, even with the important junction of Roman roads from Winchester and Silchester to Cirencester nearby. However, Mons Badonicus might also be named after the land surrounding the village of Baydon, 3 miles to the south-east, which is the highest in Wiltshire.

None of this conjecture proves anything of course but certainly Liddington Castle was an ideal stronghold from which to control this strategically important area. To all intents and purposes, it looks like any other well-preserved hillfort. It was occupied from the sixth century BC, abandoned later, and reoccupied and refortified in the early Dark Ages. As such, it remains one of the finest strongholds visible from that period today.

Reused Roman Fortifications

Perhaps most surprising of all was the apparent tendency to abandon the Roman towns and, in particular, not to refortify their walls or forts in times of trouble. The Angles and Saxons preferred open villages and, as they forced the Britons westwards, or at least came to dominate the country, so these became the usual type of settlement. As far as defences went, a palisade fence sufficed: this would not have looked too much out of place in late Neolithic times.

By the mid-fifth century, except for some towns and the former Saxon Shore Forts, there were few Roman sites capable of acting as strongholds. Apart from the odd legionary fortress, such as York or Caerleon, many older forts were built of turf and timber and would need extensive rebuilding – they may as well reuse a hillfort. There were exceptions, though. A Viking army briefly camped within the old walls at Chester in order to evade the Saxons, while in the ninth and tenth centuries some towns expanded to reuse land within the former Roman walls, as at London and Canterbury. Portchester Castle became a Saxon *burh*, but the only town where the former Roman defences successfully withstood a Viking raid was Rochester in 884.

Quite why Roman towns were not refortified is a bit of a mystery. One theory contends that perhaps the art of building in stone, either drystone or using mortar, had been lost – but then, many stone churches survive from the mid-Dark Ages. A little more realistic is the movement of people away from towns to villages, but by the eighth, and certainly the ninth centuries the growth of towns was in full swing again. On the other hand, it might simply be due to the changes in weapon technology, society and warfare in general.

On the whole, in order to defend a Roman town adequately, a degree of organization and wealth were needed to man the walls effectively. Once the Romans departed, not only was society left with a power vacuum but there is evidence that the Celtic Britons sometimes took revenge on their compatriots who had colluded with the Romans; the invading Angles and Saxons were not always unwelcome. In any case, though hillforts and *oppida* had existed before the Romans arrived, large grid-plan towns were hardly the norm. As Roman rule broke down, so too, perhaps, did the age of the fortified, and imposed, Roman town.

Saxon *Burhs*

Although the fortified towns listed in the Burghal Hidage, *c.* 910, are the best known, Saxon *burhs* first appeared in King Offa's Mercia a century earlier. Probably built to counter Viking raids at important river crossings, several strategic centres of population, such as Chester and the royal manor at Tamworth, were enclosed by a rampart and ditches. These *burhs* were often quite big, the defences at Hereford enclosed 33 acres, for example, but the internal layout was not usually so highly organized, or populous, as that of the Wessex *burhs*.

Naturally, as towns developed, *burhs* grew in size and stature, many having a market and additional administrative and living quarters. Some *burhs* extended their defences to enclose these developments, as at Hereford, while bridges over the gateways attest to the scale of the defences; perhaps they were not as impressive as those of the late Iron Age hillforts, but they were considerably better than a contemporary open village.

Originally topped by a wall-walk and parapet, and having wood and then stone revetting, the *burh* walls at Wareham are still of considerable proportions. The car park lies over the ditches.

Burhs were built in larger numbers in Wessex from the reign of Alfred the Great (871–99). Thirty of these fortified towns were listed in the Burghal Hidage, and many others developed afterwards. A typical *burh* was rectangular in shape, probably with a grid-plan street layout, and was defended by a large glacis or turf rampart, about 10 feet high with a timber palisade and wall-walk. Later, stone revetting might replace the timber. Outside this would be a ditch or two. In all, they seemed to combine Iron Age hillfort defences with Roman town layout. The finest remains of Saxon *burhs* can be seen at Cricklade, Wallingford and, especially, Wareham.

However, not unlike hillforts, *burhs* came in all shapes and sizes. There were two broad types of *burh*: the permanent settlement, which probably had a market, such as Wareham; and the smaller, less established *burh* without the regular street planning, such as South Cadbury Castle. On the whole, the latter type of *burh* did not last very long and traces of them have all but vanished.

Saxon *burhs* also made use of former Roman defences, as at Portchester and Winchester, while Iron Age defences were utilized at South Cadbury. Not surprisingly, several *burhs* were built on promontories, especially those that could control an estuary, like Watchet, but also inland, as at Wilton and Malmesbury. Harnessing nature's advantages was an age-old labour-saving solution to costly defences, and one that worked as well in the Dark Ages as it had in earlier times.

For about a century the burghal system was a huge success – and a system it most certainly was, and not a gaggle of unconnected strongholds. By the early eleventh century though, England was part of the Danish empire. Some *burhs* were abandoned, while the defences at others stymied the town's growth, but a few, such as Winchester, broke free to become thriving cities. Several *burhs* were even set up beyond Wessex and Mercia.

While many *burhs* were established fortified settlements, their eventual success as centres of population, administration, trade and manufacture can be demonstrated by the number that are still towns. Few of those originally mentioned in the Burghal Hideage have been abandoned. Indeed, many gained medieval walls or Norman castles – a sure sign of their continued importance. Their defences might now seem little better than those of Iron Age hillforts, but there is little evidence of them being overrun: the ultimate measurement of success.

The *burh* walls at Wallingford are also impressive. In addition there is a motte and bailey castle to the north of the town.

Linear Earthworks

Iron Age linear defences, such as the Chichester Dykes, and even Roman ones, perhaps Dorset's Bokerley Dyke, might now be considered pretty inferior to, say, hillforts. In many cases, this would be a correct assumption. In the Dark Ages, though, dykes (more accurately a large bank, probably with a wooden palisade, and ditch) came into their own. There are several important examples.

The east Wansdyke, and other banks along the crest of the Marlborough Downs to Savernake Forest, dates from the fifth or sixth century. As its ditch faces north, it was probably built by the Britons to stem the advance of the marauding Saxons along the Thames valley, via the Ridgeway. The west Wansdyke, running from Bristol to Bath along the hills south of the River Avon, also faces north and may have been built against Mercian Saxons a century later. Impressive though these dykes are, East Anglia also has several dramatic, massive earthworks: the Cambridgeshire Dykes. These date to the early sixth century and, as the ditch faces west, might have been built by the Angles against interlopers coming along the Icknield Way, the northern extension of The Ridgeway. Was this a counter-thrust by the Britons,

The Devil's Dyke, at Newmarket, offers a good vantage point for race-goers. The sheer scale of the Dark Age earthworks here put all their contemporaries well in the shade.

who followed up their success at Mount Badon by driving back the Angles and Saxons? Possibly, just possibly, with King Arthur at the helm?

None of these earthworks is particularly renowned, but it is a different matter for Britain's longest defensive work: Offa's Dyke. Defensive? Well, I wonder. Offa's Dyke is fully 120 miles long, although it was never continuous, the Rivers

OFFA'S DYKE (Linear Earthwork)

Offa's Dyke, the longest earthwork in Britain, runs for some 120 miles from a point north-west of Wrexham, near Treuddyn, to the low cliffs above the Severn estuary, at Sedbury. It was never a complete earthwork and is much less so today. As one would expect, many lengths of dyke have been damaged or obliterated, while there are numerous sections where its impact has been long-since lost, often when planted with trees or hedgerows. On the other hand, there are still good stretches where the bank rises to over 8 ft in height and its ditch is still in situ.

Built in the reign of King Offa of Mercia, 757–796, though never apparently completed, the dyke is classed somewhere between a defensive frontier and a boundary; too weak and difficult to defend for the former, and surely too grand for the latter. The earthworks are only

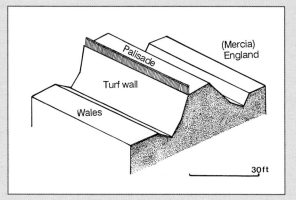

Cross-section through Offa's Dyke.

about 80 miles long, or ⅔ of the dyke's total route; rivers and gaps were always a feature. There is also the Offa's Dyke Long Distance Path, established in 1971. For perhaps the finest sections, and in countryside most appropriate to its original Dark Age setting, it is best seen between O/S map 137 map ref. 266766, where it crosses the minor road 3 miles north of Knighton, and ref. 263873, where it crosses a track, ½ mile west of Mainstone, some 3 miles north of Clun.

WAT'S DYKE (Linear Earthwork)

Wat's Dyke was probably built between 716 and 757, during a Mercian expansion westwards. It runs for about 30 miles, roughly parallel with and a little to the east of Offa's Dyke. Although less substantial than Offa's earthwork, Wat's Dyke had a western ditch defending a bank, though this is nowhere more than 5 ft high today. The whole system was originally about 50 ft wide. Only relatively short stretches remain, some of the best being at O/S map 117 refs 233697–239674, 258646–276624, and 323476 south for 3 miles, also north of Old Oswestry hillfort.

CAMBRIDGESHIRE DYKES (Linear Earthworks)

Earthworks can often be disappointing to photograph and, occasionally, to visit. Our climate is hardly conducive to their preservation, and those not covered in scrub or trees have in many cases been ploughed flat. The Saxon earthworks that run at right-angles to the Icknield Way cover the whole gamut from the magnificent to the mutilated. They are, though, clear evidence that England's Dark Ages' invaders were on the run from the Romano-Britons; possibly those led by King Arthur.

Built in the early sixth century, these dykes end in woodland, marsh or by a river. Easy to circumnavigate, one might think, but remember not only how much the landscape has changed, but also that the fens have been drained. The Saxons were no fools, these great barriers were not penetrated. A ditch protects the west side of each bank, while a palisade fence might have topped the ramparts.

The following dykes are worth visiting. (References are to OS map 154.)
Brent Ditch (ref. 515474) Best seen from the lay-by on the A11 between Stump Cross and Great Abington, it is 1½ miles long.
Devil's Ditch (refs 580648–620614) The finest Dark Age linear earthwork in Britain; it is massive and is 7 miles long. It is easiest to see beside the racecourse at Newmarket Heath.
Fleam Dyke (ref. 488601–572502, over 3 miles long) Crosses the A11 2 miles south-west of Newmarket by-pass.

Wye and Severn occasionally acting as natural barriers. Built in the eighth century, at the very least to define the boundary of Mercia, the ditch faces west – it was clearly not built to keep the Mercians out of Wales. The same can be said for the earlier Wat's Dyke, which runs pretty much parallel with, but a few miles to the east of, Offa's Dyke; it is 35 miles long.

The existence of a bank and ditch, usually of impressive proportions, shows that these linear earthworks clearly had a defensive function. Fine, but think back to the Roman frontier walls. Not only did they have numerous fortlets, turrets and forts to house the troops and guards, but each wall had a road to facilitate the movement of soldiers. The Dark Age dykes had none of these and, furthermore, if Hadrian's Wall needed about 10,000 troops to man it, Offa's Dyke – half as long again – would surely require still more. Where did they come from, and where were they stationed? Never mind 10,000 men, even evidence of a few hundred has, so far, proved elusive.

On the other hand, if linear dykes were not defences, what were they for? They would have been extravagant boundary markers – Offa's Dyke reaches parts even the most desperate of the dispossessed would decline, and some Cambridgeshire dykes are truly massive. One must not resort to sweeping statements about the use and workings of earthworks in separate parts of the country, built by unconnected peoples in different eras, but they must *surely* have been intended for defence. Did scouts patrol the lands beyond, ready to warn of an approaching enemy? If so, perhaps they ensured a yeoman militia, a sort of Dark Age Dad's Army, could assemble at the dyke to hold off an attempted assault until larger, or possibly regular, forces arrived? This is pure speculation, of course, but how else could they have operated? Perhaps Offa's Dyke was a Dark Age equivalent to the Iron Curtain, used as much as to keep Britons in, as to keep the Welsh insurgents out? Linear earthworks clearly inhibited movement and, innocuous though they may seem today, that may have been their main aim: the ancient equivalent of stop-lines, as intended to halt a Nazi invasion of Britain in 1940?

Royal Manors

Not unlike later kings, Anglo-Saxon rulers had several residences where they stayed at different times. These were not the great fortified castles of their Norman successors, but probably consisted of a couple of longhouses and, perhaps, a cattle pound, all protected by no more than a palisade fence or, at best, a bank and ditch. One can thus argue that these were not strongholds at all. On the other hand, given the turbulence of the Dark Ages, these royal manors, villas or residences were surely defended to some extent. Several have been discovered and a few excavated, but there is usually little to be seen today. Perhaps the most famous is at that of Yeavering (Northumb.) where a defended enclosure was found; this could also have been used for herding cattle. There is a little more to see at Doon Hill, near Dunbar, which appears to have a similar layout to Yeavering. Certainly, the large timber hall was surrounded by a palisade fence, but is that enough to consider it a stronghold?

There can be little doubt that Dinas Powys was a stronghold, this being one of the more extensively fortified Dark Age sites in Wales. One might suppose that it belonged to the equivalent of a king or chief. Others have been noted at Cheddar, Millfield and more recently at Flixborough. The latter was still used after Lindsey was subsumed in the Danelaw, which raises the question of whether the local ruler simply carried on as before, serving a new overall master, not unlike the early *civitates* of Roman times?

Whether royal residences or simply those of a local lord, these sites were seemingly little better defended than a village. Perhaps modest defences were required in view of the wealth that might be gathered at such a place, but even a simple bank, ditch and palisade fence had their merits in the seventh century. After all, the Britons had either been driven west or subdued, so there was no need for anything more elaborate, at least until the Vikings came.

Fortified Camps

Looking for fortified camps is rather like searching for the proverbial needle: you are unlikely to find one. Hillforts were quite often refortified, especially in the first hundred years or so after the Roman withdrawal, but a Saxon fortified

A Dark Age camp or an Iron Age hillfort? The ancestry of Clare Camp remains uncertain.

camp? Well, Clare Camp might just be one such stronghold. It gives the impression of being an Iron Age hillfort, was later known as Erbury and became a manorial compound in the fourteenth century. Another theory contends that it was actually a Danish camp.

The defences at Clare and similar camps were little more than a bank and ditch or two. As the defences were never rebuilt to anything like the scale of those at South Cadbury Castle, so we might assume any such camps were also modestly defended. The case for similar inland strongholds is very much open to question at the moment, but coastal strongholds, such as Bamburgh – obliterated by the castle – or Tintagel, did exist. These may have been combined royal manors and coastal forts, but their defences, again, relied heavily on the natural location and relatively modest man-made banks and ditches, and a judicious use of stone walls.

SCOTLAND'S DARK AGE FORTS

Just as the Picts gained control to the north of the Forth/Clyde isthmus, so the impact of the Dalriadan Scotti, initially in Argyll, continued to spread. New strongholds were quite rare but from the fifth century onwards, there was some construction. The great Pict stronghold at Burghead is probably the best known of these but, along with others, such as Dumbarton Rock, it might have been initiated late in the Scottish Iron Age. In any case, the defences were typical of that period.

The concentrating of the Britons in Strathclyde, and the Anglo-Saxon advance to the Firth of Forth, led to a not inconsiderable refortifying of hillforts. Quite a number were partially refurbished but, as in England, the defences rarely equalled those of earlier times. There were, however, exceptions. Some hillforts, such as Craig Phadrig, might even have become royal strongholds, holding a status far

BURGHEAD (Pict Stronghold)
Morayshire O/S map 28 ref. 109691
Directions: From Elgin, head west on the A96 and turn right on to the B9013 to Burghead. The remains are at the end of Grant Street.

It is hard to imagine now but Burghead was a major Pict stronghold. The town was built early in the nineteenth century, destroying the ancient defences, but a plan of the stronghold was made soon after the Battle of Culloden Moor. Little remains today, though one can certainly appreciate the magnificent location.

Burghead was thought to have been an Iron Age promontory fort of about 12 acres, enclosed by three massive ramparts 270 yd long and 60 yd wide. A wall divided the interior into two, and that is all that now remains. Thus, one of Scotland's most important historical sites was tragically and wilfully destroyed.

Yet Burghead did not go down without a fight. Following early excavations, the ramparts were thought to have had large beams protruding from the rear, secured by 8 in. long iron spikes, a technique called *murus gallicus*. Excavations in the 1960s cast doubt on this thesis, and it now seems that the beams might have supported a wall-walk. Charcoal from the rampart gave a C-14 date of third–seventh centuries AD, so perhaps a Caledonian fort was transformed into a Pict stronghold. Whatever, there is no doubt that the ramparts were consumed by fire.

Burghead is another stronghold that lays claim to be the site where St Columba supposedly converted the Pictish King Bruide to Christianity in the sixth century. This might be a myth, but one might assume Burghead's importance from the scale of its defences. Several Pict and Viking carved stones were also found here, and it is the only known Pict stronghold of anything like its size. Despite its recent fate, there can be no doubt that Burghead was of great importance to the Picts.

destroyed

0   500   1000 ft

The dividing rampart is all that remains of Burghead's once extensive earthworks.

JARLSHOF (Wheelhouses, Broch and multi-phase site)
Shetland (Mainland) O/S map 4 ref. 397096
Directions: Take the A970 south from Lerwick to the south of Sumburgh Airport. Turn right to the hotel and Jarlshof is by the coast.

Jarlshof is one of the great archaeological sites of Europe. Here, in Britain's equivalent to Jericho, one can see many phases of development, several of which overlay each other, encompassing a period of three-and-a-half millennia. Yet this great archaeological importance was never truly matched in reality. None of Jarlshof's various residences appear to have belonged to people of anything but local significance. Unlike Jericho, Jarlshof did not play any great part in history, so far as is known, but it is the combination of the remains that gives it such prominence.

In 1897 a storm blew the sand from below the ruined seventeenth-century tower-house to reveal the earlier settlements. Today, Jarlshof covers about 3 acres, but it has been heavily eroded. It was excavated in the 1930s and again between 1949 and 1952, each dig uncovering yet more dwellings. There is a museum and an invaluable guide book. Two sets of buildings date to the Dark Ages.

Jarlshof dates back to *c.* 2000 BC, perhaps before bronze first came to Shetland. The earliest dwellings are the scant remains of huts to the right of the museum, beneath the medieval farm. As one looks from right to left, so the huts' date from the Bronze Age through to the Iron Age, the latter including souterrains which, unfortunately, cannot be entered. None of these is thought to have been fortified.

A little to the north-west, and half eroded by the sea, is the broch. This had a solid wall up to 18 ft thick and a courtyard 30 ft across. There are remains of two mural cells and, given its dimensions, it may have been of considerable height; it dates to about the turn of the first millennium AD. Inside, much of the inner wall-face is obscured by its conversion to a wheelhouse, one of several outstanding examples at Jarlshof. These are the finest wheelhouses to be seen anywhere, dating from *c.* AD 200 onwards, and were almost certainly occupied during the Dark Ages. The combination of wheelhouses and tunnels gives a partial insight into domestic arrangements at that time.

At the north-west lie some late Iron Age huts and, working back to the east, there is a confusion of Norse buildings from the Dark Ages. These were discovered in the 1930s, and are some of the finest of their type. The long-house is the earliest and a multitude of later buildings were pushed out in all directions. The arrival of the Norsemen in Britain is so strongly connected with deeds of destruction that it seems strange to see a considerable settlement of farmers and fishermen. There is little evidence that Norse long-houses were fortified, but some form of defence is likely, given the violence recorded in the Nordic sagas.

Still there is more. To the right of the long-house are the remains of a medieval farm, part of which has been removed to uncover the Bronze Age dwellings; more of these may lie beneath the farm. Apart from the broch, the only certain stronghold at Jarlshof is the laird's tower-house. From the top, one gains a panoramic view of the site that helps unravel its long history.

Jarlshof, then, is unique and people from all over Europe travel to Shetland just to see it, such is its importance.

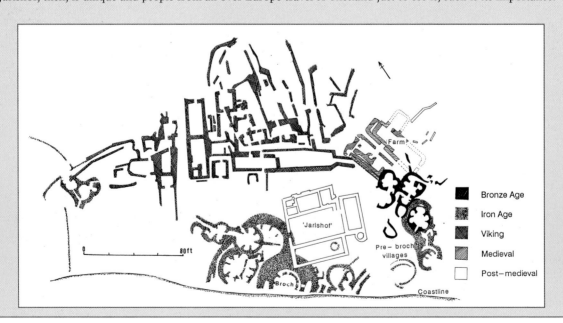

greater than anything in their former life. Of course, there were occasions when Iron Age strongholds were occupied into the Dark Ages. Duns in the Hebridean islands and Argyll are prime examples, and they continued to be built throughout the Dark Ages. At Gurness, on Orkney, Pict shamrock houses – whose name aptly describes their shape – were discovered within the earlier ramparts, while the wheelhouses at Jarlshof, on Shetland, may also belong to the Dark Ages.

As in England and Wales, the first centuries of Scotland's Dark Ages were unsettled, but there was nothing like such a profusion of stronghold building as there had been in the Iron Age. Refurbishment seems to have been the main approach for what was probably temporary defence. On the other hand, some new variations evolved.

Citadel Forts

The name says it all really. A central stronghold citadel was usually built within a range of outer defences, often at former hillforts. At Turin Hill, for example, the citadel took the form of a dun, but more often it resembled a small hillfort. As such, the combination of a new citadel plonked on top of refurbished hillfort defences smacked more of economy than of a desire, or need, for an especially secure site.

Many potential citadel forts are located deep within Pictland, so perhaps they were merely the strongholds of the local chiefs, and an external threat was regarded as unlikely. As with refurbished hillforts, their defences would hardly have been regarded with awe half a millennium earlier, but the citadel itself was

DUMYAT (Citadel Fort)
Stirlingshire O/S map 57 ref. 832973
Directions: Take the A91 north from Stirling. A farm road runs north round the bottom of the hill, about ½ mile east of Blairlogie. Ascend from there.

If you fancy a nice afternoon stroll, look elsewhere. Dumyat is 1,373 ft high and some 1,000 ft above the River Forth below. However you approach it, there is a short but distinctly steep climb.

The south and east approaches are protected by sheer rock faces, but two ruined stone walls at the north and west enclose an area of 1¼ acres. There are traces of outworks at the west entrance, all of which were probably connected with an Iron Age hillfort. There is some evidence of vitrification.

In the Dark Ages a citadel was built at the summit, measuring about 85 ft × 50 ft. The drystone wall was about 12 ft thick, but is now tumbled. It is not certain whether the outer walls were repaired, or even stood, when the citadel was in use, but that is the favoured option.

The citadel was possibly a Pict fort, and commands long views over what is assumed to have been Pictland. However, the name Dumyat translates to 'the fort of the Maeatae', the local late Iron Age tribe. Dumyat is one of many former hillforts that became citadel forts in the Dark Ages, probably as a result of the on-going conflict between the Picts and the Dalriadans that ended in the mid-ninth century.

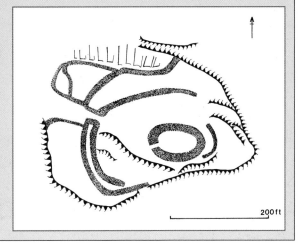

200ft

often more akin to the great drystone defences of hillforts like the White Caterthun. How effective these defences were, and how long such strongholds remained in use is not something that is really known. It is not even certain that many genuinely date to the Dark Ages, in any case. Once again, though, in a land where most brochs, duns and hillforts had become disused, such citadel forts would have been all the more impressive.

Nuclear Forts

At first sight, the difference between nuclear forts and citadel forts might seem to be pretty hair-splitting. Both have a central citadel that commands the highest point, and each is defended by outlying defences. The similarity cannot be denied, but it is the use of natural defences, joined by lengths of wall to make a series of inter-connecting courtyards round the citadel, that really distinguishes the nuclear fort. Each was a planned entity in itself, and not a cost-effective hybrid.

To no great surprise then, a solitary hill that commands the locality would make a good nuclear fort. That was exactly the choice made by the Dalriadans when they came to Argyll from Ireland, and built a stronghold at Dunadd. The

---

DUNADD (Nuclear Fort)
Argyll O/S map 55 ref. 837936
Directions: From Lochgilphead, take the A816 north. A turning along a farm road on the left, about a mile beyond Bridgend, leads to the site.

Dunadd is one of the most significant sites in Scottish history. It was fortified by the Scotti of Dalriada, possibly as a royal stronghold, and features in the *Annals of Ulster* as besieged by Picts in AD 683, and again in 736 when it was captured by the Pictish King Fergus. About a hundred years later the Pict and the Dalriadan kingdoms united under the Dalriadan Kenneth MacAlpin, and a tentatively united Scotland first came into being.

Occupying a rocky mass above the River Add, the fort covers several levels. It is cleverly designed and makes good use of natural outcrops to reduce the building required. Thus the outer enclosure has the best preserved drystone walling, and contains the foundations of two buildings and a well.

A gap through the remains of a wall leads to the

higher levels, with stairs up to the summit citadel, a former Iron Age hillfort. The defences there are disappointing, with the teardrop-shaped rampart marking the last period of occupation. Of much greater significance, just outside the citadel, is a rock carving of a Pictish boar and traces of ogham inscriptions; regrettably, these have not been translated. Perhaps the boar and the oghams were cut after the Picts captured Dunadd in 736, and represent a footprint and basin. These might have been used to inaugurate the Dalriadan kings, hence Dunadd's assumed importance.

Whatever the truth behind these carvings and indentations, they suggest Dunadd has as good a claim as anywhere to be the seat of Dalriadan power: the people behind the nascent Scotland. Dunadd is therefore unique. It is a place of such national importance that it cannot be missed. There are several outstanding Bronze Age stone circles and cairns only 2–3 miles away in the Kilmartin valley.

Dundurn nuclear fort is not unlike Dunadd in its layout, but is thought to have been a Pict stronghold. It survived a siege by the Dalriadans in 683, and might have been occupied for about a thousand years before then.

summit had once been a small hillfort, and was rebuilt as the citadel. A series of courtyards, with defences comprising a combination of rock faces and drystone walls, overlooked from above, protected the citadel. An attacking force would have to overcome each defensive line before reaching the citadel, unless an almost sheer face was to be scaled. In the use of these courtyards (or should we call them baileys?), the nuclear fort was a precursor of both the Norman motte and bailey and the concentric castles.

Abernethy's round tower is the only one still in almost-original condition.

As with any Dark Age strongholds, nuclear forts would not necessarily have impressed peoples of the Iron Age, but they can only be judged for their time and place. After all, a couple of rows of anti-tank blocks and a few pill-boxes might have prevented a small-scale beach landing in the Second World War, thanks solely to the use of guns; somehow, I do not think Julius Caesar would have been deterred by such defences in 55 BC. Horses for courses, please, and since the nuclear forts of Dunadd (Dalriadan) and Dundurn (Picts) both survived sieges, they were certainly not out of their class.

Round Towers

More usually thought of in an Irish context, and appropriately so as there are over sixty examples in the Emerald Isle, round towers were built of mortared masonry. They were not simply strongholds either, rather a multi-purpose building associated with a monastery or church, and used as a refuge, watch-

BRECHIN (Round Tower)
Angus O/S map 54 ref. 596601
Directions: Beside the west door of the cathedral in the city centre.

This is one of only two such towers on mainland Britain. It is not in original condition as the cathedral was added to it in the thirteenth century, while the conical, dunce-cap top was built a century later.

Round towers were more a refuge than a full-blown stronghold, but are most important for all that. Built of sandstone early in the eleventh century, Brechin's tower belonged to a monastery. It is about 85 ft high and has seven storeys, each reached by ladder from below. That it was a refuge is shown by its lack of windows and, more obviously, the door being some 7 ft above ground; another door was cut into the cathedral, but this has since been blocked up again. Clearly with limitations, it could withstand a short raid.

Brechin's round tower and cathedral, formerly a monastery.

tower, a store for treasure or a belfry. Nevertheless, the raised doorway indicates that these towers served some defensive function.

There are only three defensive round towers in Scotland, and none elsewhere in mainland Britain. Their design similarity, both with themselves and with Irish towers, hints that they may have been built by specialist builders. From Ireland? If the raised doorway is an important defensive feature so, no less, is the height of the tower, usually over 60 feet. Free-standing on shallow foundations, they had several wooden floors, reached from the one below by ladder, and a single window in the lower floors. Not surprisingly, there have been a few changes over the intervening centuries.

The towers at Brechin and Abernethy date to the early eleventh century, the end of the Dark Ages, while that at St Magnus Church, on Eglisay in the Orkneys, may pre-date the church of *c.* 1135, though not by much. Clearly, they only had limited defensive capabilities, perhaps being able to withstand a short raid, such as a Viking assault; the tower at St Magnus might have been built primarily with this in mind. It can only be entered from within the church, although that at Brechin was attached to the cathedral more recently.

Bearing some similarity to brochs, and the later priests' pele-towers of Northumberland, these towers were not permanent residences, and it was probably their multi-purpose nature that made them economically viable. As most stone building was associated with ecclesiastical establishments in the Dark Ages, so it is not surprising that this was the case with round towers. Even so, they were of advanced construction for the time. As for being strongholds, in contemporary Scotland they would have been almost unsurpassed in terms of stone buildings.

Wheelhouses

One might regard these as a strange inclusion here, as it is far from certain that wheelhouses were strongholds. However, the remains of a few examples can be seen at brochs, and they are considered to be a subgroup of the Atlantic roundhouse type of dwelling, to which brochs and duns also belong. Wheelhouses are only found on the Hebridean and Shetland island groups, although the secondary wall added to some brochs, as at Borwick Broch, might represent a sort of wheelhouse-type conversion.

Until recently wheelhouses were thought to have been built as brochs fell into disuse, possibly from the second century AD. Indeed, as several brochs had been converted into wheelhouse-type dwellings, it was considered possible that wheelhouses were developed from brochs, in their own right. However, this notion has begun to change. Recent Carbon-14 dating from wheelhouses has confirmed their use in the early Dark Ages and, more interestingly, shows that some date back to at least the fourth century BC. These are unlikely to remain the extreme dates. So, the former nice and neat theoretical ladder of duns, semi-brochs, brochs and finally, in the Dark Ages, wheelhouses seems to have at least a few creaky rungs!

As the name implies, wheelhouses are circular dwellings, mostly sunk into the ground, with stone piers as the spokes and a hearth as the hub. The piers divide the interior and, presumably, supported the thatch or turf roof. Not all wheelhouses had piers against the outer wall or wheel-rim – a lintel often sufficed, and these are called aisled roundhouses. We need not get too drawn into the niceties of wheelhouses for obvious reasons, but some general observations might be interesting.

There are three broad types of wheelhouse: the free-standing, such as Clettraval on North Uist; those often revetted against sand dunes, such as Kilpheder on South Uist; and those converted from brochs, as at Jarlshof. The former types probably only had the upper wall and roof visible from the outside, yet the roof might have risen up to 20 feet above the internal floor. Only the latter broch conversions probably had the slightest chance of being considered a stronghold, while artefacts suggest that some wheelhouses were more of a ritual or religious building than a residence, let alone a personal stronghold.

Brochs at Clickimin and Mousa were converted into wheelhouses, but neither retains its stone piers, although they did until the nineteenth century; however, the additional inner-wall facings are still there. By far the best example of a broch being so converted can be seen at Jarlshof. The wheelhouse phase at this great archaeological site is clearly post-broch, and is but one of many on view. The wheelhouse is no more than a house within a fortified settlement, but when built within a broch, it could just about be considered a stronghold in its own, second-hand, right.

Norse and Other Strongholds in Scotland

The Vikings settled round much of peripheral Scotland: the Orkney and Shetland islands, the Hebrides and the far north, making occasional forays inland, especially in Argyll. As in the rest of Britain, Norse settlements show few signs of

DINAS EMRYS (Citadel Fort)
Caernarvonshire O/S map 115 ref. 606492
Directions: From Caernarvon, take the A4085 south to
Beddgelert and turn left on the A498. Dinas Emrys is the
rocky hill beside the road on the left, after a mile or so.
Park at the lay-by on the left after the Copper Mine. Go
up through the trees from the north-east.

This is one of the few Welsh strongholds that genuinely
dates to the early Dark Ages. Dinas Emrys has been
partially excavated on two occasions and, although
occupied during the Iron Age, was apparently not
fortified until the fifth or sixth century.
  A low, tumbled drystone wall, linking various rocky
outcrops, encloses about 2½ acres at the summit. At the west side, a further wall was added about 100 ft lower
down the hill. The original entrances through both walls can be seen. Almost at the bottom in the south-west, a
further rampart was added that similarly linked outcrops, complete with an in-turned entrance.
  This is an attractive stronghold, but the walls are nowhere more than a disappointing 3 ft high; the scarcity of
such sites makes this an important stronghold, although it also features in legend. According to the works of
Nennius in the ninth century, Dinas Emrys was built by Vortigern, king of southern Britain, in about 430. It was he
who invited the Angles, Saxons and Jutes to help repel other invaders. To appease the gods, Vortigern nearly had
the blood of the young Ambrosius Aurelianus sprinkled over the site, but he relented and Ambrosius became the
fore-runner of King Arthur.
  There is a Dark Age cistern near the summit and the footings of a twelfth-century Welsh keep on top of the hill,
reputedly built by Llewelyn the Great. Fact and fiction are clearly intertwined at Dinas Emrys, but its position as the
finest Dark Age stronghold in Wales cannot be denied.

being heavily defended, with perhaps a bank and ditch at the most. They had the
longhouse, or drinking hall, which probably included the odd defensive feature;
on the other hand, the regularity with which halls were burned down rather
counters that theory. Fairly recently, what has been described as a small Viking
fortlet has been discovered at Udal, on North Uist; even making allowances for a
lack of detail, though, it does not appear to compare with the best Iron Age
strongholds.

  If Dunadd was the main Dalriadan stronghold, so Dumbarton Rock
(Dunbarton.) – and the associated royal residences at Partick and Govan – was
that of the Strathclyde Britons. Little of relevance to the Dark Ages can be seen
there, but one can be sure that, as with Dunadd, the defences would have been
mightily impressive for the time. As that thoroughly fortified rock was sacked by
the Vikings in 870, the fate of any other minor stronghold could so easily have
been the same.

CONCLUSION

While much of this chapter has concentrated on the strongholds of Scotland and
England, one must not assume Wales had nothing of note. Dinas Emrys has been
considered a nuclear fort, and Dinas Powys a citadel fort. On the other hand,
perhaps they should be regarded as unique in their own right, rather than being
forced into a framework that has no relevance to the people who lived in them.

There are other examples as well and, given the population movements to and from Wales throughout the Dark Ages, one might assume that defensive measures were undertaken at all levels of society from time to time.

Viewed as a whole, though, there was little innovation among the strongholds of Dark Age Britain; well, nothing that had not, or conceivably could not have, been built before. The exception is the Scottish round towers, although in England the *burhs* of Wessex were an original adaptation of older ideas, combining the defences of Iron Age heritage with a Roman-inspired interior. Considering the vast upheavals over the six-and-a-half centuries of the Dark Ages, with Angles, Saxons, Jutes, Irish, and Norse and Danish Vikings all taking turns at invading Britain's shores, it is the lack of inventive stronghold design that is most surprising. There was an obvious, and often continuing, need for defence, yet innovation was at a premium. Perhaps society was just too unsettled and fluid even to contemplate such long term projects?

In the end the *burh* system seems to have worked in southern England. Offa's Dyke kept the English and Welsh apart. The Scots and Picts united to dominate Scotland north of the Forth/Clyde isthmus and, eventually, to expel the Vikings. By the mid-eleventh century England could be viewed pretty much as a whole and Scotland was veering in that direction. Even Wales was a country of apparent principalities and, though the recently ousted Danes cast an envious eye over Britain, it was from elsewhere that the next threat was to materialize.

THE NORMAN REVOLUTION

In 1939 the German army swept into Poland and swiftly overran the land that was seemingly forever a dispensable pawn in eastern European politics. As usual the Germans claimed right to be on their side, for the somewhat artificial Polish Corridor really had separated native Germans from their homeland. Poland was later divided up between Germany and Russia, to the extent that Polish prisoners-of-war were often denied the meagre rights afforded other Allied combatants because, so it was claimed, their country no longer existed. This gave the Nazis the green light to systematically rob, ravish and dismember the tattered remnants of the Polish nation, seizing property and redistributing it among themselves as and when they wished. Rich and poor, old or young, fit or infirm, Jew or gentile – it did not matter. To the Nazis, the Poles were the scum of the earth, existing merely to satisfy the whim of the glorified master-race.

The iron grip of the Nazis was enforced by a rigid and rigorous deployment of the military, billeted in both temporary camps and more permanent strongholds throughout the land. Nowhere was free from the march of the jack-booted minions. Total devastation, or a token show of human compassion, depended entirely on the whim of the local commander. Once the armed struggle was over – and the German Blitzkrieg did not take long to comprehensively smash the Polish forces – any resistance was usually met with an horrific riposte. From the random execution of innocent civilians, to the total and complete annihilation of a village, town or district, the attempted genocide of the Jews was just one facet of Nazi brutality.

Yet, almost nine hundred years before, a blitzkrieg of not dissimilar proportions swept through England and parts of Wales. Thus far, Britain's historic eras had evolved gradually. There had been no time at which one could say, for example, 'Hey Fred, did you hear the Stone Age ended yesterday? We're in the Bronze Age now.' Even though the Romans departed in 407, the Roman way of life continued for several generations in some areas, while elsewhere Roman influence had waned decades earlier. In 1066, though, it was an entirely different matter.

True, a farmer in the wild Westmorland fells would have had no inkling of the goings-on down at Hastings on 14 October 1066. Rumour apart, he might not have known much about the sweeping, drastic changes that were under way for some time to come, but the arrival and impact of the Normans was to be measured in a handful of years, rather than decades. On Boxing Day 1066 Duke William of Normandy was crowned King William I of England, and much of the land between Christchurch and The Wash soon learnt that resistance was pretty-nigh useless and, if one enjoyed life, it was also distinctly ill advised. As with the Nazis, many Normans were only too willing to undertake acts of horrific barbarism against the Saxon populace. Yet the initial Norman invading force had numbered no more than ten thousand men.

By 1070 all of England except the Lake District was under Norman rule; they had also penetrated to the Conway valley in North Wales, forged deeply into South Wales and had spread terror through much of the land in between. The speed of the Norman conquest was not quite so rapid as the Nazi rampage through Poland, but a blitzkrieg it most certainly was to the demoralized and leaderless Saxons. Unlike the Romans, the Normans did not use the incumbent nobility to do their bidding. Rather, they were often deposed and stripped of their lands. In any case, under the new regime, all land belonged to the king; he could do as he liked with the land and all that went with it.

FEUDALISM

Before going any further, we must be certain about one thing: jolly old Saxon England was not a free and fair country, with each man entitled to his rights. Slavery was far from uncommon, encompassing perhaps as much as 25 per cent of the population. The Normans simply swept aside the old system; under the new imposed feudalism, the serf was tied to the land – and his lot, like the policeman's, was most certainly not an 'appy one.

RICHMOND CASTLE
Yorkshire O/S map 93 ref. 174006
Directions: Just off the market-place.

After the so-called Harrying of the North, or total devastation in modern parlance, the land of the Saxon Earl of Mercia was granted to the Breton, Alan Rufus. Expecting not a little resentment, Rufus built Richmond Castle in about 1071, on a cliff overlooking Swaledale, both for his protection and to secure the estate. Thereafter, history, or at least that part of it involving violent conflict, seems to have passed Richmond by.

A triangular 2½ acre bailey was created by building a stone curtain wall, with four projecting mural towers along the east and west sides. A palisade fence secured the south side, above the river, and a two-storey entrance tower covered the north angle. The two-storey Scolland's Hall was added at the south-east corner. Richmond Castle was one of the first masonry Norman strongholds in England.

The following century saw the south wall rebuilt in stone, and an enclosure, the Cockpit, built outside the south-east angle. Entered from Scolland's Hall, this was probably the private grounds of the principal resident. What is more important, the gatehouse was blocked and comprehensively rebuilt as the present, highly distinctive keep. Standing up to 100 ft high, this dominates the castle and all about, including the town that grew up within its shadow.

A few residential and domestic additions were made in the fourteenth century, and the keep was reopened as a gateway. By then, Richmond Castle was barely recognized as a stronghold and was in decay within two hundred years. Usually too far south to be involved in the Scottish wars, and too far off the beaten track to be of much importance, Richmond still retains much from late Norman times.

Starting as a Norman motte and bailey castle, being extended in the Middle Ages and finally succumbing in the Civil War, Corfe Castle was always of considerable importance. It remains a hauntingly attractive ruin.

William the Conqueror carefully divided up his new territory; he retained a quarter of the land for himself, gave a quarter to the church and rewarded his loyal followers with the rest. He appointed a hierarchy of tenants-in-chief (later known as barons), tenants and knights, who held the land for the king and in return provided knights, soldiers and taxes at his bidding. Those who fought for him in the initial invasion, or came over in the second wave, did very nicely thank you, receiving not only great tracts of fertile land, but the people to work it as well: the manor was well and truly born. On the other hand, the king ensured that his followers, in order to retain their new-found wealth, did not bite the hand that fed them; what the king gave, he could easily take away.

For the unfortunate Saxons, being tied to the land meant just that. Unlike the British, who later adopted the Roman method of allowing native rulers a degree of independence and hegemony, the Normans seized everything for themselves. The imposition of feudalism was widespread and required the Saxon serfs to work the land belonging to the lord and the church; payment was notably absent from the contract of employment. The produce from this land went to the lord, and the serfs also had other, unrewarded, duties to perform; moreover, taxes also had to be paid. Under Norman feudalism serfdom was little better than slavery.

On the other hand, providing his village escaped the ravages of the passing Norman armies, daily life probably did not change too much for the Saxon

Lydford was once a Saxon *burh*. The Normans built a ringwork castle adjoining the *burh* walls, and a keep and bailey castle was then added nearby. Like many rectangular keeps, Lydford's later served as a prison.

common-man. He still toiled away for someone else's benefit, but at least the Saxon lord was not a foreign invader. The Norman baron was expected to provide knights and men for royal service, usually forty days a year, so the hierarchy was rigidly enforced and everyone knew their place. As for the Saxons, theirs were the very lowest rungs on the social ladder – if they were lucky.

Resistance to the new order was not unexpected but was not widespread. The Danes landed in East Anglia in 1070, and joined up with the rebel Hereward the Wake. They sacked Peterborough but the Danes then went home and Hereward and his men, left holding the baby, had to retreat to their fenland stronghold in the Isle of Ely. Eventually, the Normans flushed them out but, for once, a degree of mercy seems to have been shown.

That was certainly not the case for the peoples of Yorkshire, the north-east and the north Midlands. A Saxon uprising at about the same time was subdued by a Norman response that was fearsomely savage, even by Nazi standards. The so-called Harrying of the North almost pleasingly understates the way the Normans deliberately and systematically devastated this vast area. Numerous villages and the city of York itself were razed to the ground and the inhabitants – men, women and children, whether involved in the uprising or not – were massacred. Crops were destroyed, animals slaughtered and stockpiles of food, even the seed corn, were all burnt. For those who survived the revengeful slaying and destruction, starvation was an alternative, if less immediate, death. Nothing was reputedly grown for nine long, dark years: it was a human desert. A terrible lesson was certainly and emphatically taught – and the Saxons never forgave the Norman savagery.

Then, to demonstrate that the king's power was absolute, and that he had every intention of ruling absolutely, William decided to create a private hunting ground. The whole of south Hampshire between the Rivers Test and Avon was cleared. Villages were burnt and destroyed and anybody who resisted, well . . . ; oh, and even if one went meekly, compensation was not on the agenda. The king most certainly got his way – and his new hunting ground, the New Forest. This was the ultimate demonstration of the power of the new monarch, and up to one-third of England was subject to the harshly restrictive Forest Laws at one time. Perhaps a semblance of justice was enacted when William's successor, William Rufus, met his death when hunting in that very forest.

THE NORMANS IN WALES

Despite Wales being divided into nascent principalities, there is little evidence of unity or, indeed, of a national consciousness, irrespective of current contrary trends. Wales was a much-divided land. The diverse population comprised Scots, Irish, Britons, Romano-British, Angles and Saxons, Celts and non-Celts. (People who talk about our so-called modern multi-culturalism need to open their eyes to the past. There was hardly room for all the peoples of pre-Roman times, whoever they were.) Borders meant very little to the expansively ambitious Normans. While the Cambrian Mountains held little attraction for them, at least when there were far richer and easier pickings elsewhere, the coastal lands and the Marches soon drew their less-than-welcome attention. As in England, castles sprouted up everywhere, in still greater concentrations but, like Offa and others before him, the Normans soon found that not everything would quite go their way.

On the contrary, the sheer number of strongholds, both large and small, spread throughout the Marches suggests that the Welsh were extremely tough nuts to crack. Indeed, over the next two centuries, many Norman castles were besieged and some even fell to the Welsh, such as those at Cardiff and Laugharne. Native resistance was never entirely successful, for neither the Normans, nor their Anglo-Norman successors, were ever driven out – but neither were the Welsh finally conquered until the reign of Edward I.

Credit where it is due though, the Welsh continued to resist violently. They did not entirely succumb to Norman terror as did Saxon England. The ongoing struggle may have even strengthened some principalities, in the same way that the Agricolan invasion of Scotland brought many small tribal groups together in the Caledonian confederacy. Certainly by the time of the drawn-out conflict between Stephen and Matilda after 1135, there were four main, competing Welsh kingdoms or principalities: Gwynedd, Powys, Deheubarth (mostly the south and west) and Cynllibiwg. The latter, recognized only fairly recently, occupied the centre and the south-east. These were nominally subject to their overlord English king, particularly after Henry II came to the throne, but this was often little more than a token gesture. None the less, Norman influence remained strong in the Marches and especially in South Wales, as is amply demonstrated by the number of castles of eleventh- and twelfth-century origin. It was the inability of the Welsh principalities to unite against what could be considered a common enemy that led to the extinguishing of any hopes of Wales ever becoming an independent, united country.

CHEPSTOW CASTLE AND PORT WALL
Monmouthshire O/S map 172 ref. 533941
Directions: In Chepstow, off Bridge Street.

Spectacularly sited on cliffs over the winding River Wye, with a steep scarp to the south, Chepstow's Great Tower was the first stone Norman castle built in Wales, possibly even in Britain. The castle continued to be developed for over two hundred years, and the defences were improved even after the Civil War.

The two-storey Great Tower stands at the narrowest part of a ledge, and was flanked by the current middle and upper baileys, defended by stone curtain walls. Towards the end of the Norman period, round towers with arrow-loops and a gateway were added to the middle bailey wall.

Work continued throughout the thirteenth century, with the rebuilding of the upper bailey wall, the addition of a further storey to the Great Tower, the building of the Barbican at the west gate and, in particular, the addition of the lower bailey and twin-towered great gatehouse, with its flying arch. The last decades of the century saw the domestic accommodation vastly improved, with new ranges of buildings in the lower bailey. The massive Marten's Tower, on its splayed plinth, protected not only the exposed eastern corner, but was an independent defensible residence. Further domestic buildings were added in the Tudor period until, by the mid-seventeenth century, Chepstow had become more of a great house than a stronghold.

For all its strategic importance, Chepstow Castle was never seriously besieged until the Civil War. It was held for the king and soon capitulated but in the Second Civil War Parliament turned a small battery of guns on it. Surrender quickly followed but, surprisingly, the walls and battlements were repaired and modified to withstand gunfire. Chepstow Castle then housed political prisoners until it was abandoned in 1690.

The thirteenth-century Port Wall enclosed some 130 acres, within a bend in the river. It almost adjoins the castle, and now runs as far as the railway.

NORMAN SCOTLAND

As with Wales, William I wasted no time in violating the Scottish Borders – his revenge for the Scots having taken liberties during the turmoil in northern England. He invaded in 1071, the year King Malcolm III took as his wife Margaret, daughter of Edgar Atheling – the uncrowned successor to the slain King Harold – and Malcolm was forced to pay homage at Abernethy. The Normans soon returned to England, but the seeds of intent had been sown.

Like Wales, Scotland was far from being the united country we know today. King Malcolm's influence was severely limited in Galloway, while many Hebridean islands and the Orkney and Shetland island groups were still under Norse rule. Still worse, after the events of 1071, the Scottish crown owed allegiance to the Normans, and Malcolm's son David was brought up in the English royal household: a surety of compliant behaviour – or should we say hostage?

It was, though, only after David became king in 1124 that Norman influence really spread to Scotland. In particular Norman nobles gained lands in Galloway and the north-east, the de Brus (or Bruce) family being a prime example, and with this came feudalism and the sinister symbols of the new order, castles. If feudalism controlled the people, so the new burghs – in particular the royal burghs – allowed the development of trade, but made it dependent on royal favour. With the church also under Norman influence, and without the continuous warring and troubles in Wales and – although beyond the scope of this book – Ireland, much of Scotland became another happy hunting ground, and succumbed to Norman temptations. It was, though, never to be the most harmonious or long-lasting of unions.

CASTLE SWEEN
Argyll O/S map 55 ref. 712788
Directions: From Dunadd, turn left on the A816. Turn
left along the minor road and left again on the B8025.
After 4 miles, turn left through Achanamara and follow
the road along the east shore of Loch Sween for 7 miles.
The castle is close to the shore within the Castle Sween
caravan park.

It takes a bit of time to reach Castle Sween but, with the
Paps of Jura rising to the west amid other outstanding
scenery, it is certainly worth the effort. Castle Sween is
possibly Scotland's oldest stone castle, dating to the early
twelfth century. At that time, much of Argyll was under
Norse rule, yet Castle Sween clearly displays a distinct
Norman influence.

   It is an enclosure castle, with four walls about 7 ft thick and still some 40 ft high. The main gate faces south, with
a sea-gate to the west. Wooden buildings, the slots for which can still be seen in the walls, sufficed for
accommodation. What differentiates Castle Sween from other enclosure castles on Scotland's western seaboard are
the Norman-inspired corner and pilaster buttresses. Apart from their strengthening effect, they offer a degree of
decoration to what must have been a pretty formidable stronghold.

   Fortunately, most of the original enclosure still exists, but a rectangular tower-house was added at the north-east
corner, and a smaller circular tower at the north-west. These were probably built in the fifteenth century when, via
a convoluted and nefarious route, the castle came into the hands of the MacMillans; the MacSweens, who probably
built the castle, had supported the English against Robert the Bruce and fled to Ireland as a consequence.

   Castle Sween still stands mighty and proud overlooking the sea loch. It was damaged by Royalists in 1647, but
essentially remains a Norman stronghold.

THE NORMAN CONQUERORS

One of the mysteries regarding the Normans is how a force of fewer than ten
thousand men could so relatively easily subdue a country with a population of
nigh on two million? First, once the initial victory had been secured, and their
reign of terror began to sweep through south-east England, so more Normans
quickly followed in their wake. Secondly, despite King Harold's emphatic victory
over the Norwegian forces at Stamford Bridge, near York, less than a fortnight
before the Battle of Hastings, his men and, in particular, his coterie of nobles had
been decimated. Those who had survived both battles were in no condition or
position to organize, let alone lead, determined resistance to the usurpers.

   One swallow does not make a summer, and nor does one victorious battle win
a war. Saxon England did not immediately succumb following the dramatic
events near Hastings; there were many skirmishes and dust-ups all round the
country over the next few years, some lasting a not-inconsiderable time. The
Norman armies moved rapidly to subdue these revolts, their passage through the
countryside leaving the Saxons in dread and seeking revenge. 'Living off the land'
was the usual method of provisioning an army. This innocent phrase hides dark
deeds of robbery and plunder, and often much worse, against those whose only
crime was to live on the Normans' chosen route. Despite being crowned King
William I of England, this title initially meant little to the people, say, north of

the River Trent. Even so, there are few other occasions in history when a country has fallen into the hands of an enemy as the result of a single battle. A battle, moreover, that lasted only a single day.

It has been argued that William had a detailed strategic plan to complete the conquest, following a decisive victory in pitched battle. Except in the broadest sense, that is most unlikely, since his information about the lie of the land and the depth of organization of the people would have been limited. On the other hand, he might have gambled that the planned Norwegian invasion of the north, followed by his landing in the south, would stretch Harold's resources to breaking point. Perhaps he really did expect his forthcoming victory to leave England a leaderless, rudderless ship on a sea increasingly prone to the most violent storms? If so, he was right!

NORMAN STRONGHOLDS

Motte and Bailey Castles

Duke William might not have had a cut-and-dried plan to overcome England, but he certainly had the means to impose his will. Few people with an interest in British history can fail to know about motte and bailey castles. On the face of it, this was William's trump card with which to subjugate the Saxons and was probably the single most important physical factor in establishing control. Yet it was but one of several types of stronghold used by the Normans in the initial years following the victory at Hastings, albeit the one most suited to a rapid show of force.

As with the earliest Roman forts, the motte and bailey castle was both an offensive and a defensive stronghold. Moreover, as they often towered over their

Motte castles are anything but rare in Scotland. Druchtag motte is one of many in Galloway, and shares the locality with brochs, duns, hillforts and even a modern early warning station.

locality, they left the Saxons in little doubt as to who held all the aces. Knights and soldiers could sally forth and rough up a neighbouring village or two, or forcibly extend the boundaries of land under the lord's control and then, at the slightest sign of any superior resistance, retreat into their stronghold. Furthermore, unlike the Romans, who built their own, the wily Normans emphasized their superiority by forcing the Saxons to build these new-fangled strongholds in the first place. This really rubbed salt into the open, festering wounds.

There is no doubt about it, the physical impact of the Normans on England in particular, but also on Wales, Scotland and Ireland, was enormous. Within two hundred years of their invasion, many types of castle, cathedrals, religious houses, churches, manor houses and walled towns had been built throughout the land. Never before had such a dramatic and drastic change come over the landscape. Of course, there were thousands of Iron Age hillforts and hundreds of Scottish brochs, yet the former had taken many centuries to build. Norman building was quite another matter. And yet it is easy to overstate the case, in particular with regards to the humble motte and bailey castle.

There are about a thousand motte and bailey castles in Britain. Built of earth and timber, they could be erected remarkably quickly: a fortnight for the basic infrastructure of motte, earth bank and ditch, wooden fencing and tower would not break any records. Clearly, so long as timber was at hand, the motte and bailey castle was an ideal tool for its intended task. One could easily be forgiven for thinking that, within a month of the hostile Normans arriving in a locality, they would have built their castle and England was soon littered with wooden towers standing on what appear to be upturned pudding basins. Such a scenario was repeated many, many times – but there were limits.

About a hundred motte and bailey castles had been built by the time of the Domesday survey in 1086. This is a considerable number, but hardly enough to overwhelm the country. As the twelfth century dawned, there were probably twice that number, but many of them were in South Wales and the Marches. Fifty years later, after the baronial wars and the struggle for the throne between Stephen and Matilda had died down, they had probably doubled in number yet again. Now that, you might think, is more like it – but by that time the Saxons were, on the whole, well and truly subdued. The Normans, it would seem, had managed to gain control – and even to squabble over the spoils – of England with a pretty modest number of motte and bailey castles. A sure sign of their success?

So, just what is a motte and bailey castle? Well, like most catch-all phrases, this one conceals as much as it reveals. The motte is the mound on which a tower or keep was built. Not surprisingly, this was the main citadel of the stronghold, while the bailey was a ground-level defended enclosure. The archetypal motte and bailey castle has the motte in one corner of the bailey, as at Berkhamsted. However, there were also mottes without baileys, as at Thetford, mottes with two or more baileys, as at Windsor, and even castles with two mottes, as at Lincoln.

Reconstruction of a motte
and bailey castle.

The Motte

The mottes were the distinctive half of the combination. They were not all the
same shape, nor were they all man-made, and they varied considerably in size.
With a base diameter of anything from 100 to 250 feet (though some were even
smaller), and an assumed height, complete with wooden tower, of 70 to 120 feet
(though the Thetford motte might have been as much as 140 feet high), they
were dominating symbols of oppression: a most visible reminder of where the
power lay.

Surprisingly few mottes have been thoroughly excavated, but man-made
mottes were usually built using soil and spoil from the immediate locality. The
earth would be beaten down and was often interspersed with layers of stone, or
sometimes peat, to aid rigidity. Some mottes were pile-driven, though one would
assume that the wood would soon rot. The keep, and even the curtain wall,
might be built of horizontal rather than vertical timbers, as this method would
help to spread the load and reduce the stresses on the newly built motte. It is
most unlikely that this was a universal method, but it is certainly portrayed in
the Bayeux Tapestry.

Once the wooden palisade was built round the summit, the enclosed area was
rarely large and in the main the wooden keep was regarded as a final stronghold
and look-out tower: a last refuge rather than a place to live. In time, as the motte

The twelfth-century wall and thirteenth-century tower at Coity Castle.

The Normans soon transformed Carisbrooke, a former Roman fort, into a motte and bailey castle.

stabilized, some keeps were built higher: a vertical version of the knight's residence in the bailey. Thus the keep might contain storerooms on the ground floor, with the main hall on the first floor and the knight's personal quarters on the second floor, perhaps with a pitched roof and battlements above. Even so, the motte still had its spatial and defensive drawbacks; for example, it could be undermined and few keeps were ever rebuilt in stone.

By no means all mottes were entirely man-made, though. As with our prehistoric forebears, so the Normans would use a natural rocky knoll as a motte or, more usually, use a knoll as the basis for a man-made one. This easier and, presumably, more stable expedient would obviously need to present the same psychological and physically domineering effect on the hapless Saxons.

Aside from the bailey, a motte often had several other defensive features. Usually surrounded by either a ditch or moat, the slope of the motte was also an awkward and difficult obstacle, not unlike hillfort ditches. The fence at the top would afford the defenders protection and enable them to hinder the progress of any attackers while, of course, the men on top of the tower were ideally placed to fire down missiles on an attacking force.

As usual the entrance was the potential weak spot. Entry was probably gained by easy-to-remove wooden steps, either direct from the bailey or from a bridge over the moat; some may even have had a drawbridge. Since they were built of timber, hard evidence for the layout of entrances is scarce but, as with hillforts, there were probably several options.

It would be quite a major defect if the bailey could not be observed from the top of the keep. There might be exceptions, but this seems to have been the general case: height was, after all, the motte's main defensive attribute. Of course, a motte was only one half of the motte and bailey combination, although initially it was the most strategically important component. Even so, perhaps like a hillfort, a motte and bailey castle was unlikely to be capable of withstanding a siege of any duration or ferocity. It was relatively easy to undermine, and garrisons were never big, even at the largest castles. As time passed, despite some motte keeps being rebuilt in stone or transformed in some other way, it was the bailey, or outer defences, that were substantially developed.

And the Bailey

Stripped to its bare essentials, a bailey amounted to little more than a simple hillfort: a glacis rampart with a wooden fence on top, surrounded by a moat or ditch. One might assume that, without its motte or keep, the bailey would be no more effective in a siege than a hillfort, and would probably not have the advantage of being built on a hill either. Thus both the motte and bailey would need to have their own moats to be really secure.

Some castles had two or more baileys, and these could be arranged in a variety of ways. Even the layout of the motte in relation to the bailey varied widely, as might be expected: some mottes sat in the middle of a bailey, others between two baileys, while the motte at Skipsea Castle was separated from its bailey by marshland. The Normans were no fools; they had a general plan and adapted this to the local terrain and needs.

The bailey tended to house the castle's domestic buildings. Soldiers' quarters, stores, stables, chapel, a well and possibly even the knight's residence were all built there. This layout did not change much over the centuries. Even in the greatest castles, where the keep might serve as a store, residence, chapel and fully defensive citadel, many domestic functions were still located in the bailey.

Lincoln Castle has two mottes. The multangular Lucy Tower is pictured here from the Observation Tower motte.

The Bass of Inverurie was a motte and bailey castle in Aberdeenshire. The Little Bass motte is behind.

As usual, the entrance would be strengthened, especially at the earliest motte and bailey castles. A bridge over the moat, possibly with a lifting section, was essential, and the simplest castles probably had a couple of flanking towers. In time, stone walls replaced those of timber, but many castles were either abandoned or extensively remodelled. In any case, motte and bailey castles were regarded as old-fashioned by the thirteenth century, and while some survived and were further developed, it was the bailey that, with the addition of a ground-level keep, quite literally went from strength to strength.

Many hundreds of motte and bailey castles were built through the twelfth and into the thirteenth centuries. From the Bass of Inverurie in Aberdeenshire to Carisbrooke Castle on the Isle of Wight, and from Carew Castle in Pembrokeshire to Bungay in Suffolk, they can still be seen throughout Great Britain.

Some Norman knights even saw fit to build a motte and bailey castle at a former stronghold. Although the motte was demolished in the nineteenth century, the walls of the Roman Saxon Shore fort at Burgh Castle

BERKHAMSTED CASTLE
Hertfordshire O/S map 165 ref. 996083
Directions: Just to the south-east of the railway station.

While the stone remains are quite meagre, Berkhamsted Castle has probably the finest surviving earthworks of any motte and bailey castle. Even so, these are less than complete and are atypical, though are often cited otherwise.

Built by Robert, Count of Mortain – half-brother of William I – in about 1080, the denuded earthworks supported a castle which, for nearly five centuries, was home to both the mighty and the monarchy. True to form, its up-turned pudding-basin motte is almost surrounded by a moat, and has an adjoining bailey; the whole ensemble is enclosed by an outer moat. A further rampart and a second moat, now partly obliterated by the railway, hint that this was not exactly an ordinary, everyday motte and bailey castle.

The motte had a timber keep and the bailey a palisade fence. The keep and fence were rebuilt in stone in about 1155, with the former possibly having a tower inside the shell, as at Launceston Castle. Three circular towers were added to the bailey wall early in the thirteenth century, and a three-storey rectangular keep was built astride the west wall some fifty years later.

In 1216 King Louis of France besieged Berkhamsted, which capitulated after a fortnight of almost constant bombardment from siege-engines, possibly located on the tree-covered rampart and projecting platforms outside the castle at the north-east. In any case, Berkhamsted gained much improved accommodation and at one time, as a semi-royal castle, even housed a captured French king: a rather touching reversal of fortune.

Berkhamsted's demise was less heroic. Its stones were pillaged to build Berkhamsted Place, and the railway almost did for the earthworks. Fortunately, tragedy was averted and there is no better unmodified motte and bailey castle in the land.

enclosed a motte, while a handful of hillforts similarly enjoyed a new life. An outstanding example is Herefordshire Beacon, fully 1,114 feet high, in the Malvern Hills. A strong inner bailey surrounds the motte, with the two outer baileys being defended by the Iron Age ramparts. This fortress was stormed by Owen Glendower as recently as 1405. The hillfort rampart and ditch were refurbished at Old Sarum to form the outer bailey around the massive central motte, which housed not only the keep but also a bishop's palace. The outer bailey was developed to become a town, complete with cathedral. And what of the Saxon *burhs*? Well, they might have been able to hold off the Danes, but they could not stop the Normans. Wallingford has a motte and bailey castle within the *burh* walls, as did Wareham.

Elsewhere, the Normans built motte and bailey castles within towns, as at Lincoln and Southampton: tough luck if one's house was in the way. At Chester, the castle was built just outside the town and, at a later date, the town walls were extended to encompass it. Likewise at York, where the Baile Hill motte guards the west bank of the River Ouse and forms the end of the city wall, while the renowned Clifford's Tower covers the gap between the Rivers Fosse and Ouse. At Castle Acre the castle was built with a planned town in mind. In the event, the town was not built, but, as with Roman forts, settlements often grew up beside the new castles of oppression to become new towns.

Several of the greatest castles in England and Wales had their origins as a humble motte and bailey stronghold. Quite often the motte was levelled, but others were retained. In some cases, as with Windsor Castle, the motte keep still stands as a proud national symbol to this day. At others, such as Arundel Castle, it has been swamped by later development and appears now as a mere appendage to a far greater grand design. Let us do justice to the motte and bailey

LINCOLN CASTLE
Lincolnshire O/S map 121 ref. 975718
Directions: In Lincoln, at the top of Steep Hill.

The 6 acre bailey houses the Crown Court and other former prison buildings, the castle having served as a prison for most of its life. Yet Lincoln Castle is one of Britain's most splendid Norman strongholds, with few subsequent alterations to the defences. It is almost unique in having two mottes less than a stone's throw apart.

Begun in 1068, a rectangular enclosure, incorporating the south-west angle of the Roman town wall, was defended by a rampart and ditch; the stone wall was added by 1115. A century later the north-east tower was built, the pointed towers and a since demolished barbican were added to the east gate, and an arch and portcullis to the west gate. The latter was blocked in the fourteenth century. All these defences are well preserved.

Both mottes probably date to the eleventh century, but it is not known if they were built simultaneously. The Lucy Tower stands on the larger motte, along the south wall. Its multangular shell-keep, with many pilasters, is twelfth century and, though still 20 ft high, was originally twice the size. The lower courses of the rectangular Observation Tower are also Norman, built on the motte at the south-east angle. Fourteenth-century work surmounts this and, finally, the nineteenth-century tower. From here, the views are astounding. Why two mottes though? Was one for the bishop, and the other for the king's representative, who might just find themselves on opposite sides in turbulent times?

Unique though the castle is, with its fine Norman defences, it is dwarfed by the soaring majesty of the neighbouring cathedral. Just to the east of the castle, the cathedral close was fortified in the fourteenth century, and the Exchequergate, Pottergate and Bishop's Palace can all be seen. Newport Arch, Britain's only Roman gateway over a road, is to the north of Baile Gate. Lincoln is indeed a beautiful city of many historic parts.

castle, though. It was but one of several basic strongholds that the Normans used right from the start. Simple it might have been but, without it, there is little doubt that they would not have completed their invasion of England, and later enjoyed so much success in Wales, Scotland and Ireland so quickly. Like the Roman fort a millennium before, it served its purpose outstandingly well, was ideally suited to its tasks and remains one of the most versatile and hugely successful strongholds in history.

The Ringwork Castle

The what, one might ask? Of the main Norman strongholds, this is the type about which least is known. Although earth and timber enclosure castles have existed now for over nine hundred years, the name ringwork is a recent one that helps to distinguish them from stone enclosure castles. In many cases a sort of bailey within a bailey, these enclosures exchanged the motte for a modestly raised platform and bailey or ring enclosure. This housed the keep and other buildings usually located in the bailey of the motte and bailey castle.

On the whole, few enclosure castles have survived compared to their motte and bailey contemporaries. This was probably because they were easier to modify extensively, thus obliterating their humble origins; if abandoned, an earth bank and moat are far easier to plough out to extinction. Some, such as Eynsford Castle, were soon rebuilt in stone, but others, perhaps like Saltwood or Kingerby, possibly originally had a motte that was soon dismantled.

To complicate matters, there are some castles that were formerly considered to be ringworks but are now disputed. Take the massive earthworks at Castle

Rising, for instance. With a large inner bailey flanked by smaller baileys at the east and west sides, it is hardly a typical example; the inner bailey is not surrounded by the outer ones. This castle is mostly noted for its magnificent square keep that might be contemporary with the earthworks but, with or without the keep, it must have been a fairly impregnable stronghold.

Possibly even more than the motte and bailey castle, the ringwork castle was an easy stronghold to construct. If longevity were a major concern, so rebuilding and modification was soon undertaken. As with Castle Rising, many so-called ringworks might have similarly been developed far beyond their modest origins.

Rectangular Keep Castles

If the motte and bailey castle is the archetypal stronghold of the Norman Conquest, then the rectangular keep castle best typifies the might and power of the new masters. While mottes had their little wooden keeps, it was the great stone edifices that must have really inspired fear and awe among the Saxons, and which comprise some of the most massively built strongholds in Britain.

Considering that the vast majority of motte and bailey, and enclosure, castles were built of turf and timber, it might be a surprise to find that the first, and largest, keeps were built of stone within fifteen years of the initial invasion: now

Windsor Castle and the Thames.

The decorative yet well-fortified keep at Castle Rising is almost dwarfed by the sheer scale of the massive earthwork defences. It is very similar to the keep at Norwich Castle.

there's confidence for you. Mind you, the Normans had built similar castles in Normandy long before Duke William cast his avaricious eyes towards England. So it was really only a matter of time.

The most renowned of them all, the Tower of London's White Tower, was under construction before 1080, while that with the greatest area, at Colchester, was hard on its heels. These were different in design, but formed a general pattern for such castles for more than a century. A motte was neither necessary, as some keeps were over 100 feet tall, nor desirable, as it would soon destabilize such a massive building. In the main, the keep sat on a solid base, with its thick walls splayed out at the bottom and a tower in each corner, all within a bailey.

Stairs wound up within the towers, and although external openings at the lower levels were kept to an absolute minimum, there were larger windows higher up. Entry was gained via external stairs to the first or second floor (and to the third floor at Newcastle), and these were often later enclosed into a defensible forebuilding. To Saxon eyes such a stronghold must have appeared inviolable.

By area, Colchester Castle has the largest Norman keep in Europe. It was built on the site of a Roman temple that was destroyed when Boudicca sacked Camulodunum.

This was most certainly the case in the first decades after the Norman invasion, but time waits for no man. The rectangular keep was always a compromise: part fortification, part residence for the baron or king and his immediate retinue. Conditions could be cramped, even in the largest keeps – especially when besieged. Comfort and security remain uneasy bedfellows to this day. A keep could be a dark, dank and damp place to live – but let in more light and those windows attract the attention of attackers. Security is severely undermined.

The Normans turned the Roman fort at Portchester into a mighty castle. The keep has its own inner bailey, and the Roman wall forms the outer bailey. Henry V set sail from Portchester on his way to victory at Agincourt in 1415.

As the Norman barons began to wage war among themselves, especially during the uneasy reign of King Stephen (1135–54), these castles faced their first real threat. On the whole, they survived the test with room to spare, but in 1215 a corner of the keep at Rochester Castle was undermined; its subsequent collapse ensured the castle's surrender. By then, though, the writing was on the wall for the rectangular keep, especially those protected by a bailey with a simple curtain wall.

Thereafter, and for some time previously, additional defensive measures had been taken. Rounded corners were less easy to undermine, and afforded the defenders a better view of what attackers were up to at the wall base; blind-spots were thus reduced. More importantly, keeps of different shapes were built: round, multi-sided and shell keeps were not just a swanky styling exercise, but part of a determined effort to improve on the defensibility of the great rectangular keeps.

If the eleventh century was the age of the motte and bailey castle, the twelfth century was most certainly that of the rectangular keep. Further outstanding examples were built from Newcastle and Bamburgh to Portchester and Dover, and from Goodrich to the beautifully decorated keep at Norwich. In between, there were substantial keeps, at Castle Rising and Kenilworth, and many small ones: at Clitheroe the keep's diameter was less than 15 feet. No two were ever identical and though often slighted in the Civil War, many remain as silent and eerie shells of once-mighty strongholds, of which people once stood in dread and awe.

Other Stone Keep Castles

Many of the best mottes to be seen today are those surmounted with a shell keep. Windsor, Carisbrooke, Lincoln: these and many others are crowned with a circular stone keep. Maintaining all the defensive attributes and drawbacks of the motte itself, a shell keep was not easy to undermine and, so long as the motte was not destabilized, was difficult to attack. Their good all-round visibility gave the defenders a considerable advantage.

However, a shell keep was not usually a fully enclosed building. Having a central courtyard, with rooms ranged round the wall, and seldom being as high as they were wide, on the face of it they could almost be a Norman development of the Iron Age dun. Having a blank exterior wall, probably with an extended entrance, the analogy is not so far-fetched as it might appear, although there cannot possibly have been any effective influence. The profusion of windows at, say, Windsor Castle is more recent.

Not all shell keeps were built on a motte. Restormel Castle is probably the finest example of the shell keep. It appears to have been built on a motte, but the wall was actually built inside the earthworks of a ringwork. This keep is still in pretty much original condition. There is a larger shell keep on the Isle of Bute. Rothesay Castle has an elaborate entrance forebuilding and at first sight, does not appear to be a shell keep. The remains of four drum towers mask its origins, but they were a later addition. Rothesay Castle also stands on level ground, within a moat and curtain wall. Other fine shell keeps can be seen on mottes at Tamworth and Durham, and a variation is the keep at Farnham Castle. There, a stone shell revets the motte, which had a rectangular stone keep on top; its basement is within the motte. As with the motte keep in general, though, the shell keep had both defensive limitations and, especially when standing on a motte, space restrictions. In a less-than-harmonious world, something better was needed.

CASTLE RISING
Norfolk O/S map 132 ref. 666246
Directions: Take the A1078 north from Kings Lynn. Turn left on the A149 and the village and castle are just over a mile north, on the left.

Many centuries ago the adjacent village was a port on The Wash, but it is now over 3 miles inland. The castle was built in about 1138 by William of Albini, later Earl of Arundel, as a stronghold-residence for his new wife, the widow of King Henry I.

The most remarkable feature of the well-preserved, 55 ft tall, two-storey keep is the wonderful external stonework decoration, not unlike that at Norwich Castle, supplemented with powerful towers and pilasters. The keep is entered by a splendid forebuilding, reached by an impressively decorated covered stairway. A cross-wall divides the interior, and there are few external openings. The residential quarters were on the first floor and the garderobes were divided for Ladies and Gentlemen – a seemingly rare innovation for Norman times.

All that notwithstanding, it is the surrounding earthworks that are the most impressive feature of this stronghold. The keep stands within the central bailey, defended by massive earthworks that compare with those of any Iron Age hillfort. The rampart rises fully 30 ft above the bottom of the ditch and, rather than dwarfing the keep, almost conspires to enhance its apparent size. There are the remains of the gateway and an adjoining short length of fourteenth-century curtain wall.

Beyond the gate is the smaller east bailey, with its modest earthworks: something of a cross between an outer bailey and a large barbican. Finally, to the west lies a bailey on a raised platform, which has not survived quite so well. In total, these earthworks cover 12 acres.

Despite being an occasional royal stronghold (it was once owned by the Black Prince), the mighty earthworks ultimately limited the scope for development, either as a stronghold or as a residence. By the sixteenth century decay had set in and a long retirement beckoned.

ROCHESTER CASTLE
Kent O/S map 178 ref. 742686
Directions: At the west end of the High Street.

Viewed from across the River Medway, the proximity of Rochester's distinctive cathedral and the mighty castle presents a striking and emphatic reminder of how church and state were inextricably interlinked in Norman and medieval England. In this, Rochester was not unique: the castle and cathedral were similarly close at Lincoln and Durham, but only at Rochester is there an apparent degree of architectural parity.

The bailey incorporates the south-west angle of the Roman town wall of Durobrivae. An enclosure castle with a rampart, palisade fence and ditch existed by 1086, and soon after Gundulf, Bishop of Rochester, added a stone curtain wall. Then, from about 1127 to 1140, the glorious rectangular keep, with its squared corner towers, was built. Though the Archbishop of Canterbury acted as its constable, Rochester was very much a royal stronghold.

This is one of the great Norman keeps. Standing 113 ft high with four turrets rising a further 12 ft, it is the tallest Norman keep in Britain; there are five storeys plus a battlement wall-walk. With 12 ft thick walls and entry gained through a magnificent forebuilding, complete with chapel, defence was assured. On the other hand, as the decorative stonework shows, the residential accommodation was certainly fit for a king.

Rochester Castle was besieged in 1088 and by King John in 1215. For two months it held out, until the south-east tower was undermined. Its collapse eventually brought about the castle's surrender. King Henry III had this corner rebuilt with a round tower, while the curtain wall was restored and the south-east tower and inner bailey were added. A further siege, by Simon de Montfort in 1264, saw the keep held for the king, despite the bailey having fallen.

Major repairs in the fourteenth century could not prevent the castle becoming outdated. It was in decay by the 1500s and, though considered as a potential barracks in the 1780s, it has remained unused, but certainly not unloved, ever since.

A castle fit for . . . a bishop! Farnham Castle is one of Britain's many ecclesiastical strongholds.

By the mid-twelfth century, to improve on the rectangular keep, the first circular and polygonal keeps began to appear in England, probably influenced by developments overseas. Neither type was built in anything like the numbers of the rectangular keep, and there was certainly no set format to the designs. Without a doubt the finest surviving polygonal keep is at Orford Castle. This magnificent keep is just about all that remains of a once-large royal castle, and it now stands in splendid isolation. With three turrets, externally it has about twenty sides, but it is circular internally. The keep at Conisbrough Castle has six turrets and, with its intramural stairs (rather than the usual spiral ones) bears a passing resemblance to an

Restormel Castle boasts a beautiful shell keep.

The interior of Restormel Castle.

Iron Age broch. Chilham Castle has an octagonal keep, and the remains at Odiham Castle show this was the same.

The turrets of polygonal keeps afforded better protection for the lower wall and foundations of the keep, and also improved the defenders' visibility and line of fire, than those of the rectangular keep. Another more widely used method of achieving these ends was the circular keep. By far the best preserved twelfth-century example is the massive Great Keep at Pembroke Castle. There are others at Skenfrith, Barnard and Bothwell, with several donjons in Scotland. In the main, though of Norman origin, these latter tended to be of thirteenth-century origin.

The basic shell keep was clearly derived from the wooden palisade on a motte, and followed hard on the heels of the massive rectangular keep. Polygonal and round keeps were a later development, probably derived from a combination of harsh experiences during the twelfth-century baronial wars, and influence from abroad. Not all castles, however, boasted a keep.

The great and mighty donjon at the magnificently restored Pembroke Castle. You see, it can be done!

The Enclosure Castle

At its most basic level, the enclosure castle developed from the ringwork castle. Where possible sited on a rocky mound, strong curtain walls, perhaps with a projecting tower and gatehouse, were often protected by a moat and rampart. However, the wall and its towers were not only the main defence but also, like the shell keep, provided the main accommodation.

Although the enclosure – or *enceinte* – was the basic requirement to house the garrison, there were many variations on the enclosure castle theme. Eynsford Castle had a gatehouse but no other towers, and free-standing buildings were later added within the enclosure. Framlingham Castle, in contrast, had thirteen towers along the curtain wall, one of which was extended to become the main hall. The enclosure castle at Rochester was soon transformed by the marvellous keep that so dominates the site today. White Castle had a great tower that was later partly demolished so that the enclosure walls could be linked up. As with all strongholds, it was very much a case of horses for courses.

Some of the more exciting developments with enclosure castles came in the thirteenth and fourteenth centuries, when keeps either fell out of favour, or fell foul of siege engines. The concentric castles were a development of the enclosure castle, with a sort of double enclosure. These were clearly the way ahead, with the first examples built in the twelfth century, but at that time and with the offensive weapons then developed, the stone keep was still undoubtedly the king.

Other defensive developments of the first century and a half after the Battle of Hastings, apart from the moat, included wide expanses of water to counter the siege engines and stone-throwing contraptions that were rapidly developed

---

FRAMLINGHAM CASTLE
Suffolk O/S map 156 ref. 287637
Directions: Just north-east of the town centre.

Framlingham: the very name suggests a sleepy rural market town. This may be true today but for some considerable time it was home to one of the mightiest and most treacherous families in England: the Bigods, Earls of Norfolk.

A motte and bailey castle was built here in the late eleventh century. A stone hall and chapel were added in about 1160, then in 1175 the castle (but not the hall) was demolished as punishment for the Bigods having fought against the king. On payment of a hefty fine, the Bigods regained the castle and began building the present magnificent enclosure in about 1190.

With towering walls some 45 ft high, Framlingham was an advanced and futuristic castle. The concentric defences, with twelve mostly open-backed, rectangular towers but no keep, hint at a Crusader influence. The original hall stood against the eastern wall, adjacent to the entrance and a Great Hall was built opposite; this was supplanted by the present seventeenth-century Poorhouse. There is now a mostly sixteenth-century entrance facing the town, and a postern gate and the Prison Tower extending out to the Lower Court.

The earthworks of the Lower Court and the massive outer bailey round the east, south and west sides – with the north and east further protected by the town ditch – are almost as impressive as the castle itself. In addition, the river was dammed to create a lake beyond the Lower Court, mainly to provide fish and fowl, but certainly not diminishing the castle's defensive capacity. The Bigods, however, sided with the barons against King John, and Framlingham Castle was seized for the king in 1216.

Framlingham Castle is an outstanding survivor of late Norman stronghold building. The distinctive brick chimneys, most of which are purely decorative, are clearly of Tudor origin. From the dizzying heights of the wall-head, Suffolk opens out like a map before your eyes.

during the violent twelfth century. Gatehouses gained a drawbridge and portcullis, and became ever more elaborate, and, at the top of the walls, battlements and various projecting machicolations protected the defenders while enabling them to get at the attackers. Advances in military engineering are most pronounced in times of strife, and the twelfth century was most surely that. Each offensive innovation was countered by a defensive improvement. This very serious game of cat-and-mouse was nothing new and, of course, continues to this very day.

Scottish Castles

Though there are few stone castles in Scotland from this period, there are exceptions. Rothesay Castle has already been mentioned, and Castle Sween is a twelfth-century enclosure castle. There, the inhabitants probably lived in timber lean-to buildings, similar to those in hillforts and duns well over a thousand years before. Up in the far north, Old Wick Castle is a possible Norse tower keep. Although of quite basic design, it is a forerunner of Scotland's great tower-houses and was clearly located to enjoy commanding coastal views. A drawbridge spanned a ditch, with a rampart and gatehouse beyond. Old Wick Castle is not unique, as there are remains of another promontory tower farther down the coast at Forse. These were probably the twelfth-century equivalent of the Iron Age brochs that overlook the same coastline.

Even farther north, on the tiny Orcadian island of Wyre, is Scotland's oldest stone castle. Cubbie Roo's Castle comprises a small, almost square keep about 25 feet across, with walls over 6 feet thick. Today, only the ground floor remains, but it probably had another couple of storeys, and commands the island. Outer defences included a stone wall, a ditch and an earth bank. Cubbie Roo's Castle

---

CUBBIE ROO'S CASTLE
Wyre, Orkney Islands O/S map 7 ref. 441264
Directions: Starting on Orkney Mainland, the boat for the island of Wyre departs from Tingwall, off the A965/A966 from Kirkwall. The castle is a mile walk from the jetty.

This is one of Scotland's oldest stone castles. One would perhaps hesitate to describe it as a precursor of the tower-house but, in some respects, such an assertion would not be too wide of the mark.

Cubbie Roo was Kolbein Hruga, 'the giant' or 'goblin' briefly mentioned in the *Orkneyinga Saga*, *c.* 1150, while the castle was thought a difficult place to attack in the *Hakonar Saga* of 1231. Considering the state of contemporary strongholds on the Orkney Islands, if any existed, this comes as no surprise.

A three-storey tower stood within outer defences comprising an oval stone wall, earthwork and ditch. The tower is only about 25 ft in diameter, with walls about 5 ft thick, and was probably more a refuge than a permanent residence. Today, the tower is only 6 ft high, and its cramped interior is all too apparent. The entrance was recorded as being to the first floor in the seventeenth century, and was reached by ladders, as were the upper storeys from within. The ground floor was used for storage, and a rock-cut tank is still visible. So, a forerunner of the tower-house?

The southern outer defences have been obliterated by up to five phases of later building, beginning in the thirteenth century, probably as the owner moved to the farm and long-house beside St Mary's Chapel. Cubbie Roo's Castle shows that the peoples of the northern isles did not lag behind those elsewhere in Scotland when it came to stronghold building.

might also have been a Norse stronghold, and probably featured in a couple of Nordic sagas. Scottish stone castles were rare until the thirteenth century but, with their great drystone building tradition, the necessary skills were merely dormant.

ECCLESIASTICAL STRONGHOLDS

It is surprising, in the light of today's values, how many castles were built for and by bishops. Durham Castle, for instance, was the residence of the Bishop of Durham, and Farnham Castle belonged to the Bishop of Winchester. Distinctions between heavenly and earthly lords were often quite blurred, not least in the twelfth-century baronial wars.

Wolvesey, at Winchester, is a fortified palace, with a tower and a great hall within a quadrangular enclosure. Bishops were among the richest men in the land, so they needed well-defended palaces to house their accumulated wealth. A castle was the most appropriate residence in the circumstances, although comfort was, presumably, of not inconsiderable importance.

As the sees were larger than they are today, and travel far slower, so some bishops had what might be called a series of staging posts for themselves and their retinues during their travels. Farnham Castle was one such stronghold, while Bishop's Waltham Palace also belonged to the Bishop of Winchester. The former was an extended motte and bailey castle; the latter had a tower within a quadrangle, and a large gatehouse. As with castles, these strongholds were extensively developed during subsequent centuries, but had their origins in the Norman era.

THE FORTIFIED MANOR HOUSE

This was the great compromise residence for lesser nobles and knights, uneasily balancing security and comfort. Until the thirteenth century such a proposition had been almost an irrelevance. No sooner had the Normans subdued the Saxons than two or three decades of baronial wars broke out in the mid-twelfth century. King Henry II (1154–89) put an end to all that nonsense and demolished hundreds of castles to boot, but there was more unrest later in his reign. Then, as King Richard I (1189–99) spent less than a year of his reign at home, so there was plenty of opportunity for further baronial dissent. England was seldom a haven of peace and tranquillity, and manor houses were probably built only by the lowest knights in the pecking order.

Whatever the constrictions of a castle, at least it was relatively secure. Even when Henry II was at his most destructive, there was no large-scale move towards the alternative: a modestly fortified manor house. There are, of course, many manor houses throughout

To the Saxon common-man, there was little to distinguish between the secular and ecclesiastical Norman lords. Wolvesey Palace, adjacent to Winchester Cathedral, was one of several such strongholds. No churchman had more fortified residences than the powerful Bishops of Winchester.

Weeting Castle, Norfolk, is a splendid example of a twelfth-century fortified manor house.

England, but these are mostly medieval. Weeting Castle is a twelfth-century exception, a masonry two-storeyed house protected by a moat and, presumably, a wall. Like the early stone keeps, it may have been a forerunner of things to come, but its time had not yet arrived. As for Wales and Scotland, forget it. No Norman was ever going to feel secure enough to forgo his military stronghold in those lands for many years to come.

THE WALLED TOWN

Whatever happened to the Saxon *burhs*? Earth ramparts, wooden palisade fences and ditches undoubtedly had their limitations, but when the Normans came to fortify the towns, out came the old favourites again. In some towns, such as Chester, York and London, lengths of the Roman walls still existed but, for the most part, the earth rampart, ditch and fence were the norm.

Southampton's Bargate was rather over-enthusiastically restored in Victorian times. The original Norman arch is still visible within the enlarged gateway.

If building in stone occurred anywhere, it was usually at the weakest part of a town's defences: the entrance. Southampton's stone Bargate, for example, was built in the twelfth century, while the wall was an earth bank with an outer ditch. It is unlikely that this was a rare example at that time, but the greatest advances in town defences had to wait until the following centuries.

In any case, a town's walls could be quite restrictive, both financially and physically; it was anything but cheap to keep in good repair, let alone to man it. These considerations do not seem to have been too important though, for during the thirteenth century many English towns began to rebuild in stone what existed in earth and timber. As with castle building, so town walls developed rapidly, in many cases utilising the latest defensive measures. Perhaps the only real surprise was that so few Saxon *burhs* had their walls upgraded.

CONCLUSION

Whatever and wherever the castle, it was both a stronghold and place for living and working. Whether a royal or baronial castle, it had to pay its way and, not unnaturally, a castle often became an area's economic focal point. Feudalism ensured that this was usually the case and, with a castle built in a town, or with a settlement growing up nearby, so a lord, knight or the king would be able to exert a monopoly over various trades and economic activities. As with the great country estates of the seventeenth century and beyond, the castle was always expected to make a profit.

Like the Romans, the Normans built their temporary strongholds to designs proven in European conflict. The campaign strongholds of both the Romans and the Normans were relatively quick to build, used local materials that were in plentiful supply and, most importantly, could function both offensively and defensively. Utilized in conjunction with the ruthless efficiency of the Roman army, or the more straightforward terror-tactics of the Normans, these strongholds of apparently modest strength gained a far greater menace.

In time, as the invaded area was pacified and considered safe, so these initial dual-purpose strongholds were either abandoned or rebuilt on a more permanent basis in stone. At this stage they became less offensive, more defensive, and were probably viewed as symbols of oppression. Yet this was only one attribute of the great stone Norman castles. They were also the local seat of legal, economic and physical power. Make no bones about it, a castle was not the cold and empty edifice we usually see today, but a thriving and bustling centre of an estate or an administrative county. Throughout Norman times and the early Plantagenet years, these castles never, ever lost their stronghold capabilities.

When strongholds were built (or rebuilt) in stone, so the comfort of the owner, his advisers and family became an important consideration, but the defensive stakes were always being uprated. Developments in offensive weapons and tactics leapt forward during the twelfth century and strongholds were adapted to take account of them. Earth and timber castles were unlikely to survive a siege by the effective and efficient forces of Henry II. In particular, measures were taken to prevent attackers undermining or breaking through the base of walls. Arrow-loops were built into walls enabling defenders to fire out with impunity. These and many other developments were directed towards improving the impregnability of the castle, especially as a stronghold. For the Saxons, the stone castle was always a bridge too far.

CHAPTER 5

THE MIDDLE AGES

(1201–1500)

This was the age of chivalry: a time when knights in shining armour fought duels in accordance with an unwritten code that, centuries later, inspired the noble sporting ideals of the Marquess of Queensberry. It was a time of great feats of derring-do; when the Crusades drew to their cause men driven by a higher authority to recapture Jerusalem for Christendom; and when brave, besieged defenders of a castle could surrender with honour, marching out from their stronghold, with banners held aloft, to be treated with mercy.

Such are the utopian images conveyed by the stories handed down through the generations, showing how honour and gallantry governed our ancestors' behaviour. Tales of grand castles bedecked in gaily coloured flags, playing host to tournaments, jousts or simply magnificent fairs, further enhance this impression. And what outstanding castles they were. In the Middle Ages the poor serf, tied to the land, could become a free man if he remained at large for a year and a day, while folk heroes almost vied with each other to aid the downtrodden on their way. Robin Hood was but one of many. Yet all was not as it seems.

King John was by no means the evil baddie he is often portrayed as; the barons who opposed him acted out of pure self-interest, not out of any concern for the country, still less for the common-man. Edward I, that great, chivalrous warrior king, ordered the steadfast defenders of one Scottish castle to be strung up from the nearest trees when they surrendered. It was not an isolated incident. Several south coast towns were devastated by French raids in the fourteenth and fifteenth centuries, but that was as nothing compared to the havoc and turmoil caused by English armies living off the land in France: so much for cries of St George, Harry and England. As for King Richard III, his suspected murder of the young princes in the Tower was but one of many dastardly deeds that tarnished the imagined glory of the Wars of the Roses.

The three centuries from 1201 to 1500 were marked and marred by almost continuous unrest. War was always likely to break out somewhere in Britain. Before the thirteenth century was two decades old, the barons had undermined royal authority, and a French army was on the loose. Not for the last time did the resistance of Dover and its castle save England by the skin of her teeth from

The jewel of English castles? Warwick Castle has some of the finest defences of any stronghold in Britain.

an onslaught of superior foreign forces. Naturally, the beleaguered Welsh saw England's misfortune as their opportunity to throw out the Norman interlopers, but dissent among the Welsh princes, alarmed by the growing power of Gwynedd, caused deep divisions. And once Edward I had finally made up his mind to oust Llewelyn ap Gruffydd from power in 1277, so the days of Welsh independence were numbered. It might have taken three campaigns, a massive stronghold and town building operation, and more than a few upsets along the way but, as the fourteenth century dawned, so Wales became ever more intertwined with England.

Edward then turned his attention to Scotland and invaded in 1296, after a dispute with John Balliol and King John. It took him barely twenty-one weeks to overrun the country. The small castles at Edinburgh and Stirling were no match for Edward's siege engines and singularly aggressive tactics. The war was over in no time at all and the future looked decidedly bleak for the Scots. Then, enter stage right, the ultimate local hero: William 'Braveheart' Wallace.

In 1297 Wallace defeated an English army at Stirling Bridge, and soon his marauding band – a rather less than disciplined force – was ravaging northern England. Unfortunately for Wallace, several English castles held out, including Edinburgh, Stirling and Berwick, and a year later Edward I retaliated. Wallace was defeated at Falkirk and, to all intents and purposes, that was that.

Not for long though. In 1303 Edward marched north once again, backed by none other than Robert Bruce. By and large, the English held the southern areas of Scotland with several strategic castles; as in Wales, they also began to fortify towns such as Perth, Linlithgow and Selkirk with ramparts, ditches and fences. Three years later though, Bruce swapped sides and initiated a guerrilla war against the English. Things went from bad to worse for the enigmatic Bruce, and he was reduced to watching spiders spinning webs. Then Edward I died and his less-than-determined son, Edward II, was manna from heaven, so far as Bruce and the Scots were concerned.

Slowly but surely, one by one the English-held castles fell to the Scots and, in the main, were razed to the ground. The Middle Ages was a time of great advances in military technology. The advent of gunpowder was still some way in the future, but there had been considerable improvements in siege engines and artillery, and defences against these, during the thirteenth century. Nevertheless, the Scots' method of attacking a castle relied less on a show of force and more on stealth, with a distinct touch of ingenuity and technology that would not have been out of place in Roman times: the use of rope ladders. There was, of course, more to this devastating new siege weapon than meets the eye. Iron hooks were tied to the ropes to enable them to cling to the top of, say, a curtain wall; the more men, and thus weight, on the ladder the better. Under cover of darkness and usually with the benefit of a diversionary attack, the Scots would climb their ladders unimpeded, as when Edinburgh Castle, among others, was taken. Rope ladders proved an ideal, indeed the essential, weapon in the campaign to expel the English.

After the victory at Bannockburn in 1314, Scottish raids on northern England increased markedly. Some of these had semi-official blessing, but there were also privateers, the infamous Reiver gangs, who indulged themselves purely for their own ends. For some considerable time the English seemed powerless to prevent this rampant aggression, although raids were seldom conducted against fortified towns. Carlisle, for instance, successfully withstood a siege in 1315. Berwick fell to the Scots three years later and, unusually, was garrisoned rather than destroyed. Thereafter followed two hundred years of almost continuous turmoil in the Borders, with successive raids by English and Scots; this resulted in the rapid growth of the tower-house and pele-tower strongholds that came to dominate the Borders landscape.

Newark Castle was built for the Bishop of Lincoln. It was of considerable strategic importance, guarding the intersection of the Great North Road and the Fosse Way, and overlooking the River Trent.

THE HUNDRED YEARS WAR

King Edward II did not have a particularly happy reign, with England being a far from united land. A strong leader was needed, but that he was most certainly not. He abdicated and was murdered soon after, but once his young successor, Edward III, took the reins of power for himself sparks really began to fly. He had a fairly just claim to the throne of France, where lands held by the English monarchs had dwindled considerably over the years. This position was soon

HERMITAGE CASTLE
Roxburghshire O/S map 79 ref. 497961
Directions: Take the B6399 south from Hawick. After 12 miles, turn right on the minor road at Hermitage. The castle is a mile further along.

Even today, Liddesdale can be a wild and less than welcoming place. The railway that once wound north from Carlisle to the main Borders towns has gone and so, fortunately, has the time when Liddesdale was one of the most violent and lawless places in Britain. If Reiver gangs were not causing disruption and mayhem, it was internecine Scottish wars or, quite often, English or Scottish armies on their way to or from battle. Whoever first built the castle recorded as being repaired in 1300 obviously needed a stronghold.

That, though, may have been more residence than stronghold, and Hermitage's original rectangular tower had been strengthened by the time it was granted to the Douglases. They added an enclosure at the east and west sides and, by the end of the fourteenth century, four great corner towers. Thus, Hermitage Castle became the strongest and most feared of the Borders strongholds. The great, blank forbidding walls were daunting enough, but the towers at the east and west sides were joined at the top with a parapet and flying arch, further emphasizing Hermitage's impregnability. With a projecting hoarding round the battlements, Hermitage Castle was the most formidable tower-house in Britain.

Hermitage Castle relied mainly on the sheer strength of its walls for defence, backed by ramparts, ditches and the marshy nature of the ground, for it was overlooked by hills on all sides. A liberal supply of gun-loops was added in the sixteenth century, further enhancing its impregnable reputation. Once a semblance of peace came, though, Hermitage's day of reckoning arrived; it was an uncompromising mighty stronghold, not a potential grand palace. Its time was up and, after changing hands on numerous occasions, Hermitage was finally abandoned, fortunately to be partially restored in the nineteenth century. But the legend lives on . . .

reversed, and for the next century England and France engaged in a long and debilitating struggle. In the end neither country was able to show any particularly worthwhile gain for all their efforts, let alone be able to counter the not inconsiderable costs. In any case, the English were usually at a disadvantage, for Scotland had entered into a pact with France – the Auld Alliance – to strike at England if either country were attacked. This had the effect of bestowing official, if clandestine, approval to the Reiver raids. Pitched battles on the northern frontier were few and far between though, and the Scottish disaster at Flodden Field (1513) was one of very few major extravaganzas in a rather forgotten theatre, at least as far as London was concerned.

Matters were rather different for England's southern coastal towns. The French were not prepared to hang about and wait for war to be fought solely on their soil. In the summer of 1338 the undefended port at Portsmouth was raided. Four months later, the partially walled town of Southampton, complete with its castle, was set ablaze and comprehensively sacked. The following year Harwich and Hastings went up in flames, while Rye was attacked; the French were then chased back to Boulogne, and that town was ravaged in revenge. Tit for tat.

Thereafter, the emphatic victories at Crecy (1346) and Poitiers (1356) gained England the upper hand, but by 1360 Rye and Hastings were on the receiving end yet again. Things really started to get serious from 1377 when the Spanish joined in with the French. The old favourites Rye and Hastings were plundered and burned again, as were several other coastal towns. A French force landed and moved inland to attack Lewes and, after invading the Isle of Wight, only came a cropper when they tried to attack Carisbrooke Castle. The next year the

DUART CASTLE
Mull O/S map 49 ref. 748354
Directions: From the ferry pier at Craignure, head south on the A849. Once past Torosay Castle, a road heads east to the castle above the shore.

There are fewer castles in the Western Highlands and islands than in some other parts of Scotland, but not many enjoyed a peaceful and sedate existence. Duart Castle stands proud and magnificent on its headland, dominating the Sound of Mull, the Firth of Lorn and the entrance to Loch Linnhe. On a clear day, the views are more than spectacular.

Such a location had many benefits in the Middle Ages, and not a few drawbacks. While it was a fine stronghold from which to observe all that went on, it was an obvious target for raiders. Originally built as an enclosure castle in the thirteenth century, possibly by the MacDonalds, the courtyard incorporates the remaining sections in its east and south walls. This was some 30 ft high and was protected on its vulnerable east side by a ditch.

By the fourteenth century Duart was in the hands of the MacLeans. A rectangular tower-house was squeezed into the narrow space between the enclosure and the cliff edge, and the courtyard became the outer defences; later, ranges were built round the interior. The tower-house is squat, yet of massive proportions, and needed no additional protection. Gun-loops were added later.

The MacLeans were not initially the crown's most loyal supporters, but they remained faithful throughout the wars of the seventeenth century, though Duart briefly fell to the Campbells. After the '45 Jacobite rising, Duart was occupied by government troops, and then handed over to the Campbells, who allowed it to decay. It was repurchased by the MacLean chief in 1911, and has been well restored as the clan centre and chief's residence. Duart Castle clearly illustrates the transition from simple enclosure, through tower-house stronghold, to a defensible residence of the seventeenth century.

Spanish attacked Cornwall, and in 1380 the French sailed up the Thames to burn warehouses at Gravesend, passing the advanced fort at Queenborough (Kent) on the way. It was all becoming very serious, indeed.

The next decade was decisive. England faced a very real threat of invasion. Older town defences were brought up to scratch and new defences hastily built. Rye, for example, was more than grateful for its town defences. New strongholds began to appear, and any number of manor houses and even bishop's palaces were granted permission to crenellate (to be fortified). Although the French never invaded, a revolutionary change took place at this time of frantic fortress building: many new strongholds were equipped not only to resist firearms, but were intended to harness them as part of the defences.

THE ADVENT OF GUNPOWDER

Unlike the Atom Bomb, gunpowder was not initially all it was cracked up to be; castles with great towering keeps were not rendered obsolete overnight. Cannons might have been used by the Scots to besiege Stirling Castle in 1342, and a century later King James II was almost the medieval equivalent of an armaments anorak; he even met his death when a gun exploded. But that is just the point: gunpowder was most unreliable.

It was even more so in the fourteenth century. Not only did the huge, unwieldy artillery pieces have to be dismantled and manhandled along Britain's unmade roads, but they were slow to fire, inaccurate and immobile. Worse, the essential elixir, gunpowder, needed to be mixed up on site: a most hazardous task. The

No town was attacked and sacked by the French more often than Rye in the Hundred Years War. It took several decades before Rye was effectively defended, and its Landgate is a reminder of those turbulent times.

Like Lincoln Castle, Lewes Castle has two mottes, though they are far apart. The castle gateway leads off the main street. Note its fine machicolations.

inclement British weather could never be relied on to help, either. In fact, stone-throwing artillery was quicker to fire, more accurate, less dangerous to use and had an equal range.

Not unnaturally, these factors meant that artillery was of more use to stronghold defenders in the fourteenth century. Just as in the Roman period, towers on curtain walls were strengthened to carry the new fire-breathing monsters, while the all-important task of mixing the gunpowder could be more safely undertaken in dry conditions. In addition, height gave the cannons a greater range, and while it was a thankless task to manoeuvre one about on a tower, there were conventional weapons to fall back on, such as bows and arrows and stone-throwing artillery.

Nowadays it is difficult to tell whether a tower was strengthened to carry primitive artillery, such as the trebuchet (a large catapult), or the latest cannon. Queenborough Castle, seemingly 150 years ahead of its time, might conceivably have been designed to withstand attack by cannon, or perhaps to use them in defence. As it was demolished shortly after the Civil War we cannot tell but there are other examples. Quarr Abbey on the Isle of Wight was fortified with a series of gun-loops in about 1365, but the first place to receive the familiar keyhole gun-loops, an inverted keyhole at that, was probably the West Gate at Canterbury. Towers along the city's wall were also fortified, and the

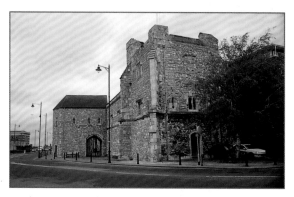

Southampton's God's House Tower housed the town's gunner and armoury.

The artillery wall at Threave Castle was the first built in Scotland.

gatehouse itself is covered from most angles by gun-loops.

The very real threat of a French invasion acted as a spur for the new artillery defences, and fortifications bristling with gun-loops sprang up in the south-east. Cooling Castle followed a year later, Bodiam Castle in 1385 and then in 1398 Cow Tower was built at Norwich as a self-contained gun-tower. Thereafter, while progress slowed as the threat of invasion receded, towns began to incorporate gun-loops in their defences. For example, by 1417 Southampton's extended God's House Tower had gun-loops on the first floor and a gun platform for cannon on the roof.

By the fifteenth century, thanks partly to the advent of corned gunpowder – mixed in advance, more consistent and safer to use – guns became more reliable siege weapons. Even so, there was no stampede either to abandon castles or to convert them to utilize firearms. The Wars of the Roses saw the royal siege train used just once, at Bamburgh Castle, but the Scots were more enthusiastic. Threave Castle incorporated artillery defences in its new curtain wall in about 1450, while Ravenscraig Castle, completed in 1462, was Scotland's first specialist artillery fort, its gun-loops having their own vaulted rooms: Britain's first casemates. In the same decade Raglan Castle was rebuilt with a full complement of gun-loops, while new castles and manor houses routinely incorporated them in their defences. The time for change was certainly ripe, but it came slowly.

Section through a keyhole gun-loop.

The traverse (foreground) and caponier (rear) guard the ditch at Craignethan Castle.

THE BLACK DEATH

Plague may have had little to do with stronghold development, but the Black Death had the most

BODIAM CASTLE
Sussex O/S map 199 ref. 785256
Directions: From Hastings, take the A21 and A229 north, and turn right to Bodiam. The castle is well signed.

Bodiam Castle is almost all things to all men: a fortified mansion; a quadrangular castle; a romantic palace or a futuristic fortress. For some, it was the most advanced stronghold of its day; for others it was a glorified luxury-residence, all dressed up to impress with fancy-dan, but militarily flawed, defences.

Bodiam was built in 1386–88 by Sir Richard Dalyngrigge (Dalling Ridge) – who had done rather well out of the Hundred Years War – ostensibly to deter French raids up the River Rother. The castle's wide moat is just one of its defensive measures.

This rectangular castle has four circular corner towers, about 60 ft tall, with the east, west and south walls further protected by rectangular towers. There was a sally-port, served by two drawbridges and a causeway across the moat at the south. There are few external windows, though the 8 ft thick walls have been considered too thin to resist even the cumbersome contemporary cannon.

The main entrance was impressively defended. It was approached by a causeway and drawbridge from the west to the octagonal islet, but one had to undertake a right-angle turn across another drawbridge to the now dismantled barbican. From there, a third drawbridge led to the twin-towered gatehouse, additionally protected by three sets of doors and portcullises, with murder holes and, most importantly, gun-loops covering the approach. The modest fire-power of contemporary guns would surely not have seriously troubled Bodiam, while such weapons would certainly have benefited the defenders, at least in anything but a full-blown siege.

Inside, the eastern range of buildings was fitted out for Dalyngrigge, with the western half for his retainers. Perhaps this was a precautionary measure, in case treacherous thoughts turned to evil deeds, but Dalyngrigge was probably looking forward to some privacy in his later years. While Bodiam Castle is in fine, even magnificent, external condition, the internal ranges were destroyed in the Civil War.

It is not beyond the bounds of possibility that Bodiam was all show and no substance; on the two occasions it was called into action, it failed miserably. In 1483 the Earl of Surrey took it for King Richard III, without trouble, while in 1643 Bodiam was quickly surrendered to Parliament's troops. That was just as well, for today its almost symmetrical, dream-like proportions make Bodiam one of the most widely known and visited strongholds in Britain. Deservedly so.

devastating effect on Britain and Europe. It first struck England in 1348, two years after the great victory at Crecy. Within a short time, over one-third of England's population was wiped out; although carried by fleas on the black rat, the plague could rapidly pass from one person to another simply through breath contact. In some areas whole villages vanished; their low grass-covered mounds remain as silent reminders of an incomprehensible human devastation. The city of Bristol all but went the same way.

The Black Death respected no one. The Scots, thinking that God had damned the English, assembled an army at Selkirk to take advantage of their desperate plight. Within days, some five thousand Scots were dead; the plague had emphatically left its calling card. On the whole, Scotland and Wales suffered less than England, but the long-term effects nevertheless multiplied. Labour was suddenly in short supply. The system of the serf being tied to the land began to break down, while cash wages not only rose, but the principle itself became imbued throughout society. This situation should not be over-exaggerated, for such changes had begun before the plague, but its extreme consequences hurried things along. Slowly but surely a mercantile economy and society were beginning to form, especially in southern England. There was to be no going back.

FIFTEENTH-CENTURY HARMONY?

Early in the fifteenth century, Owen Glendower declared himself the Prince of Wales and soon, with French and Scottish support, English castles began to fall like ninepins, including the great fortress at Harlech. In contrast, though, the Welsh also suffered some spectacular, and humiliating, failures. A garrison of twenty-eight held out at Caernarvon Castle, while only eight soldiers and a few townsfolk kept a large Welsh force at bay at Kidwelly Castle in 1403. Two years later fully twelve thousand French and Welsh troops once again failed to impress the few motley defenders. These castles were to remain a thorn in Glendower's side when he was in the ascendancy, and became inspirational beacons for the English when the tide turned.

By the end of the decade, Glendower's revolt was history and England could turn her attention back to the wars with France, not forgetting, of course, the continuing saga of Scottish Borders raiding. Considerably strengthened castles at Alnwick and Bamburgh, plus the dramatic new one at Dunstanburgh, had improved the English position during the fourteenth century. As the Hundred Years' War petered out, it appeared that things might settle down somewhat. Some hope.

Meanwhile, when the Scots were not harrying the English, they were busy fighting among themselves, and the long struggle between the Black Douglases of Galloway and the crown led to some quite horrific deeds. On one occasion, two Black Douglas brothers, dining with the king, were dragged out and beheaded: a somewhat ghastly alternative entertainment to the court jester. The Scottish royal family, in particular King James II, were active firearms enthusiasts. Indeed, James II thought nothing of, and probably even enjoyed, turning his artillery on some awkward noble's pile. Even so, keyhole gun-loops, indicating the use of

---

KIDWELLY CASTLE
Carmarthenshire O/S map 159 ref. 709070
Directions: In the town, at the north end of Bailey Street.

The semi-concentric Kidwelly Castle, with its rectangular inner bailey and impressive keep/gatehouse, gives every impression of being a late thirteenth-century stronghold. It is, in fact, built over an early eleventh-century motte and bailey castle, reputedly the most fought-over in Wales. The motte was probably the mound to the south of the keep/gatehouse, while the curved outer curtain wall is built on the bailey rampart, protected by the original ditch. The straight east side looks down over the River Gwendraeth.

The inner bailey was built by Payn de Chaworth, an old warrior-companion of Edward I, between c. 1275 and 1279. There are four mighty corner towers, of which the south-east has an adjoining, arrow-looped chapel with a splayed plinth down the hillside. Entry to the bailey was via gates through the north and south curtain walls, while the main accommodation was along the east wall.

Henry of Lancaster built the curved wall of the outer bailey with its four circular towers between 1300 and 1320. The most impressive defensive features are the north and, in particular, south gatehouses, the latter serving as the main quarters. This had doors and portcullises at either end of the passage, and could be defended in isolation should other parts of the castle fall. A century later Kidwelly survived two sieges by Owen Glendower, after which the burnt south gatehouse was rebuilt with machicolations and enhanced accommodation.

Further halls sprouted up in the outer bailey in the sixteenth century and, though modestly garrisoned, Kidwelly survived the Civil War. The town was enclosed when the castle was built, but only one gate remains, at the south end of Bailey Street.

Possibly built on the Norman motte, the well-defended entrance at Kidwelly Castle was anything but welcoming. The splayed plinth of the chapel is on the right.

firearms for defence, do not seem to have appeared before 1427, at Craigmillar Castle, along with gun embrasures and machicolations. In the long drawn out civil wars such defences were to be sorely needed.

THE WARS OF THE ROSES

The Hundred Years War finally drew to its long-awaited close in 1453. Many English nobles returned from France with considerable fortunes and were

Dolbadarn, the premier Welsh-built castle, guarding the Llanberis Pass. The circular keep stood 80 ft high and was possibly built by Llewelyn the Great. Dolbadarn was later occupied and part-dismantled by King Edward I.

Caerphilly Castle has the most extensive water defences of any British stronghold. This is the greatest non-royal medieval castle in Britain.

Conway – the ultimate Edwardian stronghold? The town walls served as the castle's outer bailey. Pictured here from the town's Upper Gateway, this was perhaps the finest fortified medieval town in Britain.

accustomed to wielding absolute power. The cessation of foreign hostilities was an opportunity for domestic peace, but it was not to be. King Henry VI was hardly the most forthright of leaders, and before long squabbling among the nobility had degenerated into another long-drawn-out conflict.

As anyone who has studied the shenanigans of this period will know, it is all rather tedious and devious. A catalogue of contradictory, treacherous and convoluted alliances and relationships, it reads more like a macabre medieval soap opera. Not everyone was involved, but the wars initiated another rash of stronghold building and the fortification of previously little-defended houses, in particular manor houses. The boundary between a manor house and a castle became very blurred, but defences were needed just in case there was an unwelcome knock on the gate at the dead of night. With no protection, one might never hear the cock crow again.

The Battle of Bosworth in 1485 brought the protracted wars to an end. Henry VII, with considerable Welsh support, was crowned king, founded the Tudor dynasty, forgave some adversaries and set about uniting the divided and depleted nobility. As the fifteenth century and the Middle Ages drew to their close, the in-fighting in Scotland, England and Wales had, at least temporarily, abated. Even the Scottish Borders were a little less violent. Of course, it did not last. Early in the sixteenth century, England and Scotland, the auld enemies, were at it again, like two bickering old women. This time, though, it was to be no neighbourly squabble.

THIRTEENTH-CENTURY CASTLES

Towards the end of the twelfth century both the motte and bailey castle at the Bass of Inverurie and Dover Castle's massive squat keep, with its four square towers exuding sheer power and impregnability, were under construction. Dover's keep was, even then, hardly the latest thing, though the rectangular towers on the inner curtain wall were bang up to the minute. Thus castle building in England and Scotland was about a century apart. By the end of the thirteenth century this was no longer the case, and Scotland could boast enclosure castles, with gatehouses and powerful donjons, the equal of any in Britain.

The experience gained from the building and besieging of castles during the Crusades would radically alter castle design in the tumultuous thirteenth century. Even before the twelfth century was over, the once-mighty rectangular keep was losing favour to the round or polygonal varieties. King John's undermining of the rectangular keep at Rochester Castle in 1215 certainly demonstrated the inherent weakness of the design; perhaps it was significant that it was rebuilt with a rounded tower. The castle keep in general, though, was far from finished.

On the other hand, a keep defended by a tower-less curtain wall, with or without a moat, was most certainly out of step with the times. King John had the outer defences at Dover Castle completed with, in the main, D-shaped towers; this, in a sense, created Britain's first concentric castle. With its great keep, inner and then outer baileys, Dover was the mightiest castle in the land. In 1215 it

BEESTON CASTLE
Cheshire O/S map 117 ref. 537593
Directions: Take the A41 south from Chester and turn left along the A534. Turn left in Bulkeley to Beeston.

For all that Beeston Castle is one of the more ruinous strongholds featured in this book, it enjoys a magnificent and spectacular location. Situated on a ridge towering some 500 ft over the Cheshire plain, not only does Beeston Castle command long views over the former lands of Ranulf, Earl of Chester, who began the castle in about 1220, it is also prominent from miles about.

Clearly Chester's crusading experiences inspired him, for Beeston was one of the earliest keep-less enclosure castles in Britain. Right at the summit, the twin-towered keep/gatehouse is flanked by a curtain wall, with two circular and singleton rectangular towers, with a deep rock-cut ditch to the south and east. The sheer cliff-faces at the north and west needed no further defending, so it was thought. The well was fully 370 ft deep.

Soon after, a curtain wall was added, ⅓ mile long, enclosing a large, sloping outer bailey. Numerous D-shaped towers strengthened the wall along the vulnerable south and east sides; again, the precipitous north and west sides were considered to be inviolable. About a third of the wall still remains, with several towers. There was a twin-towered, outer gatehouse, of which only the foundations remain.

The Chester line died out in the late thirteenth century and the castle became part of the royal estate. Much work was undertaken in the fourteenth century, but Beeston was ruinous by the reign of Henry VIII. Though occupied by Roundheads in the Civil War, Beeston was taken by Royalists who, ironically, scaled the almost undefended north cliff-face. They were besieged in 1644, but did not surrender until November 1645. The castle was slighted the following year.

withstood a siege by King Louis of France, despite the undermining of its outer barbican gateway. Such a success could not fail to be noted.

Castles with curtain walls were nothing new. They could be found from Kismul Castle, on the Hebridean island of Barra, to Framlingham Castle in Suffolk. In the 1220s two very similar and advanced castles were under construction. Dirleton Castle features a great cylindrical donjon tower, along with three smaller towers on its curtain wall. Further south, Beeston Castle boasts an even longer curtain wall with seven towers, crowning a hill 500 feet above the Cheshire plain. The defences were later enhanced with an outer wall and yet more towers. The common feature of Dirleton and Beeston was that neither castle had a traditional keep, although both were constructed within a decade of York's distinctive quatrefoil-shaped keep, on a motte, known as Clifford's Tower. Now, that was progress.

WELSH CASTLES

The areas of Britain that were still hostile to the Anglo-Normans were most likely to have castles that included the most up-to-date defensive features. In the settled south and east of England the semi-fortified manor house was introduced before the thirteenth century, but it would have been an extremely foolhardy Anglo-Norman who built one in Wales. There, the fully defended castle was still the order of the day, and that was where the latest innovations were to be found.

Since the twelfth-century baronial wars, the Anglo-Normans had not really gained ground in Wales; indeed, if anything, they had been steadily pushed back. In order to survive in a hostile environment, the Anglo-Normans continually updated their strongholds. Longtown Castle was possibly the first to be built with a round keep, while the mighty and massive circular donjon at Pembroke

Restored it might be, but the gatehouse at Pembroke Castle, seen here from the donjon, shows just how mighty were its defences.

Castle was built at the dawn of the thirteenth century. The tower keep at Skenfrith Castle had an obvious taper, or batter, to its lower courses, plus about 6 feet of earth piled against it, while Chepstow Castle was enlarged with a curtain wall and towers, barbican and new gatehouses of considerable size. That at the east was almost a keep/gatehouse and the new walls were massively strengthened at the base.

So much for the invaders' castles. What about the Welsh themselves? By no means all Anglo-Norman castles withstood a Welsh siege, and some changed hands on several occasions. The Welsh also built castles in the twelfth century, and those constructed under the aegis of Llewelyn the Great (*c*. 1200–40) and centred on Gwynedd were more than a match for those of the Anglo-Normans.

Castell y Bere not only featured a curtain wall with flanking towers but also had a circular tower/keep. Criccieth Castle had an inner bailey with two drum towers, while Dolbadarn had a great circular keep, with curtain wall and towers, that lacked nothing in comparison with those elsewhere in Britain. Dolwyddelan Castle, the presumed birthplace of Llewelyn the Great, has a tall rectangular keep, and Ewloe Castle not only had an inner bailey that enclosed a D-shaped keep, complete with forebuilding, but also had an outer bailey with another tower covering the curtain wall. Many of these castles stood on high rocky mounds and with their advanced defences were expected to resist any attack.

Nothing, though, could compare with the Earl of Gloucester's great concentric stronghold, Caerphilly Castle. This was the first of its kind to be built from

The royal castle at Caernarvon was never completed. It still exudes elegance, power and majesty.

scratch in Britain. It took about sixty years to complete and, during that time, it both succumbed to and withstood sieges. Essentially, two artificial lakes formed the outer defences, a tactic copied from the extensive water defences at Kenilworth Castle. At the east, a massive fortified barbican wall dammed the lakes, while there was an island outwork at the west. On the main island, an outer wall and bailey defended a powerful inner castle ward, with large towers at each corner. A gatehouse faced west and a massive keep/gatehouse guarded the main entrance from the dam. As far as Britain, let alone Wales, was concerned, this was years ahead of its time – yet it was but an appetizer for still richer courses to come.

THE WELSH CASTLES OF EDWARD I

Let us not beat about the bush. The ten castles built in north and central Wales from 1277 onwards, when Edward I decided it was time to put the upstart Llewelyn ap Gruffydd in his place, include some of the most magnificent, advanced and spectacular strongholds ever built in Britain. This does not mean that the likes of Conway, Caernarvon, Harlech and the unfinished Beaumaris Castles have never been bettered, just that visually, technically and militarily – especially for their time – they are unrivalled.

Despite the death of Llewelyn in 1282, it took Edward three campaigns before he could truly claim to have annexed the whole of Wales in 1296. Beginning with Flint Castle, each castle was designed and built for Edward by the Italian Master James of St George. They were not only ahead of their time, but were mightily impressive strongholds that fully served their intended purpose. Like all the best castles, they looked inviolable to contemporary eyes and acted not only as defensive strongholds but also as bases for offensive action.

Flint Castle featured an inner bailey with three towers. A fourth keep/tower had a moat that protected the harbour from which the castle could be

The formidable, almost indestructible, Harlech Castle once dominated the coastline of North Cardigan Bay. The mountains of Snowdonia are in the distance.

BEAUMARIS CASTLE
Anglesey O/S map 115 ref. 607763
Directions: Cross the Menai Bridge to Anglesey, and take the A545 to Beaumaris. The castle is at the end of Castle Street.

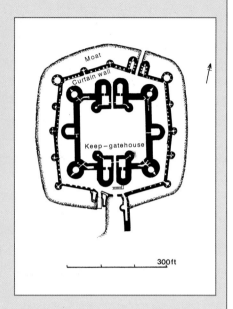

One could be forgiven for thinking that Beaumaris Castle, the technical masterpiece of Master James of St George, is something of a sham: a show-piece, but not a real stronghold. Despite a gargantuan building effort, beginning in 1295, it was still unfinished thirty-five years later. Furthermore, Beaumaris was never seriously tested.

Both castle and walled town were begun immediately after the revolt of Madog ap Llewelyn in order to finally secure North Wales for King Edward I. Built at the north end of the Menai Straits, the castle was defensible by February 1296, and work ceased two years later. By then, Edward was embroiled in his Scottish campaigns, but building began again in 1306 and continued at a leisurely pace until 1330.

Given few restrictions, Master James excelled himself with a copybook concentric castle – the finest in Britain. A moat, complete with defended dock, enclosed an outer curtain wall strengthened with twelve cylindrical towers. The outer entrances, at the north and south, were off-centre, while each tower was overlooked from the inner wall – both useful assets should the outer wall be breached, or fall into the wrong hands.

The inner curtain wall has four corner towers and one each mid-way along the east and west sides. These are two storeys high – the intended third storey was never built; the wall is 35 ft high and 15 ft thick, and some sections have an inter-mural gallery. Needless to say, there is no shortage of arrow-loops.

Undoubtedly the most impressive features of the castle are the massive inner keep/gatehouses at the centre of the north and south sides; they are not dissimilar to the singleton at Harlech. The north gatehouse is in fine condition, and had three doors and portcullises, plus an array of murder-holes and arrow-loops. The south gatehouse is rather less complete, being a storey lower, and lacks the extension into the bailey; in compensation, it has a small barbican. The main accommodation was located in the gatehouses, and these were intended to be fully defensible, even if the inner bailey were taken.

No other stronghold was such a drain on the exchequer, yet Beaumaris Castle was outdated even before building stopped. The world had moved on and left Beaumaris an almost unwanted embarrassment, though Edward could never be entirely sure of its future strategic value. In reality, Beaumaris Castle was a stronghold without a purpose. It was soon decaying and, though garrisoned by Royalists in the Civil War, they surrendered without a fight in 1646. That was its one, brief moment of action.

provisioned during a siege. A dock was a vital feature at several Edwardian castles. Rhuddlan was a concentric castle, with diamond-shaped inner defences, double-towered gateways, single towers at the other angles, a dock and a deep water channel 3 miles up the River Clwyd. Harlech Castle was washed by the sea on two sides, although it is inland today, and is another concentric castle. Its inner defences tower over the outer lines and it boasts the finest and mightiest keep/gatehouse in Britain. The last castle to be started, Beaumaris, is probably Britain's finest concentric castle and, once again, featured a defended dock.

Rhuddlan Castle had an adjoining town, though its earth and timber fortifications were hardly the last word in such defences. This was most emphatically not the case at both Conway and Caernarvon, where castles and heavily fortified towns were comparatively futuristic. While Caernarvon has the grander castle, with polygonal towers and decorative bands of coloured stonework, Conway is Britain's definitive medieval fortress town. Neither castle was concentric, but both consisted of inner and outer wards closed off by internal walls or buildings, although these were never finished at Caernarvon. The great eight-towered castle at Conway, dovetailed with exquisite perfection into the town defences, was the ultimate declaration of Edward's intent. It was built on the same rock as the abbey where Llewelyn ap Gruffydd was buried, and Edward had Master James sweep the lot away. Thus, having confined Welsh independence to history, he symbolically struck it from the landscape.

In addition to the great royal castles that ringed Gwynedd, four baronial castles were also built at Edward's behest, although these were not, of course, constructed on the scale of the other ten. Denbigh Castle not only featured a great three-towered keep/gatehouse, but also had an adjoining walled town. This was less mightily fortified than the multi-towered wall at Conway, but served the same purpose and, with its position at the top of the hill, was just as impregnable. In case that proved inadequate, Edward had several former Welsh castles extensively rebuilt, including Criccieth and Dolwyddelan Castles. Thus the ring of stone and steel round and within Gwynedd was complete: game, set and match to Edward.

CONWAY CASTLE AND TOWN WALLS
Caernarvonshire O/S map 115 ref. 781777
Directions: The castle is at the south-east corner of the town.

The massive round towers of Conway Castle stand sentinel over the river, the valley and the finest medieval fortified town in Britain. It is a matter of opinion as to whether the bridges visually add or detract from the spectacle, but the eastern approach is both awe-inspiring and regally impressive – exactly as Edward I intended.

So far as any unruly natives were concerned, both town and castle were impregnable. Indeed, the two cannot be divided, for they were built together between 1283 and 1287: a phenomenal rate of expensive work. The town wall, with its three gates and twenty-one towers – each originally crossed by a wooden bridge that could be destroyed to isolate any section of the wall – is, in effect, the castle's outer bailey. The four eastern towers, each with an additional turret, formed the castle's royal inner bailey. Here would stay the king, with further towers and buildings for his protection and comfort. A barbican led to a watergate which, like the west entrance, did not need an elaborate gatehouse as the adjacent towers gave adequate cover. A massive wall divides the castle's interior, with a simple entrance, once with a drawbridge, linking the two baileys.

The outer bailey also has four drum towers, with a barbican protecting the west entrance. This bailey contains the Great Hall and probably housed the garrison. Despite the traffic, the proximity of the town and railway, and the bridges, Conway Castle looks exactly what it is: a mighty, majestic and formidable stronghold. It was besieged in 1294 and held out; it fell to Owen Glendower in 1401 only because the garrison was at church; and finally surrendered after four months' pounding by Parliamentary artillery in the Civil War. The sheer scale of the defences was usually a sufficient deterrent to those who might fancy chancing their arm.

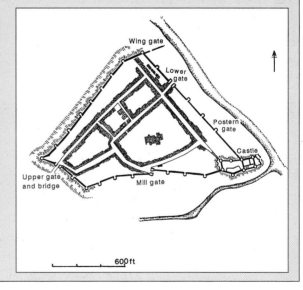

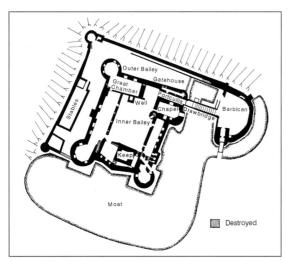

Goodrich Castle.

Denbigh Castle was not a royal stronghold, but it contributed to the ring of steel with which Edward I subdued Gwynedd.

Then, just in case other parts of Wales cared to take up the cudgels, the Marcher lords further enhanced their castles in the south. Pembroke, Chepstow, Goodrich and Kidwelly Castles were all extended and strengthened, but those were just the prominent tip of the iceberg. Many smaller castles received additional defences or improvements, such as machicolations and thickened wall bases, while fortified manor houses, such as Weobley Castle straddled the fine line between stronghold and residence, castle and house. By the mid-fourteenth century, though, out-and-out castle building in Wales was drawing to a close, and comfort had entered the equation. Barely half a century after the first Edwardian invasions, Wales was becoming as gentrified as middle England. It was, though, a peace that would not last.

It will come as no surprise that royal stronghold building in Wales was to prove extremely expensive, draining every last penny out of the exchequer. In addition, the sheer number of English men needed to build them, to say nothing of the troops required to subdue the Welsh, was, quite frankly, highly debilitating. Castles took many years, even decades, to build. Some, such as Caernarvon Castle, were sacked by the Welsh before the job was complete, and while it was not necessary to go back to square one, time and money were wasted clearing the decks again.

Building was, in any case, a long and laborious job, and villages and towns throughout the land provided their menfolk to the king's cause. Then there was the matter of troops to support the building gangs. At some locations, as many as five hundred soldiers accompanied fewer than a thousand builders on the journey to a castle site and during its construction. It was not always a case of protecting the builders from attack either; on many occasions the soldiers prevented them from absconding when they had had enough of the poor conditions, lack of pay, danger or merely being away from home for so long. Either way, castle building did not come cheap.

Nevertheless, once built, the castles of Master James of St George were impressively cost-effective to man, needing only small garrisons. Caernarvon and Kidwelly Castles were able to hold off the forces of Owen Glendower, with the fighting equivalent of two men and a dog; even if part of the outer defences fell, attackers were still at the mercy of fire from the inner line. In practice, providing the garrison could be provisioned, probably from the dock, they had a better than evens chance of holding out and tying down a large attacking force. On several occasions right up to the Civil War, Edwardian and advanced baronial castles such as Kidwelly were to prove vital, almost talismanic, strongholds to both the English and Welsh in turn. Even if they did fall, the cost exacted for the prized scalp was often phenomenally high.

FOURTEENTH-CENTURY CASTLES

When Edward I decided to invade Scotland, there were several castles in the hands of friendly lords. Still, Edward knew that a strategy similar to that used in Wales was an essential prerequisite if he were to succeed. Master James was brought forth to oversee the works, but the exchequer could not stand the strain of another castle-building programme. As a result, Edward had to rely on the same materials in his Scottish campaigns that the Romans had done 1,200 years earlier: earth and timber.

Scotland had, at that time, few stone castles. There were exceptions and, in the case of strongholds such as Bothwell Castle or Caerlaverock Castle, most noteworthy ones at that. However, even the great castles at Edinburgh and Stirling were minnows at the time compared to the mighty great stone edifices they are today.

The general trend with castles during the fourteenth century was to bring the standard of the living quarters up to a par with the defensive requirements. Initially, keeps made something of a comeback, with new ones built at Dudley and Knaresborough. The quadrangular castle then came into fashion, with four corner towers, machicolations and many other visual defensive features. Bolton Castle and Sheriff Hutton Castle were good examples of this trend, as was Bodiam Castle. On the face of it, Bodiam was revolutionary. Surrounded by a large moat, with circular towers at each corner and square ones between, the gatehouses were machicolated and gun-loops covered all angles. With hardly any external apertures, this was surely a peerless defensive stronghold. As with many other castles of the fourteenth and fifteenth centuries, though, all was not quite what it seemed.

Bothwell Castle was successively held by Scots and English. The donjon could be defended even if the rest of the castle had fallen.

Do not be fooled by the decoration. The unique magnificence of the triangular Caerlaverock Castle belied a mighty stronghold, which might have been built by either the English or the Scots.

OLD WARDOUR CASTLE
Wiltshire O/S map 184 ref. 939263
Directions: From Tisbury station, head west under the railway and turn right. Take the first left and follow the road round to the castle.

The romantic ruins of Old Wardour Castle lie within the eighteenth-century parkland setting of Wardour Castle, a grand country house. From the terrace the old castle appears to be a folly, a sham creation intended to delight genteel guests, a talking point for an evening of idle chatter. Well, Old Wardour Castle could certainly spin a yarn or two.

The hexagonal courtyard castle within its remodelled curtain wall was begun in about 1393 by John, 5th Lord Lovell, as a French-inspired stronghold-residence. It was a stylish castle, designed for comfort and entertainment, but able if needed to offer some resistance in awkward moments. The entrance is flanked by two towers, while doors and portcullises guarded either end of the passage, with machicolations above. This formed an extended sixth angle.

As was the norm, the ground-floor windows were small, but there were residential chambers at that level reached from the courtyard by several unguarded doorways. As seen today, the decoration and architecture are hardly of military function, and date from the 1570s, when Old Wardour was improved by its new owners, the Arundell family.

Old Wardour does not have a particularly distinguished history; indeed, until the late sixteenth century it was bought and sold with nary a backward glance. Its moment of glory came in the Civil War, when twenty-five Royalists held out for five days against 1,300 Parliamentarians in 1643. The position was reversed between December 1643 and March 1644, when a small Roundhead garrison withstood a Royalist siege. Tired of being held at bay, the Royalists then mined the south-west angle, causing much of the obvious destruction, and soon the siege was over. There has been no attempt to make the castle habitable since, but Old Wardour wears its considerable wounds with a distinct, vainglorious pride.

Other variations on the comfortable-castle theme came about at that time. Nunney Castle was a small but fully machicolated courtyard-type castle, with four closely spaced circular towers. Its design reflected French influence gained from years campaigning in the Hundred Years War. Not too far away, Old Wardour Castle was built at the end of the century as an hexagonal-shaped courtyard castle. Again, living quarters were far advanced from the basic provisions of castles a century earlier but even so, as would be proved in the Civil War, Old Wardour could still exact a stiff toll from any would-be attackers.

There is no doubt that these new castles were fully defensible, though how long one might hold out against a determined siege is open to conjecture. A stronghold on the outside, yet a palace within is an apt way to describe them, for even the grandly decorated Bodiam Castle was supposedly designed to resist a French raiding force. With the power of the nobility came wealth, and there was a growing desire to, if not display that wealth, at least to enjoy the comforts it could bring. Cold and draughty strongholds were all very well in turbulent times, but at others, the manor houses of even minor knights might seem rather appealing.

CASTLE OR MANOR HOUSE?

By the fifteenth century, as might have been the case with tall duns and short brochs in Iron Age Scotland, the difference between a castle and a manor house could be of little more than hair-splitting proportions. Take Tattershall Castle, for example. Superficially, it looks every inch the great keep it purports to be, towering high over the Lincolnshire fens. Four castellated and machicolated corner towers, rising to about 120 feet, guard a brick keep with walls over 15 feet thick. These give Tattershall a very powerful defensive profile. Get closer and one can see the two moats and banks, to say nothing of the guardhouse foundations; the well-nigh impregnable image is complete.

Yet it is not. The large, stately windows that grace all four sides, and even the towers, show that something is amiss. Tattershall Castle would not be a good target for contemporary burglars, nor even a disgruntled medieval mob as the very visible defences would soon put these off – but a mid-fifteenth-century army equipped with firearms? Baron Cromwell, Treasurer of England, would need to think again. Indeed, Tattershall, and many others of the hundred or so castles built in England and Wales between 1301 and 1500 were, first and foremost, increasingly impressive residences capable of being defended – but they were not solely strongholds.

It is purely an illusion, but the defensive nature of a brick castle seems to be softened somewhat; it seems less overtly challenging than one built of stone. The introduction of brick allowed a change in style and seems to signify a transformation in the role of a stronghold. The unfinished Kirkby Muxloe Castle was intended as a residence capable of being defended against, and by, firearms. The rather more complex Caister Castle put up a most impressive show when besieged in 1469; some thirty defenders resisted about three thousand heavily armed soldiers, and the castle was virtually smashed to pieces before being overcome. Herstmonceux Castle, built in the mid-fifteenth century, seems more like a great country house than a manor house, but it has a whole range of defences, including seventeen towers and numerous gun-loops. No doubt it was a luxurious residence, but the threat of French raids was very real and Lord Dacre had no intention of being caught with his pants down.

TATTERSHALL CASTLE
Lincolnshire O/S map 122 ref. 210575
Directions: At Tattershall on the A153.

Tattershall Castle is the author's favourite stronghold; its soaring outline towers high over the fens for miles in all directions. From a distance, Tattershall looks every inch a dominating, even mighty stronghold, yet it seems far less threatening from close quarters. Its plentiful supply of elegant windows suggests that Tattershall might be a very meek lamb in a sheep's clothing, a sham castle, though this impression is not entirely correct.

The tower was built between 1434 and 1445 by Ralph Cromwell, Lord Treasurer of England, and a loyal, well-rewarded comrade of Henry V on his French campaigns. The inner bailey was part of a twelfth-century castle, and the curtain wall and towers were retained by Cromwell, though only a few footings remain today. Cromwell added an outer moat, three gatehouses and bridges in the north and, of course, the main tower. Despite the tower's large windows, Tattershall still possessed some formidable defensive obstacles.

The tower is the finest brick-built stronghold of its kind in Britain. It rises to nearly 120 ft and despite the apparently undefended entrance the wall is over 20 ft thick at the base, while some impressive machicolations and battlements give all-round protection from above. Inside, its four floors contained forty-eight rooms, and some of the most lavish decoration and patterned brick-work of the age. Tattershall clearly set the standards for other fortified-luxury residences to follow.

Cromwell left no male heirs so Tattershall passed from pillar to post and back again, and was abandoned after about 1700. Lord Curzon bought and restored it in 1912, and from its turrets one can see as far as Lincoln Cathedral in the north-west and Boston Stump in the south-east.

The brick-built gatehouse, Kirkby Muxloe Castle.

While the use of brick hastened the metamorphosis from castle to palace as the fifteenth century progressed, older stone castles became ever more grand, being softened with new halls, extensions or even complete new wings. Warwick Castle maintained its undoubted defensibility, despite grand domestic additions in the late fourteenth century. The tower at Ashby de la Zouch was a throwback to a bygone age and gives the impression of being a rectangular keep, but the interior placed comfort on an equal footing with security.

Before leaving castles though, we must briefly consider the requirements of building and running one. Apart from the new castles, many older ones were substantially altered to improve the quality of their living accommodation. As the population of England and Wales fell from about five million to three million during the fourteenth century, mainly as a result of the Black Death, so the *per capita* ratio of castles, let alone manor houses, rose markedly.

Just consider how much it would cost today to build Tattershall Castle, or to vastly improve and rebuild Raglan Castle, to say nothing of one on the scale of Caerphilly Castle! Even with all the economies allowed by building machinery and using materials that are far cheaper to produce, we are talking in terms of several millions of pounds; in the case of Caerphilly, tens of millions. The drain on the national and, more importantly, local economies of the Middle Ages was immense.

Then there was the not inconsiderable matter of running a castle. In addition to repairs, heating and other domestic costs, there was also the lord's private army. Granted, the economy of the medieval world was geared to that way of life, bolstered by feudalism, but the shift away from such a world was already under way, hastened by the Black Death. The recent restoration of Windsor Castle, following the devastating fire, topped £25 million – and that was only for repairs to an admittedly ornate part of the castle. Today, it would take more than the income generated by visitors to pay for a castle if building from scratch.

FORTIFIED MANOR HOUSES

The first manor houses belonged to knights some way down the Norman pecking order, and probably dated from the latter half of the twelfth century. These manor houses were surely capable of being defended, even if only to keep a mob of aggrieved Saxon serfs at bay. A moat, with perhaps a bank and timber fence, would probably have sufficed in many cases but, as most such defences have either vanished or been comprehensively rebuilt and extended, there is some uncertainty as to how they looked.

The ruined Weeting Castle is probably a typical example. Like many other manor houses, it was strengthened with an additional tower in the Middle Ages. One manor house that has probably survived in reasonably original condition is Boothby Pagnell. The defences amounted to a moat, perhaps enhanced by a rampart, and the thick stone walls of the house itself. The ground floor housed the domestic rooms, with the living quarters being on the first floor. Although there are now several doors to the ground floor, not all are original, and there are still few windows. There are many more windows on the first floor, which is reached by external stone stairs, probably a later addition. Boothby Pagnell would never have resisted a determined and well-armed force, but it could have survived a bit of local unrest, or even a rival knight and a few men-at-arms hoping to settle an old score. It took some time before manor houses developed much beyond that level.

Towards the end of the thirteenth century a new development was appearing at manor houses: the fortified refuge tower. One of the first examples can be seen at possibly Britain's finest medieval manor house, Stokesay Castle. The original

Boothby Pagnell, one of Britain's finest medieval manor houses, front (top) and rear.

The picturesque north tower at Stokesay Castle is often regarded as Britain's first tower-house. The south tower is at the opposite end.

STOKESAY CASTLE
Shropshire O/S map 138 ref. 436817
Directions: Just south of Craven Arms, off the A49.

Stokesay Castle is a fortified manor house, not a castle. Due to regular changes of ownership and use over the last three hundred years, and the fact it has rarely been a permanent residence, fortune has smiled kindly on Stokesay and it remains the most original medieval stronghold of its type in Britain.

The first two storeys of the north tower were built by the de Say family in about 1240. This, with its northern projection, was possibly the first tower-house in Britain. It was probably a refuge for the twelfth-century timber house that stood on the site of the present hall and solar.

In about 1280 a wealthy clothier, Lawrence of Ludlow, bought Stokesay and obtained permission to fortify it in 1291. The hall, with its magnificent cruck roof and solar, was probably begun a little before that and, with its large windows, was clearly not intended to be defended. The Welsh Marches were often a less than secure and peaceful part of the country, though, and Ludlow soon added another storey and the impressive timber gallery that crowns the north tower.

A three-storey, 66 ft high battlemented tower was built adjoining the south end of the solar. Entry was by ladder from the courtyard, through a door 6 ft above the ground; this became Ludlow's personal refuge. A 34 ft high curtain wall and moat completed the surrounding defences, enabling Stokesay to resist a Marcher raid, but certainly not a siege of any duration. Stokesay Castle was a grand house that could be defended.

Fortunately, Stokesay Castle was surrendered to Parliament in 1645 without a fight. The Jacobean timber gatehouse – which would have been defensively useless anyway – had already replaced the medieval stone entrance. The curtain wall was then reduced to its present height and the moat mostly filled in, but otherwise Ludlow would still recognize his beloved Stokesay Castle, some seven hundred years later.

tower had a long hall and solar added, with a three-storey multangular tower at the south. This was further protected by a 30 feet high curtain wall and a moat. If there is doubt about the defensive capacities of manor houses such as Boothby Pagnell, those of the likes of Stokesay Castle are beyond question.

Little Wenham Hall further developed this theme. Dating from about 1280 it has three towers in an L-shape, and included the first known brick hall to be built since Roman times. There were narrow window slits at ground-floor level and arrow-loops and battlements higher up, but there is no outer wall or moat. Another variation on the tower theme adjoins the otherwise undefended manor house at Longthorpe. The rectangular tower is not simply a refuge: it has living quarters and, most impressively, medieval wall paintings in the main room. These had been whitewashed over for centuries, until just after the Second World War. It is conceivable that such paintings were fairly commonplace on the apparently bare stone walls at both castles and manor houses. We should not simply see these strongholds as the great, gaunt and bare edifices they are today. As with Iron Age brochs, some towers were undoubtedly intended to impress and to signify the status of the owner, as well as to serve defensive purposes.

Thereafter, such towers were built in the Scottish Borders, and fortified manors took on a more diverse appearance. Weobley Castle had a tower and was almost a small castle, while Broughton Castle was a house that acquired a moat, gatehouse and curtain wall in the fourteenth century. Brough Castle, which was most certainly a stronghold, was gentrified with the addition of a tower, but as the Middle Ages drew on, so the differences between manor house and castle became less and less.

Still, there was enough warring to keep minor nobles, knights and even, by the fifteenth century, the odd merchant on their toes. Gainsborough Old Hall, built in about 1470, was a luxurious house with a brick refuge tower attached, while the manor house at Cotehele was later rebuilt with a gatehouse and outer wall. These appurtenances were far from unnecessary, especially during the Wars of the Roses, when local jealousies led to more than one dignitary having to take refuge from a rival within his defended manor house. Such defences might appear modest in comparison with the great castles of the era, but they were, on occasion, just enough to save the owner by the skin of his teeth.

TOWER-HOUSES AND PELE-TOWERS

Despite the different nomenclature, pele-towers and tower-houses are, to all intents and purposes, effectively one and the same thing. If there is a difference, it is that pele-towers are relatively small (with several exceptions) and that they are English. On the whole, strongholds of this type are associated with the Scottish Borders and northern England, and are sometimes considered to be almost entirely of Scottish origin. However, fortified towers existed in central England, the Welsh Marches and even Wales before the dawn of the fourteenth century. One cannot be absolutely certain, but the tower at Drum Castle dates from about 1285 and thus may be the first Scottish tower-house. As such, it runs a pretty close race with some English towers; for example, the original (north) tower at Stokesay Castle dates to 1240.

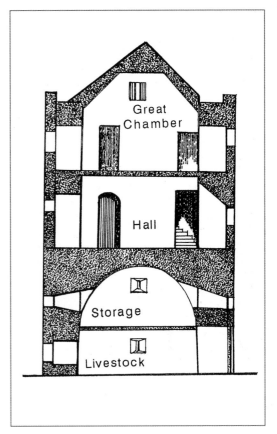

Section through a small tower-house.

It was the fourteenth century that really sparked the development of the tower-house and, at least for a while, the Scots were slow off the mark. The defeat of the English at Bannockburn saw a change in the tide of fortune in the Borders, and the Reivers and Scottish nobles soon took to raiding the south. Generally, they left castles and walled towns alone; there were plenty of other soft targets. Scruples were in short supply on both sides and the Reiver gangs would think nothing of raiding a church; even a priest could not expect to be safe from such earthly avarice.

That much is known from the Vicar's Pele, at Corbridge. Built in about 1300, it was a simple three-storey tower-house which served as the vicarage. With a room on each floor and mural stairs, this was the base model, but from then on almost anything went. Some towers were taller – Chipchase, for example, had four storeys with machicolations. A great many stood alone: stark towers amid the darkening skyline. Other towers, such as the one at Edlingham Castle which also boasted a forebuilding, were but the latest additions to earlier fortified residences. The tower at Etal Castle formed part of an enclosure, and was of keep-like proportions, though it was undoubtedly a tower-house, with an equally massive gatehouse. As with other castles, there was no absolute standard and, at times, the tower-house and castle keep became very close bedfellows.

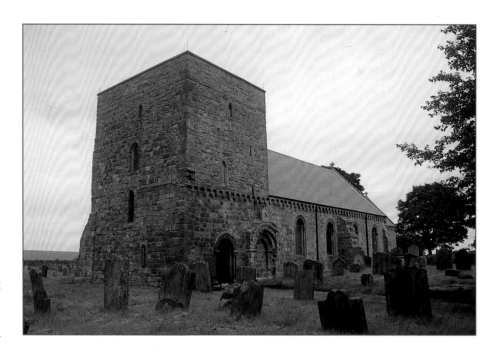

The Parson's Pele adjoins St Anne's Church at Ancroft in Northumberland – a variation on the theme of living above the shop?

The Vicar's Pele at Corbridge is separate and stands in the churchyard.

Initially, defences tended to be fairly basic: entry to the first floor was often by ladders; a few narrow windows at the lower levels; stone vaulting in the ground floor so that fire could not spread upwards; thick walls and, if there was a ground floor entrance, a heavy, iron reinforced door. A combination of these was usually enough to survive a Reivers raid. True, other property, cattle and the like, might be stolen or destroyed, but survival was the name of the game. The pele-towers of northern England varied immensely, especially in detail, and some two hundred were built between 1301 and 1500. Nor were they all situated in Northumberland and Cumberland. Turton Tower near Bolton has, like many, been extended in later years and now has large mullion windows, even on the ground floor. It is, though, undoubtedly a pele-tower or tower-house just the same.

North of the border, though, things were taken a step or two further. For a start, tower-houses can be found the length and breadth of Scotland, from Scalloway on Shetland to Cardoness in Galloway, and from Kismul on Barra to Ayton in Berwickshire. Not all of them date from the Middle Ages and many were either additions to an earlier castle, such as at Loch Leven, or have themselves been added to subsequently, in particular Glamis Castle. Towards the latter part of the Middle Ages, L-shaped towers were being built; Craigmillar Castle was one of the first, while Hermitage Castle had four tower-houses added round an earlier keep. There were other developments in the Early Modern period.

Scottish tower-houses, despite their occasional similarity to a keep, operated in an entirely different way. For a start, they were not designed to withstand a long siege so, should the king have trouble with the owner, the royal forces would soon be victorious. Moreover, comfort and ease of movement were often sacrificed for security. Going upstairs from the ground floor might have necessitated going outside and climbing a ladder or, perhaps, negotiating narrow turnpike (spiral) stairs. Manor houses in the contemporary Anglo-Welsh style do not feature in Scotland: the tower-house was their natural equivalent.

Many tower-houses were built within a barmkin, or stone walled enclosure; few survive today. Inside the barmkin stood all sorts of often wooden buildings: stables, barns, storehouses and even additional living quarters. In many cases, these additions were rebuilt in stone, as at Craigmillar Castle. Perhaps most important of all, as with an English manor house or castle, the tower-house was the centre of an agricultural estate and served many functions. It certainly did not exist in isolation.

The L-shaped tower was one of the first improvements to the simple rectangular tower-house; one existed at Edinburgh Castle – belonging to the king no less – in the 1360s. Not only did the additional wing increase the living space but, what is more important, it enabled the entrance to be covered from the flanking wall. This in turn allowed the entrance to be more usefully, but still securely, located on the ground floor. A yett (iron grille) inside the massive oak door further strengthened that potential weakspot. By the mid-fifteenth century rectangular tower-houses were old hat. Corner turrets began to appear, giving greater advantages to defenders in an on-going saga of improvements.

Preston Pele Tower is now only about one-third of its original size but it remains a splendid stronghold to visit. It is reminiscent of how historic sites were displayed in the 1950s, but is none the worse for that.

Is there a more magnificently located stronghold in Britain than Tantallon Castle, with Bass Rock behind?

RAVENSCRAIG CASTLE
Fife O/S map 59 ref. 290924
Directions: In Kirkcaldy, ¼ mile north of the harbour; it can be reached through the park from Nether Street, or off Dysart Road.

Ravenscraig's tenure in history's limelight was but brief. Built between 1460 and 1463 on the orders of King James II, it was the first new British stronghold of any size built to withstand or to dish out an artillery barrage. Unfortunately the king, a firearms enthusiast, was killed shortly after work began.

Unlike many coastal strongholds, the land approach to Ravenscraig Castle is somewhat less than enchanting. The castle stands on a rocky promontory 70 ft above the Firth of Forth, but several blocks of undistinguished modern flats have been built right in front of it, doing nothing to enhance the landward view of the castle.

By and large Ravenscraig comprises two D-shaped tower-houses, joined by a wall and gun-platform. The east tower is three storeys tall, the west four storeys; the latter stands on a higher rock. This tower was the main residential building, with a heavily vaulted basement in which to store gunpowder; this was one of several in the castle. The entrance is through the wall between the towers, this being covered by gun-loops and protected by a deep ditch; the exterior walls were up to 14 ft thick. There is a liberal supply of gun-loops and gun platforms facing the sea, presumably to engage hostile shipping, while there was a steep descent to the sea-gate.

Ravenscraig Castle was a unique Scottish stronghold but proved not to be the first in a line of development, as James II probably hoped. On the other hand, it was considered powerful enough for Parliament to order its dismantling in 1651, lest it should fall into the wrong hands. Fortunately, the job of destruction was never completed.

As fortified, yet very practical, residences, the Scottish tower-houses were destined to become the finest buildings of their type in Britain.

In addition, some tower-houses were highly complex affairs. The fifteenth-century Borthwick Castle in Mid-Lothian is a U-shaped tower-house; in other words, the rectangular tower has two parallel wings. This is one of the most magnificent examples to be seen and, with its later curtain wall, was immensely powerful. Yet nothing could be so forbidding a sight as the most daunting tower-house of the lot: Hermitage Castle. The four tower-houses of this former manor house, for that is what they amount to, combine with the massive, blank external walls to cast dread and despondency over even the most determined attackers. That these towers are linked together only serves to enhance Hermitage Castle's invincibility, with its great arched entrances adding the final defiant touch – most certainly not an empty gesture.

OTHER SCOTTISH CASTLES

By no stretch of the imagination were tower-houses the be-all and end-all of Scottish castles from the fourteenth century onwards. There is considerable variety in Scottish castle-building, from 1201 to 1500, although the tower-house certainly predominated and other types of castle were often the exception to the tower-house rule. Linlithgow Palace is Scotland's sole example of a quadrangular castle, or rather palace/castle. Initially begun by Master James of St George, for King Edward I of England, it was turned into a modestly defended but grand palace for the kings of Scotland.

Crighton Castle is a courtyard castle that started life as a simple tower-house. It was transformed into a formidable stronghold in the fifteenth century, with all sides being fully enclosed. A variation on the courtyard theme is the spectacularly located Tantallon Castle. This is almost the medieval equivalent of an Iron Age promontory fort, with 100 feet high cliffs protecting the north, south and east sides, surmounted by either buildings or earth ramparts. Ditches, earthworks and finally – and most impressively, a magnificent curtain wall defended the inland western approach. Tantallon Castle not only looks immensely powerful, with its 50 feet high wall, two end towers, and central gatehouse and barbican, each rising to about 80 feet, it most emphatically was. Built in the fourteenth century, it survived a siege by firearms in the fifteenth and sixteenth centuries, and finally fell to parliamentary forces in the Civil War after twelve days of heavy bombardment. Today, it stands proudly against the backdrop of Bass Rock, defiant to the last.

Initially, Tantallon Castle was not designed to be defended by, nor to withstand an assault from, firearms. It was an entirely different matter for King James II's mid-fifteenth-century Ravenscraig Castle – a Scottish first. Even this could not hide its tower-house inspiration, though, for two towers guard the narrow approach to its promontory overlooking the Firth of Forth. Gun-loops and platforms amply cover the entrance and all angles of the castle, turning Ravenscraig, briefly, into Scotland's premier stronghold of the day, bar none.

Despite this diversity the tower-house dominated Scottish castle-building from the fourteenth century onwards. Many owners of older enclosure castles were tempted to build a tower-house, lured by the hope of better accommodation and improved protection. Duart, Dunnottar and Urquhart are just three examples of

---

TANTALLON CASTLE
East Lothian O/S map 67 ref. 596850
Directions: Leave Dunbar, heading west, on the A1 and turn right on the A198. The castle is on the right just after Auldhame.

'It's as easy to knock down Tantallon as to build a bridge to Bass Rock': so ran a local saying, and considering Tantallon's relative success under siege, it does not over-state reality either.

Few British strongholds can match Tantallon Castle's dramatic location; it stands on a promontory 100 ft above the Firth of Forth. Bounded on three sides by sheer cliffs, and with Bass Rock as a magnificent backdrop, Tantallon Castle exemplifies the notion of the romantic ruin. The site might have been fortified in prehistory, and a castle called Dentaloune existed in the thirteenth century. All that exists today dates from the mid-fourteenth century, when Tantallon Castle was the property of the Earls of Angus.

The promontory is protected by an outer ditch, flanked by a sixteenth-century gun-looped outwork. An inner ditch, some 20 ft across, protects the massive, slightly curved castle wall, with its central gatehouse and end towers. The circular Douglas Tower, at the north, is quite ruinous, but the D-shaped south tower is more complete. The overall impact outweighs the details, though, and while the wall is about 50 ft high, the towers rise to fully 80 ft. Four storeys of living-quarters once graced the gatehouse, but of the later barbican little remains. There is not much to be seen of the range of buildings within the enclosure either.

Tantallon is a pre-gunpowder medieval castle, but proved strong enough to withstand the rather primitive early artillery. A siege in 1491 foundered on its defences, despite the use of culverins. In 1528 King James V turned his siege-train on Tantallon Castle for twenty days, and got nowhere. As he got ready to depart, the royal guns were captured and taken back into the castle. Then, in 1651, Tantallon finally fell to Parliament's General Monck, but only after a devastating twelve-day bombardment, the results of which are readily apparent.

Tantallon Castle was left to its fate by the end of the seventeenth century, and is one of Britain's most impressive ruined castles. No wonder it gained such an invincible reputation.

Scotland's main royal residence in the sixteenth century, Linlithgow Palace was lavishly decorated. It was also fairly well protected, as the gun-embrasures at the outer gateway show.

castles being vastly improved by the addition of a tower-house: a type of stronghold that was as distinctive of its age as the broch had been 1,500 years before.

TOWN DEFENCES

The decline of the Saxon *burh* was under way even by the time of the Domesday survey in 1086. Forty-eight English towns were then recorded as having defences; little had changed from two hundred years earlier. By the end of the twelfth century, about half of those towns' defences were noted as being beyond repair, yet the age of the fortified town was about to emerge again. Between 1191 and 1230, about fifty new towns were established in England, some by royal decree, such as Newcastle, but most on the initiative of the local lord. At the end of the fifteenth century, most important towns were defended by stone walls, and many had elaborate gateways, moats and additional banks as well. There were 108 walled towns in England by 1400.

Quite obviously, such defences were expensive to build, man and maintain; these costs were often paid for by a levy imposed on goods brought into the town. During the Middle Ages towns became the focal points for the produce of the surrounding countryside – the natural trading centres. If there were a perceived need for defences, either by royal decree or as desired by local dignitaries, the means would always be found.

Many towns already had a head start. Some, such as Chichester and Winchester, had the remains of Roman walls, while the Romano-Norman walls at Exeter and Chester were in fine fettle. Towns such as Southampton and York rebuilt their earth and timber defences in stone; these are still impressive today.

York's Walmgate Bar is the sole surviving town gateway with a barbican, but this was a feature of all York's bars, and others elsewhere. Monmouth has the only remaining medieval fortified bridge in Britain, over the River Monnow. The tower originally had a portcullis, and still has machicolations and arrow-loops; within the cramped confines of the bridge, the gateway would not be easy to force.

The unique, still defended Monnow Bridge, at Monmouth.

As was common practice with curtain walls at castles, town walls soon gained projecting towers, so that defenders could outflank anyone attacking the base of the wall or trying to scale it. These were never so numerous as at the latest castles, but there were a few exceptions.

When Edward I invaded Wales, he sometimes created towns adjacent to castles, and these were positively and defiantly defended. They were not a sop to the natives either, but were purely for English settlers, and there was little doubt the Welsh resented their presence. Rhuddlan's earth walls and timber palisade were never developed, but substantial walls were built at Denbigh, Kidwelly, Chepstow, Tenby and Cardigan, not only to attract people to the towns, but also to ensure these English enclaves were as safe as possible.

If these towns were impressive, they were as nothing compared to the royal towns of Caernarvon and, especially, Conway. At the latter, the town's defences formed what was virtually a large outer bailey for the castle, creating the finest contemporary fortress/town in Britain. The town wall, less than a mile in length, was bolstered by twenty-one rounded hollow towers, each traversed by a wooden bridge. Thus, if the wall was scaled, the attackers could be isolated on

The Bootham Bar, York.

Micklegate Bar, York.

SOUTHAMPTON (Town Walls)
Hampshire O/S map 196 ref. 420117
Directions: At the south end of the city, by the Town Quay.

When one thinks of Britain's great walled towns such as York, Conway or Chester, Southampton comes some way down the pecking-order. Yet, the circuit is three-quarters complete and, while not always located amidst the most scenic surroundings, there is a wall-walk and many information boards.

Today, nothing remains of the Saxon *burh* of Hamtun that extended west from the River Itchen. A motte and bailey castle was built in the twelfth century within the Norman town, that grew up beside Southampton Water. A tower block marks the site of the motte, but the stone arches of the castle's bailey wall, its Quay and Watergate, both subsequently incorporated into the town's western defences, still exist.

Southampton's pride and joy is the Bargate, the northern entrance through the earth rampart and ditch that defended the landward east and north sides of the town. It has been much altered since it was built in about 1180, but an original Norman arch survives within the extended gateway.

The earth wall was complete by 1220, but there were no waterside defences and in 1338 disaster struck. An armada of French and Genoese semi-official pirates sailed up the Solent and devastated the town. Though the north and east walls were rebuilt in stone, there was a marked reluctance to build a sea wall, as many fine merchants' houses stood along the waterfront. A resumption of French raids in the 1370s finally made them see sense, and some houses were simply built into the new wall.

By 1385 Southampton was fully enclosed by a stone wall, with seven main gates and twenty-nine towers. The wall included gun-loops and machicolations at the Westgate, and elsewhere. The God's House Tower was extended in the early fifteenth century to house the town's guns and gunner: Britain's first residential gun-tower. By that time, Southampton had probably the finest and most modern defences of any port in England.

the wall by destroying the bridges. In addition, there were three main gates and two small ones; as one might imagine, no chances were taken at these either. Conway's defences are magnificent and as French raids increased in the fourteenth century, many English south coast towns would doubtless have eagerly swapped their meagre defences any day of the week.

However, town defences were seldom kept in the pink of condition in times of peace; in the case of Southampton they were never completed. The price for such dithering was heavy for in 1338 Southampton was sacked by French raiders. Far too late, the sea-facing walls were eventually built. At least they saved the town in the future, which was more than could be said for the Cinque Port of Rye. It was seriously ravaged on at least four occasions before it gained any meaningful defences. The fear and destruction engendered by these raids did spur some coastal towns to build defences during the Hundred Years War. Great Yarmouth, for example, was enclosed, although it was not until the fifteenth century that Sandwich replaced its earth and timber walls.

Surprisingly few town and city defences have survived down the centuries. St Andrews' West Port is the sole surviving medieval town gateway in Scotland, for example. On the other hand, because many towns pulled down their walls and gateways as they expanded, especially in the late seventeenth to nineteenth centuries, perhaps we should be grateful for what remains.

The walls at York and Chester have almost complete circuits and, although they have been restored, are quite majestic and kept in pristine condition; these are the finest examples of non-military town defences. Southampton has made a commendable effort to complete its wall-walk. Other towns have good sections

WEST GATE (Canterbury)
Kent O/S map 179 ref. 146580
Directions: In the city, at the west end of St Peter's Street.

Let's be honest, only the most narrow-minded stronghold-anorak would visit one of our great cathedral cities and only look at the defensive structures. Canterbury certainly has rather more to offer. Its once-royal castle is now a disappointing, slightly squalid ruin, but there are fine lengths of the city wall and, most importantly, the magnificent West Gate.

The West Gate is Canterbury's sole remaining city gateway. Built in about 1375, it remains in original condition. It is Britain's oldest surviving purpose-built fortification to be defended by guns. The approach to the twin-towered gatehouse is covered by seventeen gun-loops, in three tiers, while battlements surmount the towers and machicolations cover the entrance. This was pretty comprehensive stuff for such a prototype. Today, it houses a museum but is rather spoiled by the continuous procession of passing traffic.

The city wall dates from the third century and, despite occasional patching up, was rather the worse for wear when the Hundred Years War flared up again in the 1370s. As Canterbury stood on the Dover–London road, the wall was extensively refurbished and towers were added, complete with keyhole gun-loops, to allow flanking fire. This wall is best seen in the south-east, near the Dane John – the original motte castle, or in the north-east. Though very well preserved, again, the roar of passing traffic is hardly appropriate.

The remains of the castle, dating to about 1100, are seemingly shoved into a corner, off Castle Street, as if the city is embarrassed by them.

remaining, Canterbury, Exeter and Norwich, for example, while several have short lengths or perhaps gateways left, usually in good order, such as Pembroke, Kidwelly, Newcastle and Beverley. These often feature in the relevant town's tourist attractions. At Great Yarmouth, however, one can still see the town wall looking as such defences often appeared until a few decades ago. Scrap yards, ramshackle buildings, rubbish and all manner of unsavoury detritus can be found beside the not inconsiderable remains. Clearly twentieth-century ideas of preservation have yet to arrive here.

COASTAL DEFENCES

The fifteenth century saw a number of important innovations in coastal defences, particularly in southern England. The long-dismantled fort at Queenborough was, presumably, intended to prevent hostile ships from reaching London. Portsmouth was becoming an important naval port by the fifteenth century and in 1420 the Round Tower was built at the entrance to the harbour; there was another on the Gosport side to guard the ends of a chain boom. This Round Tower had three gun-loops and a gun-platform by the sixteenth century, went on to form part of the eighteenth-century gun battery (which can still be seen) and was heightened in the nineteenth century. The nearby Square Tower, built in 1494, was primarily a gun-tower and was also reinforced in the nineteenth century.

A similar boom was constructed between Fowey and Polruan in 1457, with a rectangular blockhouse at either end; Polruan's, at least, was protected by keyhole gun-loops. It was a similar story at Dartmouth. In 1481 a blockhouse with gun-loops was built to protect the estuary. This was right up to the minute for the time, except that it did not cover all the possible angles of approach so, a

The West Port at St Andrews is Scotland's sole surviving medieval town gateway.

Originally built by the Romans, Chichester's defences were extensively refurbished in medieval times.

decade later, another battery was built at Kingswear, which included nine rectangular gun embrasures. In the mean time though, Henry Tudor had won the Battle of Bosworth and became King Henry VII. For a while, at least, peace with France was achieved.

RELIGIOUS STRONGHOLDS

Portsmouth's medieval Round Tower was one of a pair that guarded the entrance to the harbour.

There seems to be something of a contradiction between these two words, and yet . . . In the Dark Ages church towers, or round towers, were occasionally built to act as a refuge if necessary. The round towers at Abernethy and Brechin were most certainly intended as such, while that at St Magnus Church on Egilsay was also used, possibly against Norse heathens. Churches with semi-fortified towers provided an occasional refuge in the Welsh Marches, while the cathedral and bishop's palace at St David's were surrounded by a wall and gatehouse that would not disgrace a town. The Welsh could be relied on to hit the English at any opportunity. The Vicar's Pele at Corbridge shows that even a man of the cloth was far from safe in the Scottish Borders. During the French raid on Southampton in 1338, many townsfolk took refuge in St Michael's Church. This sanctuary did not carry much weight with the French, who monstrously butchered them anyway.

But what about those ecclesiastical strongholds that were more than simply a refuge? The Norman bishops were most certainly not pacifists. The Bishop of Durham lived in the castle next to the cathedral; should he fancy a trip to his estates in the north, he had a castle at Norham as well. He was not unique either.

The Polruan blockhouse was one of a pair that guarded the Fowey estuary. It has a gun-loop at the top.

Further south, the Bishop of Winchester had fortified residences at Farnham, Wolvesey, Bishop's Waltham, Taunton and Merdon, all dating to the Norman period and all substantially improved in the Middle Ages. The Bishops of Winchester tended to be favoured royalists, and these residences became progressively more palatial with each succeeding century. They were most certainly strongholds, and most were besieged in the Civil War.

In the main, though, there were four phases in the Middle Ages that saw ecclesiastical sites being fortified. The onset of the Hundred Years War left the south of England at the mercy of French raids, and the religious houses were as much at risk as anywhere else. The Bishop of Chichester fortified Amberley Castle, which also served in the national defence. Michelham Priory, unusually, had an encircling moat and gatehouse, and Quarr Abbey possibly included England's first gun-loops. Soon perimeter walls and elaborate gatehouses became a feature of religious houses all along the south of England, mostly for their own protection, as at Battle Abbey.

The Bishop's Palace gateway at Wells would not have disgraced any medieval town.

There were also two periods of civilian unrest in the fourteenth century: the first in the 1320s, and the second, more widespread Peasants' Revolt, in the 1380s. Churches did not escape attacks. This was not surprising as the church had amassed considerable wealth – witness the the widespread building of churches, cathedrals, monasteries and abbeys. In addition, clerics were often involved in government, either local or national, and were held responsible for the high taxation and the much resented tithes. Then, with the onset of the Hundred Years War, the French

BISHOP'S PALACE (WELLS)
Somerset O/S map 183 ref. 552457
Directions: In Wells, off the market-place.

Wells is a small, attractive city crowned by its splendid golden cathedral. It is a city of activity combined with serenity, a distinguished, almost genteel busy-ness. It is not a place where one expects to find a stronghold – an ecclesiastical stronghold at that.

The power, wealth and corruption of the clergy was not lost on the uneducated mind of the medieval common-man. While most people just about scraped by, many clergy who preached against the evils of wealth and a lascivious life were more than a little hypocritical. As became the norm, the Bishop of Wells lived in a rather grand palace, built in the early thirteenth century.

A hundred or so years later the common-man was not quite so subservient. The odd indulgent cleric had already been brought to task when, in 1341, Bishop Ralph enclosed the palace with a moat, a curtain wall and six towers; entry was via a gatehouse of considerable proportions. Arrow-loops and battlements show that while the bishop might wish to impress his neighbours, he also intended to show any unruly citizens that he could defend himself, should they ever take umbrage.

Although the curtain wall and moat could hardly hope to resist an organized military force, the gatehouse is another matter. It has a drawbridge and arrow-loops and, while it might be hard to imagine the Bishop and Dean firing arrows in all directions, it was clearly meant to be defended should the need arise.

Parliamentary troops raided the Bishop's Palace in 1643, and the drawbridge was last raised after a mob stormed the Bishop's Palace at Bristol in 1831, at a time of national agitation over the pedestrian pace of parliamentary reform. Though modest compared with other contemporary strongholds, the Bishop's Palace at Wells was built to meet an apparent need; it was not an empty gesture.

were considered to be the Pope's favourite; it was a dicey time to be a servant of the Lord.

It was not just the minor clergy that came a cropper, either. Bishops of Salisbury and Exeter, even an Archbishop of Canterbury, all met violent deaths at the hands of enraged townsmen in the fourteenth and fifteenth centuries. It was time to act. As early as 1329 the Bishop of Lincoln began to fortify his palace and the cathedral precincts. Two years later, the Bishop of Wells did likewise, and a new gatehouse was added at Bury St Edmunds, dominating the town's main street. How many cathedrals have massive stone gateways outside their precincts, in England and Scotland? They were not just for show.

Then, in the 1380s, unrest against landowners in general caused some abbeys and monasteries – which previously had been mostly open – to build enclosing walls and, most important, gatehouses. Of course, these were often mightily impressive pieces of architecture, and doubled as palatial residences, such as the gatehouse at Thornton Abbey. While they could not hope to hold an army at bay, they could, and sometimes did, keep out a local mob.

The final fortification phase concerned many religious houses in the Scottish Borders, mostly to protect them against increasing Reiver activity. In England Alnwick Abbey gained an outer wall and gatehouse, while nearby Hulne Abbey even included a tower-house. It was no different north of the border, and Sweetheart Abbey and Incholme Abbey, on an island in the Firth of Forth, were just two Scottish religious houses fortified against English raiding. Defences like these did not have quite the dignity and sanctity one usually associates with religious buildings, but then, religion and conflict have often been close bedmates.

AND FINALLY

The Middle Ages witnessed a thorough transformation of the British landscape. Feudalism in England, parts of Scotland and Wales had, like the later agricultural revolution, enabled high ranking nobles, officials, knights and the clergy to amass fantastic wealth. This in turn financed the great building programmes of the age: from the mightiest castles and cathedrals, down to the meanest manor houses, churches and town walls. Before the Norman invasion, there was hardly a castle we would now recognize as such, and stone churches were hardly commonplace. Even Saxon cathedrals such as Winchester were probably smaller than a large Norman or medieval church. But by 1500 many villages had stone churches, and only in the most remote parts of Scotland did anyone live much more than a day's walk from a stone stronghold of some sort. The impact cannot have been lost on the people of the time.

Then, despite periods of almost continuous unrest, the countryside was changed by the imposition of feudalism and the organization it brought to production. Estates went hand-in-glove with castles, manor houses and even religious establishments. Towns also gave an impetus to trade, perhaps even offering an incentive for an industrious serf to indulge in a bit of extra work. England was a fairly wealthy country towards the end of the Middle Ages and, if castles and tower-houses as centre-pieces of agricultural estates are anything to go by, Scotland did not trail too far behind.

By 1500 England's population had just about recovered to the pre-Black Death total of about five million; some way short of France's twenty million perhaps, but enough to drive the economy onwards. Wales became ever more integrated with England, and much of the social, economic, political and physical infrastructure was in place to enable the crown to pursue a wider role on the world stage, and to drive towards eventual unification. As for Scotland, well, it was still a divided country, and there was much turmoil ahead in the coming centuries, but it was increasingly an entity in its own right. In the future the need for strongholds would be just as great as before, but they had changed from austere military establishments to residences. There was, though, to be something of a reversion to type. The specialist military stronghold was to make a defiant comeback.

C H A P T E R   6

EARLY MODERN EVOLUTION

(1501–1714)

The Early Modern age was an era of European-wide renaissance in the arts, literature and sciences. Trade flourished and world horizons expanded remorselessly, while mercantile manufacture slowly took root. Barriers were continually broken down and feudalism was finally and formally abolished in England. It was a time of enlightened forward-thinking, advance and expansion; not one for harking back to the bad days of violence, petty skirmishing and parochial strife. The future looked bright and, following the very progressive lead of the Dutch, most certainly orange.

Yet in Britain, Cavaliers and Roundheads, Covenanters and Catholics, Highlanders and Lowlanders, Parliamentarians and Royalists, Jacobites and Orangemen, Levellers and Diggers all indulged in acrimonious and violent

Ightham Mote, Kent, is a splendid medieval moated manor house.

The Jacobean gatehouse at Stokesay Castle replaced one built of stone. Though it makes a pleasing picture, it would have been useless for serious defensive purposes.

conflict. There were the ravages and slaughter of the very un-Civil War and its double encores: the army revolt of 1648–9 and the Scots-backed rising of Charles II a year later. Towards the end of the seventeenth century came the Glorious – and so-called bloodless – Revolution, which was hardly glorious and was most certainly bloody and vindictive. The various forays of Cromwell, William III and James II in Ireland set man against man, family against family, and community against community; to this day the consequences are as plain as the pikestaffs with which they fought. Then there was the turmoil of the Reformation and the various counter-reformations, the periodic outbreaks of plague, principally in London in 1665, and the Great Fire that promptly burnt the city down.

In addition, England engaged in numerous wars against the French, Spanish, Dutch, Scots and, seemingly, anyone else who fancied a bit of action. Despite courting invasion on several almost calamitous occasions, this insolent bantam cock of world powers was ever more keen to enhance its international standing. The combination of all these conflicts witnessed an era as bloody as any that had gone before. Yet despite all this violence and misfortune, it was an age of enlightenment, both in Britain and in Europe. Perhaps even more importantly, it heralded a comprehensive, if slightly fortuitous, transformation in Britain: three into one shall go.

In 1501 England was virtually united under Henry VII, but as a nation-state was little more than a distinctly prickly thorn in the side of the mainland European powers; Wales was a mere adjunct, and Scotland a virtual sworn enemy. By 1714 not only was Wales formally in union with England, but the Auld Enemies, England and Scotland, were similarly bosom-buddies – at least on paper. The new, enhanced Great Britain, furthermore, was not just a country of growing influence on the European political scene, but had already ousted the Dutch as the world's foremost trading and manufacturing nation. Finally, on the back of its increasingly mighty navy, Britain was more than able to pack the heaviest of military punches. All this from three countries with a combined population less than half that of France, its nearest, greatest and almost constant rival.

Not only had the very essence of Britain changed during this period, but the world itself was opening up. In 1453 Constantinople finally fell to the Turks, an event that forced the spice traders to seek alternative routes to India. Despite what we regard as somewhat quixotic – not to say wildly optimistic – ideas as to where new passages to India might be found, these sea-faring pioneers opened up an entirely new world to the Europeans. In 1492 Christopher Columbus crossed the ocean blue, to discover first the West Indies and then mainland America. In 1497 John Cabot reached Newfoundland, while the following year Vasco de Gama rounded the Cape of Good Hope and, fortuitously, bumped into India. By 1522 a handful of the sailors who had set out to sea with Magellan finally returned, having circumnavigated the globe. Thereafter, no holds were barred in the race to exploit the untold riches of the New World. Where once sailors feared dragons, monsters, purgatory and the edge of the world, they now set forth, with due trepidation, seeking wealth, riches and power.

In time England joined in this international jolly, though more as a parasite than a full-blown member of an exclusive club, setting a controversial course that would lead to many scraps, scrapes and very close-shaves with the acknowledged masters of the world, the Spanish, French, Portuguese and Dutch. Eventually, though, Great Britain would turn it into a virtual one-horse race, but that was years in the future and, before Albion achieved parity with the main contestants, it received many a bloody nose and cauliflower ear along the way.

The combined efforts of the various explorers and the Turkish dominance of the Levant saw the focus of world trade shift westwards from the Mediterranean to the Atlantic seaboard, and finally to northern Europe. The merchant-might of Venice gave way to the mercantile manufacture and trade of Holland, which itself was virtually bullied into submission by the arrogant newcomer, Britannia. The Treaty of Utrecht in 1713 confirmed, among other things, Louis XIV's reluctant acknowledgement of the jaunty new usurper. It was the story of the old giving ground to the new – but this youngster was hugely ambitious. It wanted to lead and was not prepared to share the limelight with any old has-been country that got in the way.

THE ROSE OF ENGLAND BLOSSOMS AS BRITANNIA, FLOWER OF THE SEAS

If the foundations of England's (and Britain's) future greatness were dug during the reign of Henry VII (1485–1509), the stoutest of footings were laid by his son Henry VIII (1509–47). The latter's popular image is that of an obese monarch who, through his selfish nuptial desires, by chance saved us all from Catholicism. None of that is untrue, but it hardly opens his historical account. Despite debasing the currency and stripping the treasury bare, and creating an army of

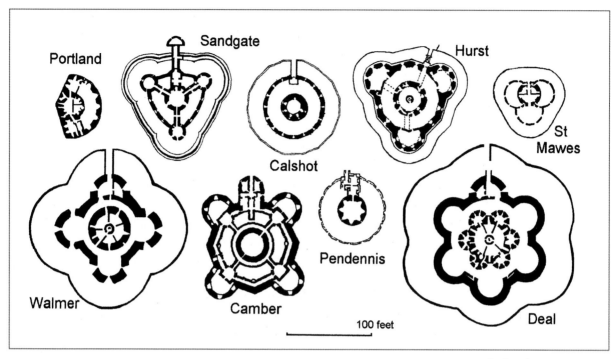

subservient lackeys, known as the nobility, enriched with lands from the dissolved monasteries, Henry was a king of no little military merit.

A cursory glance at the rise and rise of England/Britain over the Early Modern era might elicit the thought that it was all part of a very cunning plan; one, admittedly, with an alarming tendency to go wrong at regular intervals. That, of course, was nothing like the case, but Henry, at least, seems to have taken something of a long-term view of the need to safeguard his country. Alfred the Great has been called the Father of the Navy, but that is a bit like saying that Pegasus, the flying horse, was the founder of modern air travel. Henry VIII is the true Father of the Navy. During his reign England had three serious dust-ups with both France and Scotland. Crucially, it was the defeat of a French fleet off Southsea in 1545, despite the disastrous loss of the *Mary Rose*, that finally eradicated the very real threat of invasion. The navy was to be Henry's first line of defence.

Early in his reign, even before the navy had grown to significant proportions, Henry realized that he had to safeguard his own backyard. By 1512 he was engaged in a struggle against both France and Scotland, and a new gun-tower was built to guard the approaches to that oft-ravaged port in Sussex, Rye. Similarly, Norham Castle, the important Borders stronghold, was fortified with a casemated gun position. Henry was most interested in the latest military tactics, technology and developments; it was a passion that would serve him well throughout his reign.

With the Scots devastated at Flodden Field in 1513, England enjoyed nearly two decades of relative peace; all was quiet on the northern, Scottish, front. Wales was assimilated into England's fold. But then Henry took a fancy to Anne

The original Henrician
Pendennis Castle.

Boleyn, divorced his queen, was excommunicated by the Pope and big trouble
loomed on the horizon. Any chance of a reconciliation was ruined when, in
1536, piqued at the Pope's intransigence, all monasteries – Catholic, of course –
with an annual income of less than £200 were dissolved. Three years later, war
became inevitable when all the remaining monasteries, great and small, went the
same way. This was a far from unpopular act, as many had grown extremely fat
and wealthy, while stories of licentious behaviour among members of the various
religious orders were rife; they were, in many cases, far from being untrue.

Not surprisingly, the Pope was less than happy and the French were only too
pleased to do his bidding and to sort out the juvenile delinquent off its northern
shores. England still had a toe-hold on mainland Europe at Calais, and for
France, with the most powerful army backed by the finest artillery in Europe, the
Pope's demand was just the chance it sought.

Henry, despite going through wives at a considerable rate of knots, still found
the time to instigate a comprehensive set of strongholds, from Lindisfarne round
the south coast to Tenby, and built them at unprecedented speed. Moreover, his
castles – or, more accurately, artillery forts – were of revolutionary design for
Britain. They relied solely on firearms both for their own defence and to confront
foreign ships, and promptly ended any argument as to whether strongholds
should be comfortable residences. They were not.

Henry's castles, as with those of Edward I, were extremely efficient with
manpower. They usually housed a garrison, but were firstly, secondly and lastly,
military strongholds commanded and manned by full-time soldiers. Every aspect
of the design was geared to their efficient operation, and comfort hardly entered
the equation. What is more, Henry was probably involved in some of their
detail and overall design, and also in planning the general national defensive

The Henrician St Mawes Castle, from an eighteenth-century battery.

strategy, both on land and at sea. He might have surrounded himself with grovelling courtiers, but he was not prepared to rely on them when push came to shove.

Of course, everything did not go Henry's way. The French occupied the Isle of Wight for two days in 1545, and though he saw off the threat of an invasion – and was to give the Scots several more good hidings – seven thousand French troops were stationed at Leith at the time of Henry's death. With the strengthening of Berwick's defences, the English presence in the Borders was dominant but, with such a large foreign army in Scotland, it could hardly be described as secure. England might no longer be wealthy, but it had powerful defences on a national scale for the first time. When Henry VIII died, England and Wales seemed somewhat isolated, but a friendly approach was to come from a most unexpected quarter.

MARY AND MARY, MOST CONTRARY

While England had unified under Henry VIII, so King James V tried to bring the Scottish nobility to heel. His task had been eased following the slaughter of many nobles at Flodden Field, but his royal forces still had to besiege awkward lairds on several occasions. Early in the sixteenth century, a blockhouse with casemates was added to Dunbar Castle, while castles were built to exercise at least a semblance of royal control over goings-on in the Highlands; Urquart Castle, for example, was vastly expanded.

Scotland's real domestic problems began with the death of James V. His daughter Mary, an infant queen, was brought up in France, the home of her mother. Rivalry among the nobles was further heightened from 1542 by religious differences. Protestantism had taken a hold and, with an absent Catholic queen – and one, moreover, married to King Francis II of France, plot and counter-plot became almost an everyday part of life in Scottish government.

The French troops at Leith ensured that the English did not venture far beyond the Borders yet it seemed that vexatious relations between the two erstwhile enemies could become a thing of the past. In 1553 Mary Tudor eventually succeeded her father Henry VIII to the throne of England – as a Catholic queen! Mary wasted no time and soon repealed much of her father's religious legislation and began to persecute Protestants. Worse still, she married Philip II, King of Spain. The zealous blood-letting of Mary's all-too-long five years' reign almost matched that in Scotland, except that north of the border the Protestants had been gaining ground. Once again England and Scotland found themselves heading in opposite directions.

When Mary I died in 1558, Catholicism had more than made a comeback. Two years later, when Mary, Queen of Scots, left France after the death of her husband, a similar situation might have been expected in Scotland, but Catholicism was repudiated by the Scottish Parliament even before Mary landed. Scotland was, once again, about to descend into internecine strife. By then, however, the Protestant Elizabeth I had succeeded to the English throne, and soon re-established the Church of England. Had some common ground been found after all? The French army departed from Scotland's shores and, despite the Catholic queen, Protestant denominations came to predominate in both countries. In 1567 Mary, Queen of Scots, was deposed in favour of her infant son James VI, and was to spend the last twenty years of her life under house-arrest in England. The two countries seemingly edged ever-closer together.

CAMBER CASTLE
Sussex O/S map 189 ref. 922185
Directions: A mile walk south along a public footpath from the Rye–Rye Harbour road, just east of the Royal Military Canal.

What a way to celebrate a centenary of active service. In 1643, the guns having recently been removed, the lead was stripped from the roof and Camber Castle was abandoned to the elements. It had not been blown up or captured – either by foreigners or by the opposing forces in the Civil War – and, though hardly the latest stronghold, it was no more antiquated than Deal, Hurst or any other Henrician castle. No, Camber Castle, built to protect the oft-ravaged harbour and town of Rye, fell from grace and favour when the harbour silted up; today, it lies about a mile inland.

In 1514 Edward Guldeford designed the first Camber Castle, in the shape of a circular gun-tower. This sufficed until the invasion scare of the late 1530s, when Henry VIII's stronghold-building programme got rapidly underway. By 1540 the tower was heightened and a curtain wall added, with four circular bastions – backed by towers – to a design by Stephan von Haschenperg.

This complicated castle had its limitations for, in 1542/3, the curtain wall was further strengthened, and all four bastions were rebuilt to the current design. Caponiers led from the bastions to a passage encircling the tower and, with its north-west entrance also resembling a bastion, Camber is one of the more complex Henrician castles.

After 340 years' neglect, Camber Castle was consolidated and excavated in the 1980s, and is now a complete and splendid ruin. As such, it retains its basic original condition, unlike many Henrician castles. Camber Castle stands on a flat expanse of land, and is an eerie and atmospheric place to visit at dusk, especially when it is enveloped by a low creeping mist.

GOOD QUEEN BESS?

Such an assertion depends upon one's viewpoint. If one were an English Catholic at the height of the Spanish wars (which did not end with the defeat of the Armada) or, indeed, a pious and devout Puritan, then 'good' might not be the first word to spring to mind in connection with the queen. If, on the other hand, one were a merchant of the high seas, indulging in trade with, and almost entirely to the disadvantage of, Spain and its American interests, and had semi-official blessing for one's privateering business – or pirateering as the Spaniards called it – one was most certainly endeared to the monarch and her bellicose spirit.

Like her father, Elizabeth I tended to deal with foreigners in a forthright manner: action before diplomatic niceties. She had a fair grasp of international affairs and soon built on the military legacy she had inherited. She had strategically important strongholds strengthened with the latest developments in military engineering, and also ordered a review of royal castles. Any castle that was deemed surplus to requirements was to be sold. Where costs could be recovered by the sale of material – except lead, all of which was retained by the crown – demolition was to go ahead. Elizabeth was pragmatic to the last.

Thanks to the prosperous wool trade in the fifteenth and sixteenth centuries, England had become a relatively wealthy nation. During Elizabeth's reign Tudor England reached its apogee. Peace at home led to a rash of mansion building, with personal defence no longer considered essential. Overseas, the temptations of the Spanish Main were too much for both merchants and crown alike, and Elizabeth certainly did not shirk her national duties in the face of vehement threats from the Spanish king. The Dutch War of Independence was viewed as a further opportunity to put one over the Spaniards: an opportunity that was eagerly seized.

In the 1580s conflict with Spain heightened with each passing year. Then, the queen's favourite sailor, Sir Francis Drake, singed the Spanish king's beard at Cadiz, virtually ensuring not merely punitive retaliatory action but a full-blown war. At that most critical time, when the Spanish Armada sailed up the English Channel to meet and escort an army of invasion from the Spanish Netherlands, the queen held her nerve. Fate, the weather, relatively nimble English ships and some inspired seamanship averted a national disaster. The queen herself rallied her troops at Tilbury, but they were not needed. Elizabeth had squarely faced up the greatest attempted invasion for many centuries; having stared down the barrel of the Spanish cannon, she had brusquely pushed it aside and led her country to a great victory. That is how it was viewed at the time: an opinion not seriously challenged since.

UNION AT LAST, THAT DID NOT LAST

Queen Elizabeth I, alas, did not marry. In 1587 she ordered the execution of the imprisoned Mary, Queen of Scots, in case Catholics rallied round her at the very height of the Spanish wars. Ironically, it was Mary's son, King James VI of Scotland, who was next in line to the English throne. In 1603 he became King

James I of England. A strong king could probably have united the two countries, but James VI was far from that. His belief in the Divine Right to rule endeared him to nobody. Protestants and Puritans despised him, Catholics – in the Gunpowder Plot – tried to kill him, Parliament got nowhere with him and, as he only visited his homeland once after coming south to claim the English crown, he did himself no favours north of the border either.

In the 1620s James found himself at war with Spain, while the Pilgrim Fathers set off to find a purer world. Charles I was no better either. Having succeeded his father in 1625, he was soon at war with France and then, insisting on his Divine Right to rule, abolished Parliament. For eleven increasingly long years, Charles dug himself into a deepening hole. Despite being Scottish, Charles went to war with Scotland in 1640; a war he could not pay for, so he was forced to recall Parliament. Having virtually prised apart the fragile union between England and Scotland, Charles went one better. His unprincipled dealings with Parliament divided England as it had not been so divided for many centuries. Though many Scots rallied to his colours, England, Scotland and Wales were soon engulfed in a conflagration that split communities asunder and tore families apart.

QUEEN'S SCONCE
Nottinghamshire O/S map 121 ref. 791531
Directions: Head south-west from Newark Castle along Castlegate and Lombard Street. Turn right along Portland Street, and then left on Boundary Road. Sconce Hills car park is on the right, with the sconce beyond the playground.

Since time immemorial travellers have passed Newark by. Whether on the River Trent, the Fosse Way, the Great North Road or the two railway lines, Newark has been seen, but rarely visited – a town en route, but seldom a destination. In 1642, though, the Royalists built a rustic earthwork round the town's medieval wall; they, quite clearly, meant to stay.

It took Parliament's forces three attempts to shift the Royalists, and they finally succeeded in May 1646. By that time the besiegers had surrounded Newark with their own earthworks and numerous strongpoints, while the besieged, cut off from the outside, had multiplied their defences.

As might be expected, most of these earthworks are denuded today, but Queen's Sconce, built in 1644, is among the finest Civil War defences still to be seen. Clearly, as its name implies, this was a Royalist stronghold, built to command the south-west approach to the town and the River Devon. It occupies about 3 acres, being a square mound with a large arrow-head bastion at each corner. The rampart is some 25 ft above the surrounding ditch, while traces of gun-ramps and the parapet are visible. This was a long-range gun-platform with all-round, comprehensive close defence. Only plague and near-starvation forced the Royalists to surrender.

Newark is easy to overlook but it is a fine market town with a distinct royal and military past: King John died in the castle, for example. Parliament's Civil War earthworks are not so grand, but some are worth visiting. There is certainly more to Newark than is apparent from a passing glance.

Bastion and ditch, Queen's Sconce.

Quite naturally, many older strongholds were occupied during the Civil War. Sherborne Castle, like many, did not survive the conflict terribly well, but the earthwork bastion that defended the entrance remains in fine condition.

THE CIVIL WAR, 1642–6

After four years of major set-piece battles, minor battles, skirmishes and local feuds, Parliament finally gained the upper hand; the king was arrested and charged with high treason. This was a war in which firearms played a decisive part. Even so, medieval castles, town walls and modestly defended manor houses all came into their own as strongholds capable of withstanding the second generation of firearms. Some were heavily modified, others not a jot, but even a fortified manor house could prove an insuperable obstacle to artillery. For many medieval – and older – strongholds, the war witnessed their last glorious stand in action.

The imprisonment of Charles ended the war, but in 1648 fighting broke out again; this time it was Parliament versus the Army. When that was over and Charles II was crowned King of Scotland in 1651, a Scottish army, which included many Englishmen, was again drawn into civil conflict. They were not terribly successful, being heavily defeated at Dunbar, Preston and, fatally, Worcester. The uncrowned English king escaped into a long exile and Parliament – a most unrepresentative Parliament at that – was left to rule the country.

COMMONWEALTH AND RESTORATION

Reputedly the Commonwealth (1649–60) was not generally a happy time, and the reign of Charles II (1660–85), was one long jolly. Parliament ordered the destruction of many castles to prevent their reuse; regarded as wanton sacrilege today, this was often highly popular at the time. Those grim strongholds not only represented the oppression of the local community, but there was also money to be made out of the fallen stone and timbers. A government handout soon encouraged an enterprising and favourable response, just as it does today.

Yet it did not take Parliament long to fall out with other countries. Throughout the 1650s England was engaged in war, first with the Dutch and then with Spain. The return of Charles II, if nothing else, united the peoples of our three nations. Even France was almost regarded as an ally – though, of course, not one to be trusted – but periodic war kept breaking out with the Dutch. Most of the action took place at sea and was, in any case, often directed against merchant shipping; these were more wars of trade than of political hegemony.

THE GLORIOUS AND BLOODY REVOLUTION

Problems erupted again when Charles II died without leaving a legitimate heir. His brother became King James II, but he was a Catholic. In Scotland religious differences had occasionally escalated into open conflict throughout the reign of Charles II, as Covenanters and Catholics fought tooth and nail. This was to be paralleled further south when, after savagely putting down the rebellion led by King Charles II's illegitimate son, the Duke of Monmouth, James II began actively pursuing a pro-Catholic policy. This brought him into conflict with Parliament, which then took the somewhat unusual step of inviting William of Orange and his wife Mary, James II's daughter, to be joint monarchs. William landed unopposed in Torbay with ten thousand men, the navy conveniently sailing the wrong way up the Channel, and James fled. The occasional vindictiveness of the earlier Dutch wars seemed to have been forgotten.

TILBURY FORT
Essex O/S map 177 ref. 651754
Directions: Signed from the A128, ½ mile east of Tilbury.

Seen from Gravesend, across the River Thames, Tilbury Fort looks unimpressive. When viewed from its derelict and desolate surroundings it is, if anything, even less appealing. The wonder-stronghold of its age? There can surely be few aesthetically worse-located strongholds in Britain. Then, as one approaches the redoubt, one begins to get an inkling that there is something special about this stronghold after all. Perhaps it is not as depressing as first it seems.

The design alone, begun by de Gomme in about 1660, took about a decade to complete. Had it not been for the humiliation of the Dutch raid on Chatham in 1667, and the concern that London could easily have been the next target, the present fort might never have replaced its antiquated Elizabethan predecessor. Even so, Tilbury took some fifteen years to build – but what a fort!

The redoubt stands at the head of the sinuous outer moat, which is crossed by a narrow causeway. A bastioned covered-way, probably the finest still to be seen, is then encountered before crossing the bridge to the ravelin, lying in the 150 ft wide inner moat. A bridge, with two drawbridges, leads to the fort where the masonry-faced rampart is protected by two huge bastions and two demi-bastions. A fifth bastion into the Thames was begun but never finished.

Some fifty guns were mounted along the riverside rampart. Together with the blockhouses on the Kent bank, these would give any hostile fleet a very hot reception. The rampart was modified in the mid-nineteenth century to take the latest guns, and quick-firing guns were mounted during both world wars, a couple of which are still in place. The elaborate entrance and barracks add a distinguished touch of refinement.

Tilbury Fort itself is astoundingly impressive and very well preserved. It never faced a sea-borne enemy, but it lacked nothing in comparison with the best European strongholds.

While the joint monarchs were pretty much accepted in England, and the Welsh were probably past caring in any case, many Scots had other ideas. The Jacobite cause always enjoyed strong support in the Highlands and elsewhere, but Ireland was to be the venue for the final showdown. The Battle of the Boyne in 1690 saw William victorious and James flee into exile. His cause was taken up by King Louis XIV of France and in 1692 a French fleet was defeated with not a little help from the Dutch; once again an invasion was averted. That same year the massacre at Glencoe reminded the Highlanders of what was what in the new order.

The faltering Jacobite cause was taken up by James Edward, the former Prince of Wales, when James II died in 1701. Then in 1707, after one of the longest and occasionally most virulent of engagements, marriage finally took place. The Act of Union did as it said: England and Scotland finally made it to the altar. Great Britain was born. From then on, despite two further Jacobite risings, a new world power had arrived, one that was eventually to create the empire on which the sun never set. By 1713 even Louis XIV of France had to acknowledge the new cock-sure super-power.

HENRICIAN STRONGHOLDS

At the dawn of the sixteenth century, many strongholds were genteel copies of their former fortified selves. Comfort had eclipsed defensive requirements at castles and manor houses throughout England and Wales, though somewhat less obviously in Scotland; they had become first and foremost residences. In any case, an

Gun in firing position in Henrician castle.

unprepared medieval stronghold was no match for modern artillery. However, such was the rate of subsequent developments, that the great bastioned strongholds of the late seventeenth century were still capable, at least for a while, of putting up a decent show in the age of the breech-loading gun firing high-velocity exploding shells. There was, though, an interim stage, which comprehensively and impressively turned the softening of the strongholds on its head.

Henry VIII regarded his navy as the first line of defence, but the fleet needed safe anchorages and ports where ships could be re-victualled and re-armed. These could be vulnerable to a foreign power and so, in addition to a second line of coastal defences, the naval ports also needed protection. The tower at Camber Castle was built by 1514, principally to protect Rye. It was, to all intents and purposes, a fortified gun-tower with embrasures through which heavy guns could fire. This was just the start.

In the 1520s Henry authorized the strengthening of Berwick's walls, with the addition of five earth bastions. Portsmouth's defences were similarly improved but, following the dissolution of the monasteries, it was the

DEAL CASTLE
Kent O/S map 179 ref. 778521
Directions: In Deal, almost on the beach.

Fully 450 years after completion, Deal Castle is, once again, in virtually original condition. One of three inter-defensible, elaborate gun-towers built in about 1540 to protect the important, even vital, Downs anchorage between the North and South Forelands, Deal Castle was the wonder of the Tudor age.

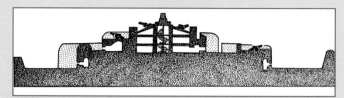

Cross-section through Deal Castle.

As with other Henrician castles, the central keep was the heart, mind and soul of the stronghold. This was protected by five lines of defence, two of which were equally valuable when it came to offence. Heavy guns were mounted on the keep's roof, while six small semi-circular bastions surrounded the keep. From these, gun-embrasures covered the inner ditch, while beyond lay six larger semi-circular bastions. Again, these served as gun-platforms, reached by two covered passageways – early caponiers – across the inner ditch from the keep's basement. These outer bastions had numerous gun-embrasures sweeping the outer ditch. A wall enclosed the castle, while an earthwork linked all three Downs castles.

Many of Henry VIII's castles were manned by, and housed, professional soldiers. Deal was no exception and was efficient in manpower terms. These strongholds formed England's first true defensive system: the first of many that were to act as a deterrent as much as to actively engage the enemy. Indeed Deal, along with the neighbouring Sandown and Walmer Castles, only saw action in the Civil War, when it held for the Royalists until the cause was lost.

By the eighteenth century Deal Castle was reduced to a mere official residence; the additional buildings of that time were bombed and removed in the Second World War. This gave the opportunity for a full restoration back to its original condition. Deal is, without doubt, one of Britain's great strongholds.

Deal Castle from the south (above), the main entrance (below left) and the ditch, showing gun-embrasures.

The Henrician Calshot Castle, seen from the Solent. The hangars behind were used during the Second World War. Flying boats were also stationed at Calshot.

threat of a French invasion that really forced the king's hand. To meet this grim and fearful reality, Henry VIII instigated the greatest royal stronghold-building programme since the time of Edward I, and it was carried out at breakneck speed. Edward's castles had been awe-inspiringly revolutionary; those of Henry VIII did not, indeed could not, look so majestic, although they were no less innovative and advanced. Height and scale, the very ingredients that are so impressive in Edward's castles, made ideal targets in the age of gunpowder. Henry's castles were low and squat, and often small. In effect they were heavily defended gun-platforms, designed to cost an invader dear should a landing party care to chance its arm.

Portland Castle guards the south of Weymouth Harbour. When it was completed in 1541 it was an essential component of the Henrician defences of England's coastline.

HURST CASTLE
Hampshire O/S map 196 ref. 319898
Directions: Either a 2 mile walk from Milford-on-Sea, or by passenger boat from Keyhaven (in summer only).

Hurst Castle is not included here just because it is an Henrician fort, despite its splendid location on a long spit far into the Solent. No, it is the subsequent developments, which by 1880 had transformed the antiquated stronghold into one of the most modern in Britain, that make it so special.

A twelve-sided, two-storey tower, with a basement, roof-mounted guns and spiral staircase – in the usual Henrician manner – formed the heart of the castle, built between 1541 and 1544. The curtain wall had three semi-circular bastions and the fort was surrounded by a moat. Give or take the odd additional temporary battery, particularly during the Napoleonic War, that was how Hurst Castle remained until the mid-nineteenth century.

Hurst Castle commands the vital western approach to the Solent and, ultimately, Portsmouth. The various nineteenth-century invasion crises led to some modest improvements, in particular the addition of earthwork batteries. However, by 1870 the castle was designated to play a key role in the extensive refortification of the Solent. Soon, it had sprouted the massive, stone casemate wings that flank and dwarf the original fort. These housed sixty-one heavy guns, latterly behind iron-shielded embrasures, that comprehensively transformed Hurst Castle into a powerful modern stronghold. A further eastern battery was added in the 1890s; the lighthouses were built twenty or so years earlier.

Early in the twentieth century Hurst Castle was provided with quick-firing guns and searchlights to counter fast torpedo boats, and formed one of several centrally controlled batteries guarding the Needles Passage. It was manned throughout both world wars, until 1956 in fact, and also boasted anti-aircraft guns. A visit to Hurst Castle can be wild and wind-swept, but can also be magnificent and invigorating. Henry VIII would have been mightily proud of its subsequent service to the country. Forts Victoria and Albert are opposite on the Isle of Wight.

As at Camber Castle, the circular tower was the heart of an Henrician castle. The magazine was in the basement and spiral stairs ran up through the floors. Each storey had gun-embrasures, while thick battlements, shaped to deflect shot, protected the gunners on the roof. The central tower was usually surrounded by low semi-circular bastions, from which more guns could pound enemy ships or land forces. Deal Castle, for example, had six inner and six outer bastions. Gun embrasures at all levels enabled the garrison to fire upon attackers from all sides, and comprehensively protected the fort. In addition, an outer ditch enclosed the whole castle.

Not only were these castles revolutionary in England, being the first to fully utilize gunpowder for both offence and defence, they also included other features, such as caponiers, or fortified corridors, which allowed the ditch to be swept with enfilading fire. Well planned to facilitate internal movement yet capable of sealing off a section should it fall into enemy hands, the detailed planning was like nothing seen before. The influence and work of a Bohemian, Stephan von Haschenperg, was very strong in all these castles, but also apparent was the overall strategy and detail work of the king himself.

Deal Castle was the largest and most vital of the Henrician castles. Deal, Sandown and Walmer Castles were three inter-defensible forts which protected the Downs anchorage off the Kent coast. Other similar castles were hurriedly built at Sandgate, Calshot, Hurst and Portland, while Camber was rebuilt with five large bastions. A string of blockhouses, small gun-platforms and forts, was built from Milford Haven round the south coast to Harwich in two remarkable years from 1538: a quite magnificent, and essential, achievement. The cost was enormous – but the price of failure would have been unthinkable.

ST MAWES CASTLE
Cornwall O/S map 204 ref. 842328
Directions: Take the A39 from Truro or Falmouth and turn along the B3289, crossing on the King Harry Ferry, to St Just. Turn right on the A3078. The castle is at a very sharp left-hand bend.

The stylish St Mawes Castle was built in about 1540 to protect the Carrick Roads and Fal estuary, in conjunction with Pendennis Castle. There is a splendid view of each stronghold from the other.

Unlike Pendennis Castle, St Mawes sits low down and is overlooked from the hill behind. It has a typical Henrician tower of two storeys plus a basement, ringed by three circular bastions in a distinctive cloverleaf shape. Guns were mounted on the roof and there are embrasures throughout the castle. The elegant entrance is at the landward side.

Down by the shore, facing Pendennis Castle, lies a small blockhouse which, like Little Dennis, was built a few years before the castle. To the south is an eighteenth-century battery that was extended in about 1905. Further batteries and searchlights were located nearby during both world wars. These housed 12-pounder quick-firing guns to counter raids from fast motor boats. Little remains of these earthworks.

St Mawes Castle led a relatively quiet existence, falling to Parliamentary forces in the Civil War without a shot being fired, although it would not have been easy prey to a concerted land attack. Rather like the Roseland Peninsula, St Mawes Castle is understated, but there is no finer Henry VIII castle in the land.

Even when the immediate threat of a French invasion receded, Henry did not slacken the pace. A castle and two blockhouses, linked by curtain walls, were added to the defences at Hull. Pendennis and St Mawes Castles were begun in Cornwall and then, in 1543, Henry demonstrated his grasp of advanced military engineering. Southsea Castle was an addition to Portsmouth's defences and featured not only a square keep and bailey, but two angle bastions in the curtain wall. These were very much the fad of the moment on mainland Europe, and thereafter all Henry's castles had angle, instead of semi-circular, bastions.

Angle bastions allowed defenders to fire all along the main walls and ramparts. In addition, they presented a small front to an attacking force, and each bastion could be covered from those flanking it. As time went on, bastions became bigger and thrust out some way from the main citadel, especially the arrowhead bastion. Thus they could be used both offensively and defensively, and should one fall it could be isolated well away from the citadel. The angle bastions at Southsea Castle were relatively small, as was the first arrow-head bastion, at Yarmouth Castle. These demonstrated that, even when faced with potential catastrophe, Henry VIII was neither dogmatic nor blinkered in his approach to strongholds that would have to withstand the ravages of ever-improving artillery.

The castles, blockhouses and town defences instigated by Henry VIII were never seriously put to the test in his lifetime, even when the French landed on the Isle of Wight in 1545. The rate of development and building from 1538 until his death shows him to have been a monarch with a rare drive and grasp of military strategy and engineering. Add to that his creation of a permanent navy, with his strongholds, in the main, being garrisoned by professional soldiers or yeomen, and England had many reasons to be grateful to the enigmatic monarch. For all his personal problems and faults, Henry VIII comprehensively dragged England out of the military Dark Ages. Though most of his castles and blockhouses soon became outdated, he laid the firmest of brand-new foundations, on which the defence of England was to rely for centuries ahead.

THE GREAT ELIZABETHAN AGE

Once things had calmed down – especially after England had ceded Calais in 1558 – and Catholicism was driven underground, the Elizabethan Age, from 1558 to 1603, became one of increasing wealth, jollity and even a degree of social mobility. Or so it is often portrayed. On the high seas, English privateers raided and plundered, mostly at the expense of Spain. At home, there were many who were only too ready to plough money into risky ventures, so awash was the country with capital. A degree of decadence filtered down the social scale; smoking became fashionable, while the Elizabethan penchant for plays and other public displays is legendary. England in the later sixteenth century must, surely, have been a magnificent place to live.

It probably was for the was reasonably wealthy: a landowner, official or successful merchant would do nicely. For the vast majority, though, religion apart, life was probably little different from that under the dowdy and dull Queen Mary. Oh, to be part of a nation rising to greatness? Many swanky Victorians gloated over a world map with one-quarter of the land coloured pink to denote the British Empire. Up and down the land, breasts swelled with national pride as Britannia ruled the waves; never mind that so many lived in dire poverty. So it probably was for over 90 per cent of Elizabethans. Francis Drake might have circumnavigated the globe and returned to great wealth and adulation in 1580, but what of the poor Jolly Jack Tars who went with him?

ELIZABETHAN STRONGHOLDS

Just as her father had done, Elizabeth regarded the navy as England's first line of defence. Increasingly throughout her reign, semi-official privateers went on the offensive; the robbery of Spanish treasure ships was, in the end, bound to lead to retribution. Elizabeth did not indulge in extensive stronghold building but, crucially, when she did, it was undertaken thoroughly and to the latest designs. Protection of the naval bases was as essential in Elizabeth's reign as it had been in her father's. The growing port of Chatham was virtually unprotected, so Upnor Castle was built farther down the River Medway. This featured a large angle bastion protruding out into the river, with a towered building along the river front. Today, it looks awkward and angular and, unlike the Henrician castles, does not appear capable of combining effective offensive fire-power with all-round defence. It was, though, an indication of developments to come.

Although England settled into a welcome internal peace, Scotland could never be relied on to play by the new rules. The border town of Berwick always expected trouble and yet, with a French army still based in Scotland, it was vital to the defence of northern England. From the late 1550s Berwick's defences were

Fisher's Fort bastion was part of Berwick's outstanding defences.

comprehensively rebuilt, using the very latest thinking in military engineering, and today we are left with the finest fortified town of Early Modern Britain.

About one-third of the old enclosed town was left outside the new, massively built ramparts, mostly near what is now the railway station, itself built over the castle. A great earthen, stone-faced rampart, about 20 feet high and 100 feet wide encircled the north and east sides of the town, while the south and west sides retained the earlier wall on the river frontage. In addition, and most revolutionary for Britain, three massive bastions and two demi-bastions, each with orillons to protect their flanks, thrust forward into the wide ditch. Though never fully completed, yet with additions such as the bank and ditch from the main rampart to the north coast, these expensive and expansive works completely replaced all the previous half-hearted attempts to update the older walls.

The massive Windmill bastion at Berwick, viewed from the top of the rampart.

Most of Berwick's defences were the work of Sir Richard Lee. Despite criticisms and subsequent alterations, they are still mightily, indeed massively, impressive. It was only the changing political climate, after Mary, Queen of Scots, had been deposed, that caused work to grind to a halt. Even so, Berwick's defences were as modern as any in Europe, and the experience gained was used in the more modest defensive works at Portsmouth. A start was made in the 1560s to remodel the town's defences using angle bastions, but it was the serious threat of a Spanish invasion, two decades later, that saw these works undertaken with any degree of haste. It was something of a double-edged sword to live in such an important naval town; yes, one had some of the finest defences in the land but, if anywhere was to be attacked, it would probably be Portsmouth.

The Elizabethan north-east bastion, at Carisbrooke Castle.

The First Dad's Army

As the 1580s wore on, it became increasingly likely that Spain would take firm action against English piracy in its American waters, known as the Spanish Main. As usual, with her finger firmly on the political pulse of Europe, Queen Elizabeth instigated the updating of older strongholds. Carisbrooke Castle received two angle bastions, Plymouth's small forts and blockhouses were improved, while those protecting London, at Tilbury, were similarly dealt with. As much as anything, though, it was the bringing to readiness of strongholds along the south and east coasts, rather than new building, that typified the urgency of the time.

The Henrician caponier at Southsea Castle.

The full-time army was far too small to man all these strongholds, so a partially trained, local yeoman militia, not unlike the Home Guard of the twentieth century, effectively became front-line troops. Apart from providing assistance to the professional troops at permanent strongholds, they manned a comprehensive and vital beacon system across southern England, and temporary defensive strongpoints of road-blocks, earth banks, ditches, tree trunks and even stakes driven into potential invasion beaches. In addition, a mobile force of thirty thousand men was stationed to counter any landing. Like their successors of the twentieth century, the force was never tested in anger.

The defeat of the Spanish Armada did not entirely end the invasion threat. Small-scale Spanish raids on the south coast increased in the 1590s. In 1595 parts of Cornwall were devastated, and stronghold building continued. A fort was built at Plymouth Hoe, while the defences of the Scilly Isles were updated and bastioned curtain walls built at Star Castle. A little later, Pendennis and Carisbrooke Castles were fully enclosed by bastioned earthworks, significantly enhancing their defensive capability and, at least in the case of Pendennis, its offensive fire-power. The expected invasion came in 1597, but the second Spanish Armada was scattered by a storm off Lizard Point. England was saved, and by the end of the reign of Good Queen Bess England was an increasingly respected nation on the world stage.

SCOTLAND

Sixteenth-century Scottish Strongholds

Almost inevitably, the tower-house continued to predominate in Scotland. Some older castles developed new tricks to counter artillery, and new strongholds were not exactly rare either. In 1528 Tantallon Castle gained extensive earthworks, backed by flanking towers, thrown up to resist the guns of King James V; more were added a decade later. Dunbar Castle received a blockhouse with casemates, while Linlithgow Palace developed more and more as a royal residence, although retaining its defensive capacity. The same was true of the Earl's Palace at Birsay (Orkney). A courtyard residence of no mean embellishment, the gun-loops along the outer walls and round the courtyard suggest that defence was of some considerable importance even in that remote spot.

Perhaps most impressive was the advanced military engineering that fully utilized firearms for defence. Craignethan Castle had a caponier across its ditch, from which flanking fire could sweep attackers intending to undermine the wall; this was probably the first in Britain. Had attacking strategies switched back from the long-range bombardment of ramparts to the older, tried and tested methods of siege? Other tower-houses gained defences capable of withstanding firearms or harnessing them for defence. Blackness Castle was given additional protection on the landward side with a strengthened wall and gun casemates. It had always been a stronghold first and foremost; now it became an even more daunting fortification.

This trend towards developing medieval strongholds to enable them to survive in the age of artillery is probably best illustrated by Stirling and Edinburgh

CRAIGNETHAN CASTLE
Lanarkshire O/S map 72 ref. 815463
Directions: Leave Lanark heading north on the A72. At Crossford, turn left on the minor road towards Tillietudlem. Follow the signs on this steep and twisty road.

It might not appear anything special today, but for much of the sixteenth century Craignethan Castle was among the finest and most powerful private stronghold-residences in Britain. Standing high on a promontory overlooking the River Nethan, the only effective approach is from the west. The owners, the Hamiltons of Finnart, were staunch supporters of Mary, Queen of Scots, and took no chances when it came to security.

A rectangular tower-house, of not inconsiderable proportions, dates to the early sixteenth century. It is a mighty affair, but there was much more to come. It was surrounded by a powerful barmkin, with towers at the eastern corners and another mid-way along the north wall. At the vulnerable west side, a massive wall completely blocked off the promontory and, along with the barmkin, was liberally provided with gun-loops. Immediately beyond the west wall, the deep ditch was protected by a full caponier, probably the first in Britain. This was not considered a success and was joined by a traverse some years later. Both remain in fine condition.

A little later a large courtyard was built further west, surrounded on three sides by a curtain wall, with flanking towers at the western corners. Defenders could thus cover all Craignethan's flanks, for this outer enclosure has over twenty low gun-loops from which to assail an enemy. Indeed, for its time, Craignethan positively bristled with gun-loops, more so than any other private stronghold in Britain.

It did not do the Hamiltons much good, though, for after Queen Mary was exiled the Hamiltons' lands were forfeited and Craignethan was slighted. The buildings in the outer courtyard date to the seventeenth century.

Castles. Both were extensively rebuilt during the sixteenth century. In particular, the artillery defences at Edinburgh are most impressive. An English force sacked the city in 1545, but the castle held out. It fell in 1573 to an English bombardment though, and it was then that the Half Moon and Forewall Batteries were built; both are still standing four-square today. The only sensible approach to the old castle was thus fully covered by artillery, and must have made Edinburgh one of the most advanced medieval castles in Britain. Stirling Castle received a bastioned curtain wall towards the end of the century, but these defences were thoroughly rebuilt in the eighteenth century.

The above were all traditional strongholds adapted or rebuilt to encompass artillery but new ones soon appeared. As the English tried to create a Borders' buffer-zone in the mid-sixteenth century, they built several earthen bastioned strongholds. Remains of the bastion at Eyemouth still lie on the headland, along with the bolder French bastion and two demi-bastions of a decade later. More impressive was the encirclement of Haddington, with huge ramparts, a bastion at each corner, a ditch and raised platforms for the massed artillery. It was every bit as formidable as it looked.

The Scots also built town defences, though it seems these were never intended to withstand a mass attack. St Andrews still retains its West Port gateway and, though it now looks pretty humble, it included gun-loops. The town was certainly not going to be taken by a band of vagabonds.

Later Scottish Tower-Houses

It is, of course, these original and distinctive buildings that really distinguish Scottish military architecture of the Early Modern period. It was not until King

CRAIGIEVAR CASTLE
Aberdeenshire O/S map 37 ref. 566095
Directions: From Banchory, take the A980 north-west, and the castle is on the left after the village of Kintocher.

Tall, stout and meatily substantial up to its fourth floor, thereafter Craigievar Castle blossoms forth with a crowning glory of turrets, towers, balustrades and gables. This stepped, L-shaped tower-house may give the impression of being a wistful recreation of a non-existent romantic past, but look a little closer. Undoubtedly Craigievar was built for comfort, but the tiny ground-floor windows, the heavily studded door with its iron yett, other heavy doors and even the laird's secret stairs all suggest that defence featured strongly in the design equation.

Completed in 1626 by William Forbes, after the Mortimers came a financial cropper, there is no finer tower-house in nigh-original condition. The levels of decoration and comfort show that Craigievar was always intended as a residence first and foremost, though the Georgian sash-cord windows and the slate roof are later additions. Those apart, Willie 'the Merchant' would still recognize his glorious tower-house today.

The Forbes family sensibly avoided the various internecine troubles – Civil War, Covenanters, Jacobites – and Craigievar was never slighted. Most of the barmkin, with its towers and rampart, has long-since been swept away, to be replaced by very fine gardens. Craigievar Castle has seemingly little in common with the grim tower-houses of the Borders but, like its southern relatives, it was built with defence from a small-scale raid in mind. Though never seriously attacked, Craigievar Castle is probably the finest example of a Scottish baronial domestic stronghold.

James VI became James I of England that attempts to control the almost constant Borders' raiding had any real effect. Until that time tower-houses had become better defended and remained gaunt and stark residences; the capacity to resist a raid was emphatically their most important function. It was a combination of the need for more living space and improved defence that led to the development of the L-shaped tower-house. During the sixteenth century still further improvements would yield considerable benefits in both matters.

First of all came the stepped L-shaped tower-house, giving something of a W-shaped floor plan. The 'step' was a small tower built in the angle between the two wings of the L-shaped tower, and it usually housed the main door. This was covered by the flanking wall. As the step was often continued to the full height of the tower-house, it also provided additional space on each floor. In many cases, the step was either square or rectangular, as at Crathes or Craigievar Castles, or rounded, as at Glamis Castle. The turrets at the tops of tower-houses, from the sixteenth century onwards, not only further improved their defensive potential, but also gave them their distinctive and magnificent fairy-tale look. There are probably no visually finer strongholds in Britain.

A rather more significant advance was the building of towers at diagonally opposed corners of the main tower: the Z-plan tower-house. These additional towers could be square or circular; it was common to have one of each. Their big

The rectangular tower-house of Smailholm Castle dominates the Borders landscape for miles about.

Greenknowe Tower, an L-shaped tower-house.

advance was two-fold: they offered a vast increase in internal space over earlier tower-houses, and enabled all four walls of the main tower to be covered from the flanks. A high proportion of Z-plan tower-houses include gun-loops.

Surprisingly, they were developed in the north-east, not in the still-violent Borders. Huntly Castle is considered to be the first; here, two towers were added to the earlier tower-house in the mid-sixteenth century. Thereafter, others quickly followed. Glenbuchat Castle was built from scratch in about 1590, and was certainly intended to be defended; gun-loops are in plentiful supply. Claypotts is another small but outstanding Z-plan tower-house, complete with ground floor gun-loops all round.

Blackness Castle guards the Firth of Forth.

The advantages of such a stronghold/residence were soon apparent and still-larger versions were built. Britain's most northerly stronghold, Shetland's Muness Castle, was an elongated Z-plan tower-house, its tower being three times as long as it was wide. It had circular towers at its north and south corners and retains several decorative gun-loops and artillery embrasures. Orkney's Noltland Castle is of similar plan and size, though it has rectangular corner towers. It dates from

the 1560s and has the gaunt, stark appearance of many Borders' tower-houses but few of the embellishments then gaining favour. It has no fewer than seventy-one gun-loops ranged in tiers, adding to the already formidable appearance. Even so, internally, comfort and appearance were not sacrificed, at least by the standards of the age.

Thereafter, all manner of variations on the tower-house theme emerged. Some featured a double step, such as Dunskey Castle, while Earlshall has a stepped circular tower in the north-east, and a rectangular one in the south-west. Elcho Castle had two towers at one end of the tower-house, which itself was extended, and two circular additions at the north. Fyvie Castle went still further, with two earlier tower-houses adjoined by curtain tiers to a central gateway tower. This was rather more palace than stronghold, and the trend continued with the grand and palatial Glamis and Blair Castles. These latter were certainly primarily residences, but the tower-house is still very much at the heart of both. Balmoral Castle was probably the ultimate recreation where, with the addition of turrets, the plain and forbidding tower-house of the Borders had been transformed into the fairy-tale palace of a queen's dreams.

Bastles

These are located all along the Scottish border, and were mostly built in the century or so after 1550. There were several hundred of these defended farmhouses; about seventy-five are left today. In essence, the bastle is related to both the small Norman manor house, such as Boothby Pagnell, and the tower-house or pele-tower. It could even be considered as the poor man's tower-house, but is only two storeys high. Some are thought to have had a thatched roof but this seems unnecessarily risky: thatch would attract Reivers like gold nuggets attract prospectors.

However, bastles were certainly refuges and as with their grander relations offered protection against the Reivers more than against any form of organized assault. The ground floor was often without windows, and had a single entrance, with a heavy door closed by wooden bars; cattle and other stores were kept there. Some had a stone vaulted roof, just in case. The first floor housed the living quarters, but even this had few windows. Today, this level is usually reached by an external flight of stairs, but a ladder was probably more common – and certainly safer – in the sixteenth and seventeenth centuries. Small openings can sometimes be found beside the upper door; whether used to observe or throw missiles at visitors presumably depended on the occasion.

It is easy to dismiss bastles as hardly deserving the title stronghold, but it all depends on the circumstances. That so many were built in so short a time suggests there was not only a need for them, but that they were reasonably successful. Reivers were

Black Middens Bastle.

likely to strike quickly, plunder and be off again into the night. If one was able to herd one's stock safely behind barred doors, Reivers would not hang about too long.

STRONGHOLDS OF THE CIVIL WAR

When the threat of invasion loomed in the Second World War, a great many earthwork defences were thrown up all over Britain, most of which have long since vanished. It is no surprise, therefore, that similar defences built during the Civil War have shared the same fate. For example, who would believe that fully 18 miles of earthworks encircled London, hastily erected in 1642 to halt the Royalist forces? The same can be said of the massive bastioned defences that surrounded Oxford, the most important Royalist stronghold, designed by the foremost military engineer then in Britain, Sir Bernard de Gomme. If precious little remains of those huge undertakings, still less evidence can be found of other minor defensive works.

Despite the extensive use of firearms and artillery during the Civil War, medieval castles, fortified country houses, town walls and even churches often proved either invincible or costly to attack. For every stronghold that had its

Civil War defences of London.

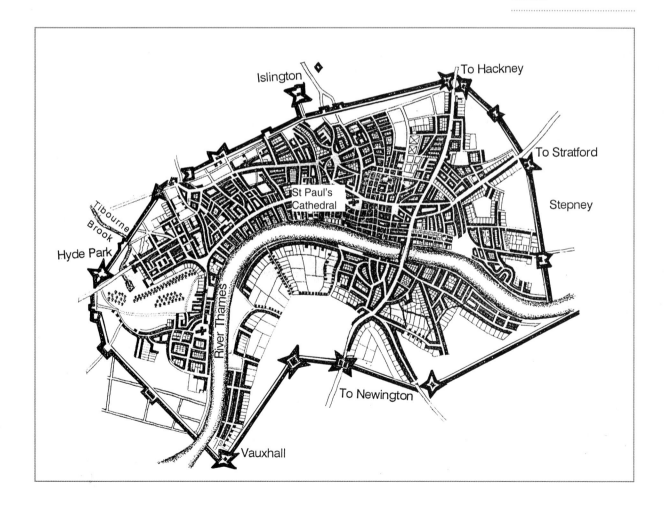

The South Gate, King's Lynn. Nearby are some Civil War earthwork defences.

defences updated (Sherborne Castle, for example, gained a bastioned artillery earthwork flanking the gatehouse), many others resisted almost unmodified. Royalist forces attacked Northampton and Coventry, and in both cases the old town walls only had earth piled in front to absorb any shot; both towns successfully survived the attack.

On the other hand, a few strategically important strongholds had their defences strengthened with bastioned earthworks. The medieval walls at Kings Lynn and Worcester were so modified, while Reading was fully encircled and had additional detached outworks. Basing House and Donnington Castle were both substantially strengthened with bastioned earthworks, and both exacted an extremely high price from the parliamentary forces for their eventual capture. It is not easy to assess the defensive potential of earthwork strongholds today, especially as so few remain. In many respects they would not have unduly impressed Iron Age man, but it was the need to withstand an artillery bombardment that made them effective.

Military tactics had changed little from pre-gunpowder days. There were still cavalry charges and, while the infantry was armed with long pikes and often fought in square formations, once engaged these set-piece battles often degenerated into an all-out brawl. In other respects, though, there had been a veritable revolution. Parliament's professional and highly trained New Model Army was unleashed at the Battle of Naseby in 1645. It brought military tactics out of the age of chivalry and downright tactical incompetence, and firmly into the age of firearms. The New Model Army was the decisive force and Naseby the pivotal battle in the Civil War, and there was no going back. The Royalists singularly failed to learn the lessons and continued to indulge in dashing cavalry charges; worse, they overlooked the impact of artillery. It was a fatal mistake; one, unbelievably, that would be repeated in the First World War.

Tall, thick stone walls were invulnerable to arrows, musket shot and even primitive cannons. Under heavy artillery fire they often smashed and, more importantly, splintered – and the resulting shrapnel could be more deadly than a whole volley of cannon shot. Cannon balls did not explode, and if one hit an earthwork, damage could be minimal. So a haphazard bombardment of an earthen stronghold, such as the surviving Queen's Sconce near Newark, might have limited effect. However, artillery and gunfire from an earthwork stronghold at troops advancing over open fields was often devastating. Defenders did not have to wait until they could see the whites of the attackers' eyes before opening fire. The farther back they were kept the better; of course, should troops reach the ditch, they would come under intensive flanking fire from the bastions. Earthworks or not, these strongholds proved to be fairly impregnable to all but the most comprehensive of assaults, or to an encircling siege, which is how the Royalist stronghold at Newark finally succumbed in 1646.

Despite the fact that older strongholds were not intended to resist primitive firearms, let alone a full-blooded artillery bombardment, some proved difficult nuts to crack. Harlech Castle resisted a siege for some time before it succumbed in 1647, while the following year Pembroke Castle held out for seven weeks. Heavy artillery was brought to bear on the Norman and

South-east side and moat, Tilbury Fort.

medieval stronghold, but it was only the cutting off of the water supply that finally caused its surrender. Similarly with Dunnottar Castle. This romantic ruin was more a fortified house than a stronghold by the Civil War. Cromwell's guns smashed it to pieces during an eight-month siege in 1651, but it was starvation that caused its downfall. It was the final stronghold to fall in the lengthy conflict.

POST-CIVIL WAR STRONGHOLDS

It was, in fact, in Scotland that some of the most advanced strongholds of the Cromwellian period were built. Many Scots had, not unnaturally, been Royalist supporters; after all, Charles was their king, while Westminster was an alien Parliament. Cromwell had to take several older castles, such as Borthwick and Edinburgh, before gaining control. He then built five massive strongholds with both defensive and offensive capabilities at Leith, Ayr, Perth, Inverness and what is now Fort William. Strategically placed, they had advanced bastioned defences and, not unlike the Edwardian towns of North Wales, they were internally planned, some having a market place, housing and other social amenities. A further twenty smaller strongholds were also begun.

None of these was completed and, once Charles II was restored in 1660, they were soon dismantled. Their regular planning harked back to Roman days – a desire to impose a design on the terrain. As far as Early Modern Britain was concerned, they formed the first planned programme of stronghold building against an internal threat. Including stone-faced ramparts and bastions,

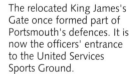

The relocated King James's Gate once formed part of Portsmouth's defences. It is now the officers' entrance to the United Services Sports Ground.

defensible barracks and all the essentials of an army of occupation, the five main citadels were certainly comprehensive, though each enjoyed only a short life.

The Restoration did not bring an end to the ongoing saga of the Dutch wars, while conflict with France was never far away. As a result, de Gomme, by then the senior military engineer in the land, was instructed to thoroughly update the fortifications at the main naval ports of Plymouth, Portsmouth and Chatham. In the 1660s the great bastioned Royal Citadel was built at Plymouth, incorporating some earlier works.

ROYAL CITADEL (Plymouth)
Devon O/S map 201 ref. 480538
Directions: At the east end of Plymouth Hoe.

The scene of history's most famous game of bowls, Plymouth Hoe is home to several blockhouses; Firestone Bay and Devil's Point still remain. These were built in about 1500 to protect the anchorage. As the naval port grew, a tower and gun-battery were placed on St Nicholas (Drake's) Island at the mouth of the River Tamar by 1549. A further blockhouse at Mount Edgecumbe, on the Cornish side, completed Plymouth's defences until after the Spanish Armada.

Then, in 1592 a fort was begun at the east end of the Hoe, at the entrance to the Cattewater. Sixty years later came the circular Mount Batten tower on the opposite bank, with its ten gun-embrasures. While Plymouth's defences did not seem obsolete, the Dutch raid on Chatham in 1667 showed what could happen if there was any laxity. A new stronghold was already underway.

Bernard de Gomme designed the Royal Citadel, which took twenty years to complete. It had three arrow-head bastions and two ravelins on the landward side, with further irregular-shaped bastions facing the water. The fort was surrounded by a ditch with counterscarp galleries, and its ornate architecture was rounded off by the distinguished and elegant entrance – unquestionably the finest at any contemporary, or subsequent, British strongholds.

Little altered, the Royal Citadel is a magnificent example of artistic military architecture. The sheer scale of its defences shows that it was not simply a pseudo-stronghold, but very much the real thing. Visiting is restricted as it is still an active military base.

Portsmouth's and Gosport's defences were similarly modified, though most of these have been lost. They included two island forts in the harbour, and an eighteen-gun battery beside the medieval Round Tower. However, as these took over twenty years to complete, some of the earlier works were either obsolescent, or virtually abandoned and in no state of readiness, even as the later building was under way.

Chatham, though, was initially treated with less urgency, and a new fort at Sheerness had not been completed when in 1667 the Dutch struck. After one salvo, most of the Sheerness guns became dislodged and the fort was abandoned within the hour. Thus ended the first of several not-so-glorious defensive actions during a week when the Dutch effectively controlled the Medway and Thames estuary. With Sheerness destroyed, the Dutch fleet promptly set off up the Medway. The prize? Most of the Royal Navy was laid up in dock out of commission. The much-vaunted chain boom was snapped in no time at all and, while the guns of Upnor Castle and several temporary batteries caused the Dutch some anguish, they were soon able to wreak havoc among the ill-defended naval ships.

Not only did the Dutch capture several large ships, including the *Royal Charles*, the pride of the fleet, but many others were burnt or destroyed. The few Englishmen who stayed to fight scuttled still more ships to prevent the Dutch towing them away. There has never been a blacker occasion in the Royal Navy's history and, what with many tales of desertion and cowardice, a more shameful time for the defences and many so-called defenders of England. The impunity with which the Dutch invaded and destroyed almost at will was an experience that was to be recalled whenever the national defensive strategy was reviewed or questioned. It was an extremely harsh, but ultimately salutary lesson.

Once the horse had bolted, it was decided to build a stable door and de Gomme was brought in. He thoroughly modified and rebuilt Sheerness fort so it

FORT CHARLOTTE
Shetland (Mainland) O/S map 4 ref. 475415
Directions: Just off the harbour road, north of Lerwick town centre.

Considering how small a town Lerwick is, Fort Charlotte is not the easiest stronghold to find. This is because it is now surrounded on three sides by houses and other buildings right up to, even touching, the main wall. It was not always so.

When it was built in 1665 to protect the anchorage of Bressay Sound, this small pentagonal fort lay to the north of what was then a tiny village, on a cliff. It had three bastions facing west and two demi-bastions to the east. By 1673 the fort was no more, having been burned by the Dutch. For just over a century it stood abandoned.

If nothing else, the Shetland Islands offer a decent anchorage in often inhospitable seas, and so the old fort was renovated, rebuilt and renamed after George III's queen in 1782. The angled seaward wall mounted nine heavy guns, with others facing all directions. Three buildings, quite typical of the time, were built round the parade ground to serve as barracks and for other essential purposes. Fort Charlotte is well preserved and is a fine example of a masonry, bastioned seventeenth/eighteenth-century fort. The buildings are still in government service.

was capable of firing at a hostile force from two sides. Two new forts were built downstream of Upnor Castle; Cookham Wood and Gillingham each had a tower, while several temporary gun batteries lined the shore. A chain boom was retained, though the siting of the new forts and batteries was such that no invaders could sail past on the opposite side of the river, as had happened with Upnor Castle.

The devastating and humiliating Dutch raid also highlighted London's lack of defences. There were still the Henrician blockhouses at Tilbury and Gravesend but, after the supposedly advanced fort at Sheerness was quickly knocked out, little hope was placed on those. A new, enlarged fort for Tilbury had been planned almost since the Restoration, and work finally began in 1670. This was to be de Gomme's finest work, along with Plymouth Citadel, and is the best example of an Early Modern bastioned fort in Britain. With a double moat, a ravelin outwork, four huge bastions and various other tricks of the trade, such as redoubts, it was a mighty obstacle for any fleet attempting to force a passage to London. Its land defences were formidable, while its two bastions and angled curtain wall, fronting the Thames, allowed for a large battery of artillery to greet hostile ships. Given the speed of contemporary sailing ships in the tight, twisting confines of the Thames, a hostile fleet would have been at the mercy of Tilbury's guns for some considerable time – probably and fatally for far too long.

Tilbury took about fifteen years to complete. Meanwhile, other coastal forts were begun, but not finished, at strategic locations such as Tynemouth and Hull. Even outlying islands gained some defences depending on their vulnerability. The Isles of Scilly had long been considered a potential advanced base for an invasion and had been fortified to varying degrees in the sixteenth century. A gun-tower was built in the anchorage off Tresco in the 1650s and named Cromwell's Castle, while an older fort was given bastioned earthworks, and renamed King Charles's Castle a little later.

It was not always the potential use for invasion that caused island groups to be fortified. Cromwell had two small forts built at Kirkwall in the Orkney

Eilean Donan Castle and
Loch Duich.

Islands, though nothing remains today, while in 1665 a fort with five bastions was built at Lerwick on the Shetland Islands (now called Fort Charlotte). Its guns covered Bressay Sound, a reasonably safe anchorage for that part of the world, but in 1673 the Dutch burned both the fort and the neighbouring village. It cannot have been regarded as too much of a disaster in the long term, for it remained derelict until 1782.

Arguably, the need for adequate coastal defence had been apparent since the Hundred Years War. Henry VIII finally built a system of strongholds capable of withstanding an attempted invasion, as a second line of defence behind his navy; the tactic clearly worked. His forts were manned by a full-time and auxiliary militia, and the system was modestly enhanced throughout the rest of the century.

There matters rested until after the Civil War when the first effective signs of a unified Britain were seen. By 1700 strongholds capable of withstanding and dishing out heavy artillery barrages protected several strategic coastal locations throughout Britain, and other places of special interest to an invader. It might have taken a combined Anglo-Dutch fleet to see off a planned French invasion in 1692 on behalf of the Jacobites, but with professional soldiers stationed throughout Britain, the chances of a successful invasion had never been slimmer. Moreover, Britain's latest strongholds were just about the equal of any in Europe. The transformation was not complete, but Britain was closer to the advanced standards of European strongholds than ever before.

Though Jacobite risings were to continue for over fifty years, by the reign of Queen Anne the union of the three countries was a reality backed by an Act of Parliament. Increasingly, strongholds were built not looking inwards, but outwards to face the world. As such, they had to keep pace with the rest of the world and yet, the next step forward was presaged by one backwards. The newly unified country, setting ever higher sights on the world stage, was still squabbling in its own back garden.

CHAPTER 7

THE GEORGIAN AND VICTORIAN AGES OF WORLD SUPREMACY

Rule Britannia,
Britannia Rules the Waves,
Britons Never, Never, Never
Shall Be Slaves.

Patriotic, nationalistic, jingoistic, arrogant: the above song could be described as any or all of those. Yet for all that, from the founding of the navy by Henry VIII until the First World War, the simplistic ideas of that joyous tune really did expound England's (and then Great Britain's) defence policy.

When George I succeeded his distant relation, Queen Anne, to the throne, the Royal Navy was internationally respected, but was some way short of being universally feared. Yet well before the eighteenth century was out, the Royal Navy was the most powerful in the world. As the nineteenth century and the long reign of Queen Victoria drew to a close, the Royal Navy was bigger than the combined navies of any other two nations. Britannia most certainly did rule the waves, and while she did so no foreign invasion was likely to land on our shores, let alone succeed in its subjugating objectives.

During the period 1714–1900, Britain was transformed from a recently united nation of modest international pretensions into the greatest power in the world. This was not the result of some grand plan, of the type pursued by Hitler, Napoleon or Julius Caesar, but came about despite timid, disunited and often lacklustre and uninspiring leadership. By a combination of accident and design, and after many expenditure squeezes, hastily followed by frenetic spending sprees more riotous than the January Sales, the Royal Navy grew big and powerful enough to safeguard our shores, and to protect the ever-more important colonial trading routes. In the days before flight, this policy most effectively thwarted the expansionist ambitions of our more avaricious neighbours.

Indeed, well before the eighteenth century, the focus of world trade had shifted emphatically away from the Mediterranean region to the Atlantic Ocean. The maritime city states of Venice and Genoa had long passed their peak. By the end of the century, the great days of Spain and Portugal were but distant memories, while Holland was too small and too constricted to remain one of the international big-boys. Autocratic and Royalist France imploded, its royal family and nobility bankrupting the country as they pursued their extravagant lifestyle, in the face of Britain's dominance of the waves and the world's trading routes. Ironically, Revolutionary France positively bristled with evil intent towards Britain, both militarily and economically, but overstepped the mark and ended up with almost the whole of Europe ranged against it.

Once Britain really got the colonial bit between the teeth, there was no holding back. France was expelled from North America and India, and while unrealistic and unsympathetic government also saw Britain summarily booted out of the USA, by the 1770s Australia and New Zealand had been discovered. Was there no limit to the ambitions of this aggressive new world power? The Colonies soon became the empire, and the Royal Navy ensured that it was Albion, with a combination of unlimited raw materials and ever-expanding markets, that gained all the benefits of this expansion. Britain's rivals were most ungraciously snubbed.

As one overseas success followed another, the eighteenth and nineteenth centuries were, nevertheless, blighted by the almost constant threat of invasion. Rather like the hypochondriac who imagines the slightest sniffle to be a bout of pneumonia, so the merest setback spawned invasion fears. If it was not the French, it was the French and Spanish, while the Dutch joined in at one stage, and even a few wild optimists in the USA fancied their chances. By the end of the nineteenth century, after giving France a going-over, the newly united Germany, initially under its expansionist Chancellor Bismarck and later the bull-headed Kaiser Wilhelm II, took to forcing a naval arms race. The outcome was never in doubt: Britain simply had to win.

THE INDUSTRIAL REVOLUTION

In terms of world domination, industry was the deciding factor. Medieval China and, latterly, Holland came close to being the first nations to embrace the ideas of industrial (as opposed to merchant) capitalism and production. Nearly, but not quite. Perhaps spurred on by the demands of the navy and especially by the growing markets and raw materials provided by the colonies, Britain's economic horizons were raised ever higher.

The Agricultural Revolution and the enclosure of villages provided a pool of surplus labour – crucially, wage labour. A ready market for one's products, buoyed by sales to the colonies, would attract sufficient capital to finance the employment of a labour force big enough to achieve production economies of scale. Add cheap transport, probably by canal, the use of some primitive water-powered machine tools, and all sorts of possibilities opened up. Before very long, handicraft manufacture was barely an economic proposition.

Most importantly, industrialism opened many opportunities to invest surplus capital, and the improvements of the Agricultural Revolution, followed by the boom of the Napoleonic Wars (1793–1815) ensured there was capital aplenty. The rapid industrial growth now took on a momentum all of its own. The drive for greater power led to the introduction of steam. Steam needed fuel – and the coal industry exploded. The higher power outputs generated by steam engines required better quality metals, which in turn needed large furnaces and accurate machine tools. None of this dynamic development was lost on the military.

WEAPONRY IMPROVEMENTS

Without any doubt, Britain led the world industrially until the 1880s. Her industries, and the taxes reaped from the vast profits that were made, enabled the empire to expand, while the Royal Navy built bigger and better ships. It might be expected that the ability to mass manufacture armaments would set Britain head and shoulders above its rivals. This was, though, seldom the case, and quite often British armaments lagged behind, rather than blazing the trail.

The extent to which weaponry and armaments improved during the nineteenth century is splendidly portrayed by the three preserved naval ships at Portsmouth. The wooden *Mary Rose* was built early in the sixteenth century, and was extensively refitted in the 1530s. She weighed about 700 tons and was powered by sail, with an arms' complement of ninety-one muzzle and breech-loaded guns. These fired a ball from a smooth bore. *Mary Rose* was one of the front line ships of Henry VIII's prestigious navy.

HMS *Victory* was built in 1765, was withdrawn from service in 1812 and remained in reserve until 1824. She, too, was a wooden sailing ship, of some 2,200 tons, with 104 guns. Despite the increase in size of both ship and guns, the basic layout of these two ships and their armament, three hundred years apart in service, would have been instantly familiar to the different crews. How that was to change.

In 1861 HMS *Warrior* took to the seas. The first large, iron-hulled naval steam ship in the world (although she still retained sail), her most innovative feature was a heavily armoured citadel, which could survive even if both bow and stern were blown off. *Warrior* carried forty heavy guns, including ten 100-pounders; most significantly many were breech-loaders with rifled barrels that spun the exploding shells for greater accuracy. While technical problems with breech-loaders took a couple of decades to sort out, rifle-barrelled guns that fired shells were a revelation; no, a revolution. HMS *Warrior* was as revolutionary as the atomic bomb at the end of the Second World War. (This analogy can be carried further: just as *Warrior* was virtually obsolete a decade later, so the A-bomb was soon superseded by the hydrogen bomb.)

What about the comparative capacities of the various guns, though? Well, a muzzle-loaded cannon on *Victory* in 1815 could fire a 32lb ball for about 1½ miles, or a 68lb ball a bare ¼ mile. One might assume the fire-power of the guns on the *Mary Rose* was somewhat less, but surely not by much. A century later a

RUTHVEN BARRACKS
Inverness-shire O/S map 35 ref. 764997
Directions: Turn off the A9 into Kingussie. Turn east on the B970 which leads back under the A9. The barracks are about 2 miles further along.

Following the 1715 Jacobite rising, the government built four barracks as part of their intention to open up the Highlands. Ruthven Barracks, built in about 1719, is the finest of these to survive, yet it was unique.

Built on a scarped hill that once housed a thirteenth-century stronghold of the Comyns and later a castle belonging to the Earl of Huntly, Ruthven Barracks commands the main north–south Highland pass. Unlike the other three barracks, Ruthven has two single barrack-blocks along the north and south faces of the enclosure. Uniquely, these did not have windows through the exterior walls, but had gun-loops on all three floors. Each barrack-block had a central entrance and staircase, with a room

Detail of gun-loops.

for ten soldiers on either side. It is unlikely, though, that Ruthven ever housed its full complement of 120 troops.

A wall, complete with wall-walk, links the two barrack-blocks and towers were built at the north-east and south-west corners; each contains a single, flanking gun-loop, in the manner of a Z-plan tower-house. The entrance is at the east, with the nearby tower serving as the guard-house; the sally-port at the west led to the stables, built by General Wade in 1734 to house some thirty dragoons.

Ruthven's moment of glory came in 1745, when Sergeant Molloy and twelve troops withstood a siege by over two hundred Highlanders. A year later, though, the Jacobites returned with artillery and the barracks soon fell, just before the fateful Battle of Culloden Moor. Thereafter, although briefly used as a rallying-point for Jacobites, Ruthven was abandoned, but it remains an attractive and impressive reminder of the days when English and Scots were far from united.

breech-loaded gun could fire a ¾ ton exploding shell some 15 miles, and with greater accuracy. As for small arms, a marine on *Victory* could fire two or three rounds a minute from his musket on a good day; by 1914 highly accurate machine guns capable of firing 600 rounds per minute were coming into use. The transformation was devastating. Strongholds and all defensive strategies would have to change emphatically to cope with the new industrial killing machines.

BERNERA BARRACKS
Inverness-shire O/S map 33 ref. 815197
Directions: Park by the school in Glenelg. Walk up the track opposite.

Today, the Bernera Barracks stands off the beaten track, seemingly a place of little importance. However, when the complex was built between 1720 and 1723, not only were the Highlands and islands far more heavily populated, but Bernera Barracks controlled the main crossing for the Isle of Skye over Kyle Rhea. A small ferry still crosses to Kyle Rhea – the only boat with a turntable deck in Europe.

Although similar in plan to Ruthven Barracks, even down to having two angle towers, the barracks at Bernera are the more usual double blocks. Each barrack-block had three storeys, a central entrance and, with four rooms per floor, housed up to 120 troops. Most surprising are the ten full-size windows in the outer walls of the first and second floors, with five half-size windows on the ground floor. These were protected by iron bars but, even so, seem a bit vulnerable considering the troops were billeted in hostile territory. The angle towers did not have gun-loops.

Unlike the other three Highlands barracks, Bernera has dressed-stone quoins, and door and window surrounds. These give a little architectural distinction, but Bernera is in a poor state of preservation. Indeed, it is currently wired-off but, especially when enshrouded in a coastal mist, the barracks evokes an atmosphere quite appropriate to the fabled magic of the '45.

The military road through Glenmore was built a few years after the barracks, which did not succumb in the '45 rebellion. The barracks was manned until the end of the century, although when Boswell and Johnson passed by in 1773, there was only a sergeant and a handful of men stationed there. Its rather gaunt, desperately sad, condition is a reminder of those grim times when Scots fought each other with an almost demonic fervour.

PUTTING THE HOUSE IN ORDER

Queen Anne was not Britain's luckiest monarch. She had seventeen (yes, seventeen!) children, none of whom survived childhood. When she died in 1714, she left no direct heir. Next in line to the throne of Great Britain was James Edward Stuart, the Catholic son of the deposed King James II, but he had no chance because a combination of the 1689 Bill of Rights and the 1701 Act of Settlement meant that a Catholic could not take the throne.

The closest Protestant heir was George Louis, Elector of Hanover, although one had to trace his lineage back to Elizabeth, daughter of James I, to justify his succession. He was enthusiastically received by Parliament, greeted with total indifference by the general population, and treated with outright hostility by the Jacobites. King George I had barely settled on the throne before the rightful heir, James Edward, landed in Scotland in 1715. A French fleet was to assist him by invading southern England and diverting government forces, but it came to naught. It did not stop a Highland Jacobite rising in the cause of the Old Pretender, though.

Although the Battle of Sheriffmuir was indecisive, the Jacobites returned home and the government sent General Wade to open up the Highlands. He built 260 miles of road, forty bridges and new strongholds at Inverness (Fort George), Fort Augustus and Fort Stalker. In addition, four fortified barracks were built at Inversnaid, Ruthven, Bernera and Kiliwhimin (the latter soon replaced by Fort Augustus). Finally, Stirling, Edinburgh and Dumbarton Castles were all refortified. This was all very promising but, ultimately, nowhere near enough. The Jacobites tried again in 1719, when supporting Spanish troops landed in Lochalsh and holed up in Eilean Donan Castle. Three Royal Navy frigates promptly blew the castle and the Spaniards to bits.

George was never popular, perhaps because he did not speak English, which allowed Cabinet government not only to take root, but to flourish. Never again would the monarchy enjoy such untrammelled power.

It was, though, the arrival of Charles Edward Stuart – Bonnie Prince Charlie, the son of James Edward – in 1745 that really set the cat among the pigeons. Perhaps because King George II was also German, Britain contrived to get embroiled in the War of Austrian Succession (1740–8). At the same time, Britain and France were at it again, battling it out in North America, India and on the high seas. In 1744 France assembled an invasion army of ten thousand men at Dunkirk to support Bonnie Prince Charlie, but England's traditional ally, the inclement Channel weather, and the Royal Navy ensured that it never put to sea.

The next year, the enigmatic prince landed in Scotland, rallied the Jacobite Highlanders to his side, won victories at Falkirk and, vitally, Prestonpans and marched south with five thousand men. The bulk of the government forces were still in Europe, so England seemed to be theirs for the taking. The Highlanders were a well behaved if rather rough and ready force, but the expected – and crucial – support from English Catholics was not forthcoming. Disheartened, the Highlanders forced a crestfallen Charles Edward to return home from Derby. George II was supposedly a weak king and his government was allegedly packing ready to leave, but this was not quite true. In any case, George II holds the distinction of being the last British monarch to lead his troops into battle, at Dettingen in the Austrian War, and he won. Moreover, large government forces were soon expected to land to counter the rebellious Scots.

It was the king's brother, the Duke of Cumberland, who chased the Jacobites back to the Highlands. En route, the Jacobites besieged several government strongholds, capturing Fort George, Fort Augustus and almost Fort William, before Butcher Cumberland caught up with them at Culloden Moor. The Highlanders with their Claymore swords and dirks were outnumbered, outmanoeuvred, outfought and then slaughtered by Redcoats armed with muskets and bayonets and, crucially, artillery. Even that was not the end of the matter.

By 1770 over 1,000 miles of military roads had been built to open up the Highlands. A new, magnificent Fort George, on the Moray Firth, became the main army base, while the tower-houses at Braemar and Corgarff were rebuilt with star-shaped curtain walls and gun-loops. This was only the start. More relevant was the ruthless hunting out of the Jacobites, and the banning of tartans and other symbols of defiance. It was a harsh and cruel means of bringing to boot and purging the dissenting Highlanders – the Duke of Cumberland was not known as the Butcher for nothing.

THE RISE AND RISE OF GREAT BRITAIN

Thereafter, Britain began to be seen as an entity, a true United Kingdom. The prospect of war with France never entirely receded though, and from 1756 to 1763 the two sworn enemies became embroiled in the Seven Years War. If ever there was a time that marked Britain's arrival as a world power, this was it. During that conflict the Royal Navy for the first time used the blockade effectively, a tactic at the heart of British power for the next two hundred years. By the Treaty of Paris in 1763, France had been ousted from India and had little influence left in North America. Britain's colonies were being transformed into the Empire.

But Britain nearly threw it all away during the American War of Independence (1776–83) when a joint Franco-Spanish invasion force was, once again, thwarted only by stormy Channel weather; this clearly illustrates just how dangerously dispersed was the Royal Navy. It simply did not have enough ships to patrol both home and colonial waters. If that set the government thinking, it was a crisis of much greater magnitude that finally provoked action.

In 1789 rebellion exploded in aristocratic France. By 1793 the revolutionary government had declared war on Britain. In what was almost a dress-rehearsal for the conflicts of the early twentieth century, Britain sent an army to Belgium, which lost a few battles and soon returned home with its tail firmly between its legs. By 1797 Britain stood alone against France and, once again, invasion loomed. The Royal Navy, as usual, was all that stood in the way, only this time there were mutinies at the Spithead and Nore anchorages. The sailors were fully justified – appalling conditions, broken promises, bad leadership, mismanagement and mis-government are nothing new. Luckily, France was not in a position to take advantage and Britain again slipped off the hook.

So the war drifted on. Nelson won the Battle of the Nile in 1798 to regain control of the Mediterranean Sea, but Napoleon was not beaten. He adopted his Grand Design in 1803, and grand it most certainly was. Fully a hundred thousand troops assembled to invade England. Had they been able to land, Britain's small regular army, inadequate defences and enthusiastic, but poorly equipped volunteer militia would have been, at best, over-stretched and at worst, completely overwhelmed.

Luck and the Royal Navy came to Britain's aid yet again, and Napoleon was never able to gain the essential control of the English Channel. In the summer of 1805 his army marched inland to win great victories at Ulm and Austerlitz, but Nelson finally ran the French navy to ground at Cape Trafalgar. It was all over in one long day, and Britain breathed another huge sigh of relief.

Despite the maritime dust-up with the USA between 1812 and 1815, the next serious threat to our shores came from, as usual, France. The appointment of Louis Napoleon as President in 1848 saw Britain anxiously glancing over its shoulder, while his elevation to Emperor Napoleon III a few years later did nothing to assuage those fears. From 1852 to 1855, though, the two wary warring nations were brothers-in-arms, seemingly united against the Russian Bear in the Crimea.

With such a long history of enmity between Britain and France, this alien concept of cooperation could not last. By the end of the decade not only were they engaged in something of a naval arms race, one result of which was HMS *Warrior*, but a Royal Commission on the Defences of the United Kingdom was appointed in 1859. The Commission's report led to the most concentrated and extensive bout of stronghold building in Britain ever. 'Palmerston's Follies' is the polite way of referring to the seventy-six new forts, built as a result of the national paranoia. We may never fully realize how effective these forts were as a deterrent, but if France, or later Germany, had any grand ambitions in Britain's direction, they certainly knew what to expect. Success would not come cheaply.

Despite the ambitions of Kaiser Wilhelm II, Britannia continued to rule the waves. During the Scramble for Africa in the 1880s, the Royal Navy ensured that it was Britain who grabbed the most. All the while, despite countless weaponry and stronghold developments, it was the might of the Royal Navy that safeguarded both the Empire on which the sun never set, and Old Blighty itself. Britain was the military kingpin but, ominously, once the American Civil War was over, in 1865, the Americans' industrial and agricultural muscle soon came to equal, and then surpass, those of the slightly ageing lady who had initiated the industrial age. By the end of the century, Germany was catching up fast. The world had indeed changed. Britain had ousted the Spanish, Dutch and French, and was now under threat herself from two newcomers. While the world has never stood still, it was changing and expanding faster than at any time in history.

Braemar Castle with its gun-looped curtain wall.
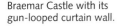

SCOTLAND THE BRAVE?

Previous chapters demonstrated how nationally planned programmes of stronghold building were a rarity. In most cases strongholds were built and used by individuals, even during the Civil War, and were usually intended to protect the owner from the unscrupulous desires of his fellow-countrymen. From the Georgian period onwards, strongholds were only built by the state and were almost entirely directed towards countering a real or perceived external threat.

The exception was the two periods of stronghold building in Scotland that followed the Jacobite risings of 1715 and 1745. Edinburgh, Stirling, Dumbarton and Blackness Castles were all further developed after the Act of Union (1707), with gun batteries and other defences, and none of these fell in the subsequent troubles. Rocked into action by the near-miss of the first Jacobite revolt, the government built four strategically placed fortified barracks, and three forts.

The barracks were self-contained and comprised double barrack-blocks, except at Ruthven, adjoining the curtain wall. Curiously, the outer barrack walls had barred windows from the first floor level upwards, again except at Ruthven, while flanking cover was less than thorough: a few musket-loops from ancillary buildings. There was no provision to fire artillery.

In view of the likelihood that Highlanders would seldom raise more than a few hundred men, and that small arms were at a premium (never mind artillery), these barracks seemed more than adequate for the job in hand. So it proved, for in 1745,

---

CORGARFF CASTLE
Aberdeenshire O/S Map 37 ref. 254087
Directions: Along the A939, south-east of Grantown-on-Spey.

Commanding the Lecht Pass through the Grampian Mountains, Corgarff Castle is a wild and lonely place. Even today, the pass is occasionally blocked in winter. Not, then, a place for the faint-hearted.

Corgarff Castle's past almost reads like a prècis of Scottish history. It was built in 1537 as a hunting lodge by Thomas Erskine, Earl of Mar, and it witnessed one of the more dastardly deeds of Scottish clan feuding in 1571. Margaret Forbes and her retinue of twenty-six were burnt to death when they were attacked by the Gordons, who simply began a fire in the latrine flues! In 1626 the Erskines regained Corgarff and built Braemar Castle, and in 1645 Montrose and his Covenanters occupied the castle prior to the Battle of Alford.

Corgarff was burnt for a second time in 1689 by the Jacobites, and in 1715 the Earl of Mar rallied his supporters before raising the Jacobite standard at Braemar. The following year, government troops burned Corgarff for the third time. It was to rise from the ashes yet again! In 1746 Lord Ancrum took Corgarff, as the Jacobite rising petered out, and it was transformed to enjoy, or endure, a further lease of life, along with Braemar Castle.

Unlike many of the region's tower-houses, Corgarff Castle is a bit of a Plain Jane. Despite its many sackings and rebuildings, there are no towers, turrets and balustrades so beloved of the Scottish baronial influence. It is a simple, rectangular four-storey tower-house, bearing the functional stamp of the Borders.

In 1748 the tower was repaired and enclosed by a star-shaped curtain wall, pierced by a liberal supply of gun-loops. At the same time two buildings were erected adjoining the tower: the bakehouse and a prison. Corgarff was garrisoned by forty troops, five NCOs and an officer as the government sought out Jacobites, and suppressed the clans and anything else associated with the rising. Corgarff the turncoat, once again.

Thereafter, its garrison dwindled, but as a finale, some fifty troops were stationed at Corgarff in the 1820s to counter illicit whisky activities. Once the troops departed, Corgarff was left to moulder away, and no wonder, for four centuries it had hardly endeared itself to the locals.

While Corgarff Castle is no dream-like fairy-tale affair, it is a well-restored military barracks in a wonderful location. Aside from Fort George, it is the finest of the anti-Jacobite government military establishments and has certainly enjoyed a most active past.

BLACKNESS CASTLE
West Lothian O/S map 65 ref. 055802
Directions: From Queensferry, take the A904 west and then the B903 into Blackness. The castle is by the shore.

Forbidding and austere, though not especially grim, Blackness Castle was a stronghold first and foremost and, until the last few decades, throughout its life.

The fifteenth-century tower-house, still with its yett, was burnt in the mid-century clan wars, and again by an English fleet at the end of the century. The barmkin, a second tower, a triangular bastion and other defences beefed-up to counter artillery were added in the sixteenth century. By then, Blackness had taken on a greater importance as the port for the nearby royal burgh of Linlithgow, complete with its royal palace.

Despite further strengthening, General Monck captured Blackness for Parliament in 1654, but Charles II had it repaired. After further reinforcements, Blackness became a gaol for Covenanters later in the century, the dank pit-prison being washed by the tide.

After the Act of Union in 1707, Blackness was one of four Scottish castles to be garrisoned, along with Edinburgh, Stirling and Dumbarton. Its guns were kept up to date, but it was not besieged in either Jacobite rising. Thereafter, Blackness remained an active stronghold, but its military importance steadily diminished; it became an arsenal in 1870. There was still further building but by 1912 the military had abandoned Blackness Castle. It was restored to its earlier profile and many nineteenth-century buildings were demolished.

Standing on a promontory jutting into the Forth, Blackness is a gloriously attractive stronghold. Inside, though, it has not been softened by use as a private residence. Four hundred years of military use is not masked so easily.

just thirteen Redcoats at Ruthven Barracks successfully withstood an assault by over two hundred Highlanders. The real question was how these forts would fare against an artillery bombardment. The answer came in 1746, as the Jacobites were pursued north by Butcher Cumberland. This time they brought artillery to bear and Ruthven fell embarrassingly quickly; it has remained effectively abandoned ever since. Bernera Barracks, in the heart of Jacobite territory, at Glenelg, continued to be occupied by a small force into the nineteenth century.

Forts were built at Inverness (Fort George) and Fort Augustus, but as pure military strongholds they were flawed. Despite its bastioned earthwork curtain wall, Fort George was overlooked from nearby high ground. This proved its undoing in 1746, and its not especially brave commandant surrendered after the Jacobites' first artillery barrage. Fort Augustus was built between 1729 and 1742 and was intended to be the military and administrative centre of the Highlands. It had all the usual defensive accoutrements of the age, with stone-faced bastioned earthworks and so forth and, in view of its importance, many buildings also displayed a degree of architectural decoration.

Fort Augustus was also overlooked by high ground, notably from the nearby abandoned barracks at Kiliwhimin. Given its importance, the defences might be expected to have to face, and resist, a heavy Jacobite barrage. One building, though, rose above the parapet: an arrogant symbol of defiance and imposing grandeur. No doubt, it duly impressed; it was also an irresistible target. Surely, one would assume, it must be the commandant's quarters or perhaps the administration centre? Unfortunately not. Blunders do not come much bigger than this: it was the powder magazine! One accurate Jacobite shot at this most tempting target and it was all over. After the rout at Culloden Moor a fair bit of new thinking was clearly required to maintain government control.

FORT GEORGE

No matter what had gone wrong with the earlier forts, it was to be an altogether different matter with the new Highlands' stronghold. Lieutenant-General William Skinner's Fort George sits on a narrow peninsula jutting out into the Moray Firth. It was built between 1748 and 1769 and featured stone-faced bastioned earthworks similar to those built at Berwick some two hundred years earlier. Cut off on the landward side by a wide ditch (which could be flooded if required), a large triangular, self-contained ravelin and other outworks, and with massive diamond-shaped bastions at each corner, it seemed that the lessons of 1746 had been well and truly learned.

A massive bastion was built at the mid-point of the two long sides, with demi-bastions at the seaward ends. There was considerable provision for both artillery and small-arms flanking fire from the bastions, while heavily defended sally-ports and a covered-way allowed for a distinctly active form of defence. Most impressively, although there were extensive and attractive barracks and other buildings for the garrison of 1,600 infantry and 80 heavy guns, there were also bombproof, casemate barracks within the ramparts. With a highly fortified magazine, Fort George was one of the world's finest strongholds and its twenty gun battery commanding the narrow passage across to the Black Isle made it the ultimate coastal promontory fortress. Indeed, it remains an active service establishment to this day.

Fort George.

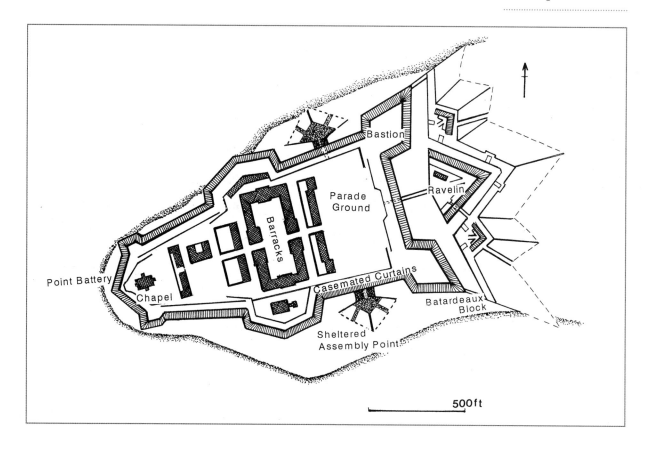

View along the south rampart, Fort George.

Entrance and moat, Fort George.

EIGHTEENTH-CENTURY STRONGHOLDS

As England, Scotland and Wales became increasingly unified, so the need for internal strongholds was drastically reduced. Suspicious eyes were, as ever, cast beyond the seas, particularly in the direction of France, and despite the favourable Treaty of Utrecht, 1715 saw the first systematic national review of Britain's military sites. For a nation that still feared an invasion, it made alarming reading. There was an unhealthy reliance on defences of medieval origin; some had been updated but most had not.

Such a situation was just about acceptable if economy was a prime consideration, but was rather at odds with a military world that increasingly embraced costly artillery. As a result of this survey, several new works were put in hand, such as the total rebuilding of Landguard Fort at Felixstowe. This forthright action was short-lived though, and there followed two further decades of neglect, decay and the manning of strongholds on a care and maintenance basis only. Despite all the official fuss, only strategic estuaries and naval ports received any worthwhile attention.

As the Royal Navy was considered to be the first (and subsequent) lines of defence, so it was essential to protect its main ports. The harsh lesson of the Dutch raid on Chatham in 1667 sat uneasily in the Admiralty's memory until well into the twentieth century. It was just as well that the Dutch were intent solely on destroying as many ships as possible rather than invading. Although the dockyard was damaged, in a sense England got off lightly. Suppose they had decided to attack London? Naval ports clearly needed full and effective protection if the Royal Navy was to safeguard Britain.

The Austrian Wars followed by the Seven Years War and the American War of Independence aligned Britain and France for another forty years of conflict. In particular, the main naval ports of Plymouth, Portsmouth and Chatham would benefit from some extensive stronghold building during that time. The threat to these ports was expected to be twofold: a blockade followed by a seaborne bombardment of the ships, port and town; or the landing of a large force elsewhere to march on the port and bombard it from the hills above, probably in conjunction with naval action. As France was ever-keen to put the upstart Britain firmly in its place, the threat could not be underestimated.

Naval Ports

The fleet that patrolled the western approaches to the English Channel, Ireland and the colonial convoys was based at Plymouth. This port was defended by several sixteenth- and seventeenth-century batteries and small forts round the harbour and, of course, de Gomme's magnificent citadel. However, the docks had expanded round to Devonport – and what if an enemy landed and encamped on the high ground to the north? The increased range of artillery meant that, should even a modest foreign force land at, say, Whitsand or Cawsand Bays, in Cornwall, it could bombard Devonport and Plymouth from the hills near Mount Edgecumbe almost with impunity.

The solution to this threat was to build the Devonport Lines: a well-bastioned curtain wall round the north and east of Devonport. This had defensive limitations as it was still overlooked by higher ground; later tinkering, including widening the ditch and strengthening the rampart, improved its defensibility, but failed to address this strategically important drawback. A few temporary earthwork batteries were also added to prevent a landing in Cornwall and to defend the high ground at the west of Plymouth Sound. For the mid-century crises these measures appeared to be enough, but with the subsequent invasion scares, new detached earthwork redoubts and batteries were built to combat the even greater perceived threat. This emphasized an important change in defence

CHATHAM FORTS
Kent O/S map 178
Fort Amherst, Barrier Road
Begun in 1756 to protect the southern end of the Brompton Lines defending the eastern approach to the naval docks, Fort Amherst became the Amherst redoubt by the end of the century, in response to the Napoleonic threat, and took its present form, complete with battery, from about 1820. Open to the public, it is now the finest of the Chatham forts.
Fort Horsted, ref. 750651
This was the largest of the detached forts built from the 1870s to the 1890s to defend the heights south and east of Chatham. Polygonal and not unlike the Royal Commission forts above Portsmouth, Chatham's forts have a lower profile and, covered in earth and spoil, are almost invisible from any distance. Most internal structures are of concrete, while the fort is divided by an earthwork traverse containing a long tunnel. Fort Horsted is currently a small industrial estate, full of garages and scrap yards: hardly the most salubrious of strongholds, but its details can be appreciated.
Fort Luton, ref. 762660
A smaller version of Fort Horsted, minus the earthwork traverse. This is open to the public as something of a theme park.
Fort Clarence, St Margaret's Street, Rochester
Not unlike a medieval keep, except that it is built of brick, Fort Clarence was situated west of the Chatham Lines to command the crossing of the River Medway. Built between 1808 and 1812, the three-storey tower has large corner turrets and, would you believe, machicolations. As such, it presents a pretty impressive sight, at least for forts of its age. The towers were for observation rather than for housing heavy guns.

tactics, away from the all-encompassing bastioned lines of the previous two centuries.

There was a similar scenario with the defences at Britain's premier naval port, Portsmouth/Gosport. The mid-century crises saw the renovation and extension of de Gomme's bastioned lines round Gosport, in particular at Priddy's Hard. These defences were modest compared to, say, those at Berwick, but they served to protect the harbour from a westwards land assault.

Towards the end of the eighteenth century, the expanding settlement of Portsea grew up around the dockyard. This, too, was enclosed by a new bastioned line to the east, adjoining Portsmouth's earlier defences. Thus in the years before the Napoleonic Wars the docks at Portsmouth were ringed by about 5 miles of bastioned defences which, combined with the low-lying land within artillery firing range, made this the most secure of all the major naval bases.

Inevitably, and sensibly, Chatham was similarly defended, with the Brompton Lines occupying high ground to the south and east of the dockyard. A bastioned rampart and ditch were deployed, with redoubts later built at each end. Batteries were built along the banks of the River Medway, further enhancing the river defences; these earthworks were successively added in response to each apparent crisis. Finally, a curtain wall with three bastions was built about half a mile to the south of the garrison at Sheerness. This served as both additional protection at the mouth of the Medway and an extension of the land defences in the manner of the Devonport Lines.

Other Coastal Strongholds

While the emphasis was on coastal fortification at the three main naval bases, during the eighteenth century other sites likely to be of interest to Johnny Foreigner were given additional, if somewhat lacklustre, protection. Outer batteries to cover the Orwell and Stour estuary were added at Landguard Fort, while the Western Heights was begun above Dover in 1778. Though initially of modest proportions, this became one of the major coastal defensive developments of the next century; needless to say, Dover was the port most coveted by any ambitious foreign power.

Batteries, temporary or otherwise, were thrown up all round Britain's coast at various times before the Napoleonic Wars. Torbay, Portland, St Ives and Milford Haven: at these and many other locations, risks could not be taken. While it was impossible to cover every inch of coast line, few estuaries or anchorages of potential use to an invasion force were left entirely unprotected.

Although it was not expected that Scotland would be invaded, especially after the failure of the '45 uprising, the useful anchorage in the far-flung Shetland Isles lacked any real protection. The seventeenth-century fort destroyed by the Dutch was comprehensively renovated and transformed into a thoroughly modern bastioned fort; it was renamed Fort Charlotte in honour of the queen in 1782. Although now surrounded by Lerwick, it is still complete and commands the Sound of Bressay. A fine example of a late eighteenth-century coastal stronghold, Fort Charlotte was quite a contrast to its mostly temporary contemporaries.

DOVER CASTLE
Kent O/S map 179 ref. 326416
Directions: Off Castle Hill Road; the A258 Deal road.

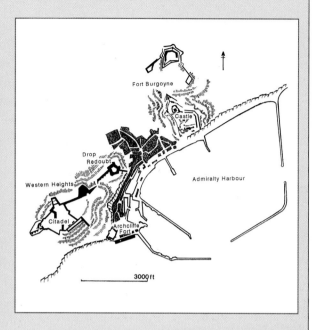

Quite simply, Dover Castle is Britain's greatest stronghold. It survived a siege by Louis of France in 1216, and served as the command centre for the Dunkirk evacuation and other major campaigns of the Second World War; it has also featured strongly in just about every invasion crisis in between.

As a result, the defences have been constantly improved and modified, and some of the Norman and medieval works have been altered, even obliterated, though much still remains. While one might bemoan this, it was no different when the original Iron Age hillfort was rebuilt as a Saxon *burh*, which itself succumbed when William I built a castle, reputedly in only eight days. All that heritage was brusquely swept aside a century or so later, when the massive keep and inner and outer curtain walls were built. That great new stronghold was designated the 'key to England' in the Middle Ages; had it not been subsequently modified, the key could easily have been lost on several occasions.

For all its strategic and symbolic importance, Dover Castle has got through life relatively unscathed, in battle at least. The siege of 1216 turned on a vigorous, determined defence after the French undermined the north gateway, which partly collapsed. Sheer brute force and bravery sealed the breach and soon the siege was lifted. In 1265 supporters of Simon de Montfort held the castle, but it was relinquished to the king, and during the Civil War some enterprising Parliamentarians talked the Royalist garrison into surrender. Thereafter, aside from an occasional strafing in the Second World War, life has been pretty considerate to the old war-horse stronghold.

The scale of the building and subsequent alterations make for a pretty complicated story. Except for a Roman lighthouse, the Pharos, only the defences built during and after the reign of Henry II can be seen today. Viewed from the Western Heights, the squat keep is the outstanding single feature. From close up, this massive edifice simply exudes power. About 95 ft tall, with walls 21 ft thick, bolstered by pilasters and with stocky corner towers, the keep is muscular rather than elegant. It was one of the last rectangular keeps to be built in England, *c.* 1180–90, and was probably the most powerful of the lot.

Surrounding the keep is the contemporary inner bailey wall, complete with fourteen square towers, including two pairs that form the north and south gates. The north barbican still stands, but that at the south was a more elaborate affair. The outer bailey wall was begun in about 1165, but was not completed from the cliff-face round the inner bailey and back to the cliff-face until a century later. This featured the earthwork spur, complete with underground tunnels, at the north, built after the 1216 siege. Not only was Dover Castle probably the most secure stronghold in England by mid-century, it was also Britain's first concentric castle.

While the following centuries saw minor additions to the fabric, such as the Tudor Moat's Bulwark, the castle seemingly languished into retirement. Then, the various mid-eighteenth-century crises saw Dover thrust into the front-line once again – a situation that lasted until after the Napoleonic Wars. France needed an invasion port and Dover would clearly have been their ideal target; it had to be held at all costs. The castle's medieval defences were drastically altered and updated; in particular, the medieval tunnels were modified, and new tunnels and earthwork bastions were built. During the Napoleonic Wars, the castle boasted 231 guns.

Still later, the defences were again adapted to mount contemporary guns but most important by far was the building of further tunnels beneath the white cliffs, from 1940 onwards. These tunnels became the Combined Headquarters for the supremely exposed, and appropriately named, Hellfire Corner sector of coastal defence in the Second World War. Thus, Dover Castle served in the front-line of our national defences until 1956, and through every major invasion-threatening conflict before; clearly it was more than an historic relic.

Dover Castle is no mere monument to Norman or medieval stronghold building. It celebrates military adaptability and ingenuity. From sling-stone to bow and arrow, and from clumsy cannon to Nazi bomber, Dover saw off and resisted the lot.

The massive earthwork bastion hides medieval and eighteenth-century tunnels. Dover's massive keep rises above, while Second World War dragon's teeth protect the flanks.

A new and enlarged Fort Cumberland was begun at Eastney Point on the south-east of Portsea island. Its five diamond-shaped bastions, ravelin and ditches offered considerable defensive cover, and there were several sally-ports to allow the garrison to seize any opportunity for counter-attacking. On the whole, though, these new permanent forts were the exceptions and, naturally, few of the earthwork batteries have survived. Indeed, little of the bastioned defensive lines at the three major naval ports remains to be seen today.

Napoleonic Strongholds

For some twenty-two years from 1793 Britain was at war with Republican France. The threat of invasion had existed before, but it was as nothing compared to the almost constant fear that persisted from 1797 to 1805. In particular, France assembled an army along its north coast to exploit any lapse in Britain's defences in 1797, 1801 and 1803–1805. Thereafter, thanks to Nelson and his fleet, that fear was to diminish, but could never entirely be overlooked.

Where would an invasion land, though? That was the pressing question of the day. Britain's east coast had many estuaries but its mud-flats and shallow tides meant that landing, provisioning and defending an army could prove hugely difficult unless a major port was taken and held. The south-east coast was the best bet, but there were many other good anchorages, bays and estuaries further

The view from St Martin's Battery to Drop Redoubt, on Dover's Western Heights. A type 23A pillbox is in the foreground, with Dover Castle in the distance.

to the west. Much guesswork concerning the likely point of invasion occupied the minds of politicians, senior forces personnel and the population at large.

Assuming an army had landed, what would be its prime target? London was the obvious one, and so mobilization centres were built along the North Downs to be manned, mostly, by volunteer militia. So grave was the perceived threat, that a large military installation at Weedon (Northants.) included quarters for the royal family should they have to leave London. Nearer the coast, temporary earthwork batteries and permanent redoubts were hastily built at estuaries all the way from the Firth of Forth round the east, south and west coasts of England as far as South Wales. Few of these remain, but the likes of Drop Redoubt, at Dover's Western Heights, still give a good impression of such strongholds. The Heights were greatly enhanced to house up to four thousand troops which, via the Grand Shaft, could quickly move to and from the town.

Fort Clarence, at Rochester. Closer inspection is at the whim of the B.T. site engineer.

In addition to these, other substantial strongholds were built and major improvements were made to older ones. The earthwork Brompton Lines at Chatham were rebuilt, revetted in brick and extended north. To further obstruct an approach on the River Medway and Rochester, several detached strongholds were built early in the nineteenth century, principally Fort Pitt. Combining bastions and casemated defensible barracks with the latest brick gun-towers, this was something of a mongrel, but it was certainly no dog. A march on London along, say, the Dover road, would be met with considerable force in the vicinity of the Medway towns.

Older strongholds were also refurbished. Extra guns were mounted at Blackness and Dumbarton Castles, in Scotland, and more recent strongholds, such as Landguard Fort, were obviously strengthened. More surprisingly, reflecting the desperation of the times, so were some pretty ancient ones. The Henrician Hurst, Deal and Sandgate Castles were modified and given additional earthwork batteries, and others were manned for the duration. No ancient stronghold was more thoroughly updated than Dover Castle though. Towers and sections of the curtain wall were lowered to facilitate artillery fire, while bastions, caponiers and other additions all continued a mighty rebuilding process begun in the middle of the eighteenth century. However much they might have changed the medieval aspects of the castle, they can still be seen today.

The Royal Military Canal, at Appledore, with a Second World War pillbox all ready for action.

The Royal Military Canal

The billeting of Napoleon's Grand Army just across the Channel really concentrated military minds in Britain. Probably the easiest and most inviting stretch of coast line for an invasion near London was between Hythe and Winchelsea. Here, in 1804, the Royal Military Canal was begun. It ran for 28 miles between these

towns, yet cuts up to 10 miles inland from Dungeness. The main section between Hythe and Rye was soon built and is still complete.

Used for military transport as well as being a defensive barrier, the Royal Military Canal was bounded by a drain and towpath on the coastal side of the 30 feet wide canal, with a rampart, the Military Road and a further drain beyond. Thus, if necessary, the canal-barrier could be defended from both sides. There were earthwork gun positions every 600 yards, while troops marched along the Military Road to man the rampart.

Fortunately, it was never put to the test, and it remains debatable how effective it would have been. It would probably not have held back Napoleon's Grand Army for very long without support, but troops occupying the high ground behind the canal could have inflicted some nasty wounds on Napoleon's men before they continued their advance on London. Some 135 years later the Royal Military Canal was refortified with pillboxes placed at strategic points, such as Appledore. Once more unto the breach . . .

Martello Towers

Somewhat more distinctive and obvious are the stumpy Martello towers that were built round the coast from Seaford to Aldeburgh; there are two more in the Orkney Islands, and one at Leith. Martello Towers were adapted from a gun-tower at Cape Mortella, Corsica, one of many in the Mediterranean region. In 1794 this tower had held off a Royal Navy force, finally surrendering to a landing party. It was an impressive lesson that was, fortunately, remembered.

Plans to build a system of Martello Towers – intended to hold up an invasion for a day or two, or until the navy arrived to sort things out – were hatched in 1803, but typically building did not begin until 1805. The first tower was not even finished before Napoleon's Grand Army had dispersed! Fears of an invasion were assuaged by Nelson's victory at Trafalgar, but did not vanish entirely until after the Battle of Waterloo. Even so, one must question whether seventy-four towers should have been built along the south coast between 1805 and 1808, with a further twenty-nine along the East Anglian coast between 1808 and 1812. The two Orcadian towers were built to protect trans-Atlantic convoys from American raiders as they assembled at Longhope Sound, during the war of 1812–15. In the end, not one was ever tested in action.

Martello Towers are oval-shaped, and stand about 35 ft high, with two storeys. They taper markedly, not unlike a broch, and their accommodation is offset so that the thickest part of the wall faces the sea. Some were surrounded by a ditch and had a drawbridge to the rear-facing door at first-floor level; others merely had a ladder. The few windows were deeply recessed and could be barricaded. Each tower consumed about half a million bricks, and room for twenty-four men and one officer on the first floor was seemingly hewn from the solid walls; the basement housed the magazine and stores. The roof was about 10 ft thick and was reached by mural stairs, and the whole tower was faced with tough cement to prevent it being scaled.

Initially each tower was armed with a single 24 lb roof-mounted gun which could be rotated through 360 degrees, although some towers later received either additional or bigger guns. The intention was to create an arc of overlapping fire with neighbouring towers, thus covering most of the coast. Even if Martello Towers never had to repel an invasion, they deterred commando-style raids and were ideally suited to being manned by local auxiliaries, with a nucleus of regular soldiers. In one respect, though, Martello Towers were innovative, in Britain at least. Designed to hinder an invasion or landing party until the navy arrived, they were an early example of combined operations.

Several towers soon gained the company of a neighbouring battery, like Hackness on Hoy, or a casemated redoubt, as at Eastbourne. Indeed, the Martello Towers need to be viewed as part of a complete defensive system of forts, batteries, redoubts, lines and mobilization centres all geared towards repelling an invading army. If the navy could not effectively blockade the enemy, nor intercept and defeat its fleet at sea, then the Martello Towers and other coastal defences would delay and obstruct the landing until greater naval forces arrived to wreck the invasion ships and an army could be mustered to prevent an inland advance.

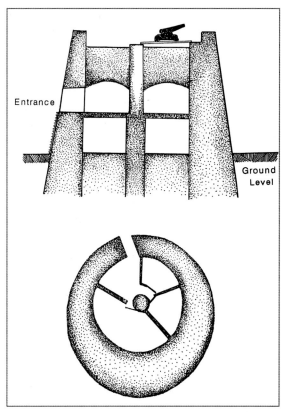

Section through a Martello Tower.

NINETEENTH-CENTURY STRONGHOLDS

For almost three decades after the end of the Napoleonic Wars, Britain's defences languished in a sea of atrophy, if not in outright stagnation. France had been decisively beaten and, with the Industrial Revolution in full swing, Britain's economy fairly stormed forwards at a rate no other country could comprehend, let alone match. State interference and expenditure were cut back on all fronts. If provision for the poorest and least fortunate of the working masses was thoroughly resented by the new capitalists, money for unnecessary defensive fripperies was positively reviled. Until, that is, the French cockerel began to strut once again, with the potential to disrupt the very markets on which Britain's economic growth was dependent.

There was no major review of national defences by the middle of the century, but the limited potential of the fortifications round Milford Haven had become quite apparent. Two gun-towers were built at Pembroke Dock, as the finishing touches to the dockyard wall. These were but part of a major overhaul of the area's defences over the next decade, which included fortified barracks, forts and batteries all along the shores of the estuary and also on two islands. Later, booms and floating batteries were added to make this south Pembrokeshire anchorage the most heavily defended outside the main three naval bases.

Seaford Martello Tower.

There was no let-up in foreign defensive innovations either, and fully casemated, bastioned forts were losing ground to polygonal forts with open casemates. Shornemead (Kent) was the first such fort to be built in Britain (1850–3), and featured three sides mounting heavy guns, with barracks along the two sides at the rear. Shornemead was fully enclosed by a ditch, the front being protected by flanking fire from caponiers, and the rear covered by the barracks. It was the start of a dramatic new trend.

Soon after, Forts Gomer and Elson marked the beginning of a new line of outer detached defensive positions round Gosport. The finest of these strongholds is Fort Brockhurst, begun in 1858. This was twice the size of Shornemead and had six sides with open and vaulted casemates, for thirty-five pieces of artillery. Its close defences were equally comprehensive. A deep moat surrounded the fort, with a large central caponier and a redan to cover the front, and two caponiers to cover the flanks. Surrounded by its own moat, a circular keep with small-arms caponiers guarded the entrance and, if under attack, there was accommodation for the garrison in casemates beneath the ramparts.

Fort Albert, on the Isle of Wight, juts out into the Solent. The Second World War battery can just be seen on the hills above.

Portsmouth was regarded as a likely point of attack, with a combined land and sea assault, so all its approaches were fortified. A rather extravagant stronghold was Fort Albert on the Isle of Wight. Jutting out into the Solent opposite Hurst Castle, three tiers of casemates rise grandly above the magazine; this is the most visible of contemporary defensive works. It was completed in 1856, yet was regarded as being hopelessly out of date – and even as a juicy inviting target – by the end of the decade. A little further east, Fort Victoria was a triangular fort, with two sides of casemates facing the Solent. This also lacked cover from both land and sea approaches, though it was not such an obvious target as its neighbour.

Finally, a bastioned casemated earthwork was built across the neck of Portsea island. The last of a dying breed, the Hilsea Lines, along with other defences that were soon to appear, were part of an increasingly powerful and complex system that surrounded the nation's main naval base. (One can still hire The Casemates musical practice rooms with no fear of being asked to turn down the volume!)

The Hilsea Lines, showing the Casemates studio.

ROYAL COMMISSION INTO THE DEFENCES OF THE UNITED KINGDOM FORTIFICATIONS (1859)

If the findings of the Commission did not make for comforting reading, at least it shook up almost every

FORT BROCKHURST

Hampshire O/S map 196 ref. 596020

Directions: Leave the M27 at Junction 11. Follow the A32 towards Gosport. The fort is on the left after about 3 miles, in Gunner's Way, Elson.

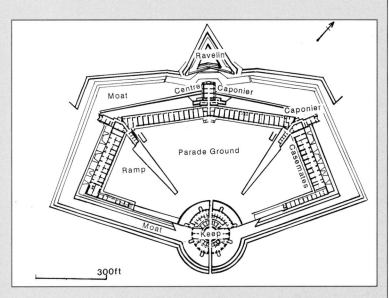

Fort Brockhurst is the finest nineteenth-century land stronghold that can be regularly visited. Traffic may roar along outside, while houses and industrial buildings jostle to hide its whereabouts, but the fort is well preserved, from its restored casemates to the cleared redan and the recreated barracks.

Built as one of the five forts of the Gosport Advanced Line between 1858 and 1862, the six-sided Fort Brockhurst was of revolutionary design; possibly, if briefly, it was the finest stronghold of its kind in the world. Effectively little more than a permanent gun platform, it was a curious mix of the contemporary and the ancient. The four outward-facing sides comprised casemates for guns or barracks when under siege, with further gun placements and open-backed casemates on the rampart above. This had an earthen parapet, and long gun-ramps leading to it – all very modern.

The circular keep was a seeming throw-back to the castles of Henry VIII, even to the enclosed shell-keeps of the Norman period, such as Tamworth Castle's; it also had its own moat. While such ancient strongholds were unlikely to have influenced the design, its mixture of gun-embrasures, loop-holes and small caponiers can be found on Tudor coastal forts. The keep housed some three hundred men plus eleven officers, with stores and buildings along the adjoining flanks catering for other essentials of military life.

Fort Brockhurst's outer defences include a fine north-west-facing redan and an all-enclosing moat, this being defended by a double-facing caponier behind the redan, and a single caponier at each adjacent angle. There is a covered-way on the outer bank. Like most of Portsmouth's outer defences, Fort Brockhurst was never effectively armed, but collectively they served as an effective deterrent – only the guns were lacking.

Pillbox and caponier, Fort Brockhurst.

The moat and central caponier, Fort Brockhurst.

PORTSMOUTH (Round Tower)
Hampshire O/S map 196 ref. 629993
Directions: At the entrance to Portsmouth Harbour, at the south end of the High Street.

Portsmouth's natural harbour has seen considerable use since at the very least Roman times. Portchester Castle served as a stronghold for nearly a thousand years, but the onset of the Hundred Years War saw the introduction of a long train of defensive improvements.

The undefended harbour and town were attacked by the French in the fourteenth century. So, with its increasing use as a port, a pair of two-storey round towers was built at either side of the harbour entrance to guard a chain boom in about 1420. Gosport's is no more, though the casemates of de Gomme's Fort Blockhouse remain, but Portsmouth's Round Tower still stands proudly sentinel today. Almost a bit too proud, for it was refaced and had a further storey added in the nineteenth century. By the sixteenth century the Round Tower had gained three ground-floor gun-loops with a gun-platform above.

Adjoining this are the eighteen casemates of de Gomme's Point Battery, built in about 1670. A flanking angle mounted four 32-pounder guns to protect the battery's outer face. The whole complex was rebuilt in the mid-nineteenth century, with the casemates deepened to take 68-pounder guns.

Next to these is the Square Tower of 1494, originally a gun-tower and the gunners' residence. By the seventeenth century it had become a magazine and, still later, a victualling store. In the mid-nineteenth century its roof was strengthened to mount heavy guns.

Further east are the late fifteenth-century Ten Gun Battery and Saluting Platform that were incorporated into the town's defences. The only surviving lengths of this, the King's Bastion and Long Curtain, are nearby. These defences were begun in the early sixteenth century, but are now as rebuilt by de Gomme. All these defensive works are close together and have several useful information boards.

aspect of coastal defence. The age of rifled, breech-loading artillery had dawned. The range of such guns was measured in miles, not yards, and it was quite apparent that current defences were too close to naval ports to keep an enemy at bay. Within a decade, seventy-six forts and batteries were either under construction or had been newly completed. Of these, only nineteen were land forts; the others were sea forts, floating or shore batteries, and gun-towers. In addition, full use was made of booms and mines in the narrow sea passages.

There has never been such a condensed orgy of stronghold building in Britain. Whether Palmerston's Follies were ever a real deterrent, we shall never know. What is certain is that, until that time, Britain had always drawn on European influence when it came to stronghold building. Not any more, though: for the first time, Britain was leading the way.

Though these batteries and forts were built at locations all round Britain, it was, as usual, the three main naval bases at Plymouth, Portsmouth and Chatham, plus Portland, that were the main beneficiaries. In particular, the whole of Portsdown Hill to the north of Portsmouth was to be defended from land attack by four main and three lesser forts or redoubts. Fort Nelson is one variant of the Gosport advanced polygonal forts, with a ditch replacing the moat. If the Portsdown forts had a weakness, it was that they could only fire their heavy artillery over land; once enemy ships got into the Solent or off Spithead, their garrisons could only watch the ensuing events.

A similar line of eleven detached forts or batteries was built to command the hills about 5 miles to the north of Plymouth's naval yards. Crownhill Fort was the keystone to this system. Other forts and batteries were built to defend

Plymouth Sound, to command the various hills and to prevent a landing on the Cornish beaches. These comprised earthworks, casemated batteries and barracks in the then advanced fashion.

While the Medway was on the whole considered to be secure, Sheerness received still further multi-casemated defences; a fort and associated shore battery also accompanied the gun-tower at Grain on the opposite bank. It was, though, the Thames itself that gained substantial new coastal defences. With the Royal Arsenal at Woolwich, all sorts of munitions and victualling stores at Deptford and, of course, the seat of power at London itself, any hostile forces had to be kept well away.

Up river from where the Thames begins to narrow, between Canvey Island and the Isle of Grain, several forts and batteries rapidly sprang up along both banks. These, with Coalhouse Fort, Cliffe Fort (Kent) and the refurbished Tilbury Fort would ensure a pretty hot reception for any foreign naval force that tried to run the gauntlet. Low, earthwork-covered casemates were not easy targets, unlike Fort Albert, while the tight weaving passage of the Thames gave little room for manoeuvre, and would make slow-moving enemy ships inviting targets. Perhaps most interesting and most innovative were the two Brennan torpedo stations at Cliffe and Garrison Point, Sheerness, both operational by 1890. The torpedoes were launched down a ramp and would be guided by wire on to hostile ships making for London.

As a result of the Royal Commission's report and at great, almost prohibitive, expense, Britain's main naval bases received the essential protection required in a rapidly changing world of mass-produced industrial armaments. Some very old dogs learnt exciting new tricks as well. For example, while Fort Albert would have been little more than a large coffin for its garrison had it been engaged, Hurst Castle on the opposite shore was fully updated. Its additional earthwork batteries were replaced in 1870 by a sweeping masonry wing on either side of the Henrician castle, comprising sixty-one casemates. Later, the gun embrasures received iron shields for further protection. Palmerston's Follies or not, as a result of the 1859 Royal Commission, the defence of naval ports was to begin not yards, nor even miles, but tens of miles away. Britons could, for a while at least, sleep safely in their beds at night.

Sea Forts

If there was one type of stronghold that ultimately deserved to be described as a folly, it was probably the six circular sea forts, four off Portsmouth, and one each at Portland and Plymouth. For a start, the ongoing on-off saga of their construction became something of a butt for nationwide witticism, while their costs rocketed well beyond even the highest estimates. (Little changes!) On the other hand, for all the misgivings of their ultimate worth, and especially the wild optimism as to how they might fare against the guns of the heaviest battleships, one can but admire the tenacity and spirit with which they were built.

No two sea forts were exactly alike, despite outward appearances. A start was made at those off Spithead and Plymouth in 1861, and they were quite an

Gun-embrasures in the
barracks wall at Coalhouse
Fort.

Spitbank Fort outside
Portsmouth harbour.

engineering and building feat. Foundations of Portland stone, granite or clay
were laid into a coffer dam, a piling enclosure dug into the sea-bed with the
water pumped out; caissons, cylinders of high pressure air, were used at
St Helen's Fort. The stone fort was built on top. Walls were about 15 feet thick,
and armoured with three iron plates, about 6 inches thick, separated by layers of
teak or a concrete and iron mixture acting as the filling in an energy-absorbing
sandwich. These were bolted on to the fort walls through a further energy-
absorbing layer of wood and concrete.

During one of the many delays, special casemates were tested at Shoeburyness and
just about survived a very heavy barrage; the days of a single lucky shot rendering a
fort defenceless were, it was hoped, long gone. That concern satisfied, building
restarted. Plymouth's fort was completed by 1870, the four Portsmouth forts at about
the same time and Portland's a little later. Inside, the two levels were divided into
casemates, while guns were mounted on the
bombproof roofs. Spitbank and St Helen's Forts were
not armoured all the way round.

Some indication of the varying size of the forts
can be gauged from the size of their garrisons.
Horse Sand and No-Man's-Land Forts (where one
can now get married!) each had a garrison of about
a hundred men, while Spitbank's complement was
about thirty. Though extremely expensive to build
and armour, the six sea forts were remarkable
engineering achievements, and their existence
doubtless contributed greatly to the cumulative
deterrent effect of the other defences at the three
naval bases.

Spitbank and No Man's Land forts guard the eastern approaches to Portsmouth.

North-east gun tower, Pembroke Dock.

ONWARDS TO THE TWENTIETH CENTURY

If the era of continuous defensive lines had about run its course by 1870 so, within a decade or two, had that of the large fort combining artillery and quarters for the troops. With France being comprehensively beaten by Prussia in 1870–71, the dark eagle of the newly unified Germany was circling ominously overhead. The German army was, unquestionably, the mightiest in Europe; should she ever have a fleet to match, Britain could be in serious trouble.

From the 1870s detached forts and batteries were built not only at the main naval ports, but also at estuaries up and down the length of Britain in an effort to protect the vital merchant marine. These often combined earth and masonry defences and presaged a nationwide move to conceal defences. Mobility was deemed to be the key and there was no longer a need for the undoubtedly expensive permanent, all-encompassing strongholds.

At Chatham, though, a ring of detached forts was built high on the ridge of surrounding hills to guard the south and east landward approaches. This crescent of forts was superficially related to those on Portsdown Hill, or around Plymouth; they still retained casemates and accommodation for the garrison, but

The enemy's view of Fort Nelson on Portsdown Hill, north of Portsmouth.

The barracks at the rear of Fort Widley, another of the Portsdown Hill forts. These face south, to Portsmouth.

they were earth-covered, making them less easy to see and, therefore, harder to destroy. Fort Horsted is the biggest, with a long dividing tunnel; it and is now an industrial estate; Fort Luton is open to visitors. These Chatham forts now appear as low grass mounds until one is almost on top of them, and they are hardly dramatic strongholds.

Almost unbelievably, London remained largely undefended against land attack until the last decade of the century, even though the capital city would be the obvious prized target of any invader. Indeed, several semi-fictitious books had appeared in the 1880s on this theme, many of them written by ex-servicemen. It became an increasingly popular subject, even being taken up by the daily press. So, from 1889 the London Defence Positions were created: a string of low profile strongholds built along the North Downs from Guildford to Dartford, then north of the Thames to the North Weald. Over thirty combined Mobilization Centres and stores were planned for a large volunteer force; the centres doubled as redoubts when necessary, and still retained casemates. Only thirteen were actually built; the biggest, Fort Halstead (Kent) was the only one retained after 1907.

CONCLUSION

In a sense strongholds had come full circle. From the earth and timber hillforts of prehistory, to the ever grander constructions of the Norman and medieval eras, there was a move back towards less visually imposing strongholds until by the 1880s new coastal and inland batteries featured a glacis rampart and ditch. True, their heavy breech-loading gun emplacements were concrete, but there

---

FORT NELSON
Hants. O/S map 196 ref. 607072
Directions: A minor road west from the B2177 Havant–Wickham road passes the Portsdown Hill forts. Fort Nelson is next to Nelson's Monument.

The western-most survivor of Palmerston's Follies on Portsdown Hill, Fort Nelson has been restored and now displays pieces from the Royal Armouries collection. A selection of guns is regularly fired at weekends.

Which is more than happened when this, or the other Portsdown forts, were in service. Fort Nelson was built from 1861–70 as a six-sided fort surrounded by a brick-faced ditch. A large caponier in the north, and two smaller ones at the adjacent angles, would cover any naughty business if an enemy reached the ditch, much the same as at Fort Brockhurst. The large rampart was to have mounted the thirty heavy guns and nine mortars to command the ground to the north, and to provide enfilading fire with the neighbouring Forts Wallington and Southwick. Except that the guns never arrived. Fort Southwick was the only Portsdown fort to be fully armed.

Brick barracks faced the south, with a redan providing flanking fire along the ditch. Perhaps most surprising, none of the Portsdown forts, whether armed or not, could fire its heavy guns at a hostile naval force trying to attack the dockyard. All the forts were prepared for defence in the First World War, but were transferred to the Royal Navy in the 1920s. During the last conflict Fort Nelson housed servicemen and was defended from air attack.

It is worth viewing Fort Nelson from the road running north beside the monument. From there, its low aspect can be appreciated. Though never used in anger, Fort Nelson could have been a vital part of Portsmouth's land defences had the need arisen. Fortunately, despite contemporary fears to the contrary, an invasion never occurred, and we shall never really know just how effective a deterrent were the Palmerston Follies in such a national calamity.

Hurst Castle, east wing casemates (left) and west wing casemates with Second World War look-outs.

were no casemates. In any case, acutely angled earth ramparts would deflect enemy shells up and over the battery, and these less-than-permanent strongholds fitted in very well with the new emphasis on mobility. Move up, hit the enemy hard, and move on before they could get you in their sights. Indeed, if such batteries were destroyed, the loss was much less drastic. By 1890 a fort cost about £45,000 to build, a redoubt only £6,000; while the latter could, at a pinch, be built within a month, forts often took years to complete.

Within two hundred years Britain had become the most powerful combined economic and military country in the world. No longer was there a general need for major strongholds to withstand and subdue internal troubles. However, despite the constant and fairly consistent rise of the Royal Navy, the fear of invasion or, perish the thought, the possible disruption of overseas trade heightened with each passing generation. Yet, as ordnance improved beyond the wildest dreams of the early gunners, so the cost of resisting the new explosive weapons proved prohibitive, especially round Britain's long coastline. Temporary batteries came to be seen as the most economic and strategically effective answer. Well-profiled ramparts and ditches more than sufficed; perhaps slings and stones would eventually replace the devastating fusillades of metal!

The era of the truly great, visually imposing stronghold was thus over. What was the point of a grandiose edifice that could simply be bombarded into submission by unseen gunners guided by maps? Of all the many strongholds built to defend Britain's main naval ports in the late nineteenth century, by no means all were armed; few, if any, ever received their full intended complement of guns and men. There was a return to basic strongholds in the technological age that, ironically, might have been regarded with disdain some two thousand years before. Yet there was to be no hiatus in development. New materials, new weapons, new technologies and new tactics ensured that strongholds had to keep running, even sprinting, just to keep on the pace. Industrialization had emphatically changed the rules. If a country wanted to compete, the stakes were only going to increase, of that there was absolutely no doubt. Stronghold Britain had every reason, and intention, to lead the way.

CHAPTER 8
STRONGHOLD BRITAIN

(1901–PRESENT)

The death of Queen Victoria at the dawn of the new century was most symbolic. The old, staid queen, Empress of India no less, had come to the throne as a teenager in 1837. Britain was then engrossed in the turmoil of the Industrial Revolution and engulfed by a rapidly growing population. It was a time of optimism and expansion for some, desolation and hardship for most. By the end of the century Britain had the largest empire in the history of the world, was second only to the USA in sheer industrial production, created vast wealth, mainly through trade with the empire – and yet restraint and sobriety in all things were the accepted norm.

In Victoria's place came a king who was all but sixty years old, yet had an altogether more extravagant and ostentatious nature. 'I've got it, so I'm going to flaunt it' might well have been the personal adage of King Edward VII. Well, Britain certainly had 'it' in abundance, in the form of wealth, and before long the few who enjoyed the lion's share cast aside the shackles of the previous dowdy decades and eagerly embraced the new age of profligacy.

Aficionados of railways, cricket and even hats regard the Edwardian era as a mythical Golden Age. For those who owned Britain's vast wealth, the Edwardian era was simply the Golden Age. The shroud of Victorian Britain had been lifted, rolled into a ball and summarily thrown away. Life was there to be enjoyed in the most outlandish way possible. Only two clouds appeared on the distant horizon: the most disagreeable notion that those who actually worked to create the wealth wanted to share in it; and an upstart nation that persisted in building battleships and was all too keen to throw its increasing weight about.

It was clear by the reign of King George V that neither threat could be ignored for much longer. As is the case today, politicians and wealthy businessmen tut-tutted at the workers' demands for a share in this vast wealth. For example, a railway fireman earned about 25 shillings for a six-day week, and the old age pension was just 5 shillings a week. In contrast, one Establishment leading-light earned just under £16,000 per year, yet still enjoyed over £15,000 after tax! Generally speaking, £1 a week was a fairly decent wage for most people. Meanwhile, a 3rd Class London–Newcastle return railway fare cost £2 5s 3d.

No wonder many of those who did the work flocked to join the new, unskilled unions; thus organized and coordinated, they were unlikely to respect and adhere to the pleas of the management, and strikes were mounted in earnest. Demands, however modest they might appear today, had to be met and government spending had to rise.

As for the German upstart, increased social expenditure by the government meant either less money for arms or the taxation of those vast salaries. Still more money was needed to maintain Britannia's rule of the waves. The alternative was unthinkable. There was never any chance of Britain being remotely interested in matching the might of the German army, but the navy was another matter entirely. It was the key to the British Empire and, more importantly, security at home. If the Royal Navy commanded the oceans, especially the home waters, Britons could expect to sleep safe at night. If not . . .

Given the social problems and unrest, successive governments were less than pleased by the provocative expansion of the German navy. After all, Britain had a vast empire to police, so it needed a vast navy; German overseas possessions were modest in the extreme. The Kaiser desperately wanted an empire – a place in the sun, as it was said – and saw Britain as thwarting him at every turn. If it was not Britain, it was France or some other old has-been nation. In any case, the autocratic German government considered overseas glories an appropriate means of distracting its population from disturbing domestic matters, such as the rising influence of socialism. The speed with which the British government went to war in 1914 likewise suggests the opinion that a short conflict – as it was expected to be – would be useful to distract the workers from their militancy which threatened the Establishment and the capitalist classes. Such a possibility, though occasionally put forward for Germany and Austro-Hungary, has never been adequately researched with regards to Britain. Perhaps the notion is too close to the truth?

Britain had other problems, too. In a world of secret alliances, ententes and other clandestine agreements, Britain's relatively open government and free press rather precluded her participation in this web of international intrigue. Then there was the matter of exactly who was the enemy. Sixty years before the First World War, Britain had been at war with Russia. Even in the 1870s France was considered the natural enemy, and that view had hardly changed. In contrast, Britain had never waged war on the unified Germany, although economic, political and naval rivalries had embittered relations. Britain seemed unsure of her allies, which might have been a decisive factor in the remorseless drift to continental war. At the crucial time Britain was sending out all the wrong signals.

Despite the deteriorating relationships between European states over the previous months, it was not until 24 July 1914 that the Cabinet formally discussed the Balkan Crisis. It was far from united on the issue and five days later the Government refused to make pledges to either France or Germany. On 1 August Prime Minister Asquith declined to commit active British support to France – yet within three days we had declared war on Germany! The political rush to human conflagration was only equalled by the popular clamour, witnessed all over Europe; if only they had known what the next four years would bring.

THE FIRST WORLD WAR

Somewhat surprisingly, Britain's home defences were in good order as Europe descended into all-out war; the only problem was that most of them faced our new-found ally, France. Modern defences were no longer the massive forts of the nineteenth century; temporary, even earthwork, batteries became the norm. The quality was certainly there; only the quantity was lacking. But in the most important respect of all, Britain's defensive strategy had not changed one iota: it still depended on the Royal Navy's command of the seas. Though the Grand Fleet spent most of its time cooped-up in Scapa Flow, and made an indifferent showing in its one major encounter with the German High Seas Fleet, it maintained an ever-tightening blockade of Germany. This guaranteed not only our ability to last the distance, but effectively precluded any real chance of an invasion. Of course, there were scares and skirmishes, but while the Royal Navy held home waters, Britain was safe. But, did it?

The first naval dust-up came in August 1914. In the Battle of Heligoland Bight three German cruisers were sunk for no British losses. A month later three Royal Navy cruisers were torpedoed without riposte. Public confidence in the navy was further shaken in November. First of all, von Spee's squadron defeated an undergunned force at Coronel, off the Chilean coast. Two days later another German squadron shelled Great Yarmouth. Where was the navy when they were most wanted?

December saw an improvement in British fortunes, as von Spee was defeated at the Battle of the Falklands; even so, by the time his ships had been rounded

---

LANDGUARD FORT
Suffolk O/S map 169 ref. 284318
Directions: From the A45 Ipswich–Felixstowe road, follow the signs to the ferry terminal. Continue along Langer Road to Landguard Point. The fort is signposted.

The important Orwell/Stour estuary has been defended in the vicinity of Landguard Fort since the mid-sixteenth century. This was initially a temporary arrangement, but a permanent fort existed by 1628. The Dutch attacked in 1667 by land and sea, and up to three thousand troops were repulsed; after the earlier débâcle at Chatham, this was welcome news in London. Even so, that fort did not inspire the confidence of the inspecting officials during the review of Britain's military sites in 1715.

The present pentagonal bastioned fort was built between 1717 and 1720, and it was the first large stronghold to be completed as a result of the review. Initially, Landguard Fort boasted twenty large guns to cover the estuary; a sea battery was added by mid-century, considerably enhancing the fire-power. Still there was more for in about 1780 extensive outer defences and a land-facing battery enabled the whole complex to house up to two thousand troops, and to mount some 115 guns.

The advent of the Napoleonic Wars saw the external batteries removed, to be replaced by a battery of 42-pounders at the south rampart. Then, in the 1870s, the prominent granite-faced casemates and caponiers were built, with further batteries added in the 1890s. The fort was rearmed early this century, housing a marine mining establishment, and was manned throughout the First World War. Further look-out towers, anti-tank blocks and the adjacent Darrell's Battery – mounting twin 6-pounders – were built in the Second World War, when the Home Guard manned the fort.

Landguard Fort's location is, shall we say, less than endearing, but there are many neglected twentieth-century defences nearby. A front-line stronghold for some 250 years, the fort amply demonstrates the changes in military engineering over that time.

up, they had sunk seventy merchantmen. Then, in mid-month, Whitby, Scarborough and Hartlepool were all victims of hit-and-run raids. The Royal Navy missed out again, which did not augur well, although the Hartlepool coastal batteries – comprising just three guns – put up a fiery show, hitting the German battleship *Blucher* several times. Even so, it appeared that the Germans could raid the east coast with impunity. A month later, a further attempted raid was intercepted at Dogger Bank; *Blucher* was sent to the bottom and that was the end of that embarrassing nuisance.

The decisive naval action of the war came in mid-1916. The German High Seas Fleet left harbour with the intention of drawing the Royal Navy into action and luring them on to the minefields off Jutland. Heavy weather and thick mist ensured that neither fleet really knew what they or each other were doing, the flashes of exploding ships often being the only sign of the enemy's presence. Had Germany won a decisive victory, Britain's home defences would have been more than sorely tested. As it is, the details of this encounter read like the endless statistics of a televised football match. Team A had more possession, corner kicks, shots on goal and territorial advantage, but still lost 3–2. So it was at the Battle of Jutland. The Royal Navy lost fourteen ships, the Germans twelve. Less crucial, at least strategically, 6,097 British sailors died, but only 2,551 Germans. On paper then, a slender German victory?

Yet the Germans scurried back to port and Britain claimed the battle honours. Were we so desperate for some good news? The High Seas Fleet emerged on only three other occasions, and hastily retreated each time rather than risk another battle. That was the crux of Jutland. In its immediate aftermath, the Royal Navy still had twenty-four undamaged Dreadnoughts, the largest and most powerful ships afloat, while Germany had just ten. The Royal Navy, Britain's first line of defence, did not exactly emerge from the war with flying colours but, by remaining the dominant force at sea, it ensured that invasion was never a serious proposition.

Tommy Atkins' Lament

When I was young, I went to fight
For country and for king.
We fought the Hun on Flanders' fields,
To halt the Kaiser's men.
I went over-the-top in a bayonet charge
And died in a sea of mud.
The Army sent my uniform home
In tatters, all covered in blood.

Not every Tommy Atkins was a lion, and not all the officers were donkeys – least of all the junior officers who died in their tens of thousands. There was, though, something a little odd about green-behind-the-ears, fresh-from-public-school subalterns leading battle-hardened Old Contemptibles to slaughter after slaughter. War is seldom heroic, rarely glorious. Yet each and every combatant deserved every medal and citation bestowed in the so-called War to end all Wars.

The real donkeys were the staff officers encamped miles behind the front lines, hatching ill-planned and senseless schemes that would at best gain little and usually ended up with hundreds more casualties. Such men were instantly recognized by their vainglorious medal ribbons, and nearly all returned home unharmed, unlike most combatants.

For over three years the Germans sat back and defended their spoils. Fighting a war on two fronts limited their offensive options. Ypres, Passchendaele, the Somme, Verdun – at all these battles, and more, Allied troops were senselessly slaughtered; it was they who were weakened from battering against the Hun's iron wall. Well, not quite iron, for the Germans quickly learned that extensive and comprehensive fieldwork defences were far more suited to modern war than the permanent, all-encompassing strongholds of yore.

The late nineteenth century had seemingly seen the demise of the grand stronghold. Mobility and heavy interlinking fire were the yardsticks of the modern age. Yet the Belgians built underground forts at Liege, Namur, Maubeuge and Antwerp, fully expecting them to resist any attack. Once the Germans turned their massive howitzers, firing armour-piercing, delayed-action shells, on the forts, they were simply devastated. To the tune of the Schlieffen Plan, the German army remorselessly swept forwards, to be halted only by fieldwork defences consisting of trenches, dugouts, barbed wire, mobile batteries and much heroism. Several lessons should have been learned: each attack must have a single clear objective, and thorough preparation and adequate resources and men were essential. If only . . . The donkeys tried one grandiose, ill-conceived scheme after another but until March 1918 – when the Germans showed how it should be done – the Western Front remained almost static. The recent trend towards justifying the former official line – that the generals had no option but to conduct the war as they did – is nothing more than a sop peddled by fourth-rate, mealy mouthed apologists. They do nothing but tarnish the efforts of the millions who suffered and died on the Western Front.

One may think that this had little bearing on events in Britain, but if the Allied land campaign reads as an endless catalogue of disasters, there was one important, probably vital, success. Except for Ostend, none of the Channel ports fell into German hands. Britain thus was able to retain control of the English Channel, crucial for the movement of troops to Europe, and absolutely essential to prevent an invasion. Had more ports fallen, with the Royal Navy kept at bay, Britain's coastal defences might have been sorely tested.

Coastal Defences

Once war was declared, it was all-systems-go. The British Expeditionary Force was relatively small – indeed it was positively minute compared with the German army. Experienced men were held back to train the tidal wave of recruits, while the new temporary defences, older forts and other fixed positions all had to be manned. Earthwork and semi-permanent batteries were relatively easy to erect, and guns were readily available. Still, there was no point in manning them with keen novices and so, even though they were desperately needed in Europe, two

How the Germans would have enjoyed destroying the Forth Bridge! Inch Garve island was one of several in the firth that was heavily defended to prevent any sea-borne attempts.

full regular divisions were retained in the first months of the war until the Territorials were ready.

The possibility of invasion was, obviously, treated very seriously, both by the government and in the popular mind; such fears were not exactly assuaged by the German hit-and-run raids. Pretty soon, some 150,000 troops formed a mobile Central Reserve, in addition to the the 300,000 who manned the coastal defences. Oh how the commanders in France would have loved an extra half million expendable trained men.

Conscription was introduced in 1916, yet the slaughter in France continued unabated. At that time, central command believed that Germany could invade Britain and land some 150,000 troops in the twenty-four hours before the Royal Navy arrived to do anything about it. As a result, the Central Reserve was increased to 300,000 troops. Somewhat conveniently, the theoretical German landing force was halved when still more troops were needed overseas in 1917 and another 150,000 went abroad.

Coastal defences had, on the whole, become integrated into a national defensive system; important naval bases had long been secured by extensive outer, inner and land defences in this manner. An invasion force would doubtless prefer a port to a beach, and none was more enticing than the Channel ports. These were protected by the Dover Patrol, which amounted to some 400 assorted ships, along with vast minefields, batteries, projected gun-towers and other similar features, all of which effectively put the attractive south coast out of German reach.

There were, though, other estuaries, in particular the Orwell, Humber, Tyne and Forth, though the further away from London, the less appealing they were to the Germans. The Thames estuary was heavily fortified with numerous temporary batteries along both shores, while older forts, such as those at Tilbury and Coalhouse, were modified and armed with the very latest weapons.

Landguard Fort, at the mouth of the Orwell, was rearmed and supplemented by the nearby Brackenbury Battery. Before long, all ports, estuaries or possible invasion beaches gained earthwork batteries, and at some places further measures were taken. The Humber estuary served three major ports and was an important anchorage; thus, it was an inviting target. Batteries were built along Spurn Head and the river's banks, but it was the construction of two sea forts – Bull Sand off Spurn Point and Haile Sand off Cleethorpes – that were the most remarkable fixed defences of the great conflict.

The shifting sands of the Humber estuary were hardly conducive to such works, but the forts were laid on masonry foundations, stood four storeys high and were covered in 12 inch thick armour plating. Each was armed with four 6 inch guns and played a leading role in a locally comprehensive defensive system. That they were never then put to the ultimate test was, thanks to the naval blockade, a mere fortune of war.

Still further north, the Tyne estuary was defended by the usual combination of temporary batteries and minefields, but there were also plans to build four turrets, each with two 12 inch heavy guns. These Tyne Turrets would have been the crowning glory of the usual defences, but they were barely begun before the end of the war, and were never completed. The important Forth estuary, with the naval anchorage at Rosyth, made good use of the islands in the firth. Batteries and searchlights were mounted on these islands and along both shores to protect the base; this in turn allowed naval ships to further extend their protective range. Such measures were the principal means of deterring a German landing, and

---

TYNEMOUTH CASTLE (Priory and Battery)
Northumberland O/S map 88 ref. 374695
Directions: Near the North Pier.

Standing at the northern extremity of the Tyne estuary, this commanding location initially housed a Saxon monastery. Then, in about 1095, Robert de Mowbray built an earthwork enclosure, bounded by cliffs on three sides. At the same time a Benedictine priory was built and the two maintained close links, financial and reverential, for several centuries. The castle was refortified in the late thirteenth century and the impressive three-storey gatehouse, complete with barbican, was built a century later.

Then, in about 1545, faced with a Franco-Scottish alliance, Henry VIII had the castle ringed with one of Britain's first bastioned earthworks, and built the Spanish Battery lower down the cliffs. At the end of the seventeenth century Sir Martin Beckman built a central redoubt with a rear bastioned rampart: Clifford's Fort. This, though much rebuilt, is all that remains of his various coastal defences.

These works were beefed-up during the Napoleonic Wars and were thoroughly overhauled and brought up-to-date in the late nineteenth century. All of which begs the question, what are Tynemouth Castle and Priory doing in a chapter devoted to the twentieth century? Simple: the enhanced batteries were a vital component of the First World War Tyne defences, while plans were hatched to build four batteries of 12 inch ex-naval guns – the so-called Tyne Turrets. They were hardly begun before the end of the war and the unfinished project was scrapped in the 1920s.

The castle also served in the Second World War: it is one of the few sites to be defended through nearly all the major invasion crises over more than eight hundred years. The seemingly strange mix of religion and military was not thought quite so odd during the Middle Ages, and certainly adds distinction today.

similar schemes could be found in various stages of completion all round the coast of Britain.

This was all well and good, but what about protecting the coastal defences, especially from a landing party? Defence in depth was the key. Magazines were, to no great surprise, usually located underground, while the perimeter of even the most basic temporary battery was secured by trenches, barbed wire and pillboxes. A combination of these had been used to overcome the South African Boers, but it was the use of reinforced concrete that was the essential ingredient in a war of heavy armour.

Not that these early pillboxes were identical to the more familiar Second World War versions. Those built in East Anglia were often round, and many were built of concrete blocks – a method of construction that was unlikely to withstand contemporary shells. Pillboxes in the south were usually hexagonal and, right from the start, most pillboxes formed part of comprehensive defensive systems. Their effectiveness was clearly demonstrated by the Germans in Flanders. So while coastal defences protected the bases of Britain's first line defence, the Royal Navy, these were, in turn, shielded by defensive systems proved on Flanders' fields.

Inland Defences

These defences were not considered to be entirely sufficient, though. Suppose the Germans had managed to land 150,000 troops, and the Royal Navy had been defeated at Jutland: what then? However one looked at it, London had to be the obvious target. York or Manchester are fine cities, but, as Bonnie Prince Charlie found out, what does one do when they have fallen? No, the seat of power surely had to be the objective of any invasion.

The London Defensive Positions had mostly been abandoned early in the twentieth century, and although redoubts and other fixed strongholds were hardly ideal in the current war they were still better than nothing. They were supported by stop-lines, the modern equivalent of permanent, linear defensive fortifications. They were a simplified version of the defences on the Western Front, with systems of trenches, barbed wire, earthwork batteries and the occasional pillbox. There were three lines in East Anglia, from the North Weald outwards, and several in and across Kent.

Mobility in the First World War still, mostly, relied on the horse so, as in Flanders, it was expected that stop-lines would do just that. Effectively, as improvised trench systems, their job was to delay the invading forces until the mobile reserves could be brought into play. It was assumed that, at whatever cost, the Royal Navy would be able to intervene to prevent the Germans landing a constant stream of reinforcements and supplies. Thus, so starved, their invasion force would eventually succumb to the inevitable.

Aerial Defences

In early 1915 Germany launched the first Zeppelin raid on London. Such attacks were never anything like so numerous or effective as the heavy air raids of the

Bull Sand Fort, one of two that guarded the Humber estuary, with Spurn Head behind.

Second World War, but it was not until September 1916 that the first dirigible was brought down. For over two years, Zeppelin raids, sometimes involving a dozen or so airships, were directed against London and other conurbations. Flying at 20,000 feet and often guided by moonlit railway lines, they were generally out of reach of the few aeroplanes held back to counter them. There were hardly any guns and searchlights and, until near the end of the war, no batteries that could upset their secure and stately progress across the sky.

Of course, Zeppelins could carry only a modest bombload, and rarely did they drop more than a few pounds. On the other hand, they caused a degree of consternation and disruption among the defenceless civilians, especially as there appeared to be nothing that could be done about them. One counter-measure was based on the belief that blind people had superior hearing, so some were recruited to listen out for the distant throb of Zeppelin engines. Each was issued with a stethoscope to aid their hearing, and had a pole attached to his or her head to indicate the direction and, would you believe, compass bearing of incoming Zeppelins. Desperate measures, indeed.

In 1917 Zeppelins were superseded by twin-engined Gotha bombers. Hunting in flights of about twenty, these packed a harder, more accurate punch than the Zeppelins had done and, though flying at a height that could be intercepted, Britain's air defences were still inadequate. At first, daylight air raid precautions were almost laughable: a policeman riding along on a bicycle crying out a warning, or a bugler in the back of an open car. Less funny was the lack of effective anti-aircraft artillery and, especially, adequate shelters. Stronghold Britain was wide open to air attack. It was fortunate that Germany's resources and determination to carry out this strategy were strictly limited.

In any case, as Britain did not reply in kind, it retained the moral high ground, invaluable when it came to encouraging the Americans to enter the war. By the end of the conflict, about a thousand civilians had been killed and three thousand injured. That was bad enough, yet it was only one-twentieth of the British casualties on the first day of the Battle of the Somme.

INTER-WAR INERTIA

Few people were really fooled. A war to end all wars was a most unlikely notion. The catastrophic conflict had been debilitating for all the participants and nobody wanted to see its like again, but before long troops from some eighteen countries had invaded Soviet Russia. There was absolutely no chance that war would ever end.

For the first time in Britain's history, the whole country had been mobilized in a concerted effort to defeat Germany: whether on active service, home defence or simply involved in war production. It had been a truly national effort and, bolstered by conscription, included those who were non-too-fussy about getting involved in imperialist conflicts. War and warfare had been through a revolutionary change since the late nineteenth century, yet senior commanders hardly seemed to have noticed. After a brief hiatus while the various combatants recovered, the development of armaments, tactics and, most important, air strategy gathered pace again, at least in some quarters. Britain had much in its favour: a new Royal Air Force, home defences in considerable depth, and unquestionably the mightiest navy in the world. None of these came cheap though; much was scrapped or mothballed, and development of armaments, machines and tactics often stagnated.

The Greatstone-on-Sea sound mirrors, near Lydd. These are the finest examples still existing.

Several airfields that opened in the First World War went on to become the foundations of the junior service. Keen to make a mark and establish itself, the RAF occasionally encouraged or patronized innovative projects, but the 1920s was not a time of plenty and government was always strapped for funds. Even so, aerial bombardment was rightly considered a serious threat to Britain's sovereignty and the means to counter it had to be found. Sound mirrors began to appear along the south and east coasts, such as those at Greatstone-on-Sea. These consisted of concrete bowls or lengths of wall that could locate approaching aircraft at about 15 miles away in ideal conditions. In 1930 that was a reasonable warning, but no more. As aircraft speeds increased, and they did so quite markedly thereafter, such hit-or-miss notice was almost useless; 10 miles could easily be covered in 2 minutes by a fast aircraft. Something else was needed, and fast.

The masts of the Swingate Chain Home radar station, near Dover, are still used today.

Radio Detection and Ranging (radar) stations came into operation from the mid-1930s, as part of the new national plan for air defence. From the Tyne to the Solent twenty Chain Home stations were built to cover this area. The three 250 feet masts at Swingate near Dover can still be seen. These were soon joined by a series of Chain Home Low stations, to detect low flying aeroplanes. Still later, in 1941, Chain Home Extra Low stations came on stream to give full air cover over England, at least.

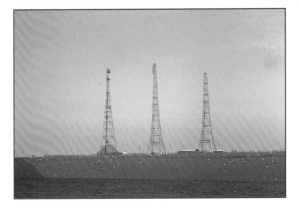

Britain could now detect hostile aircraft, but something still had to be done about them. Anti-aircraft batteries were established although, far more often, basic plans and locations were approved, just in case. But this was little more than a hope-to-hit option; it was far better to get fighter planes in amongst the feared bombers. At a time when appeasement of the growing menace that was National Socialist Germany was an immensely popular government policy, a few far-sighted individuals instigated a number of aeroplane-related projects, including engines, armament and bombers. Most important, though, were two fighter planes: the Hawker Hurricane and the Supermarine Spitfire.

It might seem strange that, in a book on Britain's strongholds, the emphasis has moved from mighty land fortresses to flying machines and radar stations with little or no fire-power or protection. Ever since the time of Henry VIII, the Royal Navy had been Britain's first line of defence; by the Second World War that was no longer the case. Air power and the ability to retain a semblance of control over the country's air-space was suddenly all-important. The naval bases could have all the outer, inner, land and sea defences they liked – but an enemy could simply fly over and blast the lot, defences, ports and ships, to smithereens. Warfare had changed emphatically and, in the coming conflict, dramatically.

THE SECOND WORLD WAR

During this war, far more than ever before, Britain became a genuine, comprehensive island stronghold. Following the actions of the German Condor Legion and its aircraft in the Spanish Civil War, it was very clear that, this time round, the civilian population was not going to get through virtually scot free. Fearful of being bombed in its ports, the Home Fleet once again moved to the inadequately defended Scapa Flow. This made sense in many ways, since nobody was exactly certain how ships would fare against air attack; moreover, unlike in the earlier conflict, Germany's surface fleet was now modest, mainly comprising a handful of pocket-battleships.

It did not take long for all the impetus and urgency of September 1939 to dissipate; the feared German bombing, horrifically directed against Poland, never came and there was an inactive stalemate in France. The Phoney War was at once a blessing in disguise and a time when it was felt that Britain had rather jumped the gun. Unable, or even unwilling, to do much in France, the Allies were totally powerless when it came to helping Poland, the invasion of which had caused Britain to declare war. This brief calm before the terrifying storm was put to good use by building a more complete system of coastal, inland and air defences than ever before, including mining the beaches, while the production of fighter planes and other armaments steadily got underway.

The first clear sign that Stronghold Britain's defences needed shoring up came with the sinking of HMS *Royal Oak* in the assumed safe anchorage of Scapa Flow. After this débâcle, the Flow's eastern approaches were to be permanently closed by barriers and not just blockships. This was a lesson put to good use at

SCAPA FLOW (Naval Anchorage)
Orkney Islands O/S map 7

No sooner had the natural anchorage of Scapa Flow been chosen as the base for the Grand Fleet in the First World War than a false sighting of a U-boat sent the ships scuttling away for the winter. By the time they returned, a few batteries had sprouted up, booms, torpedoes and mines defended the main passages, and blockships closed the remaining gaps between the islands. With the onset of the Second World War, the building, rebuilding and re-equipping of Scapa's defences began again, but at less than the rapid pace that was necessary. Then, in October 1939, Lieutenant Prien expertly took U-47 through Kirk Sound, between Lamb Holm and Mainland, and sank HMS *Royal Oak*. Again the Home Fleet dispersed as the passages were blocked with booms, anti-submarine nets and yet more blockships, while heavy guns and anti-aircraft batteries ringed the Flow. In addition, two Fleet Air Arm squadrons were based on Mainland while the fleet was in harbour, with RAF fighters at Wick. Scapa, at last, became a secure naval stronghold.

Almost none of these defences remain today, except the rusting hulks of the blockships but, with the horse well and truly bolted, it was decided to firmly slam the stable door. The Churchill Barriers linked the islands of Mainland–Lamb Holm–Glims Holm–Burray–South Ronaldsay: in total, about 1.5 miles. A quarter of a million tons of rubble formed the base, the water being up to 60 ft deep, and some 66,000 concrete blocks, of 5 to 10 tons, completed the job. The tiny island of Lamb Holm was heavily quarried.

Quite appropriately, Italian prisoners-of-war undertook most of the work, and the chapel they built stands as a grand memorial to those not-so-grand times, on Lamb Holm. After the war these barriers formed causeways for a road between the islands. They remain as a remarkable memorial to the men who built them, the men who died in the *Royal Oak* and the skill of Lieutenant Prien, enemy or not.

other naval ports, for if an undetected U-boat could pierce seemingly impregnable defences once, they might do so again and again. In April 1940 a joint Anglo-French expedition to invade Norway ended in catastrophe, although the Royal Navy performed quite well, but the balloon would now, suddenly and violently, go up in France.

The Battle of France

Almost out of the blue, the Nazi Germans launched Operation Sickle Cut in May 1940. Within days, it was apparent just how and why the Poles had been so comprehensively swept aside the previous September. Despite the painful and succinct lesson dished out to the Belgian forts in 1914, the French preferred to hark back to the eventual but costly success of the Verdun forts. A fixed line of defence, of a scale and depth unknown in history, was thus built during the inter-war period.

The Maginot Line had everything. It was a system of deep and strongly protected forts, with only the gun cupolas visible, and had far-reaching advanced defences and observation posts, including anti-tank obstacles and machine-gun nests. Moreover, each fort could bring its heavy guns to bear on its neighbour, to bombard an airborne landing, while the fort itself would remain unharmed. What with the Germans' West Wall, it appeared that fixed defences were back in favour. The French claimed that the Maginot Line was inviolable; it could, so it was said, even withstand the devastating Blitzkrieg tactics.

There were, though, a couple of drawbacks. The Maginot Line ended abruptly at the Ardennes Forest: an error of cataclysmic proportions. It was expected that, for the third time in seventy years, the Germans would attack through Belgium. So, as the Blitzkrieg began on 10 May, British troops advanced to the River Dyle. The French, meanwhile, boasted about the impregnability of the Maginot Line; the Germans, it seems, were quite happy to believe them. But then the Germans did exactly what the French had thought impossible; the seven Panzer Divisions of Army Group A drove through the Ardennes Forest, in a militarily daring and tactically brilliant move. Simultaneously, a ferocious attack was unleashed on the Belgians, capturing the assumed impregnable fort of Eben Emael by the simple expedient of landing glider-borne and parachute troops on top, who placed explosives in the exposed gun barrels. The Nazis swept all before them. By 19 May Army Group A had reached the Channel coast, splitting the French forces and surrounding the Anglo-French army to boot. The Belgians surrendered on 27 May, the day after the Dunkirk evacuation had begun. As for the Maginot Line, well, the French were right, it did not fall to a full frontal assault; the Germans simply went round it. By 6 June, it was effectively all over; on the 22nd France signed an Armistice.

Blitzkrieg

The secret of the German success was their combined land/air operations. Prior to an advance, the Luftwaffe would bombard the target, while the troops and tanks went forward under air cover. There was no respite for the embattled Allies. The French air force constantly and consistently came a cropper, rarely able to match the battle-hardened German pilots. The RAF, in contrast, and despite the rather haphazard reputation gained in the Battle of France, gave as good as they got. But it was like throwing sand in the wind. Instead of the coordinated air support enjoyed by the Germans, the Allied troops were all too often left open to air attack. Then, when they counter-attacked, the RAF either missed the target, was nowhere to be seen, arrived after the attack had ground to a halt, or, worst of all, bombarded Allied troops. It seemed to the soldiers on the ground that the Army and RAF commanders could never get their act together, either in concerted attack or defence.

It was not always the fault of the RAF, though. They had some truly awful aeroplanes to put up against the well-proven aircraft of the Luftwaffe. Even the Hawker Hurricane, the very plane that was shortly to prove decisive, was slower than the German fighters. On occasions, pilots returned to their airfields out of ammunition and almost out of fuel, only to find it in German hands. Despite the fiasco that was the Battle of France, an important lesson had been learned: control of the skies was vital. In the next phase of war, it was the simple fact that Britain refused to cede control of the air that ensured her survival. Individual or groups of strongholds were of little or no consequence. In the coming campaign there had to be a total, comprehensive Stronghold Britain on land, sea and in the air. Survival depended on a level of coordination never before utilized in the defence of a country. The harsh lessons learned in northern France and Belgium had to be applied with an immediate, unhesitant effect. There would be no second chance.

Once housing massive 14 and 15 inch guns, St Martin's Battery on Dover's Western Heights is now a silent shell. The guns could attack enemy shipping in the English Channel or bombard the French coastline.

'This was their Finest Hour'

Churchill was quite right. Without question, to survive the gravest of invasion threats in the summer of 1940, all the many components of Stronghold Britain had to pull emphatically together. There had never been, and probably never will be, another occasion quite the same. It really was all or nothing and, however tight the margin, Britain's continued survival was the base on which eventual victory was built.

Until the Second World War, Britain's first line of defence was the Royal Navy. Retain control of home waters and invasion was little more than a distant threat. The Nazi German navy was hardly a match for the Royal Navy, but it had little need to be: the ante had been upped. As the northern French ports fell so, for the first time this century, control of the all-important English Channel was lost. The Home Fleet was based at Scapa Flow, they hoped out of bomber range. This was the crux of the matter: it was control of the skies, not the sea, that would determine whether or not the German plan for the invasion of Britain – Operation Sealion – would go ahead.

The portents were not good; in fact, they were downright dicey. Despite having home advantage and the benefit of radar, whose contribution was immeasurable, the figures still did not add up. At the outset of the Battle of Britain, the RAF had 2,913 aeroplanes, fewer than 800 of which were Spitfires or Hurricanes; the rest ranged from the distinctly mediocre to virtual flying coffins. Some pilots had battle experience, but for most a quick, truncated training course was their lot. This thin light-blue line faced a similar number of aeroplanes, many of which were bombers or dive-bombers, but all were of proven, up-to-the-minute design. To cap it all, most German pilots were battle-hardened and had all the confidence that success brings. In the Battle of France, the ratio of RAF/Luftwaffe kills was fairly equal; if this remained unchanged, numerical supremacy was emphatically in German favour.

That the Battle of Britain was won (or at least not lost) is one of the most significant facts in world history. The story, embellished or otherwise, has been told on countless occasions, but the effects of not conceding air superiority over England in the summer of 1940 were to be felt the world over. We must not doubt for one minute the consequences of failure. The German preparations for invasion were nowhere near as thorough or sophisticated as those of the Allies some four years later; neither, though, were the land defences as well established. Hitler had assembled some 250,000 troops, including airborne divisions, supported by hundreds of tanks, rocket launchers and five hundred guns, for the initial force alone, all to be transported across the Channel in a fleet of barges. Given Britain's hastily contrived defences and woeful lack of equipment, the prospect was more than a little daunting. Everything hinged on the forthcoming struggle for the mastery of the skies.

Fortunately, the Germans, hitherto the most meticulous of planners, had confused objectives. The Battle of Britain erupted in July, with the Germans intermittently raiding shipping and coastal towns. On 31 July Hitler ordered a massed air offensive and, by the end of August, the bombing attacks on airfields were having a seriously debilitating effect. In a single week one-fifth of the RAF's fighters were lost. Britain was fast running out of planes, many of which were destroyed on the ground, and, worse, pilots.

Then, as had happened on numerous occasions before, fate intervened. Previously, the Channel weather had helped out just as foreign forces were preparing to invade. On 24 August a German pilot dropped his bombs on London. Churchill ordered an immediate retaliatory raid on Berlin. A foolhardy thing to do, one might have thought, given the morale-sapping demonstration of

---

WEST BLOCKHOUSE BATTERY
Pembrokeshire O/S map 157 ref. 817037
Directions: From Haverfordwest, take the B4327 to Dale and turn right towards St Ann's Head. About ¼ mile after passing Broomhill Farm, turn left and then right to West Blockhouse Point and the battery.

The government had ambitious plans for the Milford Haven defences in the mid-nineteenth century, probably as a result of the so-called invasion of Pembrokeshire by French vagabonds in the Napoleonic Wars. The comprehensively planned defensive systems were never completed but some interesting structures were built, not least the island forts on Thorn Island and Stack Rock.

West Blockhouse Point overlooks the entrance to the natural anchorage of Milford Haven, and is an ideal spot from which to command the passage. A battery existed there in Henry VIII's reign, but this was long-since overgrown by the time the current L-shaped battery was built in the mid-nineteenth century. A two-storey barrack block housed the garrison and the fort was protected by a ditch. An open battery was built on the cliffs early this century. Initially, the main armament comprised six 68-pounders, these being replaced by 80-pounders in 1881. Twenty years later 6 inch breech-loaders were installed, lasting until the battery was abandoned after the Second World War.

Not the easiest stronghold to visit, West Blockhouse nevertheless has spectacular coastal views and is slowly undergoing restoration.

destruction that the Luftwaffe had already dished out. Hitler was enraged and soon the Luftwaffe changed tack and concentrated on bombing London. The respite for the beleaguered RAF was beyond value. As daylight bombing raids turned into the night-time Blitz, and spread to many other cities in a spasmodic and haphazard fashion, the cost in lives and human suffering grew to obscene levels. But the RAF was able to recover and survive. Had Operation Sealion gone ahead with the RAF effectively destroyed, the cost would have been incalculable.

Coastal Defences

In the summer of 1940 Britain had little option but to pull together to survive. Even so, just as the Germans had been less than single-minded in their aerial campaign, so the politicians and military displayed an uncertain approach as to the best means of resisting an invasion, expected to land somewhere between Brighton and Folkestone. Initially, it was intended to encircle all major and minor south and east coast ports with a comprehensive system of emergency batteries, booms, mines and anti-aircraft guns. Prospective landing beaches were protected with land and sea mines, scaffolding, pillboxes, anti-tank blocks and obstructions and barbed wire; there were even experiments with equipment designed to set the sea on fire. The Royal Navy supplied some five hundred redundant guns from old warships, but the coastal and port batteries were still woefully short of armament, especially the essential anti-tank guns. Later, the twin six-pounder gun became widely used, replacing many of the older weapons.

Coastal batteries had to be rather better defended than the simple open earthworks of the First World War. For a start, enemy aeroplanes were unlikely to ignore them, so cover was essential for both guns and gunners. A typical battery might consist of two ex-naval guns covered by a reinforced concrete casing. There would usually be a concrete watch-tower, searchlights and an underground magazine. The battery would be protected from land assault by a combination of earthworks, barbed wire, tank-traps and pillboxes. Trenches and dugouts might also contribute to a local defensive system, itself part of the national network.

Aside from the emergency batteries, older strongholds were also used to differing degrees. Some forts simply had guns and look-outs placed on top or within them, as at Tilbury or nearby Coalhouse; such adaptation was relatively easy. Others had batteries built adjoining or outside the earlier defences, as at Landguard Fort. On the other hand, the older forts surrounding the naval bases often had little more than a few token anti-aircraft guns, their primary function being forces accommodation.

Some ancient strongholds also found themselves pressed into active service. Dover Castle gained new gun positions, anti-tank obstacles and a pillbox. Most ingeniously, Pevensey Castle had pillboxes built into its Roman and Norman walls. The skill with which these were concealed was in direct contrast to the mutilation and wanton damage done elsewhere in the name of the war effort. The Fal estuary in Cornwall was protected by several new and older batteries, both featuring at St Mawes Castle. A new battery was built below Pendennis Castle

The Half-Moon Battery is just below the Elizabethan ramparts at Pendennis Castle, and its observation post is built into the ramparts. The battery was used throughout the Second World War.

with the look-out post sited within the Elizabethan rampart, itself an addition to the Henrician stronghold. Combined with minefields and booms, the old and the new were adapted to the demands of total war on land, sea and in the air. There were many, many other similar examples at numerous ports and estuaries.

Anti-tank blocks at Taddiford Gap, Hampshire. These were intended to look like innocent beach huts to the enemy.

The two pillboxes beneath the bridge guard the road, railway and River Test, near Southampton.

Just because Operation Sealion was postponed until the summer of 1941 and then, with the German invasion of Russia, cancelled indefinitely, it did not mean that coastal defences were never put to the test. German E-boats, U-boats and, of course, aeroplanes were a constant headache and regularly probed and prodded their capabilities. Although both men and guns were transferred away in 1943, the devastation caused by E-boats at Slapton Sands in Devon in 1944, during the preparations for D-Day, signalled the dangers of letting the guard slip.

Still later, coastal batteries in Kent and Essex were strengthened to combat the V1 flying bomb campaign in 1944. Not only did they act as advance look-outs, but they also marked the outer limits of a whole barrage deployed between the coast and London. They were a mixed blessing, though, for aeroplanes in pursuit of these deadly new weapons were hampered or fired upon by the coastal batteries on more than the odd occasion.

Finally, some of the most fascinating coastal defences were the army and navy anti-aircraft sea forts in the Thames estuary and off the east coast, built from 1942 onwards. The navy forts consisted of two concrete towers, armed with anti-aircraft guns, which were towed out and sunk into the sea-bed. The army forts were more sophisticated, consisting of seven two-

The nineteenth-century casemates at Coalhouse Fort were strengthened to take Second World War guns.

storey steel towers, each carried on legs and connected by girder bridges: science-fiction enters reality. They carried both anti-aircraft and heavy guns to counter ships either raiding or laying mines. On a clear day these structures can still be observed off the north Kent coast.

Make no mistake, the network of coastal defences, ranging from primitive trenches to the latest electronic outpost, played a vital part in resisting the Nazi threat. Whether a genuine deterrent or an active defensive post, or even the morale-boosting exercise of simply doing something, everything, from a roll of barbed wire to the great 14 and 15 inch guns at Dover, had its place in the grand scheme of things. Today, the remains of this system are often in poor condition, and much has been lost forever. Coastal erosion and nature have taken their toll, and much has been salvaged or vandalized. The irony is that while two thousand-year-old defences can still be admired, many of those built barely sixty years ago, and which faced far greater offensive threats, have vanished; their presence often unrecorded owing to the haste of their construction during a national crisis. After the disastrous Battle of France, Britain put the weeks following Dunkirk to very effective use.

Some of the most ingenious – and most sensitively located – pillboxes can be seen at Pevensey Castle. The finest of all is this brilliant adaptation of a Roman bastion.

Inland Defences

Should the Germans have invaded in 1940, the principal inland defence was a hastily created network of stop-lines. These comprised a mixture of natural barriers, particularly rivers, backed by fixed defences consisting of thousands of miles of anti-tank ditches, often supported by pillboxes and other obstacles. It was the greatest system of defensive earthworks ever built in Britain, and was probably the shortest lived. Today, even knowing the route of stop-lines, one would be very lucky to find even an anti-tank ditch, as most were filled in well before the end of the war.

Tests conducted in 1941 had shown that the most effective anti-tank ditch was V-shaped, 18 feet wide, 9 feet deep and with 2 feet high ramparts on either side. Prior to these tests, ditches usually had a vertical face on the defenders' side. Ditches were often dug by contractors with excavating equipment, mostly in a zigzag pattern; one machine could dig about 300 yards per week. Despite the wooden templates used in their construction, most ditches were anything but the correct profile and dimensions. (It is comforting to know that, even in Britain's darkest hour, builders still failed to work to the prescribed standards, within cost constraints and to time, despite supervision by Royal Engineers.)

The most vital stop-line of all was the General Headquarters Line that ran from Bridgwater Bay, across to the south and east of London, then up through Cambridge and York to Edinburgh. This was supported by a web of secondary lines. The premise was that the Germans would be delayed by road-blocks and local volunteers at towns and villages, while mobile reserves moved up to counter the threat. This rather simplistic scenario seems, with hindsight, to be either daringly or mindlessly optimistic, but the Germans would certainly not wait politely until Britain was ready, so such stop-lines and tactics were all that could be done in the time available.

A change of command just as the Battle of Britain got under way saw a change in this strategy. Mobile offensive action became the new tactic, in particular to hit the enemy hard before a firm foothold was established. The stop-lines network was relegated to secondary status and new construction was limited to creating strongpoints at specific strategic locations; armour was transferred to forward, often coastal, positions. Once the Germans had landed, they would target airfields on which they could land reinforcements; however well the Royal Navy managed to blockade the coast, the Luftwaffe could simply fly over the top.

In mid-1941 all work on the stop-lines ceased and pillbox construction was halted soon afterwards, although not before some 18,000 had been built. Many were heavily, some brilliantly, camouflaged and, while they often appear in isolation today, in Britain's darkest hour they were but one component in a fairly comprehensive local defensive system. Concrete dragons' teeth, trenches and other anti-tank obstacles were often combined with pillboxes, barbed wire and road-blocks to halt, or at least delay, the expected marauding motorized advance parties or even paratroops. Though rarely, if ever, tested these defences, usually manned by the Home Guard, had to be prepared for the real thing. It could have happened at any time.

Airfield and Anti-Aircraft Defences

Nobody could be sure, but in 1940 it was thought that just five thousand paratroops would be able to overcome seven important fighter bases and virtually render Britain's air defences useless. Once the airfields were captured, supporting troops and equipment could be flown in. Such a scenario was justified by the events of May 1941 when German paratroops landed on Crete's three airfields. In fact, they only managed to capture one, but that was enough to bring in reinforcements which soon swept the British from the island. So what had seemed to be a quite fantastic military proposition became a reality in the heat of battle. Fortunately, in Britain measures against such a daring plan had been in hand for some time and airfields were provided not only with adequate external defences, similar to those round the coasts, but internal ones.

Trenches, dugouts, Stanton personnel shelters and bunkers were built at and round airfields to provide cover from both air and land raids. Pillboxes, gun-posts and other positions were sited to counter paratroops, both as they descended and once they had landed. Underground battle headquarters were built to be used in the event of an attack. Again, cover and mobility were the main factors, while the operation centres were often widely dispersed, sometimes even outside the base, making them difficult for the enemy to locate. It was intended that, even if the enemy gained control of an airbase, they would not simply be able to begin using it immediately.

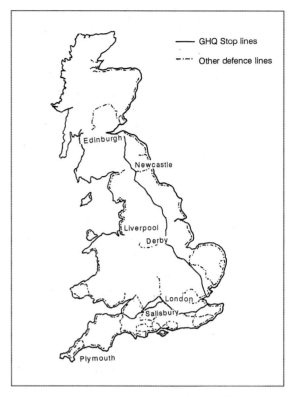

Map showing the location of the main GHQ defence line.

Although the risk of invasion receded dramatically once the Germans invaded Russia, the raiding and bombing of aerodromes was a regular occupational hazard. Anti-aircraft batteries were provided, generally having between four and eight guns, similar to those placed in large numbers all round Britain. Unlike the latter, gun emplacements on air bases did not need separate external defences, merely concrete gun-mountings (and sometimes not even those). Later in the war, mobile gun and rocket batteries were an increasingly frequent feature of defences, particularly to counter the V1 flying bombs.

The value of the anti-aircraft batteries has been questioned on several occasions since the end of the war. While the cost of such operations was of gargantuan proportions when evaluated against the number of planes shot down, the morale value of being seen to be actively engaging the enemy and the effects of a barrage in preventing accurate bombing were priceless. Knowing that the Germans were not quite having everything their own way reinforced the island stronghold mentality. However small, everyone's bit counted in the end.

Other Strategic Locations

Air raids could halt everything, though. Protection for the civilian population was essential and ranged from large public shelters and seventy-nine London tube stations to the almost ubiquitous Anderson Shelter. The latter were earth-covered corrugated iron affairs that were dug into gardens; they were, by far the most

Dragon's teeth, or 'pimples', such as these at Wilton, were intended to hinder Nazi tanks.

Much larger anti-tank cubes, such as these at Chesil Beach, can still be seen all round the British coastline.

popular of all. During the London Blitz less than 5 per cent of people used the tube stations, 10 per cent other public shelters, and nearly 30 per cent used personal shelters. The remainder slept on the floor or in their beds. The Nelsonian spirit was clearly far from dead.

Barrage balloons were a familiar sight all over our island stronghold. Their aim, like the anti-aircraft fire, was to force the bombers to fly higher, thus reducing their bombing accuracy and putting them within the best range of the guns. As with the gun batteries, their impact cannot simply be measured by the number of planes they ensnared.

Another activity that brought ingenuity to the fore was the use of decoy sites. Many fighter bases had a dummy station, and there were even mock army bases, mostly associated with preparations for the invasion of Europe. Often, of course, all was to no avail, but there were some quite remarkable successes, and during the Battle of Britain, some dummy stations were claimed to have been attacked far more often than the active ones. Considering how desperately Fighter Command was struggling by the end of August, these dummy stations might conceivably have even saved us from invasion.

Some of the most inventive decoys were the Starfish sites. There were about sixty close to ports and other strategic locations all round the country. A network of remote-controlled pipes and explosive devices combined to create

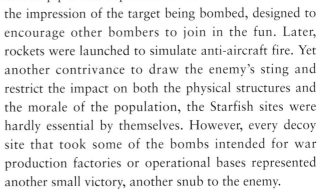

the impression of the target being bombed, designed to encourage other bombers to join in the fun. Later, rockets were launched to simulate anti-aircraft fire. Yet another contrivance to draw the enemy's sting and restrict the impact on both the physical structures and the morale of the population, the Starfish sites were hardly essential by themselves. However, every decoy site that took some of the bombs intended for war production factories or operational bases represented another small victory, another snub to the enemy.

London Underground stations aside, there is often little to be seen of many larger Second World War shelters. However, there are some underground strategic command centres open to the public. The secret wartime tunnels beneath Dover Castle housed Britain's foremost military command centre and initially used casemates built during the Napoleonic Wars. The Dunkirk evacuation was coordinated from these. Given their forward position, more tunnels were dug under the castle from 1941 onwards. The vast complex became the combined headquarters for the absolutely crucial Dover sector of Britain's defences. Still later, these tunnels were used to plan for the invasion of Europe.

Shelters and barracks,
Lympne Airfield.

The civilian equivalent of Dover's tunnels, the appropriately named Cabinet War Rooms in London, are also open. Here can be seen the bombproof rooms where Churchill and his senior staff (and occasionally politicians) worked during raids. Nearby, at Horse Guards Parade, is the underground Admiralty Citadel, still with gun-loops in its exterior walls. There were, of course, other underground complexes, from which a semblance of organized resistance could be maintained if the worst came to the worst.

Pillboxes

The very nature of twentieth-century warfare brought about a swift and often devastating end to the grandiose fortresses of previous centuries. Small defensible locations became the norm, many of which have since been wiped clean off the face of the earth. The most enduring reminder of the all-encompassing nature of Stronghold Britain during the Second World War is the humble pillbox. Although also built in the earlier conflict, often to a circular design of concrete blocks (from which the name was derived), it is those of the 1939–41 period that are by far the most universal. They were built at Dunnet Head, Lowestoft, near Land's End and at the Lizard Point: all the four extremities of Britain. There were over seventeen thousand more in between, with others on the Isles of Scilly, Man, Wight, Sheppey, Anglesey, Orkney and Shetland. A pretty comprehensive cover, then.

Initially, pillboxes were mostly constructed of concrete poured between wooden shuttering; the walls were about 18 inches thick, reinforced with steel bars. Using this method, they could easily resist small-arms fire, or even withstand a direct hit from larger calibre weapons. A pair of pillboxes could be built by a small gang of men in some four to six weeks, but before long this rather leisurely approach was soon turned upside down.

Following the evacuation from Dunkirk, the military undertook the building of pillboxes and other defences. The sheer quantity required led to shortages: of concrete – met by reducing the thickness of pillbox walls or floor; of steel – even bed-springs were used as reinforcement; and of wood. As a result, corrugated iron or bricks were sometimes used as shuttering, occasionally being left in place as camouflage.

Most pillboxes had a gun-loop through each outward facing wall, often with a blast-wall protecting the entrance. The vast majority of pillboxes were intended for infantry rifle use; the bigger the gun-loops, the more vulnerable they were to enemy fire or a well-directed hand-grenade. An important feature of many pillboxes was an internal wall to prevent ricochets or a single grenade knocking the box out of action.

A casual acquaintance with these often decrepit and vandalized artefacts might suggest that most were identical, but there were about ten main types of pillbox, with others of a more specialist nature. The most common of all was the hexagonal Type 22, found all over Britain. The Type 26 was either square or rectangular, the Type 24 was an irregular hexagon, often with walls 3 feet thick, while the Type 25 was circular. Those were the most widely used pillboxes. The Type 23 was rectangular, but half open to house an anti-aircraft gun, the Type 28 was about 20 feet square, with 3 feet thick walls, and was also used for an anti-aircraft gun. The Type 28A had an additional infantry section on the side. Another variant was the Vickers Machine-gun Pillbox, with a large embrasure. Many airfields were defended by octagonal Type 27 pillboxes, some of which had two storeys and an anti-aircraft gun. While these encompass the main types of pillbox, even these had individual differences.

Pillboxes usually formed part of a local defensive system that might utilize a multitude of natural or artificial defensive barriers. They were found in linear defences, such as the Royal Military Canal and the stop-lines, and at strategic positions, such as cross-roads or coastal, air base or other military establishments. Pillboxes were the universal infantry stronghold, and could be manned by regulars, auxiliaries and the Home Guard.

It was usual to camouflage pillboxes. They could be disguised as a beach hut on the coast, a small garage in a town, a workshop in a village or an earthen mound in open countryside. Many have been destroyed since the war, but others survive, complete with fifty years' natural growth to help conceal their whereabouts. It was in camouflaging pillboxes that many ordinary people came to play their little, often ingenious, bit towards defeating the enemy.

Finally, there were several specialist pillboxes. The Pickett-Hamilton retractable pillbox seemingly combined an ingenious Heath-Robinson design with serious military engineering. It housed up to five men and was sunk into the ground. Initially using a winding mechanism, this pillbox could be raised above ground level or lowered in about ten seconds, making it ideal for airfields, where they could be found in clusters of two or three.

The Tett Turret had a concrete turret which sat on top of a concrete pipe sunk into the ground. It could house two men and had a 360 degree field of fire. Its advantage was its concealment but, in addition to the cramped conditions, it was

difficult to enter and was prone to flooding. It was
suitable for use at aerodromes and strategic junctions.
The Alan Williams steel turret was another variant on
this dynamic theme.

Once again, it is easy to criticize, even scoff at, the
strategy that thought hastily dug ditches, anti-tank
blocks and pillboxes could ever stop the highly
disciplined attacking tactics of German Blitzkrieg. After
all, by mid-1940, nothing else had, not even heavily
armoured forts, so why should the military equivalent
of a wing and a prayer be any more successful? For
once, we can smile as historians and academics debate
and score points off each other, with pet theories and
notions as to the likely success and suitability of such
defensive tactics and fortifications. The point is that if
the Germans had invaded, and the combination of
temporary defensive lines and strong-points had not
held out, then they might not have been here to argue
the matter.

Scapa Flow

At the outbreak of the First World War, this Orcadian
anchorage, despite its notorious currents, became the
base from which the Grand Fleet imposed its
blockade of the German High Seas Fleet. Despite this,
it was virtually undefended and an alleged sighting of
a U-boat sent the fleet scuttling away; it did not
return until 1915. By then a series of batteries, booms
and other underwater obstacles and blockships helped
to create a safe anchorage. By 1939 Scapa Flow's

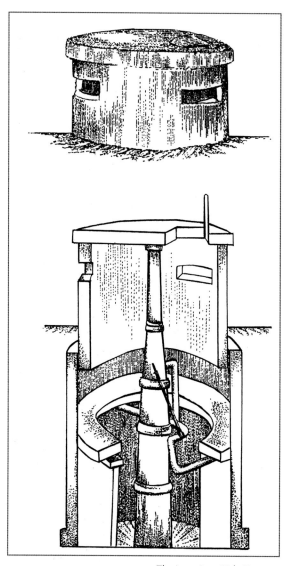

The ingenious Pickett-
Hamilton pillbox.

defences were almost back to square one, save for the rusting blockships. As
the Home Fleet moved north again, so the land, air and other defences were
quickly established – but tragically not well enough. In October 1939 a
German U-boat skilfully negotiated its way though the blockships at the
eastern approach and sank HMS *Royal Oak*. Again, the fleet withdrew, but
soon work began to link the southern islands together, permanently blocking
off the Flow: the Churchill Barriers. Eventually, every single approach to the
flow was closed by a combination of booms, blockships or permanent barriers
and submarine nets, all covered by gun batteries, along with heavy anti-aircraft
batteries encircling the whole anchorage. A Fighter Command aerodrome was
also built in Caithness specifically to provide air cover. Although air attacks
were a fairly frequent occurrence, there were no more major disasters at Scapa
Flow.

After the war the gun batteries were maintained until 1957, and a fuel depot
on the island of Hoy was kept open until 1979. Since then, the anchorage has

Camouflaged pillbox at Beaulieu.

A Pickett-Hamilton pillbox.

been used during NATO exercises and an occasional Royal Navy ship still turns up. Almost all the defences have now gone, but the Churchill Barriers remain, linking the southern islands with the Mainland, and act as a solemn reminder that this was the senior naval base during the world's two greatest conflicts.

POST-WAR STRONGHOLDS: THE NUCLEAR AGE

During Neolithic times the introduction of the bow and arrow must have ruffled a few smug and self-assured feathers. The advent of metals began a revolution in weaponry, though the simple sling might have been responsible for some of the more extensive additions to hillfort defences. No doubt the chariot and metal-tipped javelin caused a few upsets as well, while Roman artillery and siege tactics added further complications to stronghold building.

In the Middle Ages gunpowder turned the world of strongholds upside down. The nineteenth-century development of breech-loading, rifle-barrelled guns that fired explosive shells turned it inside out and changed forever the notion of strongholds as grand edifices. The aeroplane, with its ability to drop high explosives really put the cat among the pigeons. Yet in all these cases new strongholds could still resist the new weapons, at least for a while.

Once the first atom bomb had been dropped in 1945, it was apparent that all contemporary strongholds were immediately and irrevocably obsolete. Considering the after-effects of a nuclear explosion, it is still unlikely that any stronghold could do more than put off the worst until another day; the inhabitants would have to emerge sooner rather than later. This notion seems to have been quickly realized for, apart from building its own nuclear arsenal, Britain's network of coastal defences, built up over centuries, was formally stood down in 1956. Three years later anti-aircraft guns were replaced by guided missiles, and technological and scientific progress has barely slowed since, Cold War or not.

At the front line are the monitoring and signal stations – effectively the modern equivalent of the Roman signal stations or King Harold's scouts who watched over the south coast. While some of these stations were all too visible, like the former Fylingdales 'golf balls' on the North Yorkshire Moors, others are some 120 feet below ground, as at Pitreavie (Fife); many are quite small. In any case, permanent patrols of aeroplanes loaded with electronic aids of immense complexity have probably been the most important of the lot.

Clearly though, this was nowhere near enough. In 1961 the massive Burlington underground bunker was completed near Corsham in Wiltshire. This has miles of tunnels, and cuts beneath the renowned Box railway tunnel. It was intended to be the ultimate refuge for the prime minister, and the heads of the armed forces and all major government departments in the event of a nuclear attack. In addition, there was a full range of supporting services, to enable fully five thousand personnel to survive for a year or more. That figure, more than anything, gives some idea of the sheer size of Burlington.

Burlington would be the central source of authority in the aftermath of a nuclear strike. As it was expected that there would be a gradual build-up to such an event, ministers would have transferred to Burlington as the skies darkened. While parts of Britain perished, the heads of government would have survived to mastermind the rebuilding of the nation. Oh, the joys of power! (Mind you, if a nuclear bomb had been dropped close to the bunker, they would have been the first to perish.)

In addition to the Burlington bunker, seventeen underground Regional Seats of Government were built throughout Britain in the 1950s. It was hoped, for nobody could really know, that some form of basic administration and order could be maintained. Pie in the sky? Fortunately we never had to find out.

As with all previous strongholds, nuclear bunkers varied in size and scale, could be as much as 150 feet below ground and were entered down a ramp and through a concrete door heavily encased in steel. Inside were decontamination rooms, engine and generator rooms and ventilation ducts, while the accommodation and working quarters were lower down. One such bunker, at Crowborough, has thirty-five rooms on three levels, for up to 150 people.

A much bigger version is the Troy Wood secret bunker, which could accommodate three hundred people. Built in 1952, it became a nuclear command post in 1968; like several others, it was sold off once the threat from the Warsaw Pact countries had apparently vanished. Fortunately, it is now a museum, while others are open at Kelvedon Hatch and Mistley (both Essex).

TROY WOOD (Nuclear Command Bunker)
Fife O/S map 59 ref. 553090
Directions: Take the B913 from St Andrews. Turn left on the B940 towards Crail for 1 mile.

Never mind the Blitz; forget the Doodlebugs; put the V2 rockets out of your mind. Despite the devastation, destruction, doubts and distress they caused, that would be as nothing compared to the weapons Troy Wood was designed to withstand. Only a few years ago this top-secret Regional Command Centre was one of seventeen intended to house senior government and armed forces representatives in the event of the unthinkable: a nuclear strike. Nowadays, one can see and contemplate just what might have been, and feel relief that we never came to the brink.

It all looks innocent enough on the surface but underneath that relatively inconspicuous calm a two-level underground bunker, encased in reinforced concrete, was the intended base for maintaining a semblance of control in east Scotland. There was accommodation for about three hundred personnel who, assuming a progressive build up towards nuclear conflagration, would have taken up residence before the big day arrived. On the other hand, if a strike came somewhat out of the blue, with only the fabled two-minute warning, then the modest skeleton staff would be the lucky few. I gather there was hot competition for the gardening jobs.

Nowadays dedicated to displaying equipment from the Cold War era, Troy Wood vividly portrays an unreal world; one from which you and I were excluded, yet one that sought to protect civilians. Sold in the early 1990s for just £125,000 – despite being refurbished at a cost of £5 million some three years before – Troy Wood shows just how profligate governments can be with money – our money. On the other hand, few of Britain's defences were ever cost-effective.

Such bunkers would never deter a nuclear strike, but might just have saved civilization had the world finally gone raving mad. Still might, in fact, for Troy Wood can be reinstated if things take a turn for the worse.

These bunkers cost millions of pounds to build and many have been sold for the equivalent of a song. But even while they were being considered for sale, a new bunker beneath the Ministry of Defence in Whitehall became operational in 1992; it cost a whopping £126 million. With a bit of luck, this too will be nothing more than a white elephant.

A miniature variation on this theme was the 872 Royal Observer Corps bunkers all round Britain, designed to monitor the effects of a nuclear strike and its fall-out. These often housed only three men, in cramped conditions and, with no decontamination rooms, they could hardly have been expected to survive for long. While they might seem almost farcical today, they were a crucial part of the apparatus once deemed essential to ensure some form of life continued following a nuclear Armageddon.

Of course, all military establishments still need defending, both against a potential enemy strike and terrorist attacks. Indeed, in view of the threat posed by the latter, many military sites that were formerly enclosed by little more than a fence are now afforded highly visible protection. To no great surprise, the best and most comprehensive of these are in Northern Ireland. There, combinations of concrete road blocks, barbed wire fences and heavily protected guard posts are directly derived from those intended for use should the Germans have invaded in the Second World War.

FINALE

In the age of inter-continental missiles that can carry either conventional or nuclear warheads, the stronghold has almost returned to its prehistoric roots. Defences of barbed or razor-wire on top of fencing, with relatively simple guard posts, are the modern equivalent of a ditch, bank and palisade fence, with guard huts. For all the developments in long-range weaponry, local defence is still of some importance.

This may be part of a general trend, for strongholds have gained successively more sophisticated defences to counter new weapons, only to revert subsequently to seemingly inadequate ones. While massive bunkers deep underground are the only possible means of surviving a nuclear attack, they would be of limited use in a conventional war – as demonstrated by the Maginot Line. The underlying fact remains that, no matter how ineffective a stronghold's defences might appear to be against weapons of another age, even those of an earlier time, it was the ability to withstand an attack using contemporary weapons and tactics that was of paramount importance. If an older stronghold could be adapted to resist later weapons, that should be regarded as a bonus.

In any case, throughout history the stronghold has been envisaged as a deterrent as well as a secure place. Presumably, prehistoric man built his defended settlement in the hope that it would deter people from chancing their arm, however enticing his herd of cattle. If necessary, the stronghold would be actively defended and, with a bit of luck, its fixed defences would give the home team a definite advantage. The Romans certainly located their strongholds to show the locals who was boss. If the natives fancied it, they could have a go – but the price exacted for failure was very high indeed. This was the case right through to the Second World War.

It was only in the nuclear age that strongholds became irrelevant as a deterrent. No matter how many underground bunkers Britain could muster, they would never put anyone off attempting a nuclear attack. Only the certain threat of immediate and equally devastating retaliation could do that. Had there been a winner, they would have very little to celebrate. While the Saxons were aware that Norman revenge would be devastating had they attacked a castle, it was the scale of the defences that usually diluted any extreme acts of bravado. There have always been exceptions, especially when, as with the Spanish Armada, it was considered that the English navy and coastal defences were incapable of resisting a combined land and sea attack – pity about the weather! Indeed, the time to attack was when the defences were thought to be inadequate, or when the attacking forces far outnumbered the defenders; with hindsight, one wonders what Earl Haig would have to say on the matter.

That is quite enough discussion of the whys and the wherefores of strongholds. It is far better to do than to talk; even better is to do with some understanding. So, go and seek out, examine and enjoy Britain's vast and varied array of strongholds. There are many thousands of them, from the slightest Neolithic camp, through the mightiest medieval castle, to the all-encompassing defences of Stronghold Britain in the Second World War. Each has its story to tell, but one must always remember the bigger picture. Nothing exists in isolation.

Even more important, whether they be derelict, restored, a museum or converted to another use, remember that all strongholds were working

Troy Wood entrance and missile.

environments devised for a specific purpose. They were built, lived in and manned by real people; few British readers will not have relatives who were involved with a stronghold of some sort in the twentieth century. One must envisage and recreate strongholds in the mind's eye as living places, not as the cold and empty ruins they now often appear. Strongholds and the people connected with them formed and forged our history. In them the past awaits to give you a fascinating, exciting, challenging and most enjoyable present.

The light has gone out,
The flame has died.
The spirit lives on
Though empty inside.
Dark to the eyes,
Dank to the smell,
T'was a living hell,
A place built to die.

GLOSSARY

Bailey or Ward	Castle courtyard.
Ballista	Siege weapon similar to a large crossbow.
Barbican	Outwork protecting an entrance or gateway, usually at a castle.
Barmkin	Wall enclosing the courtyard round a Scottish tower-house.
Bastion	A defensive projection beyond a rampart or curtain wall, allowing flanking fire.
Battlements	Parapet of wall or building, comprising merlons (walls) and crenels (gaps).
Belgae	People of mixed Celtic-German origin who came to Britain in about 100 BC.
Berm	The flat ground separating a rampart from its ditch.
Bi-vallate	Hillfort with two ramparts.
Caisson	Large cylinder used to lay underwater foundations; kept watertight by air pressure.
Caponier	Covered connecting passage, often offering flanking fire along a ditch.
Carbon-14 Dating	(Also Radio-carbon 14 (RC-14) dating.) Method of dating organic matter. There is a fixed proportion of Carbon-14 to Carbon-12 in a living organism. Once dead, this proportion is not maintained and falls to about half the former level in about 5,700 years; this is known as a half-life. By measuring the 14C:12C ratio in organic matter, an approximate date of death can be calculated. It cannot be determined with absolute accuracy, and is usually expressed scientifically as, for example 500BC±100, that is 600–400 BC.
Casemate	Vaulted chamber in the thickness of a wall or rampart, often with a gun embrasure.
Celtic Fields	Small rectangular fields defined by lynchets and dating from the Bronze and Iron Ages.
Celts	Peoples from central Europe who possibly came to Britain early in the first millennium BC.
Chevaux de Frise	Upright stones, or wooden stakes, protecting a stronghold from a mass charge.
Cliff-Castle	Cornish promontory hillfort.
Coffer Dam	A piling enclosure into the seabed with the water pumped out, used to lay foundations.
Counterscarp Bank	A bank on the outer edge of a hillfort ditch; the product of clearing out the ditch.
Counterscarp Gallery	Defensive position on the outer lip of a ditch or moat.
Cursus	Neolithic avenue bounded by banks and ditches; some are several miles long.
Curtain Wall	Wall or rampart surrounding a castle courtyard; some have mural towers.
Dalriada	Kingdom of Scotti tribe from Ireland in western Scotland, from about the fifth century AD.
Donjon	Principal tower, or keep, of a castle.
Druids	Celtic priests, probably late Iron Age.

Dyke	Boundary wall, in Scotland. (Not to be confused with a ditch or watercourse.)
Enceinte	Fortified, encircling enclosure.
Flanker	Gun emplacement covering rampart from the flank, or shaft, of a bastion.
Forebuilding	Additional building enclosing the stairs entrance to a castle or keep.
Glacis Rampart	Stone-, earth- and spoil-covered rampart.
Galleried Wall	(Broch or dun.) Hollow wall, or two walls tied together with cross slabs.
Gun Embrasure	Opening in a wall, splayed on the inside.
Gun (or Arrow) Loop	Narrow opening in a wall.
Hut Circle	The wall footings of huts, often now turf-covered.
Hut Platform	A platform cut into the side of a hill, on which a hut was built.
Intermural Cell	Small room within the thickness of a wall.
Keep	Principal tower at a castle.
Machicolations	Projecting stone gallery with holes for dropping missiles on attackers.
Mangonel	Torsion-powered stone throwing siege engine.
Midden	Rubbish tip.
Motte	Mostly artificial earth mound of Norman castles.
Multivallate	Hillfort with more than two lines of ramparts.
Orillons	The two spurs of an arrowhead bastion, protecting the flankers.
Picts	Dark Age inhabitants of north-east, central and possibly north Scotland.
Portcullis	Iron or wood grating, dropped vertically to secure the entrance passage at a castle.
Rampart	A defensive bank, often made of earth; the usual defences of a hillfort.
Ravelin	Outwork with two faces forming a projecting angle, outside the ditch.
Redan	Fieldwork with two faces forming a projecting angle.
Redoubt	Outwork or fieldwork, often without flanking defences; a small defensive position.
Revetment	The facing of a rampart, which may or may not have been structurally supporting.
Sally-Port	(Postern Gate) Small gate to enable defenders to sally forth and attack.
Scarcement	Ledge projecting from or cut into a wall, possibly to support a floor.
Scots or Scotti	Tribe from Ulster that settled in Argyll in the fifth century AD.
Souterrain	Drystone underground passage or cell, used for storage.
Storage Pits	Holes in the interior of a hillfort, often quite deep, used for the long-term storage of grain or salted meat. They could also be used as rubbish pits.
Timber-Lacing	Horizontal cross-timbers through a drystone wall, possibly connecting vertical posts at the front and rear. They were essential to prevent the wall's collapse.
Trebuchet	Stone-throwing catapult siege engine, worked by counter-weights.
Univallate	Hillfort with a single rampart.
Vitrified Fort	A timber-laced wall that had been burnt, usually at a hillfort. The heat fused the stones or rubble together.
Yett	Hinged iron grille at tower-house door.

GENERAL
INFORMATION

The strongholds mentioned in this book all stand on public, private or common land. Most have public access, but not all. If in the slightest doubt seek permission from the nearest house or farm. I have visited thousands of historical sites throughout Britain and I have never yet been refused entry.

Many strongholds are in the care of English Heritage, Historic Scotland or Welsh Heritage (CADW), especially the prehistoric, Roman and Dark Age sites. At many sites an entrance fee is required, but all three state organizations offer annual, or short-term membership rates that give considerable savings; these can be obtained at any manned site. These organizations usually provide excellent interpretation facilities at their manned sites, with good guides, although regrettably many unmanned strongholds do not have a noticeboard. Even so, these three are worthy organizations, especially at a local level. For once, many private and non-state historical bodies trail far behind their state-run counterparts.

When visiting strongholds, a good quality road atlas is vital, as directions are generally given from the nearest town. The relevant Ordnance Survey Landranger map, at 1:50,000, is quoted for each stronghold. These maps are not essential for locating a stronghold, but they will enable you to appreciate a stronghold within its environment. These maps are widely available, or can be borrowed from a library. A compass might also be handy for a few strongholds. For readers unfamiliar with the six-figure map reference numbers, say 012345, the first two figures refer to the vertical grid reference found at the top and bottom of the OS map. By dividing the distance between the vertical lines 01 and 02 into an imaginary ten, the third figure (2) is approximately one-fifth of the way across. Numbers 3 and 4 refer to the horizontal grid lines across the map, also found at the edge. The last figure (5) is, once again, an imaginary line between the horizontal grid references of 34 and 35. By drawing these two points together, you will find the location of the stronghold. Have a couple of goes and it soon becomes second nature.

It goes without saying that under no circumstances must you damage, dig into or remove any material whatsoever (unless it is litter) at any stronghold. There are no treasures to be found, so digging will do nothing but cause irreparable damage, while even tidying up a bit – clearing stones and so forth – will hinder any future excavations. If you were at a museum, you would not tinker with the displays, would you? These strongholds are even more valuable; they are our past, present and future. Treat them with the utmost respect. Resist walking on stone walls, even if they are tumbled. Unless they have been secured, drystone walls are liable to collapse at some time.

Also, treat our countryside as you would your most prized possession; it is, after all, irreplaceable. Close and secure all gates, do not trample crops and never chase livestock; keep your own animals and children under control. These are all straightforward, common-sense matters but, as any farmer and landowner will tell you, there's always one idiot about. Make sure that idiot isn't you.

USEFUL TELEPHONE NUMBERS

For readers intending to visit several strongholds or other historic sites, either during a year or for a holiday, it is worth considering joining one of the following organizations. Their relevant handbooks give important information on site opening times, costs and other sites in their care.

English Heritage	0171 973 3000	National Trust	0171 222 9251
Historic Scotland	0131 668 8800	National Trust for Scotland	0131 226 5922
Welsh Heritage	01222 500200	Landmark Trust	01628 825925

For overseas visitors, especially those from the USA and Canada, the Great British Heritage Pass can be obtained from your nearest British Tourist Authority office before departure. This is invaluable for those wishing to explore Britain's heritage off their own bat. If you intend travelling round Britain by train, ensure the strongholds you visit are near a railway station; regrettably, public transport, like so much else, has changed for the worse. Oh, and unless money is of no concern, always ask for a cheap ticket, not the ordinary full fare; there are also a variety of railway rover tickets available. If travelling by hire car, then the Ordnance Survey Road Atlas of Great Britain, at a scale of 3 inches to the mile, is undoubtedly the finest of a wide range of such maps, and can be obtained from most good High Street book shops.

STRONGHOLDS MENTIONED IN THE TEXT

Note: Places are listed under their traditional counties.

Stronghold	Type	County	O/S Map	Map Ref.
Abernethy	Round tower	Perthshire	58	189164
Acton Burnell	Manor house	Shropshire	126	534019
Almondbury	Hillfort and castle	Yorkshire	110	153142
Alnwick Castle	Castle	Northumberland	81	187137
Am Baghan Burblach	Hillfort	Inverness-shire	33	832199
Ambleside Fort	Roman Fort	Westmorland	90	376033
Appleby Castle	Castle	Westmorland	91	685200
Arbury Banks	Hillfort	Hertfordshire	153	262387
Arbury Hill	Hillfort	Lanarkshire	72	944238
Arundel Castle	Castle	Sussex	197	019074
Ashby-de-la-Zouch Castle	Castle	Leicestershire	128	362166
Aydon Castle	Castle	Northumberland	87	002663
Badbury Rings	Hillfort	Dorset	195	964030
Bamburgh Castle	Castle	Northumberland	75	184350
Bar Hill	Roman Fort	Dunbartonshire	64	707759
Barbury Castle	Hillfort	Wiltshire	173	149763
Barcombe Hill	Roman signal station	Northumberland	86	783668
Barmekin of Echt	Hillfort	Aberdeenshire	38	725070
Barnard Castle	Castle	Co. Durham	92	049165
Basing House	Manor house	Hampshire	185	663526
Bass of Inverurie	Motte and Bailey Castle	Aberdeenshire	38	781206
Battle Abbey	Abbey	Sussex	199	749157
Battlesbury Camp	Hillfort	Wiltshire	183	894456
Bayard's Cove Fort	Fort	Devon	202	879510
Beacon Hill	Hillfort	Hampshire	174	458572
Berry Pomeroy Castle	Castle	Devon	202	839623
Berwick	Barracks	Northumberland	67	994535
	Town Walls	Northumberland	67	994535
Bishop's Palace	Palace	Orkney	6	449108
Bishop's Waltham Palace	Bishop's Palace	Hampshire	185	552173
Black Middens	Bastle	Northumberland	80	775898

Stronghold	Type	County	O/S Map	Map Ref.
Blair Castle	Castle	Perthshire	43	866662
Bolton Castle	Castle	Yorkshire	98	034918
Borgadel Water	Dun	Argyllshire	68	625061
Borwick Broch	Broch	Orkney	6	225168
Bothwell Castle	Castle	Lanarkshire	64	688593
Bovisand Fort	Fort	Devon	201	486507
Bradwell	Roman Fort	Essex	168	031082
Braemar Castle	Castle	Aberdeenshire	43	156924
Bragor Broch	Broch	Ross & Cromarty	8	286474
Bratton Castle	Hillfort	Wiltshire	184	901516
Bredon Hill	Hillfort	Worcestershire	150	957401
Broch of Burraland	Broch	Shetland	4	446231
Broch of Burrian	Broch	Orkney	5	762513
Brough Castle	Castle	Westmorland	91	791141
Brough of Stoal	Promontory hillfort Yell	Shetland	1	547873
Broughton Castle	Castle	Oxfordshire	151	418382
Broughty Castle	Tower and battery	Angus	54	465304
Bungay Castle	Castle	Suffolk	156	336896
Burgh Castle	Saxon Shore Fort	Norfolk	134	475046
Burnswark	Roman Practice Camp	Dumfriesshire	85	185785
Burra Ness	Broch Yell	Shetland	1	556957
Buzbury Rings	Hillfort	Dorset	194	919060
Caer Caradoc	Hillfort	Shropshire	137	478952
Caer Caradoc	Hillfort	Shropshire	137	310758
Caerhun (Canovium)	Roman fort	Caernarvon.	115	776704
Caerlaverock Castle	Castle	Dumfries-shire	84	026656
Caernarvon	Roman fort	Caernarvonshire	115	485624
Caernarvon Castle	Castle	Caernarvonshire	115	477626
Caerphilly Castle	Castle	Glamorgan	171	155870
Caer-y-Twr	Hillfort	Anglesey	114	219829
Caister Castle	Castle	Norfolk	134	504123
Caldicot Castle	Castle	Monmouthshire	171	487885
Calshot Castle	Castle	Hampshire	196	488025
Cardiff Castle	Roman fort and castle	Glamorgan	171	181766
Carew Castle	Castle	Pembrokeshire	158	045037
Carisbrooke Castle	Castle	Isle of Wight	196	486877
Carlwark	Hillfort	Derbyshire	110	258815
Carn Brea	Hillfort	Cornwall	203	473350
Carn Euny	Iron Age village and fogou	Cornwall	203	403288
Carn Liath	Broch	Sutherland	17	871013
Carreg Cennen	Castle	Carmarthenshire	159	668191
Castell-y-Bere	Hillfort	Merionethshire	135	667086
Castle Acre	Castle and bailey gate	Norfolk	132	819152
Castle Ditches	Hillfort	Wiltshire	184	963283
Castle Greg	Roman Fortlet	Mid-Lothian	65	050592
Castle Haven Dun	Dun	Kirkudbrightshire	83	594483
Castle Tioran	Castle	Inverness-shire	40	662724
Castle-an-Dinas	Hillfort	Cornwall	200	945632
Caterthun, Brown and White	Hillforts	Angus	44	555668/ 548660

Stronghold	Type	County	O/S Map	Map Ref.
Chalbury	Hillfort	Dorset	194	695838
Chanctonbury Ring	Hillfort	Sussex	198	139120
Cherbury Camp	Hillfort	Berkshire	164	373963
Chester	Castle and town wall	Cheshire	117	405658
Chew Green	Roman forts	Northumberland	80	787085
Chilham Castle	Castle	Kent	179	066533
Chipchase Castle	Castle	Northumberland	87	882757
Chun Castle	Hillfort	Cornwall	203	405339
Chysauster	Iron Age village	Cornwall	203	473350
Cissbury Ring	Hillfort	Sussex	198	140080
Claypotts Castle	Castle	Angus	54	453318
Cley Hill	Hillfort	Wiltshire	183	839448
Clickimin	Broch and fort	Shetland	4	465408
Clitheroe Castle	Castle	Lancashire	103	742416
Clun Castle	Castle	Shropshire	137	299809
Coalhouse Fort	Coastal Fort	Essex	178	690768
Conisborough Castle	Castle	Yorkshire	111	515989
Cooling Castle	Castle	Kent	178	755760
Corbridge	Vicar's Pele	Northumberland	87	987644
Cotehele	Manor House	Cornwall	201	422685
Cow Castle	Hillfort	Somerset	180	794374
Cow Tower, Norwich	Gun tower	Norfolk	134	240091
Craig Phadrig	Hillfort	Inverness-shire	26	640453
Craigmillar Castle	Castle	Mid-Lothian	66	288709
Cranbrook Castle	Hillfort	Devon	191	739890
Crathes Castle	Castle	Aberdeenshire	45	735968
Criccieth Castle	Castle	Caernarvonshire	124	500377
Crickley Hill	Hillfort and causeway camp	Gloucestershire	163	928161
Crighton Castle	Castle	Mid-Lothian	66	380611
Crownhill Fort	Fort	Devon	201	487592
Dane's Dyke	Hillfort	Yorkshire	101	213712
Danebury	Hillfort	Hampshire	185	323376
Dartmouth Castle	Castle	Devon	202	887503
Denork	Hillfort	Fife	59	455137
Devil's Dyke	Hillfort	Sussex	198	260110
Din Sylwy	Hillfort	Anglesey	114	586815
Dinas Powys	Fort and ringwork	Glamorgan	171	148722
Dirleton Castle	Castle	East Lothian	66	516839
Dolbadarn Castle	Castle	Caernarvonshire	115	586598
Dolwyddelan Castle	Castle	Caernarvonshire	115	722523
Donnington Castle	Castle and earthworks	Berkshire	174	461692
Doon Hill	Dark Age royal enclosure	East Lothian	67	686755
Drum Castle	Castle	Kincardine	38	796005
Drumcarrow	Broch	Fife	59	459133
Drysllwyn Castle	Castle	Carmarthenshire	159	554203
Dudley Castle	Castle	Staffordshire	139	947907
Dun Burgidale	Dun	Bute	63	063660
Dun Grugaig	Dun	Inverness-shire	33	851159
Dun Mor	Broch	Tiree, Argyllshire	44	046493

Stronghold	Type	County	O/S Map	Map Ref.
Dun Skeig	Hillfort and dun	Argyllshire	62	757571
Dun Torquill	Dun	Inverness-shire	18	888737
Dunagoil	Hillfort	Bute	63	085530
Dunbar Castle	Castle	East Lothian	67	678793
Dundurn	Nuclear Fort	Perthshire	51	707233
Dunksey Castle	Castle	Wigtown	82	004534
Dunnottar Castle	Castle	Kincardine	45	881839
Dunstanburgh Castle	Castle	Northumberland	75	258220
Durisdeer	Roman fortlet	Dumfries-shire	78	903048
Dyke Hills	Oppidum	Oxfordshire	164	572937
Dymchurch	Redoubt	Kent	189	129321
	Martello Tower	Kent	189	102294
Earith Bulwark	Civil War Sconce	Huntingdonshire	153	385758
Earl's Palace, Birsay	Palace	Orkney	6	248277
Earlshall Castle	Castle	Fife	59	465211
Eastbourne Redoubt	Fort	Sussex	199	623995
Edinburgh Castle	Castle	Mid-Lothian	66	252736
Edinshall	Hillfort and broch	Berwickshire	67	772603
Edlingham Castle	Castle	Northumberland	81	116092
Eggardon Hill	Hillfort	Dorset	193	541948
Eildon Hill	Roman Signal Station	Roxburghshire	73	555328
Eilean Donan Castle	Castle	Ross & Cromarty	33	881258
Elcho Castle	Castle	Perthshire	53	165211
Elsdon Pele	Pele tower	Northumberland	80	936934
Embleton Parson's Pele	Pele tower	Northumberland	75	230225
Etal Castle	Castle	Northumberland	75	925394
Ewloe Castle	Castle	Flintshire	117	288675
Eynesford Castle	Castle	Kent	177	542658
Farnham Castle	Castle	Surrey	186	839474
Finavon	Hillfort	Angus	54	506556
Forse Castle	Castle	Caithness	11	224338
Fort Albert	Coastal Fort	Isle of Wight	196	328890
Fort Cumberland	Fort	Hampshire	196	682991
Fort George	Fortress	Inverness-shire	27	762567
Fort Victoria	Coastal Fort	Isle of Wight	196	336897
Fort Widley	Fort	Hampshire	196	077065
Fyvie Castle	Castle	Aberdeenshire	38	764323
Gainsborough Old Hall	Manor House	Lincolnshire	121	815895
Gatehouse Bastle	Bastles	Northumberland	80	787889
Giant's Grave	Hillfort	Wiltshire	173	166632
Glamis Castle	Castle	Angus	54	386480
Gleadesglough, Akeld Hill	Hillfort	Northumberland	75	949290
Glenbuchat Castle	Castle	Aberdeenshire	37	397149
Golden Hill Fort	Fort	Isle of Wight	196	338878
Goodrich Castle	Castle	Herefordshire	162	579199
Goosehill Camp	Hillfort	Sussex	197	830127
Grain Tower	Tower	Kent	178	890772
Greenknowe Tower	Tower-house	Berwickshire	74	639428
Grosmont Castle	Castle	Monmouthshire	161	405244
Guildford Castle	Castle	Surrey	186	999495

Stronghold	Type	County	O/S Map	Map Ref.
Hackness	Martello Tower	Orkney	7	338912
Ham Hill	Hillfort and Roman fort	Somerset	193	478169
Hamble Common Camp	Hillfort	Hampshire	196	482062
Harding's Down	Unfinished hillfort	Glamorgan	159	437906
Harehope	Hillfort	Northumberland	75	956285
Harlech Castle	Castle	Merionethshire	124	581312
Hembury	Hillfort	Devon	193	113033
Herefordshire Beacon	Hillfort	Herefordshire	150	760398
Herstmonceaux Castle	Castle	Sussex	199	646104
High Rochester	Roman Fort	Northumberland	80	833986
Highdown	Hillfort	Sussex	198	093043
Hilsea Lines	Linear defences	Hampshire	196	660043
Hod Hill	Hillfort	Dorset	194	857106
Hoga Ness	Broch	Shetland	1	557005
Hole Bastle	Bastle	Northumberland	80	867846
Horsey Hill	Civil War Sconce	Huntingdonshire	142	222959
Hoxa Broch	Broch	Orkney	7	425940
Hoxa Head Battery	Gun battery	Orkney	7	410943
Humbleton	Hillfort	Northumberland	75	967283
Keiss Brochs	Road broch	Caithness	12	348615
	Harbour broch	Caithness	12	353611
	Coast broch	Caithness	12	353612
Kenilworth Castle	Castle	Warwickshire	140	278723
Kents Cavern	Cavern	Devon	202	934641
Kingerby Castle	Castle	Lincolnshire	112	056928
Kings Lynn	South Gate	Norfolk	132	620191
Kingswear Castle	Castle	Devon	202	881509
Kintradwell Broch	Broch	Sutherland	17	929081
Kirkby Muxloe Castle	Castle	Leicestershire	140	524046
Knaresborough Castle	Castle	Yorkshire	104	348569
Knockfarrel	Hillfort	Ross & Cromarty	26	505585
Ladle Hill	Hillfort	Hampshire	174	479568
Landguard Fort	Coastal fort	Suffolk	169	284318
Launceston Castle	Castle	Cornwall	201	330846
Linlithgow Palace	Palace	West-Lothian	65	003775
Little Wenham Hall	Manor House	Suffolk	155	081392
Llanstephan Castle	Castle	Carmarthenshire	159	352102
Loch Leven Castle	Castle	Kinross-shire	58	138018
Longthorpe Tower	Tower	Northamptonshire	142	163983
Longtown Castle	Castle	Herefordshire	160	321291
Ludlow Castle	Castle	Shropshire	138	508746
Lydford	Castle and Saxon *burh*	Devon	191	510846/ 509847
Lympne	Roman Fort	Kent	189	117342
Maiden Castle	Hillfort	Dorset	194	669885
Maker Heights	Gun batteries	Cornwall	201	438512
Mam Tor	Hillfort	Derbyshire	110	128837
Manorbier Castle	Castle	Pembrokeshire	158	064978
Martinsell Hill	Hillfort	Wiltshire	173	177639
Merdon Castle	Castle and Hillfort	Hampshire	185	421265

Stronghold	Type	County	O/S Map	Map Ref.
Middleham Castle	Castle	Yorkshire	99	128875
Mid-Howe Broch	Broch	Orkney	6	371306
Midsummer Hill	Hillfort	Herefordshire	150	760375
Mingary Castle	Castle	Argyll	47	503631
Mither Tap o' Bennachie	Hillfort	Aberdeenshire	38	683224
Monnow Bridge	Town bridge	Monmouthshire	162	513126
Mote of Mark	Dark Age fort	Kirkudbrightshire	84	845540
Mount Batten Tower	Tower	Devon	201	486532
Mount Edgecumbe	Tower	Cornwall	201	458526
Muness Castle	Castle	Shetland	1	629013
Needles Batteries	Gun batteries	Isle of Wight	196	291850/ 293849
Ness of Burgi	Blockhouse	Shetland	4	388084
Newark Castle	Castle	Nottinghamshire	121	796540
Newhaven Fort	Fort	Sussex	198	448007
Noltland Castle	Castle	Orkney	5	429688
Norham Castle	Castle	Northumberland	75	907467
North Berwick Law	Hillfort	East Lothian	67	555842
Nunney Castle	Castle	Somerset	183	737457
Nybster	Broch and fort	Caithness	12	370632
Odiham Castle	Castle	Hampshire	186	726519
Okehampton Castle	Castle	Devon	191	584942
Old Oswestry	Hillfort	Shropshire	126	295310
Old Sarum	Hillfort and castle	Wiltshire	184	138327
Old Wick Castle	Castle	Caithness	12	369489
Orford Castle	Castle	Suffolk	156	419499
Oxwich Castle	Castle	Glamorgan	159	500862
Oystermouth Castle	Castle	Glamorgan	159	613883
Pembroke Castle	Castle	Pembrokeshire	158	982016
Pembroke Defensible Barracks	Barracks	Pembrokeshire	157	961030
Pembroke Dock	Gun towers	Pembrokeshire	158	964038/ 955036
Pendennis Castle	Henrician Fort	Cornwall	204	824318
Pennard Castle	Castle	Glamorgan	159	544885
Pennymuir	Roman camps	Roxburghshire	80	755138
Pen-y-Gaer	Hillfort	Caernarvonshire	115	750693
Pevensey Castle	Saxon Shore Fort	Sussex	199	644048
Portchester Castle	Saxon Shore Fort	Hampshire	196	625406
Portland Castle	Castle	Dorset	194	684743
Poundbury	Hillfort	Dorset	194	682911
Preston Tower	Tower	Northumberland	75	189255
Prestonbury Castle	Hillfort	Devon	191	747900
Raglan Castle	Castle	Monmouthshire	161	415083
Rainsborough Camp	Hillfort	North'ptonshire	152	526348
Ravenglass	Fort and Roman bath house	Cumberland	96	088961
Rawlsbury Camp	Hillfort	Dorset	194	767057
Reculver Roman Fort	Fort	Kent	179	228694
Restormel Castle	Castle	Cornwall	200	104614

Stronghold	Type	County	O/S Map	Map Ref.
Rhuddlan Castle	Castle	Flintshire	116	024779
Ringmoor	Iron Age Settlement	Dorset	194	809085
Risbury Camp	Hillfort	Herefordshire	149	542553
Rothesay Castle	Castle	Bute	63	087645
Rough Castle	Roman fort	Stirlingshire	65	843799
Royal Military Canal	Linear defence	Kent/Sussex	189	Various
Rybury Camp	Hillfort and causeway camp	Wiltshire	173	083640
Scratchbury Camp	Hillfort	Wiltshire	184	913443
Sgarbach	Dun	Caithness	12	373637
Sherborne Castle	Castle	Somerset	183	647167
Sherrif Hutton Castle	Castle	Yorkshire	100	652661
Skenfrith Castle	Castle	Monmouthshire	161	457202
Skipness Castle	Castle	Argyllshire	62	908577
Skipsea Castle	Castle	Yorkshire	107	163551
Smailholm Tower	Tower	Roxburghshire	74	637346
South Kyme Tower	Tower	Lincolnshire	130	168497
Southsea Castle	Castle	Hampshire	196	642980
Spetisbury Rings	Hillfort	Dorset	194	915020
Sron Uamha	Hillfort	Argyllshire	68	612060
St Andrews	Castle and West Port	Fife	59	513169
St Anne's Church, Ancroft	Pele Tower	Northumberland	75	002452
St Anthony Head and Zone Point	Battery	Cornwall	204	850310
St Catherine's Hill	Hillfort	Hampshire	185	485276
St Catherine's Castle	Coastal fort	Cornwall	200	118580
St John's Point	Hillfort	Caithness	7	310752
St Magnus Church	Refuge tower	Orkney	7	466303
St Mary's Chapel	Chapel	Orkney	7	443262
Stirling Castle	Castle	Stirlingshire	57	790941
Stockland Great Camp	Fort	Devon	193	226027
Strathgarry	Dun	Perthshire	43	890632
Sudbrook Camp	Hillfort	Monmouthshire	172	505873
Sweetheart Abbey	Abbey	Dumfries-shire	84	966664
Tamworth Castle	Castle	Staffordshire	139	206037
Tenby	Castle and town walls	Pembrokeshire	158	138005
The Birrens	Roman fort	Dumfries-shire	85	218753
The Wrekin	Hillfort	Shropshire	127	629082
Thetford Castle	Castle	Norfolk	144	874828
Threave Castle	Castle	Kirkcudbrightshire	84	739623
Thundersbarrow	Hillfort	Sussex	198	229084
Tolquhon Castle	Castle	Aberdeenshire	38	874286
Totnes Castle	Castle	Devon	202	800605
Tower of London	Castle	London	177	338806
Traprain Law	Hillfort	East Lothian	67	581746
Tre'r Ceiri	Hillfort	Caernarvonshire	123	373446
Tregeare Rounds	Hillfort	Cornwall	200	032800
Trusty's Hill	Hillfort and Pict	Kirkudbrightshire	83	588560
Tutbury Castle	Castle	Staffordshire	128	210293
Ty Mawr	Iron Age village	Anglesey	114	212820

Stronghold	Type	County	O/S Map	Map Ref.
Tynemouth Castle	Battery	Northumberland	88	374695
Ugdale Point	Stack fort	Argyllshire	68	784285
Upnor Castle	Elizabethan Fort	Kent	178	758706
Urquart Castle	Castle	Inverness-shire	26	530285
Walbury	Hillfort	Berkshire	174	373618
Wallingford	Saxon *burh* and castle	Berkshire	164	610898
Wallingford	*Burh* and motte and bailey castle	Berkshire	175	610897
Walmer Castle	Castle	Kent	179	778505
Warbstow Bury	Hillfort	Cornwall	190	202908
Wareham	Saxon *burh*	Dorset	195	921875
Warwick Castle	Castle	Warwickshire	151	284047
Weeting Castle	Manor House	Norfolk	144	778891
Weobley Castle	Castle	Glamorgan	159	478927
West Hill Camp	Hillfort	Northumberland	75	910295
White Castle	Castle	Monmouthshire	161	380168
Winchelsea	Town gates	Sussex	189	903179
Windmill Hill	Causeway camp	Wiltshire	173	087714
Windsor Castle	Castle	Berkshire	174	970770
Winklebury Hill	Hillfort	Wiltshire	184	952218
Wolvesey	Bishop's Palace	Hampshire	185	484291
Wooler	Hillfort	Northumberland	75	984273
Y Pigwyn	Roman marching camp	Brecknockshire	160	828312
Yarmouth Castle	Henrician Fort	Isle of Wight	196	354898
York/Jorvik	Viking centre	Yorkshire	105	602523

INDEX

(Page numbers in **bold** refer to site details; page numbers in *italics* refer to illustrations.)